CW00969499

Luisa Gandolfo is the Altajir Lecturer in Post-war Recovery at the University of York. She holds a PhD in Arab and Islamic Studies from the University of Exeter.

PALESTINIANS IN JORDAN

The Politics of Identity

Luisa Gandolfo

I.B. TAURIS

LONDON · NEW YORK

Published in 2012 by I.B.Tauris & Co Ltd
6 Salem Road, London W2 4BU
175 Fifth Avenue, New York NY 10010
www.ibtauris.com

Distributed in the United States and Canada
Exclusively by Palgrave Macmillan
175 Fifth Avenue, New York NY 10010

Library of Modern Middle East Studies 128

ISBN 978 1 78076 095 7

A full CIP record for this book is available from the British Library
A full CIP record for this book is available from the Library of Congress

Library of Congress catalog card: available

Typeset by Newgen Publishers, Chennai
Printed and bound by CPI Group (UK) Ltd, Croydon, CR0 4YY

CONTENTS

ACKNOWLEDGEMENTS

By its nature a study of identity, I foremost must thank those who participated in the study. Your insights guided the book in new directions and I hope your contributions will facilitate a deeper understanding of contemporary Jordanian society and the Palestinian diaspora.

My profound thanks are also extended to Professor Nadje Al-Ali and Professor Tim Niblock for their invaluable critiques, which refined the study to its current form. In addition, I would like to extend my thanks to Maria Marsh and Hannah Wilks for their keen eyes and sage editorial advice.

In addition, I profoundly thank Adnan for his unstinting support and encouragement; his wisdom countered many an intellectual tangle that could be resolved only through the union of history and anthropology.

Finally, my deepest gratitude goes to my mother, Maria-Antonietta, for her unending love and understanding. It is certain that without her this book would not have been possible.

Luisa Gandolfo, 20 July, 2011

They all have the full rights of citizenship and all its obligations, the same as any other citizen irrespective of his origin.

They are an integral part of the Jordanian state. They belong to it, they live on its land, and they participate in its life and all activities.

Jordan is not Palestine, and the independent Palestinian state will be established on the occupied Palestinian land after its liberation, God Willing.

There the Palestinian identity will be embodied.

King Hussein's Speech, 31 July, 1988

1

THE EMERGENCE OF THE PALESTINIAN COMMUNITY IN TRANSJORDAN

In entering a province one has always the need of the goodwill of the natives.[1]

The words of Machiavelli are on first sight so removed from the formation of Transjordan as to seem incongruous. Published in 1532 in the Florentine Republic by a diplomat and political philosopher, the construct of a twentieth-century Middle Eastern kingdom can be viewed as quite disparate. The fact that Machiavelli addresses acquired, as opposed to constructed, principalities through *The Prince* does not lessen its pertinence: for the Hashemites, governing a purposefully delineated state comprising Bedouin tribes, Palestinian refugees, Circassians and Chechens, required a stability dependent on the support of the 'natives', in this instance the Bedouins. Yet while their domain of dominance has been the government and military, their minority status amidst increasing grassroots unrest raises the spectre of the goodwill losing its permanence. The aftermath of the region's partition by the British authorities in 1922 brought into existence the semi-autonomous Emirate of Transjordan and rendered residents of Palestine not only stateless, but subjects in the new Kingdom. At the end of World War I, the area that encompasses Israel, Jordan, the West Bank, the Gaza Strip and Jerusalem was granted to the United Kingdom by the League of Nations under the Mandate for

Palestine and Transjordan and while King Abdullah I was the head of state, the remainder of Palestine continued under the British High Commissioner, Sir Alan Cunningham, until 1948. The Mandate over Transjordan drew to a close on 22 May 1946 and within 72 hours the Hashemite Kingdom of Transjordan grasped independence. When the following year's United Nations Partition Plan divided the former Mandate area between the Jewish and Palestinian population Transjordan assumed a ringside seat to the political unrest and a responsibility for the victims of the conflict fleeing Palestinian towns and villages. While for some Jordan became a state en route to a new beginning in the West, for others it became a second homeland, that over the years they would dominate, challenge and contribute to as the Jordanian state progressed.

The annexation of the West Bank by Jordan in 1950 altered the demographic structure of the Kingdom: for the indigenous Transjordanian population – estimated at 450,000 in 1948[2] – the addition of 900,000 persons (roughly half of whom were refugees) would have lasting socio-political consequences.[3] More advanced in terms of education, healthcare, employment, trade unions and newspapers, the Palestinian population contrasted with the predominantly nomadic, semi-nomadic, and sedentary Bedouin tribes.[4] Having sustained the Arab struggle against the emergent Israeli nation, the Palestinians had developed not only skilful economic competition, but also a political awareness that was more cognizant than that of their Jordanian counterparts.[5] Guided by Western political ideologies, the political identity of the Palestinians was conducive to a reluctance to integrate into the Jordanian system and concepts of trade unionism and democracy rendered them critical of a monarchy that relied on the support of tribes and the military as a source of power.[6] Unable to assent to a primitive, tribal and autocratic monarchy, the Palestinians struggled with the existing institutions of administration.[7] For their part, the Hashemites strove to incorporate the Palestinians into the state and by 1964 the government had created a moderately high level of employment and prosperity. Yet while the infrastructural issue was resolvable, 'political homelessness'[8] would prove less surmountable and would bear a significant impact through the creation of a bi-national discourse within the country.

Palestinians in the Jordanian Military (1926–1968)

Transjordan's first monarch was assassinated in Jerusalem on 20 July 1951 by a Palestinian contingent operating under the financial auspices of benefactors residing in Egypt. Having ruled for 15 months, King Abdullah I was killed as rumours of a joint Jordanian and Lebanese peace treaty with Israel gained momentum. The circumstances of Abdullah's assassination emphasized the threats the state confronted during early independence as the plot demonstrated the lengths to which Jordan's enemies would go to destroy the monarchy. The Palestinian element emphasized the animosity held for the Hashemite family by the Palestinian population who perceived the king as an impediment to the establishment of an independent Palestinian state.[9] Amongst the convicted were a distant relative of the Mufti and a close confidant of the monarch, Abdullah al-Tall. Having fled to Cairo in the immediate aftermath of the assassination, he made connections with West and East Bank Palestinian dissidents[10] and in the long term consolidated the foundations of Jordanian distrust of the Palestinian community. Equally, it marked the beginnings of the two groups' struggle to exist side by side, establishing and asserting identities, and achieving acceptance and integration without relinquishing hope and support for a Palestinian homeland.

Following Jordan's annexation of the West Bank, Abdullah confronted the challenge of absorbing the West and East Bank Palestinians into Jordanian society. The skills brought by the Palestinians were crucial to the Kingdom's evolution towards a viable state, yet all the while the king was aware of his support base in the East Bank and the destabilizing effect of the nearby Palestine conflict. To upset the former or become entangled with the latter would have produced devastating results and in turn Abdullah sought to integrate the Palestinians into not only political circles, but also the military, to the chagrin of Jordanians, for 'with the incorporation of Palestinians, the Legion had lost its homogeneity.'[11] The disdain with which the Palestinian presence was regarded in military circles is ironic: the earliest recruits of the Legion were a force of 50 gendarmes employed by the Karak administration to collect fines and taxes and detain criminals.[12] Within a short time, the overwhelmed force prompted British officer Frederick Peake to resort to Arabs who had served in the Ottoman army, many of whom were recruited from Egypt, Sudan, Syria and Palestine.[13]

The Arab Legion was founded on 1 April 1926 as the Transjordan Frontier Force (TJFF), a multinational unit associated with the imperial forces in Palestine. With the majority of its 1,000 men drawn from Palestine, Syria and Lebanon,[14] the Transjordanian contingent was represented by the Circassians.[15] By 1929 the Arab Legion resembled a police force in its duties and equipment as opposed to a regular army, having been reduced from 1,300 to less than 900 in all ranks including a number of Syrian and Palestinian recruits.[16] Post-independence, the Jordanian armed forces confronted an increasing population and technical branches that necessitated more staff, a need met by numerous Palestinian refugees and Palestinians from the West Bank. While many of the new recruits had been technicians in the employ of the Palestinian Mandate in areas of public service and utilities, they came to almost exclusively compose the Legion's maintenance workshops.[17] Indeed, far from homogenizing the Jordanian military, the Palestinians bolstered the corps.

The transformation of the Jordanian Army into a national army incorporating the growing Palestinian population demonstrated not only the integration of the two communities within the Kingdom, but also the problem of 'nationalization'. Far from being the model of acceptance, the move to incorporate Palestinians was calculated according to Transjordanian interests. The Palestinian presence denoted integration and cohesion, but its real value resided in the opportunity to defend the Kingdom, while preventing them entering into the army officer corps and presenting a threat to the military status quo, since the majority of Palestinians were allocated administrative and technical positions:

> the monarch has been careful to retain the traditional tribal element as the preponderant one in the operational ground force units, namely, infantry and armoured car regiments. In doing this, the monarch [King Hussein] has managed to continue to

identify himself with the traditional forces in the Legion, while
at the same time he had led the process of a viable integration of
the various elements in the country that is so essential to political stability.[18]

Just as the Arab Legion afforded a means to integrate the Palestinians,
so too did the Jordanian National Guard question the extent to which
the Palestinian community could contribute to and defend Jordanian
state interests. In January 1950, prior to the annexation of central
Palestine to Jordan, the government issued the Law of the National
Guard that inaugurated a new military force in the Kingdom.[19]
Initiated by a British officer, John Bagot Glubb, the new legal stric-
ture enabled military conscription to control the tribes and integrate
them within the nation-state.[20] Considered the foremost authority in
pacifying Bedouin tribes, Glubb had previously excelled in neighbouring Iraq during the 1920s and he sought to apply his methods to the
integration of Palestinians in the new Guard. Glubb's insight into the
position of the Palestinians in the region prompted the frank conclusion that the isolation of Palestinians from Jordanian affairs would
benefit Jordan's unscrupulous neighbours as they sought to instigate
animosity between West Bank and East Bank:

> One of the major points they used to stir up resentment was
> that the Jordanian government did not trust the Palestinians.
> The Arab Legion was depicted as a purely East Bank army.
> The Communist went farther. They labelled the Arab Legion –
> 'The Anglo-Hashemite Army of Occupation in Palestine.' [The
> Palestinians] could not be half-citizens. We must make them
> feel trusted, and the first sign of trust was to arm them.[21]

It was a risky move and one that did not pass without resistance,
particularly from the government that feared arming the Palestinians
would not protect the Kingdom, but rather place it in further jeopardy. The Law also encountered resistance from West Bank Palestinian
notables not yet reconciled to unification.[22] Yet the real task was not
protecting Jordan from forces within, but from damage to relations

with neighbouring states, new and old. In particular, border infiltration into Israel by armed members of the National Guard gained significance in October 1953 when 66 civilians, including children, were massacred by Israeli forces in the West Bank town of Qibya.[23] Both Jordan and Palestine were becoming rapidly embroiled in an internal impasse over policy and security on the Israeli border. Vehement in their cries for better arms and training, the Palestinians deplored the Jordanian civilian and military evasion of confrontation with Israel. Impassioned by both the experience of losing their homeland and suffering previous Israeli violations, the gulf between the peace-seeking Jordanians and the retribution-hungry Palestinians within the Kingdom widened.

Viewed by many as 'the protector of Israel from Palestinian infiltrators,'[24] the onus for events was placed on the Kingdom. Jordan was not acting (or not) alone, for the British command was perceived as equally weak, restricting the army from engaging in action against the Israelis.[25] Opposition MPs, predominantly from the West Bank, called for the Legion to be given a free hand to retaliate with force against Israel and the then representative of Nablus in the Jordanian parliament, Qadri Tuqan, contended that 'only a daring will and the power of the fist will be able to drive back the frivolous, despicable, and treacherous Jew. As long as the Arabs concede a lot, the Jews will go on running wild.'[26] If the Hashemite's gentleness proved contentious for the Palestinians, it was no less comforting to the regime: challenged on its borders and within, Jordan assumed a stance that would characterize its foreign and domestic policy, treading the fine line between loyalty and stability. Unable to satisfy all (or none), ultimately she risked the wrath from within over that which shared its western border.

The protests and demonstrations that followed the Qibya massacre brought the Jordanian government under increasing pressure from Arab governments to withdraw the National Guard from Arab Legion supervision, itself under British officers, and place it under joint Arab direction and leadership. After the British Mandate, the Jordanian army remained under the auspices of a Joint Defence Board that stipulated that British officers would fill the top positions.[27]

Glubb had come to represent Jordan's reliance on Britain and in turn became a liability for Hussein in an atmosphere of increasing nationalism. Galvanized by the rise of Nasserism, Glubb was duly dismissed and deported on 2 March 1956.[28] With the final vestige of British presence removed, the regime could reorient itself towards an intraregional approach to domestic politics and for the Transjordanian population, the proposal offered by the Arab governments proved tantalizing. Subsisting on little or no wages under the British employ, a sympathetic stance vis-à-vis Israel provided an additional allure for the people and a problem for the new monarch. In a preventative step, the Guard was integrated into the Arab Legion in May 1956, two months after the expulsion of Glubb from the Kingdom. The juxtaposition of the two forces yielded 'an essentially élite regular force of beduin [sic], tribesmen and Transjordanian peasants with a territorial frontier force wholly consisting of settled Palestinian agricultural peasants and a few townsmen.'[29] Yet in the midst of Palestinian integration was a scheme that brought credence to the suspicions within Jordanian society. The withdrawal of British officers brought enticing opportunities to a generation of young men, ideologically inspired, albeit 'from the dynasty's viewpoint, of doubtful political loyalty.'[30] Lieutenant Colonel Ali Abu Nowar quickly rose in prominence and formed the Fourth Infantry Brigade, composed almost exclusively of Palestinians. On the surface a simple military division, it was a military nucleus primed for a coup d'état, concurrent with a group of Free Officers as the base for a future regime.[31] The coup attempt of April 1957 ultimately failed due to the loyalty of the king's Bedouin ground operational units who upheld the status quo. Once more, the clear distinction between Bedouin and *hadari*[32] proved a defining factor in the ill-fated attempt and the subsequent downfall of Abu Nowar and his cohorts and imparted a warning to a Palestinian community disillusioned by its leaders.

The National Guard had failed to 'Jordanize' the Palestinians and the resulting bitterness lingered on its closure in 1966 following the Israeli raid on the West Bank village of Samu, in which 15 Jordanian soldiers and three civilians died.[33] Its successor, the compulsory national military service (*al-Khidmah al-Watiniyyah al-Ijbariyyah*) applied to Jordanians between 18 and 40 years,[34] yet despite the trans-formation, the Arab Army remained a Transjordanian affair. In the political arena, the Palestinians were making more progress and by expanding the political establishment to incorporate a large number of Palestinians, Hussein limited the spread of dissent 'held by the discontented and alienated among them into the army officer corps, particularly now that the *Jeish* comprises so many more [...] person-nel who are Palestinian.'[35] In 1964, 'the discontented' found a greater medium to impart their restlessness and realized the threat to inter-nal stability through the Palestinian Liberation Organization (PLO).[36] The emergence of an organized, external leadership in Palestine altered circumstances considerably, providing dispossessed Palestinians with a vociferous, united voice. The PLO dominated political discourse and within the next six years the Kingdom tasted civil war. The tremors of political disquiet would shake the state to its political foundations, engulfing in its progress the futile militaristic bids to integrate the Palestinians during the previous decades.

The Velvet Glove of Pluralism and the Steel Fist of Security

Subsequent to partition, the Palestinians living in the territory annexed to Transjordan were rendered 'stateless'. In 1928 the introduction of the Transjordanian Citizenship Ordinance stipulated that those residing in the Kingdom in 1924 were eligible for Transjordanian nationality.[37] Concurrent with Abdullah's desire to absorb the refugees and improve the position of the Palestinians, the Passport Amendment Ordinance No. 11 of 1949 was passed and enabled Palestinians to gain a Jordanian passport.[38] To facilitate maximum legal and social movement, restric-tions imposed by the Foreigners Law of 1927 were rescinded in the case of Palestinian applicants and the movement was consolidated by the Additional Law No. 56 of December 1949, which amended the original Citizenship Ordinance of 1928 and presented Palestinians with *ipso facto* Jordanian nationality.[39] But it was not a limitless gesture, for those arriving in the Kingdom after 1948 would remain 'Palestinians' despite their integration into Jordanian society and acceptance of Jordanian citizenship. Between those arriving prior to 1948 and after, the national sentiments were shared towards the homeland:

> It accurately reflected the totally different circumstances under which those Palestinians arrived. It reflected as well the state of mind they brought with them. Whether they fled to the West Bank and Jordan to escape fighting or to avoid living under Israeli rule, or were forcibly driven out by Israelis, all left unwillingly. They arrived embittered at their loss and determined to go back eventually.[40]

Almost 30 years on, the dynamic has markedly evolved as subsequent Palestinians forged their way in the host state. In 1967 the Kingdom braced itself for a new influx following the Six-Day War (*an-Naksah*) as the Israeli annexation of the West Bank and Gaza Strip resulted in the registration of 140,000 of the 240,000 citizens of the West Bank as UNRWA refugees. The impact was to be lasting: by 1999 Jordan was host to 1.52 million Palestinian refugees, 1,512,742 of whom were registered with UNRWA, 1,012 with UNHCR, 4,325 seeking UNHCR refugee status and a further 800,000 'displaced persons'.[41]

The Gulf War (1990–1991) prompted a renewed wave of refugees and the temporal variance proved conducive to distinct internal divisions with respect to the Palestinian perception of and relationship to Jordan. 360,000 Palestinians arrived from Kuwait, Iraq, Saudi Arabia and the Gulf states. Of those, 300,000 remained in Jordan, while 40,000, holding valid Israeli-issued documents, resettled in the West Bank.[42] While the pre-1948 residents identify themselves as Jordanian and thrive commercially, professionally and politically, the post-1948 refugees did not live in camps and constitute the 'silent minority', though they have enjoyed equal success in terms of integration. Resentment persists amidst the refugees of 1967 and 1990–1991, as a high proportion of the refugees of 1967 remain in the camps, 'disgruntled, unsettled, despondent, militant or potentially so.'[43] For those entering after the first Iraq War, though affluent and educated, despondence was still held following their return to Jordan during the mass expulsions by Saddam Hussein.

After citizenship was granted to the Palestinians, the next step was parliamentary representation. For this purpose, the Chamber of Deputies (*Majlis an-Nawab*) was dissolved as from 1 January 1950 and new elections were fixed on 11 April 1950. By a decree on 13 December 1949, Article 20 of the Chamber of Deputies Electoral Law, no. 9 of 1947 (*Qanun al-Intekhab al-Majlis an-Nawab*) was amended to extend franchise to the Palestinians.[44] Simultaneously, an Annexe to the Electoral Law no. 55 of 1949 (*Qanun Idafi al-Qanun al-Intekhab al-Majlis an-Nawab*) stipulated that 20 members were to be elected to the Chamber of Deputies, representing 'the western region' (*al-mantaqa al-ghariyyah*). Despite the equal representation given to the Palestinians in the lower elected Chamber of Deputies, no such provision was made with regard to the Chamber of Notables (*Majlis al-A'yan*). Nominated by the king at his discretion, the Chamber remained a deliberating body and representation was predicated according to area rather than the population.[45] Later, under Hussein, senior posts in government and administration continued to be monopolized by Transjordanians,[46] while the Palestinian opposition and those Arab countries contesting the annexation continued against a backdrop of increasing Israeli resistance. As Abdullah prepared to modify the parliamentary model, new elections were scheduled for August 1951 and on 17 July 1951 the former Lebanese First Minister, Riad as-Solh, was assassinated in Amman by a member of the Syrian National Party. Three days later, Abdullah was killed in Jerusalem.[47] The assassinations marked a turning point in Palestinian resistance: no longer peaceful, they entered a phase of violence that would form the backdrop to their political integration within the Jordanian parliament and administration.

Increasingly accountable to the Chamber for their policies, the early parties heralded the emergence of a semi-organized public opinion in the country and the growth of a separate Transjordanian nation-state identity.[48] Significantly, in May 1949 three Palestinians were appointed to the Jordanian Cabinet, a year after the onset of the Palestine War: Ruhi Abdel Hadi, Musa Nasir and Khulusi Khayri represented a change pending a permanent legal-constitutional arrangement as the newly annexed territory held twice the population of the Kingdom east of the Jordan[49] and gradually the number of senators rose to 20, seven of whom were Palestinian. During the 1940s and 1950s, the Palestinian presence in Jordanian politics was characterized by the vociferous group press for policies, despite the absence of a clear agenda.[50] The exigency for enhanced governmental participation was felt nonetheless through the fervent organization of forces so numerous that 'their numerical strength (and perhaps even the resultant emphasis on the Palestinian problem) makes it possible to view the parties [of the Jordanian National Movement] as primarily belonging to the West Bank.'[51] Political ideology, nationalism and patriotism were associated with opposition to the Jordanian regime, particularly with the struggle to democratize political and public life, and parallels were drawn with the political agenda of the Communists.[52] For the majority of Jordanian rule, the Ba'ath party and the Arab Nationalist movement, which had supporters in Dheisheh, were illegal. Parties were initially very small, with membership in the Communist Party nudging 2,000 in the West Bank, while for the Ba'ath there were a few hundred – and fewer still during periods of unrest.[53] Between 1950 and 1970, Palestinian nationalism had yet to gain momentum as it did after the 1967 War and was seldom endorsed by the nationalist parties and movements active in Jordan.[54]

Despite the political stagnation, the period was marked by a surge in the popularity of Marxist, Ba'athist and pan-Arab ideologies within the Palestinian communities in and around Jordan. As many Palestinians pinned their hopes of repatriation on external forces, Palestinian intellectuals in Beirut endorsed the belief that the aforementioned doctrines would benefit the Palestinian cause through the revival of Arab society as a whole. Correspondingly, others looked to Nasser as the leader who would liberate Palestine. Such approaches would prove futile, essentially 'non-Palestinian solutions to the Palestine question [and] tied the recovery of Palestine to external Arab regimes and outside ideologies. Even the most Palestinian organization of the time was little more than an instrument of the Arab states.'[55] By the late 1950s distinct Palestinian political movements began to evolve. Fatah, committed to remaining independent of Arab regimes, and whose interests were not concurrent with all Palestinians, favoured direct military confrontation with Israel. Equally, smaller movements that emerged from the pro-Nasserist Arab national groups in Beirut moved towards a Marxist analysis of society and social action and the belief that a free Palestine could be achieved through a revolution in the Arab countries.[56] But as new ideological directions emerged, the Palestinian movement as a whole remained a disjointed outfit, lacking a distinct, united objective.

In 1964 the Arab League created a separate entity for the new generation of Palestinians educated in Cairo and Beirut and responsive to the political ideologies under debate. The Palestinian Liberation Organization (PLO) functioned under Egyptian control and its military faction was appended to the Egyptians, Jordanian, Iraqi and Syrian armies.[57] Hussein's approval of the PLO demonstrated the necessity 'to accommodate the almost unanimous Arab position that the Palestinian identity should be asserted' for 'the Palestine problem had not been resolved and [the] unity of the West Bank and the East Bank would not prejudice the ultimate solution to the Palestine problem.'[58] Had the Jordanian government objected to a Palestinian entity, it would have isolated itself from other Arab nations and distanced its Palestinian population. But despite its support, Jordan remained cautious and imposed a number of limitations, placing the Palestine Liberation Army (PLA) under the direction of the United Arab Command (UAC), prohibiting interference in the domestic affairs of the Arab states and the exercise of territorial sovereignty in the West Bank.[59] Seeking to contain the Palestinian movements further, Hussein initiated a seven-point agreement in November 1968, forbidding members of organizations to carry arms or wear uniforms, enjoining them to carry Jordanian identity papers at all times and mark cars with Jordanian license plates, be tried under Jordanian legislature for crimes committed on Jordanian soil, desist from halting and searching cars, and avoid recruitment competition with the Jordanian army. Lastly, disputes between the Palestinian organizations and the Jordanian government would be resolved between Hussein and the representatives of the relevant Palestinian movements.[60]

Over subsequent years, the limitations would be repeatedly flouted. Between 1967 and 1970 the PLO established a quasi-autonomous administration in Jordan, prompting clashes between the PLO militias and the Jordanian army. As Palestinian leaders sought the right to

conscript and tax Palestinians living in Jordan and commenced unsanc-
tioned incursions into Israel,[61] they signalled a threat to Jordanian sovereignty and a threat to the Kingdom's stability, for had Israel retaliated
the West Bank would have provided the foremost location of confrontation. The Arab League's designation of the PLO as the legitimate representative of the Palestinian people at the 1974 Arab League Summit
in Rabat included those who had adopted Jordanian citizenship and
heightened the ambiguity of the Palestinian-Jordanian relationship. In
turn many Palestinian-Jordanians responded with ambivalence towards
its formation, while outrage poured from the East Bank when 'some East
Bank Jordanians [...] wanted to remove Jordanian citizenship from the
Palestinians and call new elections in the East Bank alone.'[62] Realizing
the serious implications this would have for the state, Hussein and
Prime Minister Zaid al-Rifai shunned extreme methods. The Jordanian
government could only regulate its Palestinian citizens if it addressed
the issues engendering the unrest – that is, Palestinian rights, the West
Bank and relations with the PLO – for '[f]ailure in this regard would lead
to a growing divergence of interests and aims between the Palestinian
base [and] a divergence that the existence of an autonomous Palestinians
body (such as the PRM or PLO) would exacerbate.'[63]

By 1970, the utilization of Jordanian territory to attack Israel
in the Jordan Rift after 1967 (with the consent of the government)
presented a threat to internal security. The aftermath of the 1970
ceasefire generated unease amongst the Palestinians confronting the prospect of exclusion from the negotiations. As Hussein
and Nasser accepted the Rogers Plan and a ceasefire took effect, it
was anticipated that an Israeli withdrawal from the Jordanian and
Egyptian territory occupied by Israel in 1967 would follow in return
for a comprehensive peace settlement. In contrast, the Palestinian
organizations regarded acceptance of the Plan as a betrayal of the
Palestinian cause and evidence of collusion with the United States.[64]
As Yasser Arafat and the PLO fielded demands by Nayif Hawatmah
of the Popular Front for the Liberation of Palestine (PFLP) and
George Habash of the Popular Democratic Front for the Liberation
of Palestine (PDFLP) to overthrow conservative Arab regimes as a
precondition for an assault on Israel, they remained dogmatic in the

fight against Israel, while maintaining distance from Arab politics. By August 1970, the PFLP and PDFLP had attempted to overthrow Hussein as a preliminary step towards a radical Arab front willing to confront Israel.[65] The realization of the possibility of the Palestinian forces being used against the state compelled Hussein to launch an all-out war against the Palestinians, resulting in thousands exiled, wounded, and killed, and the crushing of the organizational infrastructure.[66]

While the overall goal of the November 1971 Arab League's Joint Defence Council in Cairo was to surmount Israeli aggression, additional talks addressed the issue of aggression from within and in Jordan's case, the question of Palestinian organizations and their quest for a 'state within a state'. Despite the agreement on the Seven-Point Plan between Hussein and Palestinian leaders, the intervening three years brought little change, culminating in September 1970 with the outbreak of the Jordanian Civil War, which demonstrated the drive and disregard for Jordanian authority of the Palestinian movements. Seeking to contain the internal threat, Jordanian Prime Minister (and at that time also Defence Minister) Wasfi Tal agreed to draw up a document that would recognize the PLO as the representative of the Palestinians, with the caveat that it would operate only in its capacity as a political body in Jordan.[67] Yet while the accord was finalized, opposition to the initiative continued and as Tal left the negotiations the six gunmen – members of the newly formed Black September (the following year to be of Munich Summer Olympics infamy) – moved in for the kill. What followed brought the Palestinian struggle to a new nadir: as one of the killers knelt to lick Tal's blood from the floor, the Prime Minister's wife screamed 'Palestine is finished!'[68] And in Jordan it was: already exiled to Lebanon after the failed coup of Black September, the remaining forces relocated to the burgeoning 'state within a state' operating from the 16 UNRWA Palestinian refugee camps in Lebanon.

With numbers nudging 300,000 and power transferred from the Maronite-dominated Deuxième Bureau to the Palestinian Armed Struggle Command in accordance with the Cairo Agreement (1969),[69] the battleground had shifted from the Kingdom to Lebanon. But Arafat remained unrepentant as he claimed responsibility for the assassination – and it would not be the last. Territory was no longer an issue: one month later, the Jordanian ambassador (and later Prime Minister) Zaid al-Rifai was wounded in London by a Black September gunman, while in 1973 Fatah members were arrested during a plot to seize hostages at the U.S. embassy in Amman, and an assassination attempt on Hussein at the 1974 Rabat Arab Summit was also thwarted.[70] Arafat's acceptance of responsibility, combined with his high profile in the realm of Palestinian resistance, rendered him the icon of violent, national struggle. But to assume Arafat as the sole force behind Black September would be a flawed, almost facile pursuit. From a perspective of semi-vindication for Arafat, Said K. Aburish poses the question, 'could Black September have taken place without Arafat's knowledge and approval? Amazingly [...] yes.'[71] Arafat's role was nominal in a group that comprised members of the DFLP and PFLP, including Abu Iyad, Kamal Adwan, Abu Jihad, Ali Hassan Salameh (under whom the assassination of Tal was enacted), George Habash and Khalid Al Hassan: 'except for suggesting the use of a new name, the final decision to create Black September was carried without his (Arafat's) vote.'[72] From leader to minor participant, Aburish demotes Arafat further: 'Even after twenty years no evidence has been uncovered to suggest that Arafat was personally involved, or that he approved any one single operation. But he was in a position to stop the operations, at least most of them, and that he did not do.'[73] The extent of Arafat's involvement in each act is superfluous to the main point; that he *was in a position to stop* the actions of the factions indicates a position of authority and power. That Arafat proceeded to become the most influential and enduring icon of the Palestinian struggle does not sit easily with the apologetic image of a man with no vote and no power of approval. On an organizational level, the PLO made attempts to return to Jordan after the assassination of Tal and even enlisted the assistance of King Faisal of Saudi Arabia in an active role to work out an agreement. It was to no avail. For Jordan, the loss of Tal was grave, but Hussein (and to a degree Jordan) gained immensely through the expulsion of the PLO to Lebanon. Hussein's alliance with America brought money and technology that would expand Jordan on an international level and the U.S. government re-equipped the Jordanian army on the military front. Hussein 'could only look on with relief and despair' as Black September kidnapped and killed 11 Israeli athletes at the Munich Olympics.[74] Jordan, for now, was safe.

Jordan had passed through one of its greatest challenges since independence, but to external observers Hussein had triumphed where Lebanon's leaders had failed. By avoiding Israel and Syria, striking a balance between the Transjordanian and Palestinian components of his Kingdom and aligning with Iraq, Egypt and the smaller Gulf states in the 1980s, Hussein offset declining relations with Syrian and Saudi Arabian reticence that had lingered since the expulsion of the Hashemites from Mecca and Medina in the 1920s.[75] Nevertheless, Black September had divided Palestinian and Jordanian society and the legacy would be far-reaching. By November 1974, the consequences were tangible in parliament: once composed of an equal number of East and West Bankers, it was dissolved by the king and a new cabinet was formed by Zaid Rifai, in which only three out of 19 cabinet members were Palestinian. As internal affairs calmed and the Kingdom began to reap the fruits of its new unions, the government stance vis-à-vis the Palestinians relaxed and the number of Palestinians in the cabinet readjusted to the pre-1974 level.[76] While politically Jordan has readjusted, the tensions between Palestinian-Jordanians and Jordanians in the Kingdom continued and proved less flexible than cabinet seats.

The Difficult Alliance

Arising from politics, culture, resentment, anxiety and history, the tensions between the Palestinian-Jordanians are viewed distinctively by each community. Politically, the Palestinians emerged from their perpetual struggle into a new life in Jordan with a passion for politics and Palestinian nationalism that could not be quelled by Abdallah I. Although the Hashemites sought to integrate the Palestinians into the Jordanian nation-state, the Palestinian national aspirations rendered assurances of 'Jordan and Palestine were always one people and one country'[77] vain. The disassociation between the Palestinians and Jordan manifested prior to Israel's takeover of the West Bank in 1967, a disassociation that rendered Jordan a weak, non-threatening entity in comparison with its neighbours, for 'if you offended the Jews, you were punished by the occupation forces; if you offended Syria or the PLO, someone would burn your car; but you could say whatever you wanted about Jordan and nothing would happen to you.'[78] By the 19th year of Transjordanian administration, the West Bank bore few signs of Jordanization and West Bankers viewed the Jordanians more as occupiers than countrymen, while holding contempt for the Arab Legion.

The early years of coexistence were marked by social, educational and cultural schisms whose traces remain 50 years on. In 1948, East Jordan was largely rural, the people lived in villages or Bedouin tents and though a number of small towns existed, such as Irbid, Amman, Salt and Karak, they were inhabited by only 30,000 people and had few urban characteristics.[79] Palestine, meanwhile, had a distinctly urban centre with concentrations in port cities and towns such as Haifa, Gaza and Jaffa and in the principal towns of Jerusalem, Nablus, Nazareth and Hebron with populations ranging from 20,000 to 65,000.[80] The Transjordanians regarded the modern mode of living and values held by the Palestinians with disdain. Believing their new compatriots had veered from the simple life of the quintessential Arab, they regarded themselves as righteous and reserved contempt for the Palestinians who had lost their homes to the occupation.[81] Abidi's observances in the 1960s demonstrate an animosity in abundance on both sides through Jordanian quips of '[h]ow fine was our life before union!' as Palestinians lamented their new surroundings and 'ridicule[d] the tribal life and customs of the Transjordanians [and] refuse[d] to be at the receiving end.'[82] Despite variances in living standards, the Palestinians brought positive ideas, methods and skills that would transform Jordan within decades.

Integration emerged in the education, employment and economic sectors to name but a few. The educational advantage of the Palestinians over their contemporaries was drastic and combined with their political savvy, they swiftly learned the value of education as a weapon against the occupation. While discord reached the streets and negotiation tables, so too the Palestinians used their expertise to gain positions in the business and employment sectors. Integral to the formation of self-identity, education provided the means for social mobility and an opportunity to alleviate the circumstances of the refugees.[83] Prior to the first Gulf War, the rewards of pursuing the educational approach were evident as families capitalized on their academic prowess and attained prosperity. The aftermath of the Gulf War emphasized their socially elevated status, as, on entering Jordan in 1991, an element of resentment prevailed – less at the loss of their homeland to the occupation, than at the decline in social standing following their expulsion by Saddam Hussein. Once more starting afresh, education became an investment for the next generation and (not without a hint of irony) the Palestinians became regarded as the 'Jews of the Arab world'.[84] For Palestinians in the diaspora, the mantra of 'the children are our house'[85] suggests the onus placed on children to 'rescue their family from miserable conditions through education.'[86] During conflict, however, the Palestinian educational lead diminished in comparison to their Arab counterparts and figures compiled in 1980 revealed the ratio of students in the population to have risen to 17.5 per thousand in Egypt, 16.1 in Syria and 16.5 in Jordan.[87] While Jordan's sum continued to rise in the 1990s, the majority of Jordanian students were of Palestinian origin.[88] Likewise, in terms of faculty Palestinian-Jordanians occupy a higher percentage of places in both public (51 per cent) and private (71 per cent) universities.[89]

In terms of employment, the 1960s defined Jordan as a premium exporter of migrant workers, the majority of whom were Palestinian. It is worth noting that prior to the arrival of the Palestinians, the concept of the worker's union was absent; as the Palestinians arrived, the new workers gradually reintroduced their unions in Jordan.[90] As early as the 1950s, an increase in emigration was noted and the 1961 census ascertained that 61,000 Jordanians were employed abroad.[91] Among them were skilled, semi-skilled and non-skilled labourers, technicians, professionals and semi-professionals, all impacting the labour market before the regional division of labour between oil-rich and labour-exporting states reached a pattern of development. Into the 1970s, Jordan proactively provided employment opportunities for the refugees, with 'self-sufficiency' being a key component in rebuilding their lives. Those who were not able to support themselves received rations and education, while others received vocational training from the UNRWA. Of the 1,344,576 Palestinian refugees, 722,687 resided in Jordan, though the Secretary-General of the United Nations dismissed 'the widespread assumption that the refugees [had] been stagnating in idleness in the refugee camps.'[92] In particular, Jordan gained praise for its control of the unemployment levels as the refugees 'were rapidly achieving the capacity to support themselves [and] the social and economic aspects of the refugee problem in Jordan [...] were well on the way to a partial remedy.'[93]

Regardless, the government established development plans and an increase in the numbers of Palestinians employed to harvest crops seasonally and install irrigation works, greenhouses, food-processing factories, warehouses, metal fabrication workshops and textile plants, and garages soon followed.[94] Businesses were established on a small scale with shops in the shanty towns of Amman and on a grand scale with the Arab Bank founded in 1930 by a Palestinian peasant, Abd al-Hamid Shuman.[95] The decrease in the Palestinian presence on the relief rolls after 1967 illustrates that many former refugees had taken advantage of the emigration of Jordanians to the oil states and found employment in the local economy.[96] Equally, the increase in disposable income was aided by remittances from the Gulf states after a growth in oil exports raised demand for labour in the urban areas.[97] Despite their efforts, the Palestinian refugees are impeded in their bid for employment as figures demonstrate that less than 10 per cent of the 35,000 government employees are of Palestinian origin and holders of temporary Jordanian passports. Prohibited from seeking employment in the public sector,[98] the result of such obstacles is the restriction of opportunities to escape the camp system and establish an independent future, which in turn contributes to the wider disillusionment amongst camp residents.

Yet just as Jordan has endured unrest and influxes, to an extent the demographic changes have been conducive to a resilience reflected in the political and social sectors that enrich private sector potential.[99] The influx of Palestinians nonetheless disrupted the equilibrium of an economy that had a low absorptive capacity with respect to the majority of refugees. With little or no assets and dependent on UNRWA, the refugee population looked to labour migration for its livelihood. In the three years preceding the 1967 War, an annual average of 26,000 Palestinians (predominantly West Bankers) left the Kingdom for Kuwait and Saudi Arabia.[100] The extent of the labour migration was reflected throughout the 17 years of Transjordanian rule as its population increased by 100,000, despite a 3.5 per cent annual rate of natural growth.[101] Moreover, data for Jordan demonstrates that the outflow influenced the relative weight of employment in the public sector, as figures rose from 34 per cent in 1972 to 46 per cent in 1986 – a growth attributed to the 'readjustment' of the state's economy in the wake of its new role as labour provider to the Gulf states.[102]

Forging their new life in Jordan were two categories of Palestinian refugee: the camp resident and non-camp refugee. Of the former, only 1 per cent of camp refugees had a professional background (businessmen, clerical workers and skilled professionals) in contrast to 60 per cent of Amman-based refugees. Prior to the 1967 War, 51 per cent of non-camp refugees originated from large cities with 66 per cent being home-owners. By comparison, 80 per cent of camp residents had previously owned their own homes.[103] Geographical factors and the spirit of competition in Palestine had granted the non-camp resident Palestinians an enviable economic status. The multitude of professionals and trained civil servants coupled with finer training and experience enabled them to outclass the Jordanians in the professional and business sectors.[104] The Palestinian success story was not without challenges, however, and in the 1960s discrimination re-emerged with renewed vigour. The Palestinians of the West Bank believed the Transjordanian government attributed more resources to the development of the area of Jordan than the West Bank as new educational and health institutions, agricultural projects and small-scale factories were located in the East Bank.

Abidi reasons that the government's actions rested on the rationalization that 'the East Bank had remained relatively underdeveloped for long and deserved more attention [and] the West Bank is nearer to Israel and hence insecure.'[105] Just as each side sees sound rationalizations or economic discrimination, the encouragement of the economic development of the East Bank was most prominent around Amman and at the cost of the outlaying regions. As a result, Amman flourished as the core power centre and brought about a reorientation of West Bank traders towards the capital.[106] The stream of workers, largely Palestinian refugees, is reflected by the population growth between 1949 and 1961 as Amman swelled from 43,000 in 1944 to 246,000 in 1961 and 350,000 in 1967, with Palestinians constituting approximately 75 per cent of the final figure.[107]

The subsequent boom in the 1970s brought a thaw in the tensions between the Palestinians and Jordanians as the elite and labourers of both communities enjoyed the economic climate and free enterprise system. Jordanian and Palestinian businessmen established joint enterprises and worked cohesively while the abundance of job opportunities mitigated both Jordanian covetousness of the Palestinians' prominence in business, and Palestinian antipathy towards the Jordanian monopoly of power. As the elite traded involvement in political activity for economic advancement, so too did the refugees pose less of a political liability as the economic and social benefits of increased government spending offered partial compensation.[108] The link between economy and politics prompted warm overtures from the Palestinian community towards the government, particularly from the middle classes. Close family ties between Palestinian and Jordanian families and a strong interest in Jordan's political stability encouraged a growing identification with the monarchy in the midst of relinquishing the animosities rife following the 1974 Rabat Summit.[109] Despite enthusiastic sentiments, the Palestinian identity was still vital and the events of Black September underscored the divisions between the two communities. Although economically bonded, two separate nationalisms took hold and as the Jordanian identity grew with each act of Palestinian defiance, so too did its counterpart appeal to a new generation and ensure fresh rifts with each economic flux.

Inevitably, the 1990s ended the honeymoon period and reintroduced disillusionment on the tail of the unsuccessful resolution of the Arab-Israeli conflict. Jordan had been exposed to the frustration of the Palestinian majority of its population and the steady population rise negated income gains and created a dearth of young people. Unable to sustain the increase, external investments declined and Jordan retaliated with a series of unpopular reforms, bureaucracy reductions and a cut in subsidies in line with IMF and World Bank demands.[110] The reforms were a blow to the indigenous Transjordanians, the support base of the monarchy, as adequate finances still failed to flow in. Sour relations between the Palestinians and Israelis after 1996 further quashed Jordan's hopes for economic dividends from its 1994 treaty with Israel and previously buoyant expectations that the Kingdom could serve as a 'hinge state' between Israel and the Arab world proved erroneous.[111] By 2000, the collective GDP of Syria, Jordan and Lebanon peaked at $42 billion, less than half of Israel's $112 billion.[112] As in the 1960s, the limitations of the financial golden period combined with the issue of identity were evident. Regardless of their social status, government efforts to persuade the Palestinians to accept the Jordanian identity through economic prosperity were doomed and pecuniary offerings proved a fickle placebo, particularly when the main desire remained statehood.

Cohesion and Discrimination in Jordanian Society

For certain Palestinian-Jordanians, the dichotomy between the two groups remains imperceptible, manifested through the responses 'Jordan and Palestine are one' and the notion of 'brotherhood'. Inevitably, the divisions remain perceptible and, for those of the schismatic inclination, the dichotomy rests with origin: the Transjordanians from the nomadic tribes of Syria, the Hejaz and the Nejd, and the Palestinians from Arab nomads, Cannanites, Hebrews, Syrians, Romans, Byzantine and Greeks.[113] Comprising also the Circassians and Chechens in their midst, Abidi suggests the ethnic diversity of Jordan is conducive to additional schisms of Arab-Circassian and Christian-Muslim. The sources of these tensions are not wholly religious and derive from the degrees of modernity and difference in the economic status of the groups concerned. In the case of the Arab-Circassian disparity, the tensions arise from the Arab assertion that the Circassians are not of their own race; conversely, the Circassians demonstrate little enthusiasm to be identified as Arabs.[114] Writing in 1965, Abidi's observances – while poignant – demonstrate positive change in Jordanian society, for any hints at schisms between the

Circassian and Chechen communities and Palestinian/Jordanian are met only with incredulity. But while certain rifts have healed, others have opened in their place.

Christian communities have long flourished in the area that is now the Hashemite Kingdom of Jordan, notably in and around the provincial towns of Karak, Madaba, Salt and Amman. Jordan's history as a transit country has provided a rich and varied tapestry of cultures and faiths, the most notable being the majority mixed-faith Palestinian community that is estimated to comprise 60 per cent of the Kingdom's population. The peaceful mélange of faiths is illustriously exhibited in the capital by the numerous spires that stretch alongside minarets towards the skies of Amman. The Christians of Jordan and Palestine deserve more than a passing nod as they transcend the boundaries of ethnic, religious and national identity within Jordanian society. While Jordan has long sustained a Christian community, the Palestinian debut facilitated the rise of a new identity which continues to complement the existing Jordanian Christian identity – that of the Palestinian and Palestinian-Jordanian Christian identity. Multifarious and vibrant, the political and cultural aspects that have sustained and evolved the identity shall be charted, culminating in a debate addressing the future of the community in Jordan. The Christian Arabs originate from three areas: central Palestine and the Galilee and the middle and south of Lebanon; southern Syria; and the Caucasus. The greater majority of Christians in 'Amman and Zarqa' are originally refugees from 1948 or arrived by internal or external migration.[115] Although there is no reliable data relating to the religious affiliation of the populations in Palestine prior to the British census of 1922, estimates of the Christian population in the year 1900 in all of Palestine, including Galilee, the Mediterranean coast, Jerusalem, the West Bank and Gaza Strip, range from a high of 18 per cent to a modest 10 per cent.[116] According to recent sociological studies in the Palestinian territories that incorporate East Jerusalem, the West Bank, and the Gaza Strip, the Palestinian Christian population has dropped to a mere 2.4 per cent of the total Arab population.[117]

Yet the exact number of Christians present in the Kingdom is disputable: Valonges estimates that Christians in Jordan constitute

3 per cent of the total population,[118] while the 1994 census concluded the figure at a mere 2.4 per cent, with more than half of
them of Palestinian origin.[119] Among this multi-denominational
population, Greek Orthodox is by far the most popular affiliation,
with 75 per cent of Jordanian Christians members of the Eastern
Orthodox Church. Following the 1948 War, the Greek Orthodox
Church was placed under the supervision of the Jordanian government, which governed religious expression under the Mandate
government. While Jordanian efforts to nationalize the Orthodox
Church were initiated, a reluctance to interfere in the internal affairs
of Christians caused the endeavour to flounder. The uncertainty
continued until Israel's occupation of the West Bank and Jerusalem
nullified Jordanian authority, though the question of 'how much
intervention' persisted. When Patriarch Benedictos passed away in
Jerusalem in 1980, the Monks of the Holy Sepulchre called for the
election of a new Patriarch. The move was greeted with threats of
election boycott by the Arabs if their rights were not restored and
petitions were presented to the king and government. Responding
to the challenge, the government naturalized a number of Greek
monks, enabling them to meet the voting criteria. The elections
resulted in favour of Deodoros against Bishop Fasilios and Bishop
Germanos, and Deodoros was formally elected by royal decree on
21 February 1981.[120]

The Armenian Orthodox Church forms an exception in the
Christian communities of Jordan and their acceptance of Jordanian
identity is guided more by conformism than willing assimilation. As
Haddad notes:

> The problem for them is the association of the Jordanian iden-
> tity with its basic characterization as Moslem, which they reject,
> essentially when it is fundamentally defined through its Arab-
> Moslem identity. They have a national identity that is linked to
> their being Christians and followers of the Armenian Orthodox
> Church, and this plays an important role in their socio-cultural
> and political organization.[121]

On matters of identity, it is possible to distinguish commonalities between the Palestinian refugees of 1967 and the Armenian Orthodox community: the reluctance to embrace Jordanian culture and society as a new home and future and the creation of communities that maintain an element of 'home' for the old and new generations alike. This is particularly evident in Harat al-Arman in Amman, the refugee camps that have become villages and towns and the continuance of diaspora organizations that maintain links with Armenians and Palestinians worldwide.

In contrast to the Greek and Armenian Orthodox community, the Protestants in Jordan have encountered a cooler reception. Stigmatized by connotations of colonialism, anti-Arabism, conspiracy against Islam and links to Judaic sects, they confront mistrust not from the wider Arab community, but from the older Christian churches. Unlike the Greek Orthodox Church, which enjoyed cohesion soon after Jordanian independence, the Protestants have experienced rejection and alienation that escalated in the aftermath of the creation of the Israeli state. The defeat of the Arab armies, the success of the Jewish immigrants in displacing the Palestinians and the preaching of missionaries adhering to the Old Testament (and referred to the return of the Jews to the Promised Land) lent credence to the notion of a Protestant conspiracy against the Arabs, Moslems and Christians alike.[122]

The Jordanian Christians are largely pro-Hashemite and the dynasty remains the guarantor of Jordan's ethnic and religious balance, including the 2,000-year-old Arab Christians. Within the administration, the Jordanian Christians have secured high positions: in November 2004 the government appointed a Christian Deputy Prime Minister, Marwan Moasher; two Christian ambassadors from the same tribe were appointed to Washington and Paris; while the Christian community is allocated six of 55 seats in the appointed Senate and at least two cabinet posts. In the military, Christians can reach the highest rank of general commander of the army, while the private sector has proven equally fruitful, with almost 40 per cent of private economic power guided under the ownership of Christian businessmen.[123] More recently, however, the Christian population has dwindled: in 2001, the figure stood at approximately 120,000, compared with 115,000 in 1961, and while the general population has trebled, the Christian population rose little. The most likely cause of limited growth is migration, yet Jordan as a predominantly Islamic country yields a hospitable environment for Christian coexistence, particularly as the process of democratization and growing freedom actively encourages Christians to create and expand their economic ventures.[124] Jordan is not immune to the financial crises and it is pecuniary, rather than political, impulses powering the move. Educated and ambitious, the new generation of Christians are seeking their futures outside the Kingdom and as the Jordanian economy continues to prove fickle the decline will inevitably follow apace.

Prisms of Identity

The majority of the Palestinian diaspora community comprises the refugees of Lebanon and Jordan, many of whom remain in the camps. As the number of Palestinian refugees increased, a strengthened sense of Palestinian identity was nurtured by the belief in a physical return to Palestine and the establishment of a stable Palestinian state, which would provide amenable living conditions, legal equality and a viable future for subsequent generations.[125] Since their arrival, refugees have resisted the process of complete assimilation into the host states more vehemently than their middle income and elite contemporaries. The prospect of being 'swallowed up in Jordan'[126] fuels refusals of resettlement and their insistence on the right of return under to international law. The refugees are distinguishable from their compatriots in the Kingdom through the following figures: while 14 per cent of refugee citizens who still reside in the camps largely oppose Jordan's conciliatory approach towards Israel and seek for a right of return, the Palestinian middle class, many of whom have established roots in Jordan, are less likely to leave.[127] While indicative of a direct correlation to socio-economic conditions in the host state, the concentration of Palestinians in and around the refugee camps has been integral to the development and consolidation of the Palestinian national identity[128] and defines the degree of integration of the Palestinian community in the host society. According to research conducted in 1994, three main factors determine the status of Palestinian refugees in host states: the external character of how they are legally defined; conflict of interest at state level; and the inherent contradiction between the Palestinians' interest in maintaining the refugee identity and securing civil rights.[129]

Occupying a grey area of identity, the middle class Palestinians arrived in Jordan as small merchants and lower-level government employees who subsequently achieved a level of economic success and integration. While hostility was felt on arrival, it is speculated that it has receded, save only for those actively engaged in the Palestinian movement.[130] For many, their Palestinian background is present through assisting in the refugee camps, at social events and family gatherings. For others, the connection is not so strong. Yet the middle class is fully capable of transforming the Palestinian identity to suit not only their new environment, but also their lifestyle. A blend of Jordanian characteristics with Palestinian cultural traditions, the capacity of each determines the strength of Palestinian identity in the individual. Residing in a limbo between the elite's capricious, ever-changing identity and the steadfast loyalty of the refugees, the middle class present an interesting case.

The final group, the Palestinian-Jordanian elite, comprises families drawn from powerful positions in Palestine and acquainted with the monarchy. Distinguishable from the middle class in the sense that many of the latter confronted the challenge of re-establishing in a new country, their ties to the regime can be traced to the early years of Jordanian independence. Prominent families such as the Nashashibis launched alliances with the monarchy and acknowledged the annexation of the West Bank by Jordan in 1950 and in return they gained access to high positions in Jordanian society, a continuation of that which they maintained in Palestine. As the elite passed the early years in favour with the monarchy, the shift in the political atmosphere raised the question of whether societal comforts struck a higher priority than the Palestinian struggle. As sectors of the elite made strategic or sincere choices a discourse on the Palestinian, Palestinian-Jordanian and/or Jordanian identity was taking place simultaneously.

As members of Palestine's indigenous ruling classes allied with Abdullah, they faced a dilemma following the Jordanian annexation of the West Bank in 1950. Confronted with accepting the Hashemite hegemony and the benefits that would follow through participation in the Jordanian government, the alternative was a continuation of the struggle for an independent Palestinian state and against the Israeli occupation.[131] Just as the former promised security and the standard of living to which they had become accustomed, it also denoted the relinquishment of the opportunity to assist the Palestinian people. And the latter option was no more palatable, implying the loss of land, estate and power; in contrast, the benefits were of the non-material kind, affording the right to speak for the Palestinians as a whole.[132] In the end, those who chose to play an active role in the struggle were either deported or forced into exile, while others later made peace with the monarchy in the 1960s. Meanwhile, those who originally chose the Hashemites continued to excel within the Jordanian government and diplomatic sphere, while rejecting demands from their Palestinian-Jordanian constituents for a resumption of the nationalist struggle.[133] In the latter instance, identity could be bought – or at least stifled – for the right price, be it wealth, power or social status.

A Battle for Amman, Jordan and Palestine

> If I am not for myself, who is for me, but if I am for my own self, what am I? And if not now, when?[134]

While peace was being brokered in the early- to mid-1960s, by the end of the decade the schism between Palestinians and Jordanians was becoming an open rupture. If the events of the Jordanian Civil War proved an irreparable explosion in tensions, the Six-Day War provided a steady striking of the match. The conflict transcended the loss of the West Bank and East Jerusalem as the Six-Day War undermined Jordanian military might, straining relations between the Kingdom and its Palestinian inhabitants on the one hand and Israel on the other, and emphasized both the Kingdom's fragility as well as its dependence on external relations with Israel, the United

States, Egypt and Syria. The legacy was social, cultural, political and nationalistic: not merely the loss of a land, it was the loss of a union and ultimately, a people.

The War roused an animosity that brought blame upon both sides in the Kingdom: had Hussein been stronger, the territory would not have been ceded; had the Palestinians desisted from provoking Israel through 1966 and 1967, the conflict might (the term can be applied loosely) not have occurred. The clash of narratives characterizes Palestinian-Jordanian and Jordanian discourse – the Battle of Karameh, fought in the eponymous Jordanian town between the Jordanian army, the PLO and the Israeli Defence Forces on 21 March 1968, being a foremost point of contention – yet the competing narratives concerning the Six-Day War bore graver implications and emphasized the rupture between Hussein and the PLO. The tussle for power was perceived by the Palestinians in Jordan as a means to ensure political and national survival, but for Hussein the hijackings, makeshift military camps and attacks on his convoys connoted only attempts at domination, uprising and usurpation. Fundamentally, the nation was at stake: for the Palestinian-Jordanians, Palestine; for Hussein, the Kingdom. Neither would relinquish their objective and both had populations counting on their success.

Just as Israel had grown weary of attacks by Fatah, so too was Jordan exhausted under the yoke of retaliation. In November 1966, three Israeli soldiers were killed by a mine; in response, 21 Jordanian soldiers were killed and 37 wounded in an Israeli attack in the West Bank village of Samua.[135] Between 1967 and 1971, Arafat sustained a campaign of bombing and shelling kibbutzim in the West Bank, and Israelis reciprocated. For those inhabiting properties in the West Bank area, the repercussions were borne once more, economically and structurally: 'I don't remember getting a penny from my farm in '67 to '71 because that was a continuous active front. Those who paid for it were the Jordanians who helped the Palestinians.'[136] The Kingdom's subsequent engagement in the Six-Day War was reluctant; just as Israel advised against participation, the Jordanian population called for action in the name of Palestine, the preservation of Jordanian territory in the West Bank and East Jerusalem, and the desire to support Egypt. Confronted with either civil war and inevitable loss of territory on the one hand, and engagement in a war in which victory was uncertain, Hussein chose the former and on 30 May 1967 committed to a defence pact with Nasser in Cairo. What followed transcended Hussein's portents, for within six hours of battle being joined the Jordanian air force was defeated, within 24 hours the West Bank was lost, and by the third day Jordanian ground forces had capitulated in Jerusalem.[137] The king had seized the gauntlet cast down by Nasser and roundly lost.

In later recollections, an ambiguity remains regarding the apportionment of culpability. Although Hussein initially hints at Palestinian involvement, he later cites Egypt: 'I looked at the internal scene in Jordan. [...] Jordan had been attacked by Israel time and time again *for actions that might have originated elsewhere.*[138] So in the eyes of Israel, we were one, we and Egypt.'[139] On this point, Hussein exercises a level of restraint with the truth, for Jordan had served as a launch-site for Palestinian attacks on Israel; more accurate would be the argument that if Jordan and Egypt were cohorts against Israel, the Palestinian resistance made three. Jordan and Egypt entered the conflict under diverse impulses – for the former the battle was a reluctant tussle in defence of what it already held; for the latter it was a show of might, regardless of the consequences. Any commonality between the two resided in the tendency to enter a fray unprepared and against what one might expect to be their better judgement:

> Five years of fighting in the Yemen had left the Egyptian army exhausted, its ranks seriously depleted and much of its military equipment worn out or damaged beyond repair. The Egyptian army was, they stress, ill-prepared and ill-equipped to challenge, let alone defeat, the well-supplied and well-trained Israeli Defence Forces (IDF).[140]

And it was not only Egypt's involvement that proved questionable. Three years after the completion of the contested Israeli National Water Carrier (NWC) that diverted water from the River Jordan, attempts at sabotage continued. With its waters coursing through the

Kingdom, Jordan confronted a dilemma: to allow Israel to siphon the resource would consolidate their amity to the surrounding Arab states, while at the same time sharing – or losing – water, or ally with the neighbouring states in the Six-Day War and prevent further water carriage into Israel. The construction of the NWC transcended the issue of supply and demand: for an investment of $175 million, Israel nurtured strategic plans, the ramifications of which would be felt into the twenty-first century. The Six-Day War facilitated their aspirations and having secured the West Bank Israel gained the Mountain Aquifer and the accompanying ability to restrict Palestinian water supplies and divert resources to Israeli suppliers. Despite the gain, as the population of Israel continues to grow, supplies continue to be drawn from the Rivers Jordan and Yarmouk, and the East Ghor Canal, resulting in the depletion of the Dead Sea and the Sea of Galilee.[141] By entering the war against Israel, Jordan risked a heavier loss through a plan proposed by the Arab states to divert the Hasbani and the Banias from the River Jordan. Had it proceeded, the Kingdom would have lost half of its water supply.[142] For Jordan, the conflict was replete with conflicting demands from competing factions: the Palestinians, who did not long for assistance, but rather *expected* support; Egypt and Syria, allies who also expected loyalty and ergo, action; Israel, the foe with the promise of power and potentially, U.S. support. Equally, energy and territory represented economic and nationalistic concerns and last, Jordan's integrity as a nation carved by Western tacticians led by an appointed monarchy in a region jostling under the banner of Arab unity.

To fail would be costly, yet fail she did. But the loss by the Kingdom was shared by its neighbours as the Palestinian resistance, disgruntled by a quivering show of (reluctant) support, commenced action within the host states. The aftermath of the War saw the Palestinian population of Jordan increase from 650,000 to 850,000;[143] homeless, stateless and ripened by nationalist rhetoric the Palestinian movement in the Kingdom located a ready source of recruits. For Hussein, the battle for Jordan was just beginning. As the region recovered from Israel's quick, but devastating, victory, 1967 represented a turning point in the Palestinian cause. Israel had asserted her might and the Palestinian predicament became ever more bleak – and central to the region's political discourse. For a moment, the threat of the activities of the Palestinian movements faded and a unity emerged. But Israel's policies could not reconcile the long-term objectives of Hussein and the Palestinian groups and as 'the confrontation between the king and the Palestinians became imminent, their goals and means of resistance [were] diametrically opposed. One can then predict with accuracy [that] the liquidation of Palestinian organizations became the priority task of the Hashemite king's policies.'[144] The war had provided only an interlude in the tussle between Hussein and Arafat and tensions continued unabated after the battle with Israel had been lost with the boldest act yet: the hijacking of international airlines.

As the refugee camps mutated into guerrilla strongholds, their guardians did not shy away from attacking the monarch's convoy, or establishing checkpoints that would challenge even Jordanian government ministers. Arafat's fiefdom, comprising training camps, prisons, courts and arms stores, financed by extortion, kidnappings and carjackings,[145] was presided over in the manner of a monarch: granting divorces, blessing marriages, passing death sentences and issuing pardons. Emboldened, Arafat considered himself 'stronger than the king.'[146] Hussein was losing control and the popularity of the resistance fighters ensured that strongholds such as Karameh remained unassailable. In November 1968, the Jordanian army entered the camps of Jabal Ashrafiyeh and Jabal Hussein, testing the warning by Arafat that those 'attempt[ing] to stab the Palestinians in the back, [would] pay very much dearly [for] his betrayal.'[147] The Palestinian activities in Jordan were financed not only through nefarious means, but also from external donors. In March 1969, Saudi Arabia levied a tax on Palestinian workers in the Gulf that would generate a $12 million annual grant to the PLO, in addition to almost 30 truck loads of arms to be distributed in the camps of the Jordanian capital.[148] By the following year the *fedayeen*, emboldened by victories in skirmishes with the army, ventured from the camps and into Amman.

In the events that followed Arafat veered from caution; Jordan would not be a substitute state, but rather a battleground. Despite awareness that the support of Hussein would have been a boon, the reluctance of the monarch to commit to the Palestinian cause failed to present an

impediment. Arafat's inability to acknowledge stately etiquette escalated hostilities through 1970, for the Palestinian leader perceived but
one state: Palestine, and 'in his strict Palestinian nationalism there
was an acceptance of reason of state [though] [t]hat acceptance was not
applicable to the two "sanctuaries", Jordan and Lebanon.'[149] The clashes
through June 1970 consolidated Hussein's stance in opposition to the
Palestinians and as the wider region looked on, Jordan emerged as a
study in conservative regime survival.[150] On 6 September, Palestinian
impudence reached its zenith with the hijacking of five planes, three
of which landed in Dawson's Field on the outskirts of Zarqa. The
holding of 600 hostages juxtaposed with the presence of 52 guerrilla
groups and 44,000 abrogations of Jordanian law[151] shifted from the
domestic arena to the international stage, and Hussein's powerlessness
in restraining his subjects inspired fresh humiliation. Yet Hussein did
not respond quickly – perceiving the significance of the juncture and
the opportunity to oust the PLO from the Kingdom, it was not until
17 September that the decision to enter Amman and confront the
fedayeen was issued.

While the Palestinian fighters operated from parts of Amman,
Irbid, Jerash and Zarqa, the intervention and isolation enacted by
Jordan's neighbours presented an added threat in terms of regional
position and security. Widely regarded as a civil war, this definition
has been refuted with the contention that the conflict was neither a
'civil war' nor a police intervention. According to Lunt, the noncom-
mittal stance of certain Palestinians negated the former, while the
absence of restraint in the case of the army refuted the latter. One
further disqualifier can be added: the intervention of regional actors
in deciding the conclusion of the hostilities. Ostensibly a struggle
for dominance between the *fedayeen* and the Jordanian state, Black
September confirmed new lines of alliance in the region: between Syria
and Iraq in support of the Palestinian fighters, and Jordan and Israel in
opposition. The Kingdom was presented with the prospect of not only
rebellion within its borders, but encroachment by the 25,000-strong
Iraqi Expeditionary Forces around Mafraq and Zarqa, four Syrian bri-
gades – including a Palestinian Liberation Army brigade – on the border, economic isolation and the possibility of Saudi intervention on

the side of the Palestinians.[152] In addition, Libya and Kuwait severed financial assistance and diplomatic ties at a time when over 50 per cent of Jordanian annual revenue derived from aid provided by the Arab states.[153] The conflict concluded before the latter could be enacted, but the nature of the Jordanian victory brought confirmation of old suspicions and a renewal of present bitterness.

The intervention of Israel arrived at the behest of the United States following a request by Hussein to President Richard Nixon, as well as Britain, the Soviet Union and France. Operating as a proxy, Israel agreed to commence strikes against the Syrian ground force between 19 and 20 September 1970; within 48 hours, Syria had withdrawn her troops from Jordan and within four days of the incursion the Jordanian army celebrated success.[154] For Israel, intervention had become a necessity, for had Jordan fallen to the Syrian army or Palestinian fighters the threat to the Israeli state would have edged closer. Similarly, it was not merely close ties to the United States that motivated Prime Minister Yigal Allon's agreement; aware of domestic disdain at the risk of Israeli lives and expenditure for the sake of a neighbouring Arab state, Israel attained American support and military equipment for the endeavour.[155] But while the Israeli foray was brief, its intervention provided confirmation of the (clandestine) alliance between Israel and the Hashemites. In her moment of need, Jordan looked to Israel, which duly responded, openly consolidating and affirming an 'intelligence relationship'.[156] Jordan had proved that national security was prized above fraternal relations, and 2,000 fatalities and a country plunged into electricity, communications, food and water shortages[157] had demonstrated the lengths Hussein would go to ensure the future security of the regime, monarchy and Jordanian nation.

Having issued a statement of ceasefire on 25 September, Arafat required a swift exit. His salvation arrived in the form of Sheikh Saa'd Abdullah Assalim, the former Emir of Kuwait, who concealed and smuggled the Palestinian leader to the airport in a manner befitting a farce, rather than the culmination of several years of civil unrest: 'Sheikh Saa'd stripped down to his underwear and gave Arafat his top robes. Arafat then travelled to Amman airport disguised as Sheikh Saa'd and in a Jordanian armoured personnel carrier!'[158] As Arafat slinked off to Cairo free from punishment and 3,000 Palestinians languished in jail, the Jordanian army was unfulfilled and sources interviewed at the time reveal a modicum of frustration: 'All we talked about all day long was what we would like to do to those damned Palestinians.'[159] If the Six-Day War sowed regret and defeat, Black September proved a bittersweet victory. A brief redemption, its legacy has been the continued sentiment of frustration coupled with a latent insecurity. For many of the Jordanians interviewed during fieldwork, Black September is the foundation for distrust and the justification for a multitude of denials of citizenship rights, healthcare and education. The victory over the *fedayeen* is hollow, however, for Jordan risks its long-term prospects for domestic security – keeping the Palestinian refugees in a state of disenfranchised limbo is not durable and in the light of the Arab Spring of 2011, the regime must progress from 1967 and 1970–1971 towards a united, cohesive dynamic between Palestinian-Jordanians and Jordanians alike.

Dissolution and Disillusion (1980–2000)

The mid to late 1980s were to prove tumultuous for the Hashemite monarchy. The Intifada in December 1987 was an unanticipated development amidst dire economic circumstances in the Kingdom. A rebellion against Israel, the uprising raised both opportunities and dubious implications. The West Bank rebellion not only questioned Israeli presence in the Occupied Territories, but also the 'Jordanianess' of the territory as disenchanted Palestinians looked to the PLO as a representative.[160] The result of a car accident in Gaza, the Intifada morphed towards a political mobilization of the territories and the subsequent shift in Palestinian power from the diaspora to Palestine enabled Arafat and the PLO to establish itself in the region with greater strength.[161] Similarly, Hussein could conduct clandestine peace talks with Israel while renouncing the West Bank, recognition of the PLO and addressing the final status of the territories.[162]

As the Intifada continued, Hussein considered the options. Relinquishing the West Bank Palestinian issue would permit him to hold parliamentary elections for the first time since 1967. Previously regarded with caution due to the monarchy's (questionable) support base amidst the majority Palestinian population, the elections were a significant component in Jordan's evolution towards a nation-state.[163] Now Hussein could express his true intention, and did so within four months of the Intifada on 7 June 1988 at the international summit in Algiers. The same year the king exhibited a reluctance to undertake Palestinian affairs for the foreseeable future and in April 1988 he delivered a series of speeches to tribal conventions around the Kingdom that pledged Jordan's support for the PLO as the sole legitimate representative of the Palestinian people and his support for the end of the Israeli occupation. Two months later in Algiers, and a month before disengagement, he denied that Jordan had annexed the West Bank and that the union was based on the demand of the Palestinians in response to issues that were no longer applicable to the then current situation.[164]

Whether the Intifada was the catalyst for Jordan's subsequent disengagement is questionable. Certainly, events such as the April 1988 bombing of an Amman driver's license office, purported to be the first of many attacks to follow by Black September, motivated Hussein to strengthen security at the refugee camps and arrest scores of Palestinians linked to radical leftist groups.[165] As the West Bank demonstrated an increasing allegiance to Arafat and his pictures flooded the streets with slogans calling for an independent Palestine, Hussein was slipping from view and towards despondency, for '[t]he PLO had risen again from the ashes. Similar to a seesaw, when Arafat was up, Hussein was down.'[166] Viewed thusly, it is plausible that the disengagement was the outcome of a desire to ensure the survival of the Hashemite monarchy, consolidate its territory and usher in the beginning of a new political life through a conclusive divorce from the Palestinians and the issue of representation.[167] Yet as Hussein was a renowned politician and statesman it is unlikely the severing of the West Bank would be conducted in a fit of pique. An alternative theory runs as follows: Jordan and Israel had enjoyed an affable relationship and as Kuwait and Saudi Arabia reneged on a ten-year aid commitment consolidated in Baghdad in 1978, Israel became not just a valuable ally, but a gateway to financial security as its industry and ties with the United States grew stronger by the decade. The Jordanian territorial position was vulnerable and as the Arab world endorsed the Palestinian cause, pressure on Jordan increased with the promulgation of the concept of 'Jordan is Palestine' by the Likud party from 1977 onwards. If the Kingdom feared a Palestinian uprising to overthrow the monarchy, then an even greater fear was a singular convergence of interests between the Palestinians and Israelis that could wipe Jordan completely off the map.[168]

In his analysis of Jordanian foreign policy, Jarbawi notes that the Kingdom's three consistent objectives have been to maintain Hashemite rule, consolidate Jordanian territory and to assume a greater role in the region as a whole.[169] Constrained from both sides, it was crucial to deal separately with the Zionists and the Palestinians. Focusing on the Palestinians, Jordan sought to eradicate their identity through the suppression of Palestinian ambitions, as a means of maintaining stability within Jordanian society.[170] It was in this atmosphere that Hussein announced on 31 July 1988 that there was to be 'a dismantling [of] the legal and administrative links between the two banks' and that 'maintaining the legal and administrative relationship could constitute an obstacle to liberating the occupied Palestinian land.'[171] Shrouding the move with sympathetic nods to the Palestinian cause and the state's obligation to assist in their quest for a homeland, Hussein cut ties with the West Bank in what he hoped would become a challenge for the PLO and precipitate their downfall by hastening Palestinian loyalty back to the Hashemites.[172] Alas, it was not to be: in effect the king provided the PLO with a redemptive opportunity and assisted the Palestinians. The 'poisoned chalice' truly had spilt on its way to the receiver.

The disengagement also resounded in terms of Jordanian interests, for the loss of thousands of Jordanian salaries was speculated to undermine an economy damaged by the Intifada and the notion of the PLO salvaging the financial loss of Hashemite subsidies was dubious.[173] Claiming to work in the interests of the Palestinians, the severance made travel more problematic with the introduction of new travel documents and in turn, employment opportunities were affected by the travel restrictions. For West Bank Palestinians, contrary to removing obstacles to the establishment of an independent

Palestine, the disengagement was 'a Holocaust [...] King Hussein has decided to destroy us.'[174] And the question remains: was this the move of 'an impulsive decision-maker, with judgement especially flawed on Palestinian-related issues'[175] or a statesman looking to the very entity from which the disengagement he purported was to save his brothers? That Hussein had ruled and prospered for 47 years in a troubled region indicates shrewdness combined with an intuitive nature. Hussein has been recognized as a politician 'who often takes decisions "by feel"'[176] and his priority was (at that time) to secure the Kingdom by the best possible means. On 26 October 1994, Jordan ended its 46-year history of war with Israel through a treaty that Rabin promised would bring 'an honourable peace, a balanced peace and a peace that will last.'[177]

Whether this peace would prevail within Jordanian society was doubtful, yet Hussein was willing to risk the unrest for the long-term gains a pact with Israel would bring. Jordanian-Israeli peace acted on economic and strategic weaknesses at a time when the Kingdom's overall security was open to compromise as the turmoil of the 1980s gave way to the Gulf War in 1990. The treaty was, however, not a new direction for Jordan. As far back as 1970 when the events of Black September shook the Kingdom, Israel was prepared to deploy forces to repel a Syrian invasion from the north that sought to divert Jordan's military attentions away from its conflict with the PLO. Assistance from Israel, whether at the behest of the United States or otherwise, undoubtedly helped maintain the security of the Hashemites. It was evident that Jordan's state of aggression towards Israel was futile and the chances of defeating her remote and costly. The vulnerability of Jordanian security was an ailment that an alliance with Israel (and thereafter the United States) could ease, since acquiescence would provide military hardware, including F-16 aircraft as well as the removal of over $700 million of Jordanian debt to the United States.[178] Moreover, companies that had previously avoided investment in countries with the potential to engage in conflict with powerful states (such as Jordan, pre-1994) would reassess their options as peace offered assurances. Two years after the signing of the treaty, this theory was proven as 'foreign direct investment in Jordan increased more than 14 times to $43 million between 1994 and 1995.'[179]

Despite the gains,[180] peace with Israel did not solve Jordan's security problems. On a regional level, tensions rocketed as Palestinians denounced the treaty, declared a general strike in the West Bank and Gaza Strip and burned Hussein's image during anti-Jordanian demonstrations. Once again a rupture in the Palestinian-Jordanian relationship threatened the stability of the area and though public support was expressed in the Kingdom, private unease prevailed. Many Jordanians questioned the return of territory that left some Jordanian land 'leased' indefinitely to Israeli farmers; others complained that the peace dividend was not as extensive as anticipated and Jordan's debts remained unresolved. But the treaty raised a more poignant dilemma: obliged to demonstrate allegiance to the United States (and to an extent Israel) King Abdullah II must balance ties with Israel and the West while nodding to Arab nationalism and the Palestinian cause. During the recent Iraq conflict this was particularly in evidence as the United States looked to Jordan as a regional ally and Jordan reciprocated, permitting 4,000 U.S. troops to conduct regular exercises in its southern desert, in addition to 200 British troops and 50 vehicles. Economically, Jordan stands to gain very little by espousing the war. Surviving on imports of cheap Iraqi oil, the war could cost the Kingdom upwards of £650 million per annum.[181] In turn, the influx of refugees placed a greater pressure on Jordan's economy that sustained Palestinians, Kurds, Egyptians and Sudanese. However, as shall be explored shortly, Jordan has gained from the influx, both in terms of economy and state infrastructure.

The treaty with Israel brought a brief stability to the Kingdom, but the repercussions of the reorientation continues to bode ill for relations between the Hashemites, the Palestinians and to a lesser extent the Jordanians, rendering an already fraught society more fragile. The city of Ma'an has provided a focus for unrest since the 1989 riots levelled against rising fuel prices, the 1996 bread riots and a series of pro-Iraq rallies that resulted in the death of a 22-year-old man after Hussein visited the area in 1998. Hussein's response to the demonstrations was unequivocal:

This is the third time. Not the first or the second. This means if a seed of evil is spread it will cause us great deal of trouble. We hope the time will come when we do not have any troublemakers and malicious or ungrateful persons or anyone who does not believe in this country and does not have any allegiance to this country.[182]

The people of Ma'an remained fractious and on 10 November 2002 a futile military operation to capture Muhammad Shalabi (Abu Sayyaf), a cleric connected to the militant Islamist group *al-Takfir wa al-Hijra*, was made.[183] The subsequent arrest of 'Ma'an's Robin Hood'[184] transformed the area into an 'arms-free zone' and weapons were submitted under an amnesty that pledged compensation in return. In a region in which weapons had been carried for decades as a matter of tradition the move proved questionable. One theory attributes Jordanian actions to U.S. advice in the aftermath of the killing of an American diplomat, as the temporal proximity of the designation of Abu Sayyaf as a 'scapegoat' afforded 'a gift for Washington to show they were combating terrorism.'[185] Already awkward bedfellows, the Jordanian-Israeli alliance fuelled contempt held by the Palestinians towards the regime and ultimately enhanced Palestinian solidarity within the camps.

Conclusion

By the passing of Hussein on 7 February 1999, Jordan had survived economic, political, social and military upheavals. The state's reluctance to 'divide its indigenous and Palestinian citizens, because the country had cohesive élite [*sic*]'[186] and the withdrawal of Jordan's claim to the West Bank in 1988 demonstrated a self-preservation that would not pass without internal censure, notably by the Muslim Brotherhood. While the dissolution consolidated relations between the Palestinian-Jordanians, the repercussions for West Bank Palestinian residents in the context of citizenship was less amenable as those loyal to the Jordanian state were rendered stateless for a second time. By the end of the twentieth century, the 'velvet glove of pluralism that soften[ed] the steel fist of the most sophisticated security apparatus in the Arab Levant'[187] had ensured political life continued as the elite rallied to the new king in a bid to ensure their future, common interests.

The 2000 Intifada provided Arafat with the means to mobilize Palestinian society anew and to pressure Israel into accepting the Palestinian Authority's demands for the creation of a viable Palestinian state.[188] If the 1988 Intifada shook the Kingdom, the next was a flame that scorched the border. Where rioters once held stones, now they held rifles, pistols, hand-grenades and mortars, ironically courtesy of Israel under the 1993 Oslo Peace Accords that envisaged an armed Palestinian force strong enough to defend Arafat's regime against local opposition.[189] The repercussions were not felt in open hostilities in Jordan, but through subtle disdain as many Jordanian-Palestinians had relatives in the West Bank. In turn, the Israeli response to the uprising prompted calls for a severance of ties with Israel. Yet the idea of a rejection of ties with Israel provoked unease amidst the Jordanian authorities who feared a deepening of ethnic divisions and clashes with the local Jordanian minority.[190] Criticism quickly spread to Queen Rania, who is of Palestinian origin, from both Palestinians and Jordanians alike. Dubbed the 'handbag queen', her absence from the region during Israeli assaults on the West Bank, including her home town of Tulkarm, incensed Palestinian-Jordanians. For Jordanians, the disapproval manifested itself at a football match between a refugee camp team, al-Wihdat, and one composed of mostly local Jordanians, al-Faisali. Amidst chants of 'Get rid of Rania, Abu Hussein, and we'll send you a couple of real Jordanian girls instead!'[191] a Jordanian journalist commented, 'Rania means well, but the Intifada is putting a terrific strain on her loyalties.'[192] Whether a ribald provocation in a competitive sporting environment or a genuine reflection of animosity towards the monarchy from both sides, one in resentment and the other in ridicule, continuing unrest suggested the latter pervades as a significant contributory factor towards ongoing divisions.

2

CITIZENSHIP AND NATIONALITY IN JORDAN

The legal code of Transjordan emerged from a melange of European and Ottoman law; occasionally a willing adoption of new principles, it was equally the result of capitulation. During the nineteenth century, the Ottoman Empire was compelled to amend its legal system, resulting in the modification of the nationality laws. Sampled from the French and Belgian Codes, the Ottoman Civil Code of 1867–1877 emerged in Transjordan through the Egyptian Civil Code.[1] Central to the new system was the default application of European Codes for cases that lacked reciprocal laws and precedents from European courts – notably French courts – in legal decisions for new Arab courts.[2] Under the British Mandate, the Jordanian Citizenship Law was imposed in agreement with the decisions of the Council of the League of Nations in September 1922. In turn, the Transjordanian government adopted the Ottoman Code and established the court of appeal, courts of first instance, four civil magistrate courts and a Department of Tribal Administration to mediate inter-tribal disputes and cases between the Bedouins.[3]

Under this system, power principally resides with the monarch who is closely supported by the National Parliament (*Majlis al-Umma*), which is subdivided into the House of Lords (*Majlis al-A'yan*) and the

House of Representatives (*Majlis al-Nawab*)[4] and it is here that the laws are formed.[5] According to Article 95 of the Constitution, both the Senate and *Majlis al-Nawab* must submit legislation to the government in the form of a draft law. Both houses of Parliament initiate debates and vote on legislation, while proposals are referred by the Prime Minister to the *Majlis al-Nawab* for the deputies to accept, amend or reject the submission before referring each proposal to a special committee in the Lower House for consideration. If successful, the proposal is directed to the government to be drafted in the form of a bill and re-submitted to the *Majlis al-Nawab* for approval once more; if accepted, it is passed on by the House Speaker – an elected official – to the Senate for debate and a vote. If approved, the bill is presented to the king, who either grants consent by royal decree or returns the bill unapproved with justification for his rejection. In this instance, the bill is returned to the *Majlis al-Nawab*, where the review and voting process is repeated. Should both houses unanimously pass the bill by a two-thirds majority, it becomes an Act of Parliament, which constitutionally countermands the monarch's veto. Any bill refused by the Senate is returned to the *Majlis al-Nawab* for amendment. Should discrepancies arise between the two houses, a two-thirds majority vote in a joint session of Parliament is sought.[6]

The activities of Parliament and the sectors therein operate under the auspices of the monarch, who in accordance with the Constitution must be a Muslim of sound mind and born to a legal wife and of two Muslim parents.[7] As the Head of State, the monarch is immune from any consequence or responsibility[8] and has the authority to ratify and proclaim legislation and order the necessary administration of the law, in addition to establishing elections to the *Majlis al-Nawab*. The king also opens and convenes the sessions of the *Majlis al-Nawab* and can postpone or end the sessions at his discretion. Moreover, he holds the power to dissolve both the *Majlis al-Nawab* and the *Majlis al-Umma* and dismiss any of its members. Conversely, he can appoint and dismiss the Prime Minister and the ministers and accept their resignations in the light of the recommendation of the Prime Minister as well as retaining the power to pardon or reduce sentences meted out by the courts.[9] Finally, in his role as the commander-in-chief of the armed forces, he can declare war, peace and sign agreements and treaties.[10]

Post-independence, the legal system retained aspects of the British Mandate that were visible in the Transjordanian Nationality Law, 1928. The Law laid the foundations for future decrees regarding nationality, citizenship and naturalization and heralded Jordan's role as a host state for Palestinian refugees in the region. Under Article 1:

> All Ottoman subjects habitually resident in Transjordan on the sixth day of August 1924, shall be deemed to have acquired Transjordan nationality. For the purpose of this article the term 'habitually resident in Transjordan' shall be deemed to include any person who had his usual place of residence in Transjordan for the period of twelve months preceding the sixth day of August 1924.[11]

That the Nationality Law acknowledged the inhabitants of Transjordan as Ottoman subjects is noteworthy. By addressing the subjects as 'Ottoman', by that point an obsolete entity, the Law emphasizes the absence of a location in terms of identity through the avoidance of the term 'Transjordanian'. Rather, it grants Transjordanian national-ity to all Ottoman subjects who were residing in the region on the given date and raises the question of belonging through Articles 2 and 3, and the offer of a choice of Transjordan or an alternate former-Ottoman state as a homeland and nationality for those 'habitually resident in Transjordan [...] who decided within a period of two years to opt instead for Turkish nationality or for the nationality of one of the states previously in the Ottoman empire in which the majority of the population was of the same race as themselves.'[12] In doing so, the rudiments of national identity were sown into the minds of the newly independent subjects.

To become a 'Transjordanian' as opposed to 'Turkish' or 'Syrian' would require a wilful decision on the part of the individual, a choice that would form the basis for a future Jordanian national identity and one that would evolve over coming years and adapt to new changes. In terms of identity, this occurrence elicits further questions regarding the Palestinians who assumed Jordanian nationality in the subsequent years: could additional aspects of their Palestinian identity be considered 'Jordanian'? Do individuals recognize traits they perceive as being predominantly 'Jordanian' percolating into their lifestyle and if so, do they resist or embrace it? Moreover, the issue of how important it is to be 'Jordanian', 'Palestinian' or even 'Palestinian-Jordanian' holds its roots in the Transjordanian Nationality Law of 1928, which initiated the Jordanian identity and emphasizes the contrast between the Palestinian identity and the relatively nascent Palestinian-Jordanian identity.

Choosing a nationality bears implications not only in terms of identity, but of geographical locality. As Article 4 stipulates, those 'who opted for Turkish nationality, for the nationality of one of the states previously in the Ottoman Empire in which the majority of the population was of the same race as themselves shall be obliged to leave Transjordan'.[13] In 1954, the Transjordanian Nationality Law was amended with the additional clauses of the Jordanian Nationality Law,[14] which clarified the terms under which an individual could assume Jordanian nationality. Moreover, it adapted the legislation to encompass the recent influx of Palestinian refugees into the Kingdom by broadening Article 3 to cover 'anyone carrying a Palestinian passport issued before 15 May 1948 – provided that he is not Jewish – and habitually residing in Jordan during the period 20 December – 16 February 1954'.[15] The Nationality Law introduced new facets to the concept of Jordanian citizenship: gender, terminology, discrimination and nuances of Arab unity were concealed within its clauses. By substantiating the Jordanian identity through a criterion by which individuals could be accepted or repudiated at will, a system was promulgated that has since been deemed 'a sexist piece of legislation' and condemned by numerous civil rights groups. Placing applicants within predefined categories of *urduni*, *ajnabi*, *arabi* and *mughtarib*,[16] it differentiates between those in possession of Jordanian citizenship under the stipulations of the Jordanian Citizenship Law of 1954; persons who are not Jordanian; any individual whose father is of Arab origin and carries the citizenship of one of the member states of the League of Arab States; and 'any Arab born in the Hashemite Kingdom of Jordan of the

usurped part of Palestine and who emigrated from the country or was
expelled, including the children of such a person wherever they may
have been born.'[17] Additional clauses address the expressions '*fuqdan
al-ahaliyya*' – loss of capacity – and '*sinn al-rushd*' – age of majority.[18]

The new measures signified that women would be denied equal
rights to their male applicants and in cases in which the woman was of
Jordanian origin, she would be denied the privilege to pass on Jordanian
nationality to her children. Due to the patriarchal nuance of the legislation, the children of a Jordanian male born in any country outside the
Kingdom become eligible for Jordanian citizenship.[19] In contrast, the
children born of a Jordanian mother and, for example, a Kuwaiti father,
who are resident in Jordan, will still receive treatment that is equal, or
less than, that which is granted to an *ajnabi* (foreigner). Aside from the
issues concerning identity that the child would confront growing up in
Jordanian society sans citizenship, there is a practical array of repercussions that include the absence of a right to enrol in the school system,
social entitlements and/or political rights.[20] For Jordanian women married to Palestinian refugees the situation is graver, a point acknowledged by Refugees International in their in 2003 report:

> In Camp A,[21] there are 'mixed' families, i.e., women with
> Jordanian citizenship married to Palestinian men. It is antici-
> pated that these 'mixed' families will be allowed to resettle in
> Jordan within weeks. While women with Jordanian citizenship
> are free to leave Camp A, their children cannot since accord-
> ing to Jordanian law, children take the father's citizenship. As
> a result, these children are considered Palestinians rather than
> Jordanian citizens. It is for this reason that Jordanian women
> remain in Camp A.[22]

In such instances, the women were compelled to live in the refugee
camp due to the patriarchal nature of the legislation. Although the
alternative of relocating to a secure environment is available, it comes
with a price: leaving their family in the camp.

Equally intriguing is the stance adopted on dual Jordanian-Arab
citizenship, an act that not only prohibits the applicant applying for

Jordanian citizenship, but is conducive to the nullification of existing Jordanian citizenship.[23] In line with the Provisions Regarding
Citizenship Among Member States of the League of Arab States
signed by the governments of Jordan, Syria, Iraq, Saudi Arabia, Egypt,
Yemen, Lebanon and Libya, it is in conjunction with Article 2 of the
Pact of the League of Arab States and signifies an agreement to adopt
the Provisions formulated by the Council of the League of Arab States
at its 21st Ordinary Session.[24] Article 1 of the Provisions stipulates
that 'for the purpose of the Provisions of this Agreement any person who is a citizen of a member state is considered to be an Arab',[25]
and from this point the Jordanian Citizenship Law nurtures a unique
understanding of the notion of Arab unity.

Ideologically United, Legally Divided: Arab (Dis)Unity

The 1954 Law redefined the legal category of 'Arab' at a time when the
political environment surrounding the new Kingdom was replete with
an Arab nationalism that was gaining popularity through the charis-
matic promulgations of the Ba'ath Party and the Egyptian President,
Gamal Abdel Nasser.[26] According to Article 4 of the Law, an Arab
who resides in Jordan and has resided there for 15 consecutive years
has the right to acquire Jordanian nationality provided 'he' gives up
his original nationality in accordance with his country's laws.[27] Critics
of this clause emphasize the disparity between the four years' consecutive residency required for non-Arab applicants in comparison with
the 15 years stipulated in Article 4, contending that despite the rhetoric of Arab unity, the legislation prohibits dual or multiple Arab-Arab
citizenship, thereby hindering the realization of Arab unity on a state-
to-state level.[28] This is ironic, given that Jordan is part of the founding
bloc of the League of Arab States in 1945.[29] Having adapted its legislation to prohibit dual nationality between Arab states, it lies in contrast
to the League, despite the Agreement that '[t]he naturalization of a
citizen of any member state of the League of Arab States in another
member state is not permitted except with the express agreement of
his Government in which case his previous citizenship will be fulfilled after obtaining his new citizenship.'[30] Why non-Jordanian Arab

applicants endure a stringent process of naturalization is unclear, but the introduction of the term 'Arab' to the amended 1946 Constitution in 1952 strengthens the suggestion that the introduction of 'Arab' was impromptu, a nod to the rise of Arab nationalism, rather than a genuine gesture of Arab unity.

The decision to restrict Arab applicants from maintaining their original citizenship is tied to concerns regarding national security, and by restricting and discerning who becomes Jordanian a degree of control is exercised. For the threat is not merely in terms of fundamentalism – as witnessed in the 9 November 2005 bombings in Amman – but rather domestic stability. As can be observed in the revolutions that swept the Middle East and North Africa in early 2011, domestic unrest arises from socio-economic factors: the absence of opportunities in education, employment and healthcare augment the likelihood of an uprising. As the country with the highest proportion of Palestinian refugees, in addition to Iraqis, Kurds and Sudanese, Jordan has developed a heightened awareness of the strained economy and social pressures. The ability to ensure that citizenship is granted to the few, rather than the many – regardless of the degree of need – is justified as a slight, but significant, measure to redress the balance.

That the applicant must wait a further 12 years before they might assume positions in the public office (such as political, diplomatic or bureaucratic) or stand as a candidate for election in the *Majlis al-Nawab*[31] contributes a sense of displacement, since a non-Jordanian Arab applicant must wait a total of 27 years before participating in Jordanian society.[32] It is noteworthy, however, that the Constitution does not strictly prohibit non-Jordanian Arabs from assuming a ministerial role within the 12 years of naturalization. Under Article 42, 'No person shall be appointed a Minister unless he is a Jordanian', a point that is reiterated by Article 75 i(a), 'No person shall become a Senator or Deputy who is not a Jordanian'.[33] And it is not only Palestinians who are discriminated against by the Law: the exclusion of Jews from Jordanian citizenship has been condemned as lending 'credence to official Zionist and Israel citizenship legislation in that the Jordanian law unjustly discriminates against Jews and the Israeli law – against non-Jews.'[34] It must be observed, moreover, that the

clause prohibiting the admittance of Jewish applicants into the citizenship process was added in 1954 – the 1949 addendum did not
exclude Jewish applicants. During the post-war struggle for territory
and statehood, the subsequent exclusion of Jews constituted part of
the offensive against Zionist colonial settlement in Transjordan and
claims asserted in the 1950s on Jewish-owned land in the country.[35] In
July 2009, the Jordanian Minister of Information, Nabil Sharif, countered further claims by The Israel Land Fund that ownership of properties purchased during the Ottoman rule remained viable. Having
(re)claimed land in the West Bank and East Jerusalem, the Fund
endeavours to (re)acquisition properties to be inhabited by Eastern
European settlers (*olim*). However, under Jordanian administration,
transactions finalized through Ottoman and British Mandate agreements are legally nullified and Israelis are prohibited from buying
properties in the Kingdom.[36] In contrast, it is noteworthy that while
Israelis are denied property rights in Jordan, factories and industrial
projects funded and owned by Israeli citizens[37] are in operation.

Deconstructing Jordanian Citizenship

After 1948, the controversial sentiments of Article 3(2) echoed the
consensus of the surrounding Arab regimes. But in 1950 Transjordan
put national preservation before regional loyalties and hosted a series
of meetings and correspondences with Israeli negotiators, much to the
chagrin of British associates and Arab League cohorts. On 1 April
1950, after whispered concerns from Syria, Lebanon and Iraq on the
ambitions of Abdullah to realize the dream of a Greater Syria (at any
cost, including that of the Palestinians and their future state), the Arab
League prohibited all member states from conducting political, military or economic negotiations with Israel.[38] Though Transjordan sub-
scribed to the resolution, clandestine relations continued and affirmed
Abdullah's ambivalence towards the Arab League: dreams of territorial greatness soon dwarfed the ideologies followed by his subjects and
states loyal to the League.

The fickle nature of Abdullah is visible through a number of legal
decrees, particularly Article 16 of the Nationality Law, through which

'[a]ny Jordanian may renounce his Jordanian nationality and acquire the nationality of an Arab State'. That the regulations have not been altered by subsequent monarchs to encourage unity through nationality, identity and assimilation within the region is indicative of Jordan's relationship with its neighbouring states. Since its formation under the rule of Abdullah I, the Kingdom has associated with states that at best attract controversy and at worst contempt from Arab regimes. Notable among these controversial relationships are Britain, Israel and the United States. In comparison with the measures imposed on non-Arab applicants, the exclusion is particularly rigorous, given Article 6 of the Provisions Regarding Citizenship Among Member States of the League of Arab States: 'The naturalization of a citizen of any member state of the League of Arab States in another member state is not permitted except with the express agreement of his Government in which case his previous citizenship will be fulfilled after obtaining his new citizenship.'[39] Thus, to be naturalized into the Jordanian state would require the consent of both the original state from whence the applicant came and of Jordan, which Article 16 expressly forbids.

The complex nature of the legislation is attributable to the influx of Palestinian refugees from Palestine and the Arab states seeking refuge and economic opportunities. During the 1950s, the Jordanian government commenced a dual policy to encourage the political integration of the refugees and contain Palestinian separatism through the bestowal of Jordanian citizenship. However, neither declarations of policies nor constitutional law succeeded in bridging the mutual antagonism between the annexing regime and its annexed subjects.[40] On 20 December 1949, the Additional Law 56 was introduced and provided Palestinians with a passport and the means to travel between the Arab countries in search of employment, thereby introducing economic benefits and political rights that would facilitate the refugees' absorption within the new framework.[41] Moreover, it eliminated the Ministry for Refugee Affairs, confirming the refugees as an integral part of the Jordanian community.[42] As a ruse to quell unrest in the camps by easing the freedom of circulation and right to employment, the new law was partially successful. Officially, it made the search for employment simpler and removed the obstacles that previously exacerbated the predicament of the refugees in addition to losing their land and homes. Alternatively, it was largely ineffectual since the passports were marked in a manner specific to the Palestinian holder, issued as they were under article No. 3, as opposed to article No. 1, which applied to citizens of Transjordanian origin.[43]

Although Plascov states that 'it was not a calculated policy but sprang mainly from the emotional reactions of two competing sections of the population', Additional Law 56 can be regarded as an interim measure. Introduced with the objective of assimilating the Palestinians further into Jordanian society, it would quell the dissent stirring in the camps. Following the annexation of the West Bank in 1948, Abdullah I was a leader hoisted upon a despondent population and it was crucial for the monarch to present annexation as a response to Palestinian desires and not an enforced move. The unfortunate truth was that the Palestinians accepted Abdullah's domination due to an absence of alternatives and by the early 1950s the rancour manifested itself in demonstrations against the monarchy and the British. Protesters in Salt denounced the king and demanded a republican regime, while Palestinian deputies attacked Britain in the Parliament.[44] The passport issue was a careful move by the monarchy to calm a rapidly expanding population and a facilitating factor in Abdullah I's passage towards a 'Greater Syria'.

Gender, Marriage and Children: A Legal Perspective

The Nationality Law of Jordan has attracted criticism from the UN Convention on the Elimination of All Forms of Discrimination Against Women (CEDAW), the press, ministers and the Jordanian Queen Rania. Provisions in the law constrain the conduct of women while allegedly maintaining the 'cohesiveness' of Jordanian society as 'one unity'. Since nationality is conveyed through the male line, a Jordanian woman marrying a non-Jordanian is forbidden to pass her nationality to her 'foreign' husband.[45] Although in this instance the terminology cites 'foreign', it encompasses not only *ajnabi*, but also *arabi*. Once more, the differentiation applied by Jordanian law between *urduni*, *ajnabi*, *arabi* and *mughtarib* (Jordanians, foreigners, Arabs and *émigrés*) reinforces the precedence patriotism and nationalism hold in a society that strives for 'one unity' – a unity that does not include the children of Jordanian women married to Palestinians. In such an instance, Sonbol relates how 'one feminist leader in Jordan was granted residency for her Philippine domestic servant but was denied a residence permit for her unmarried daughter whose deceased father was a Palestinian American.'[46] Although it is possible for husbands of non-Jordanian origin to circumvent the citizenship restrictions placed on women, it comes at a price: requiring investment in the country, residence for at least four years with the intention of permanent residency and a legal means of employment that does not compete with Jordanians in the same field of occupation and includes a work permit verified through official ministries.[47] While Jordanian women cannot petition for citizenship on behalf of their non-Jordanian husbands, once the 'foreign' husband has met the stipulated requirements laid out above, in addition to satisfying the requirement of 15 years of continuous residence, the woman can confer citizenship upon her husband, and thereafter their children.[48] Given the lengthy stipulations, applications for citizenship by non-Jordanian spouses take years to process and often prove futile, rendering the husband, and children, foreigners.

One of the greater tragedies to derive from the nationality and passport legislation is the absence of equal rights and opportunities for the children of mixed marriages between Jordanian women and non-Jordanian men. The amalgamation of the Palestinian presence in the Kingdom, the inclusion of Palestinians in the category of 'foreigner' and the geographical proximity of Jordan to conflicted states once more emphasizes the link between the citizenship process and concerns for state security. In 2004, the Minister of Interior, Samir Habashneh, expressed this anxiety when he declared that the government had no intention of offering Jordanian citizenship to the children of Jordanian women married to Palestinian men until a peace settlement is reached in the Palestinian conflict. The comments were made during a speech at a two-day seminar on the Elections Law in which Habashneh revealed that 60,000 Jordanian women were married to Palestinian men, rendering the question of citizenship to be 'no longer possible because it means offering the

citizenship to around half a million Palestinians in Jordan'.[49] Given
that each family on average holds 6.5 children and the Palestinian
refugee population in Jordan is estimated by the UNRWA to be
1,930,703, it would herald a tremendous surge in the Palestinian-
Jordanian community – an already dominant contingent that gener-
ates unease for ethnic Jordanians.

Despite the restrictions on the maternal line, the Jordanian
Nationality Law offers extensive protection for children born of a
Jordanian father:[50] they can retain citizenship even after the Jordanian
father rescinds his citizenship and adopts that of a foreign country.[51]
Conversely, the children of a Jordanian woman have no opportunity to
assume residency status and nationality through maternal associations
to the Kingdom and any passport bears the stamp 'children are not
included due to the different nationality of the father'.[52] The Jordanian
Nationality Law reiterates that nationality is tied to the land and the
nation only if the nation is regarded from a patriarchal perspective.

Patriarchy determines not only the position of women as mothers,
wives, children, and siblings, but also in a legal context. According to
a report by the United Nations Development Fund, women as citizens are 'conflated with children needing care and control' and on
this premise, Arab states have justified laws that prevent a woman
from fulfilling her independence in matters of the family, work and
society.[53] The patriarchal stance exists in conjunction with the element of kinship and at its most fundamental patriarchy privileges
male and elder rights, who in turn utilize the rhetoric of morality to
consolidate actions taken against women. The influence of patriarchy
is as tangible as the permanence of kinship: family structures, values
and terminology have been critical to survival in the societies of the
region. Demonstrated through political nepotism, as family members
are recruited to fill high-ranking positions, mobilize support through
family units, dispense goods and services through family-based networks, and employ terminology to justify their leadership, thereby
reinforcing the 'family' as a political unit of society.[54] Although it is
indisputable that patriarchy is a key component in the state system
the role of religion is equally, if not more, significant in the sustenance
of patriarchal structures.[55] Given that family is linked to political

identity, the Arab nation descends through patrilineal kin groups. In turn, citizens must belong to a male-defined kin group to participate in a religious sect, to be part of the nation and to acquire the rights and responsibilities associated with citizenship. By preventing women from assigning citizenship to their children and non-Jordanian spouses, the link between religious identity, political identity, patrilineality and patriarchy is reinforced through religion, nation, state and kinship.[56]

Ironically, maternal ties can only be used as the basis for nationality in the case of illegitimate children whose mother has been killed by her kinsmen in an 'honour' killing, before she has applied for child citizenship. The Jordanian National Committee for Women has issued a recommendation to amend Article 13 of the Jordanian Nationality Law to permit the Council of Ministers to grant the children of Jordanian mothers married to non-Jordanians nationality should the council find the action suitable. Should the amendment prove successful, it would ease the predicament of women by reviewing on a case-by-case basis, as opposed to a 'blanket change,' which enhances the possibility of rejection by the government.[57]

That *shari'a* enables a woman to exercise her right to choose her residence and domicile vis-à-vis her future husband and that such 'conditions must be honoured by the husband, otherwise a wife can apply for the cancellation of the marriage contract',[58] scuppers once more the necessity for male kin approval. The alternative is by agreement with the Passport Department director, who can issue a passport for a one-year period.[59] This is limited in practice, however, particularly for Jordanian mothers abandoned with their children in Jordan by non-Jordanian husbands. Moreover, the annual provisional renewal makes it difficult for the children to move and travel and increases the burden of the mothers, who must go through the process of passport renewal with additional expenses.[60] Notwithstanding the scope that this aspect of *shari'a* offers, it remains a discriminatory legislation that penalizes the Jordanian woman. By not explicitly stating that the husband granting the permission must be a Jordanian citizen himself, it is plausible that a Jordanian woman entering a marriage without a passport will be reliant upon the goodwill of her non-Jordanian spouse who may be resident in the Kingdom. In such instances, the union affords more power to the non-Jordanian man than the Jordanian woman – an ironic twist borne of the patriarchal foundations of the Passport Law.

In accordance with Islamic *fiqh*, 'the child belongs to the marital bed' (*al-walad lil-firash*). While there is no direct reference to the male, the interpretation is that the child belongs to the father.[61] In defence of the governmental position on Jordanian Citizenship Law, Sheikh Khayyat advocated that under Sura 33, verse 5:

> If this means that the children would follow the nationality of their mother – in the sense of being traced to her – this is rejected by Islam. Almighty God says: 'Call them by the names of their fathers: that is [more just] in the sight of God.'[62]

Despite the opportunity to enact positive change through measures recommended by CEDAW, signed by Jordan in 1980 and ratified by the government in July 1992, the regime has remained somewhat dogmatic. Of the three reservations expressed in relation to the Convention (citizenship, clauses in the Personal Status Law, housing and women's mobility), the Kingdom has complied with only one, when the Cabinet lifted reservations on the clause relating to the mobility of women in accordance with Article 15(4) on 10 February 2009.[63] While a positive move, Jordan's stance on citizenship has not altered; rather, in recent years it has regressed, rather than progressed.

Under CEDAW, basic human rights must be equally enjoyed by men and women and particular emphasis is placed on economic, political, and social equality.[64] Reservations regarding Article 9(2) – Nationality of Children – were confirmed upon ratification,[65] and reaffirmed in a subsequent memorandum submitted by the Jordanian Ministry of Foreign Affairs that maintained the recommendations by CEDAW would not be followed due to conflict with *shari'a* and the Jordanian Citizenship Law. As Amawi observes, on closer scrutiny, the reservations are not based on *shari'a*, but a patriarchal nationalism; in turn, there is no discrepancy between Article 9(2) of CEDAW and the principles of *shari'a*. Specifically, Article 9(2) states that 'parties shall grant women equal rights with men with respect to the nationality of their children.'[66] While *shari'a* does not explicitly address the issue of nationality, but rather that of '*nassab*', which establishes linkages between the child to the father, it is argued that Jordanian trepidation is without foundation as Article 38 of the Jordanian Civil Code stipulates that 'every person shall have a name and a surname and his surname shall be attached to the names of his children.'[67] Consequently, paternal linkages based on blood ties to the father would not be denied if the mother passed her citizenship to her child who holds the surname of the father.[68] Yet this does not repudiate the issue of kinship and the continuity of Jordanian paternal lineage; it is increasingly evident that despite religion being the impetus behind citizenship and passport legislation, it is more likely to be based on the 'higher national interest'[69] of the country.

In addition to the argument that nationality entitlements would strain the limitations of the Kingdom's meagre resources,[70] the reservations illustrate Jordan's perception of women as a potential risk to national interests, since 'Jordanian woman do not possess the intellectual capacity to discern the intentions of their suitors'.[71] If security measures are to be considered seriously, the issue of the child remains. Though at first sight a twee notion, it is invariably a reality: children are the future and to emerge into adulthood sans full citizenship rights due to the origin of one's father is conducive to a heightened awareness of being 'other' – a circumstance that does not foster societal cohesion and domestic stability. Further questions concerning a woman's right to vote, occupy a seat in parliament, fulfil administrative posts, choose a partner and become a mother also linger, in addition to the darker aspect of Jordanian legislation: the reluctance to actively prohibit honour killings.[72]

Despite conceding that 'the Jordanian Citizenship Law is a sexist piece of legislation', Samir Habashneh and the wider Jordanian government have done little to address the legal predicament. The legal code regarding citizenship, elections, national health insurance and social security results in the diminishment of women's rights and increase the despondence regarding future welfare.[73] Yet it is not only women who are at risk: while in 2006 tentative steps were taken, in 2009 the government commenced a broader initiative through the removal of Jordanian citizenship from Palestinian-Jordanian citizens in the Kingdom. Although the creeping process of rescindment has occurred over the past decade, the stipulation that Jordanians of West Bank origins would have their nationality withdrawn demonstrates an increasing boldness on the part of the Jordanian regime – particularly as the move has no legal basis. Under existing Jordanian law, Jordanian citizenship can be rescinded providing the individual is in the employ of the civil service of a foreign authority or government. In turn, the individual would be advised by the Jordanian government to terminate their role and, if the citizen does not comply, the council of ministries would commence rescindment.[74] The process is at once simple and devastating:

> The revocations of citizenship that the Jordanian authorities have carried out since 1988 contradict the written law and the constitution. [...] It is now a more simple matter to revoke a yellow card-carrying citizen from his citizenship than it is to revoke their driving license! With the revocation of a driving license, the citizen has the right to challenge the revocation in a court. The inspection and follow-up department is the only government department that is not subject to judicial review. [...] It is also important to mention that there is no refugee law in Jordan. As such, once the citizenship is revoked, the Palestinian refugee is left with no political, civil or economic rights.[75]

The crux of the Jordanian argument rests with the failure to possess a valid Israeli-issued residency permit for the West Bank; whether the individual has been resident in Jordan for ten or 50 years is seemingly irrelevant. And the process of rescindment belies the understanding that the move is not legally sound: as opposed to a blanket initiative of recalling nationality documents, the act occurs only once the individual attempts to renew a 'passport or driver's license, or registering a marriage or the birth of a child at the Civil Status Department'.[76] According to Human Rights Watch, between 2004 and 2008 approximately 3,000 Palestinian-Jordanians have been stripped of Jordanian citizenship, though Jordanian officials have yet to perceive the negative implications of the move: for some, it is a matter of security; others, in the interests of the Palestinian people; and for yet others, a non-issue entirely.

As late as August 2010, the Jordanian Minister of Information and Communication, Dr Nabil Sharif, refuted claims that the citizenship of Palestinians who entered the Kingdom during the 1950s is being revoked: 'There is no decision of this nature at all. We do not withdraw nationalities of [...] Palestinians or Jordanians of Palestinian origin.'[77] It is worth noting that as Sharif denied the initiative, the number of Palestinian-Jordanians affected surpassed 3,000. While Sharif touched upon the aspect of Palestinians of West Bank origin, it was those already in possession of Israeli permits whom he addressed: 'If they were all to abandon these permits and go anywhere else they would only contribute to the confiscation of Arab land, to confiscation of Arab rights.'[78] Sharif's advice sits uncomfortably with the findings of the Human Rights Watch report released in January 2010, particularly the accounts by citizens who have been affected. For example, Fadi entered the East Bank in 1968 aged 17 from Nablus; both he and his father held Jordanian passports. In 2007, while updating the identity documents of his children, he was informed that he must update his Israeli permit in order to retain Jordanian nationality.[79] As yet unsuccessful, both Fadi and his family were rendered stateless, caught in a bureaucratic limbo between the Jordanian and Israeli officials.

Whether denying or defending, Jordanian rhetoric rests on the notion of 'Palestinians interests'. Since 1948, the Kingdom has morphed from a empathetic surrogate to an admonishing matron, dispensing advice and measures that are for the common good – even if the reality of being rendered stateless and subject to discrimination is far from positive. A year prior to Sharif's dismissal of the rescindment, the Jordanian Interior Minister, Nayef al-Kadi, defended the measure as overdue:

We are only correcting the mistake that was created after Jordan's disengagement from the West Bank. We want to highlight the true identity and nationality of every person. Our goal is to prevent Israel from emptying the Palestinian territories of their original inhabitants. We should be thanked for taking this measure. Jordan is not Palestine, just as Palestine is not Jordan.[80]

Likewise the Director of the Governor's Office at the Follow-Up and Inspections Department (FID, *al-mutabaa wa al-taftish*), Ghazi Odwan, reasons that 'the main reason behind the loss of nationality is due to the negligence of Palestinians and their failure to have concern for their Palestinian Identity; they indifferently stopped visiting the West Bank for years which encouraged the Israelis to cancel their ID cards.'[81] Odwan, al-Kadi and Sharif are far from alone in this view, which renders the announcement in February 2011 that Jordanian citizenship would be conferred on senior Palestinian Authority officials, including President Mahmoud Abbas and his sons, Mohammed Dahlan and Nabil Abu Rudeineh, paradoxical.[82] Moreover, the absence of accountability presents the Palestinians in Jordan with a frustrating quandary: their loyalty is demanded by the regime, while scant loyalty is conveyed in turn; provided with nationality, they are rendered stateless on a non-legally based whim. Despite proclamations of fraternity, the schism between the Palestinian and Jordanian communities is widening, evidenced during events such as the al-Faisali and al-Wihdat football matches. From bureaucracy to bottle-hurling, the Jordanian regime is working against its objective of domestic stability: rather, it is unnecessarily creating a *bête noire* that is nurtured through enacting measures of disenfranchisement.

The Intifada and its Legacy

In 1988 King Hussein announced the 'dismantling [of] the legal and administrative links between the two banks.'[83] The separation of the West and East Banks bore implications not only for the region's politics, but the citizenship status and identity of West Bank residents. Jordan's annexation of the West Bank on 24 April 1950 prompted a demographic transition in the Kingdom's structure through the absorption of the Palestinian refugees who had fled to the West Bank and Jordan following the 1948 Arab-Israeli war. The rising Palestinian

population in the East and West Bank consolidated not only the political unity of the Transjordanians, but also facilitated the emergence of
a configuration of Jordanian national identity and culture. Ultimately,
it would become increasingly exclusivist and over the coming decades
vast sections of the Jordanian citizenry would intensify the schism
between the Palestinian and Jordanian communities.[84] Born of a desire
for consolidation and legitimacy, the annexation would prove a swift,
but enduringly imprudent strategy for Jordan.

After several years of forceful negotiations between the Kingdom
and the PLO to reach an agreement on a Jordanian-Palestinian con-
federation in 1985–1986, the divorce from the West Bank (with the
exception of its religious ties to Jerusalem) emerged from an agreement reached in February 1985. The Amman Summit Accords failed
and collapsed the following year as a result of the Jordanian-PLO
rivalry for supremacy in Palestinian affairs[85] and the eruption of the
Palestinian Intifada in 1987 negatively impacted the king's plans for
partnership with the Palestinians in the West Bank. By the spring of
1988, it was clear that the unrest would endure and as the Intifada
rejuvenated the position of the PLO, so too did it perpetuate a rise in
antipathy towards the monarchy and government from the Palestinian
community in Jordan, the East and West Bank.[86] The emphasis
placed by local leadership on the role of the PLO as the representative of the Palestinians living under occupation rather enhanced the
political might of the organization – to the chagrin of the Jordanian
regime.[87]

Returning the Palestine question to the top of the Arab agenda,
the Intifada afforded the opportunity to draw both regional and international attention to the issue. Yet while Hussein provided a positive
endorsement of Arab unity and the future of the Palestinian state at
the Algerian Arab summit in June 1988, the speech was a prelude to
the official disengagement that would take place four weeks later: 'If
today [...] it is the wish of the Palestinian people's representatives to
separate from Jordan, we are willing to bless and respect this desire,
just as we blessed and respected the decision by the Palestinian people in 1950 to unite with Jordan.'[88] The final point is significant:
the act of annexation held no basis in international law and was the

result of the de facto act of Transjordan as 'conqueror'.[89] That the neighbouring Arab countries and the United States denied formal recognition of the move, and only Britain and Pakistan consented, indicates that Hussein was on perilous territory from which to compete with the PLO.

Since the 1974 Rabat resolutions, Jordan had maintained that the PLO had been imposed on the Occupied Territories by the Arab League (a decision about which they had not been consulted). The Intifada, however, disproved this claim and in May 1988, Hussein conceded that the Palestinians had 'elected the PLO' as their sole representatives and that 'from this premise [Jordan] could not carry any more burdens'.[90] In the months leading up to the severance, Hussein exhibited a perceptible offensive towards the Intifada and criticism of Jordanian nonchalance as events unfolded. Although at the Algiers Summit[91] he accentuated Jordan's active support during the uprising, that he felt the urge to reiterate this point demonstrated an awareness of the regime's declining favour. Jordan continued to act as a conduit for assistance in the West Bank, but the population had bolstered their contempt for the erstwhile monarch.[92] Hussein's trepidation was not without basis, for the 1987 Intifada in the Occupied Territories was the match by which the Jordanian tinder box could raze the monarchy and the government. Given the demographic imbalance between the Palestinian and Jordanian components of the population, the Intifada exposed Jordan's vulnerability and provided a golden opportunity to flee the growing Palestinian unrest and prevent a spread of the discontent to Jordan. It had negatively affected the king's plans for partnership with the Palestinians in the West Bank and as the PLO gained popularity, they vocalized the growing schism between the monarchy and their Palestinian counterparts.

From the outset, the immediate impetus for the disengagement lay with strategic interests in the context of preventing an escalation of public hostilities. For Hussein, it was essential to assist in the liberation of the occupied Palestinian land and make the point that the decision to dismantle Jordanian legal and administrative ties with the West Bank had been 'to support the steadfastness of our brothers and we respond to the wish of the Palestine Liberation Organisation

[...] and to the Arab orientation to affirm the Palestinian identity.'[93]
Furthermore,

> To leave the labyrinth of fears and doubts [about the competition
> between the Jordanian Government and the PLO in particu-
> lar, for the representation of the Palestinians in the West Bank],
> towards clearer horizons where mutual trust, understanding and
> cooperation can prevail.[94]

Although the sentiments befitted the gesture, the move was shrewd:
as support grew for the PLO, the Kingdom began to perceive political unity with the West Bank as a threat rather than a benefit.[95] To
concede the West Bank rapidly, while the aftermath of the widespread
unrest of the 1980s was still fresh, belies self-interest on the part of
the government and Hashemite regime rather than concern for their
Palestinian brothers. While the disengagement surprised international
observers, for Jordan it was the next logical step in a move to protect
the internal dynamic and the severing of ties became deeply institu-
tionalized in Jordanian behaviour and discourse.

Relations with the West Bank had come at a high political and
economic price and the government seized upon the disengagement
process as a pre-emptive defence that could reduce the involvement
and interaction between Palestinian-Jordanians disillusioned by the
regime in Jordan, and the East Bankers engaged in the Intifada.
Working on past experience, the regime viewed cross-bank relations
warily: liaisons had been conducive to multiple security infiltrations
against Israel across the Jordanian border by Palestinian and Jordanian
inhabitants, a development that contradicted Jordanian foreign policy
with Israel.[96] And it worked both ways, as the disengagement prevented future Israeli expulsions of Palestinians under the 'Jordan
Option', an initiative that promotes the Kingdom as an alternative
Palestinian state. Jordan needed a modus operandi by which the
unrest in the Occupied Territories could be divorced from the socio-
political demands of Jordanians of Palestinian origin. The disengagement provided such a formula: once the West Bank, Palestine, was
recognized as distinct and autonomous from the East Bank, Jordan,

the Jordanians could legitimately support the Intifada as an external event. Concurrently, this would satisfy the Arab consensus, while dele-gitimizing Palestinian political activity in the East Bank.[97] The disen-gagement sent an unmistakeable signal of Jordan's stance towards the West Bank and the Palestinians: no longer responsible for the West Bank, Jordan joined the ranks of Arab states offering vocal support to the Palestinian cause, yet in reality little assistance. A succinct appraisal of the Palestinian predicament is afforded by Goodwin-Gill: 'Just as Israel has denied citizenship to the majority of Palestinian Arabs, the Arab countries have, for the most part, consistently rejected local inte-gration and citizenship as a solution to the problem which, in their view, can only be resolved by repatriation and self-determination.'[98] Just as Jordan was distancing itself from the West Bank to maintain favourable relations with Israel, so too was it fighting the slogan of 'Jordan is Palestine' that was rapidly gaining popularity not only with its Israeli architects, but also in Palestinian circles.

Despite efforts to deny the correlation between the disengagement and the perceived domestic threat posed by citizens of Palestinian ori-gin, the redefinition of state borders could not escape the question of national identity. While in the past Jordan has emphasized common-alities over differences and encouraged unity over division, after the severance it became crucial to distinguish between the Palestine issue and the Palestinians living in Jordan. Although Lynch proposes that one was 'a question of foreign policy, the other a question of domestic politics', it can be contended that on this point no divergence emerged. Intrinsically linked to Palestine, the progress of the peace talks resounds within Jordan, as was demonstrated after the Jordan-Israel peace treaty in October 1994. The West Bank may have been severed, but the Palestinians within Jordan would forever be a reminder of Jordan's obligation to the cause.

By 1988, the deadlock between the PLO and Hussein had reached its zenith. Although he pledged to assist the PLO in its endeavours for a Palestinian state, it was clear that Hussein's motives were removed from such cordiality. The Palestinians had been clear in their demands and the ensuing withdrawal indicated that the PLO was ready to take over the administration and liberation of the Israeli-occupied West

Bank. The PLO 'had spent ten years on the touchline abusing the referee; now the time had come for them to shoot their own goals.'[99] Under a cloud of mistrust and scepticism, the PLO succeeded Jordan as the protector of the Palestinians and many of Arafat's colleagues and supporters feared they were witnessing the opening move in yet another strategy to remove the PLO from the region.[100] A campaign to cast aspersions on Jordan's disengagement soon followed, originating from sources in favour of the 'Jordan Option'. Yet the challenge lay in the PLO's ability to retain control over the West Bank and its inhabitants: Israel's stake in American policy was a strong factor in the talks and determined not only how the negotiations would progress, but with whom. If Israel succeeded in locking the PLO out of the peace process and Israeli military opposition prevented the PLO from administering the West Bank, a high proportion of the West Bank Palestinians could ultimately conclude that they were better served under Jordanian administration, and that it was Hussein who could improve their circumstances and end Israel's occupation. Should such a development ensue, the PLO would have confronted deep divisions amidst the Palestinians that would be open to exploitation by Jordan, the United States, Israel and Syria, who advocated that the PLO divest its mantle as the sole legitimate representative of the Palestinian people and withdraw from the peace process.[101]

When Hussein failed to consult the PLO before announcing Jordan's decision to nullify its administration of the West Bank, the ambiguity of his intentions was rendered stark. Had he intended to assist the PLO, the move would have been discussed in advance with Arafat, to grant the PLO time to formulate a strategy for the unfolding situation.[102] This view is countered, however, by a report in which the British Prime Minister Margaret Thatcher is alleged to have advised Hussein against disengagement, implying that a form of consultation, however limited, took place. Had this been the case, the absence of a PLO representative prior to disengagement validates the notion of a unilateral agreement on withdrawal, one in which Jordan initiates and enacts, yet does so without regard for her Palestinian counterpart.

For many Jordanians and movements such as the Muslim Brotherhood, readjustment in defence of the disengagement proved problematic. Having supported the unity of the two banks for 21 years, the decline of the concept of a unified Palestinian-Jordanian population was lamentable, since it had held 'fundamental, constitutive normative principles of Jordanian discourse and institutions'.[103] Displeased by the move, the Muslim Brotherhood maintained that 'we are in the two Banks one nation in blood and in family. We are one people not two.'[104] This contention, raised in parliament and coupled with the principle of calling for Islamic world unity, reaffirmed the Muslim Brotherhood's stance as an opponent to the regime, but also as the voice of the Palestinians, in both the East and West Banks.[105]

Having objected to the dual nationality certain Palestinians chose to adopt, memories of the *fedayeen* and the criticism to which their king had been subjected continued to rankle. Aware that the PLO's most strident overseas supporters and Hussein's harshest critics would not sacrifice their livelihoods to return to a liberated Palestine,[106] the severance with the West Bank satisfied the leftist bloc and halted accusations of a Jordanian 'creeping annexation' policy. While in contravention of the Ba'athist philosophy, the disengagement was viewed as a defence against Israeli bids to erode the Palestinian identity,[107] providing cover for Hussein's actions and reinforcing that the move was in the interest of the Palestinians and their identity, as opposed to Jordanian domestic stability, identity and nationalism, as well as relations with influential states such as Israel and the United States.

An alternative perspective comprises the legal and constitutional conditions. Seen in this light, the king's declaration of disengagement contravenes Article 1 of the Jordanian Constitution, that is: 'The Hashemite Kingdom of Jordan is an independent Arab state. It is individual and no part of it may be ceded.'[108] Under the amended Constitution of 1 January 1952, which came into effect following the unity of the two Banks, the West Bank remains part of the Hashemite Kingdom. The only legal and constitutional way in which the annexation of the West Bank can be nullified is through legislation passed by the National Assembly – that is, the Senate and the House of Deputies – and the king. Since Hussein had dissolved the House of Deputies, the Senate was also suspended and, consequently, the disengagement is nullified.

In January 1991, the Jordanian High Court refused to review the government's denationalization measures since the decision was an act of state and therefore not subject to review by the court. Moreover, the king's speech has not led to any formal changes in the Jordanian Nationality Law as, according to Articles 18 and 19, a person can only be divested of his or her Jordanian citizenship if that person serves in a foreign army and refuses to leave that army after being asked to do so by the Jordanian government; serves a hostile state; commits an act against the security of Jordan; or has obtained citizenship under false documents.[109] For this reason, advocates of the invalidity of the disengagement challenge the 'general conviction' that the West Bank Palestinians no longer retain the rights and obligations of Jordanian citizenship. [110] As the rescindment of Jordanian citizenship from Palestinians of West Bank origin continues, denial has given way to a more formal (though unofficial) endorsement of the absence of Palestinian-Jordanian legitimacy and in turn, the contra-disengagement argument is undermined.

Waiting for Palestine: the Passport System

While the validity of Jordanian disengagement remains ambiguous, the impact was tangible, bringing about substantial changes in the passport system. In a press conference on 7 August 1988, Hussein confirmed that Palestinian holders of Jordanian passports in the West Bank could retain their documents 'until such time as the Palestinian state hopefully is created [then] Palestinians have their own passports representing them as citizens of that state.'[111] Jordan has continued to issue Jordanian passports to the West Bank Palestinians, with a significant reduction in the term of validity to two years, as opposed to five years for Jordanian citizens. The replacement of passports with travel documents triggered further bureaucratic complications as the temporary passports curtailed visits to the East Bank to a maximum of 30 days at a time. Longer stays necessitated a permit and exceptions were made for matters involving the health of family members, a measure that placed them on an equal standing with Gaza refugees.[112]

The limitations imposed by the procedure afflict all areas of Palestinian life in Jordan, from healthcare to schooling and government appointments. Those Palestinians from the West Bank and Gaza who choose to reside in Jordan on a temporary passport are not entitled to health care fee exemptions and must rely upon UNRWA clinics and governmental health centres which still demand reimbursement. Previously assisted through fee exemptions granted by al-Dewan al-Malaki/Royal Court subsidies, during the rule of King Abdullah II, 'Abd al-Ra'uf al-Rawabdeh's government terminated the fee exemptions.[113] In terms of higher education this places Palestinian-Jordanians on a par with applicants from the wider MENA region, and to attend a university in Jordan they must endure intense competition for the 5 per cent of the seats allocated to 'Arab foreigners'. If successful, they are defined as 'foreigners' and pay a higher quota of fees, up to $60 per hour of tuition. However, since holders of Palestinian Authority travel documents are submitted for entry through the Palestinian Embassy, they are often excluded from the list and obliged to attend private universities with higher fees.[114] Despite this hindrance, the Palestinians have sustained the highest per capita rate of university graduates in the Arab world.[115]

Supplementary to the temporary passports, the government distributed a series of cards that distinguish between the categories of Palestinians in the Kingdom: Green Cards were issued to West Bankers enabling them to visit Jordan and return to the West Bank; Blue Cards to Palestinians from Gaza, also permitting visits, and Pink Cards enabling Gazans to temporarily reside in the East Bank. Yellow Cards were allocated to holders of permanent Jordanian passports and of a national identity number, as well as a family reunification permit provided by the Israeli occupation authorities.[116] The cards are sub-categorized according to the applicant's background and entitlements: five-year passports with a national identity number are distributed to Palestinians who have resided in Jordan since 1948 and Jordanian East Bankers with a family book and full access to services. Jordanian-Palestinians that have resided in the Kingdom since 1967 require a supplementary Yellow Crossing Card for family reunification, but hold the same rights as the aforementioned group. Palestinians who have resided in the Kingdom since 1967 and in the West Bank specifically, as well as Jordanian-Palestinians who hold permanent residence in Jerusalem, are granted a five-year passport with a national identity number, but no family book, which registers the civil status of the family members. Accorded a Green Card, employment requires a work permit, university education is charged at the rate for foreign students and ownership of property is possible only with the approval of the ministerial council. The Palestinians of Gaza must be permanent residents of Jordan and carry a two-year temporary passport, without a family book, and can only cross with a Blue Card for family reunification purposes; other than that their rights are equal to the above noted group. Finally, Palestinians of West Bank or Gazan origin must have permanent residence in either the West Bank or Gaza and hold a Palestinian authority passport. They have permission to enter and are regarded in the same as any Arab in Jordan and provided there is a valid residency they can access facilities permitted for foreigners.[117] Administrative documents, such as driver's licences, were also brought under a new regime, requiring the applicants to attend in person in Amman to renew them.[118]

The decree not only terminated Jordan's administrative ties to the West Bank, but also nullified the citizenship rights of an estimated three-quarters of a million Palestinians who were ordinarily resident in the West Bank, with the exception of the 1948 UNRWA registered refugees in the West Bank camps. The national change affected the lives of hundreds of thousands of families, yet was not debated in the House of Representatives and was not proclaimed by law.[119] On this premise, Shehadeh argues that because the Jordanian Nationality Law remained unabridged, the West Bank Palestinians did not formally lose their Jordanian citizenship. However, the reality is that they are no longer regarded as absolute Jordanian citizens and are considered stateless individuals.[120] Enshrined as the ultimate act of Arab patriotism and pro-Palestinian magnanimity, the disengagement stripped the Palestinians of their rights and obliged them to eke out a stateless existence in Israel, until the official establishment of the state of Palestine in the indefinite future. The cost, effort and limitations incurred by the temporary documents casts doubt on how far the severance was a sacrifice of the West Bank Palestinians by Jordan. The move remains a significant component in the ongoing relations between Palestinian-Jordanians and ethnic Jordanians and had a substantial influence on the evolution of Palestinian identity in the Kingdom.

New War, New Influx: The Iraq War (2003–2011)

A haven for refugees fleeing through, or to, the Middle East since the 1900s when the Chechens and Circassians settled in Amman having fled the armies of the Tsar,[121] the Kingdom was sought once more by those in need upon the establishment of the state of Israel 1948. Since then thousands of Palestinians have fled over the border in search of a secure future amongst fellow Palestinians. The Lebanese Civil War (1975–1991) added to the increasing number of refugees seeking protection in Jordan, but the next wave of *émigrés* was to be one of the largest and most diverse.[122] During the Gulf War (1990–1991), Kuwait expelled 300,000 Palestinians who had been living in Kuwait since 1948 and over the subsequent decade over one million Iraqis entered Jordan, fleeing the regime of Saddam Hussein, with figures nudging over 700,000 by 2007 and 450,000 by 2011.[123]

In the aftermath of the Gulf War, migration flows into the Kingdom transformed the trend of labour supply and demand as previously the Gulf states had absorbed the excess of Jordan's labour market after each new flow of migrants by employing the skills of qualified individuals and offering financial rewards for their experience. However, the international embargo imposed upon Iraqi oil during the ten years after the war destabilized the economy, prompting an exodus of several thousand Egyptians and Sudanese to relocate to Jordan seeking new employment.[124] The diverse influx of refugees during this period closely correlates political and economic factors that conditioned the out-migration of these groups, their reception and their subsequent livelihoods in Jordan. The dynamic between Jordanian society and the Iraqi community is linked to wider regional events: simultaneous to the Gulf crisis, Jordan was entering the peace process and the combination of events created a contradiction as Jordanians and Palestinians united against the Gulf War, while remaining divided over Jordanian peace proposals. The Kingdom's approach to the invasion of Kuwait prompted the belief among Iraqis that Jordan would afford not only a lucrative, but a stable and positive reception. It was not to be. Although Jordan initially supported Iraq and skirted international sanctions to provide for its neighbour, following Hussein's invasion of Kuwait Jordanian allegiance was (reluctantly) and rapidly switched to the Western forces. King Hussein's political indecisiveness rested on ensuring the best possible outcome for Jordan, while encouraging the flow of Iraqi refugees into the already replete country.

By the second Gulf War in 2003 Iraqis constituted the third main refugee group in the world, while Jordan had ceased to enjoy the dependency of migrant earnings that contributed to the boom in remittances between the years 1972 and 1991, when it reached a peak in 1984 at $1.2 billion, or 25 per cent GDP.[125] In addition to 300,000 'returnees', 1.5 million Iraqis moved through the Kingdom, with 300,000 remaining.[126] Of the 300,000, only 30,000 have legal status as labour migrants, while the remainder eke out a livelihood in the informal economy in competition with the Egyptians.[127] In 2003, a study of the socio-economic profile of Iraqi migrants with asylum seekers at UNHCR in Amman revealed the typical profile of Iraqi forced migrants to be male, between 25 and 45 years old, who, if married, have left their family in Iraq until stable foundations have been laid for their arrival.[128] This hoped-for stability could be through employment, migration to another country or recognition by UNHCR of their refugee status. The majority of migrants were male, with women in the marginal minority of 44 per cent. However, while it may seem that there is an almost equal male–female ratio presence, it is more likely that those women who were present approached the UNHCR on a more frequent basis, thereby seeming of a greater number.[129] On a religious level, 67 per cent of the migrants were Shi'a, followed by Christians (13 per cent), Sunnis (12 per cent) and Sabeans (8 per cent). In this context, it is important to note their religious affiliation with regards to their livelihood strategy once in Jordan. As foreign NGOs are prohibited by the authorities from establishing projects aimed at assisting Iraqis, Church charities are the only ones permitted to provide aid 'in kind'.[130] Originating from the historic relationship developed between the Hashemite state and the Christian Church organization,[131] Jordan's vibrant and well-integrated Christian community can be viewed as an obstacle for many Iraqis seeking assistance from the available organizations. A number of respondents interviewed by Chatelard expressed reservations at approaching the organizations, believing that their services were reserved for Christians alone.[132] While the charities aim to bring aid to all in strife, the reality is that their services are rendered more willingly to Christians than to Moslem Iraqis. Aid opportunities are further limited for the Moslem Iraqi community as Shiite Islam has no indigenous followers in Jordan, no official status and therefore no established social institutions and no legal possibility to register any in the future.[133] Alternatively, Sunni mosques and charities, zakat[134] committees or medical facilities – such as the Islamic Hospital – provide Sunni Iraqis with relief.

Aside from the internal mechanisms – upon whom the onus of refugee welfare rests – the external framework for providing relief and support for migrants, Iraqi or otherwise, remains riddled with flaws. The countries of the Middle East maintain a cautious approach towards the issue of asylum, indicating the close connection between the plight of refugees and the politically sensitive and still unre-solved Palestinian issue as the cause. Anxieties include domestic and regional constraints such as the limited resources available and the economic burden new migrants would bring to the host countries, the necessity of maintaining good relations with neighbouring states and the fear of becoming a 'dumping ground' of rejected refugees from other states in the region.[135] These concerns are reflected in the behaviour of the host states: the initial eagerness to assist was gradu-ally replaced by an over-reliance on bodies such as the UNHCR. As the UNHCR displayed an effective approach in dealing with the refugees, local authorities adopted an increasingly passive attitude and a reluctance to change the status quo.[136] The consequences of this approach saw a reduction in commitment towards the issue of refugees, a growth in restrictive practices against them and a rise in expulsions. The predicament was further exacerbated by the growing sense of urgency conveyed by Western countries to reduce the mass movement of people from the Middle East towards their borders.[137] In turn, a number of flaws emerged in the migrant system. Primarily, while the refugees attained some level of protection, the formal structure within which policies were formulated remained inarticulate and weak.[138] Furthermore, the practices of governments remain inconsistent and discretionary, thereby enabling the condition of refugees in the Middle East to remain unstable. Defined as the 'main constraints'[139] of the host nations, the following factors can be viewed as conducive to a reduced level of cohesion, both in terms of legal protection and social integration: limited finances, security concerns, weak domestic legal systems and low human rights awareness.[140] Such factors contribute to the disillusionment of many Iraqis, on varying levels of the social scale, who arrived in Jordan with high aspirations for a secure future.

The Iraqi refugees in Jordan represent an example of Jordan's stance on the allocation of citizenship to non-Jordanian Arabs. Under the Agreement of 5 April 1954 on Provisions Regarding Citizenship Among Member States of the League of Arab States, the signatories were cautioned against 'the naturalization of a citizen of any Member State of the League of Arab States in another Member State' unless it is with 'the express agreement of his Government in which case his previous citizenship will be nullified after obtaining his new citizenship.'[141] Jordan opted to retain its original legislature from 1928, which limits the access of non-Jordanian Arabs to Jordanian citizenship until the applicant has been ordinarily resident in the Kingdom for 15 years or more.[142] Reminiscent of the Palestinian refugees in Jordan, the Iraqis confront an equally gruelling 15-year wait before gaining full Jordanian citizenship. Moreover, they must decide between retaining their Iraqi nationality, in the hope of a future return, or rescind their Iraqi passport in order to accept the Jordanian offer extended after 15 years.

Prior to 2007, the breakdown was most perceptible in the cases of the refugees residing in the Al-Ruweished camp, where individuals endured sexual harassment, lax security and poor medical care. The camp, which held at its peak 2,000 Palestinian and non-Palestinian refugees, was located 350 kilometres east of the capital and managed by the Jordan Hashemite Charity Organization (JHCO).[143] By

February 2007, Jordan held 22,000 registered Iraqi refugees whose educational, medical and legal needs were met through various NGOs, including Save the Children, Caritas, UNICEF, the Noor Al Houssein Foundation, the Jordanian Red Crescent, Mizan, the Jordanian Women's Union and the National Centre for Human Rights. Among the most prominent contributors are UNHCR, UNICEF and the United States Agency for International Development (USAID); in 2007, 61 per cent of UNHCR's operational budget was granted directly to Jordan, while the following year the U.S. Congress approved $200 million in supplemental aid funding for Iraqi refugees, $110 million to the Jordanian government and another $45 million to existing USAID programs in the Kingdom.[144] That the aid is directly bestowed to the Jordanian government and used thereafter to renovate schools, hospitals and water systems has prompted the realization that it will not be to the Iraqi community's benefit (due to relocation in a third country), but rather resident Jordanians. As a consequence, 'Schools built in expectation of hundreds of poor Iraqi students may end up serving only handfuls, or none at all.'[145] Yet despite the high injections of fiscal aid the consequences of the Iraq conflict has not left the Jordanian economy unscathed and an estimated $1 billion per annum is dedicated towards refugee services and resources.[146] On a grassroots level, the pinch has not passed unnoticed: during the course of fieldwork, respondents frequently noted the rising cost of commodities and real estate, a change that is – justly or unjustly – attributed to the affluent stratum of Iraqis entering the Kingdom.

While security can be bought through the $150,000 residency permit, obstacles persist, both officially – from November 2006 Iraqi refugees aged 17–35 were denied entry[147] – and unofficially, due to a distrust originating from the 9 November 2005 Amman bombings (enacted by Iraqi members of Jordanian Abu Musab al-Zarqawi's al-Qaeda in Iraq) and/or rumours of a burgeoning Shiite Crescent arcing from Iran, through Iraq into Syria, Lebanon and the Gulf.[148] The resultant discrimination is diverse, including:

[A] prohibition on opening *huseiniyat* (Shiite houses of prayer); teachers telling Shiite children they are not true Muslims;

preachers giving Friday sermons in support of jihadis in Iraq (at a time when these were explicitly targeting Shiites); popular use of the derogatory term *rafidin* ('rejectionists') to describe Shiites; and border officials often asking entering Iraqis whether they are Sunni or Shiite.[149]

But such antagonism was not always present; rather, the close ties between the two countries encouraged many Iraqi refugees to seek asylum in the Kingdom. Jordan was aligned with Iraq from the onset of Baghdad's conflict with Tehran, even before the actual outbreak of war in the summer of 1980.[150] From the outset – and with the exception of Jordan's final decision during the first Gulf War to side with the West – the relationship showed signs of the turbulent affection of the two states striving for mutual gain through cohesion. The relationship was based upon a mutually beneficial premise: Iraq, unlike Syria, was not a frontline state and as a consequence was less immediately implicated in Arab-Israeli issues, so that differences regarding Israel were less inclined to strain the relationship. For Iraq, the additional benefit of splitting Jordan from Syria was perceived as a great gain; for Jordan, the advantage lay in the fact that the Saudis were more at ease with the Kingdom's relationship with the Iraqis in the 1980s than they had ever been with the Jordanian-Syrian relationship in the previous decade.[151] By 1989, the friendship was consolidated through the Arab Co-operation Council, along with Egypt and North Yemen. Through the union, it was hoped that greater trade links would be established, with Iraqi and Jordanian protagonists leading the way, and Iraq would provide an expanded market for Jordanian exports, jobs for the unemployed skilled workers of Jordan and business opportunities for the private sector.[152] The project was short-lived and in the aftermath of the Iraqi invasion of Kuwait in August 1990, all remaining economic and political aspirations were quashed.

It is, then, a cold economic and political relationship rather than one based on fraternity as King Hussein endeavoured to portray in his speech of solidarity shortly before the invasion of Kuwait. Despite close affiliations, the Gulf War necessitated a split to preserve Jordanian economic interests. In spite of strong recommendations from the

United States during the Gulf War, Jordan flouted the embargoes and granted political asylum in 1995 to Saddam Hussein's sons-in-law, Lieutenant-General Hussein Kamel Hassan and Lieutenant Saddam Kamel Hassan.[153] King Hussein welcomed the defectors and declared, 'A new era and a new life for the Iraqi people.'[154] Emphasizing that Jordan would not stand by and witness the demise of its neighbour, he continued, 'This is a matter that we do not contemplate because we are with the people of Iraq [...] until the long night of their suffering ends.'[155] In reality, self-interest prevailed as, should Jordan remove all ties with Iraq and endorse the embargo:

> Such a step will break the back of the Jordanian economy. The imposition of sanctions by Jordan against Iraq might not cause major damage to the Iraqi economy, or to its military effort, but it will devastate the Jordanian economy and cause a loss in excess of half a billion dollars a year.[156]

In the context of Iraqi refugees in Jordan, this indicates the priorities of Jordan: the well-being of the country, its economy and inhabitants. Next comes the Palestinian issue, which at its most ubiquitous dominates the internal social sphere, the stability and security of the state, and the relations of the country on a regional and international level. Last is the welfare of the non-Jordanian/Palestinian citizens, which is subject to the circumstances of the above points.

And therein rests the exceptionality of the Iraqi case that distinguishes its influx from that of the Palestinians. Over the past decade, Iraqis have entered Jordan in a steady flow, in contrast to the Palestinian refugees who have entered in waves and trickles since 1948. Moreover, the Iraqis in Jordan are en route to a third country and the Kingdom provides a mere stopover; for the Palestinians, Jordan has become either an adopted homeland (though rarely a substitute for the real one) or an enduring limbo with a return that remains elusive. Lastly, the Palestinian refugees are represented at all socio-economic levels of society; from the elite to unemployed camp residents, they are marked in their pervasiveness while the Iraqi community remains polarized between those in abject poverty and their compatriots sustaining a

lavish existence. Affluent businessmen managing multi-million dol-
lar enterprises that trade United Nations-approved goods to Iraq via
Amman or highly educated professionals who have accepted menial
jobs to support their families in Iraq are equally present. Then there
are the street vendors who use the lax immigration rules to spend
a few months selling cigarettes and chewing gum in the old town
before returning home. While the prosperous reside in luxury apart-
ments and villas, the latter lodges in dilapidated hotels or share a
crumbling bedroom with other compatriots. For many Iraqi refugees
the onus lies not with the United States, but rather with the under-
funded aid agencies or Jordan's bursting refugee capacity. The Iraq
conflict emphasized the crisis point that refugee mechanisms have
reached, not only in Jordan but in the wider Middle East. To date,
internal and external displacement has been limited and the conflict
has not reached the neighbouring countries. Yet the situation in Iraq
has not reached a complete end and as long as uncertainty remains,
individuals will continue to journey to an area where stability and
safety is (perceived to be) guaranteed. Equally, the volatility does
not provide an incentive to the refugees residing in Jordan, be it in
squalor or opulence.

   Under such circumstances, the Jordanian government must adopt
new measures to increase its capabilities to absorb and facilitate
the Iraqi refugees. According to Zaiotti, the application of the
're-engagement scenario' under which the UNHCR and local authorities, unsettled by the deterioration of the condition of refugees and
the possible destabilizing effect it could have on the region, would
attempt to address the problem by amending their relations and
adopt a more proactive stance towards one another.[157] Furthermore,
local governments would be involved if they discern these initiatives
as fostering their interests in the long-term.[158] This process would
ultimately lay the foundations for the resumption of the socialization
mechanism that was in its infancy during the early 1990s. Through
cohesion, Zaiotti reasons, the internalization by local authorities
of the standards of the refugee regime could increase, ensuring a
gradual change in practices and policies.[159] The frustration borne
of the Jordanian citizenship process is antagonistic to Palestinians

and Iraqis alike, though to date the Palestinians have been the more vociferous of the two as the struggle to recoup the homeland is a longer and more arduous process. Unless the citizenship stipulations are reduced to stand in line with those for non-Arab applicants, disillusionment will continue to grow within the refugee and low-income sectors of Jordanian society.

Citizenship rights in Jordan remain strangers to amendments that promote equality. The few changes that have occurred have taken place under dire circumstances and under a duress heightened by security interests, as opposed to the welfare of citizens and potential citizens. Iraqis, Sudanese, Palestinians and others endure a process that is more arduous than that which is enforced for the foreign/non-Arab applicant, and contrary to increasing the Kingdom's population in a manner that would foster a cohesive environment. Although the Provisions Regarding Citizenship Among Member States of the League of Arab States sought alignment to the wider region's systems, the Jordanian regime favours self-preservation, a feature that has persisted since the reign of King Abdullah I. That the Kingdom's geographical and demographic proximity to the Palestine-Israel conflict compels the state to view domestic and security issues with greater discernment is clear, and for this reason Jordan has consistently nurtured a strict approach to applicants and citizens. Nevertheless, there is little to suggest that Jordan would lose through compromise. To reduce the duration from 15 years to 8, for example, and increase the current period for foreign applicants by four years would place the two on an equal footing. Security would be maintained and the equal duration would work towards a containment of the inferior treatment accorded to non-Jordanian Arab applicants. The imbalance of the rights of women and children under the Nationality Law also demands amendment. Providing an identity to children lacking a steadfast identity in Jordan would address the schism between Palestinians and Jordanians and promote inter-communal cohesion. The correlation between citizenship rights and the Palestinian-Jordanian relationship is considerable and the long-term future of domestic relations would benefit from less stringency and more equality to guarantee an integrated and collaborative society.

3

A MULTIFACETED NATIONAL CONSCIOUSNESS

The Arab land is my homeland,
From Damascus to Baghdad,
From Egypt to Yemen,
From Najd to Tetuan,
No religion separates us,
The Arabic tongue unites us.[1]

The relationship between the Jordanian establishment and the Palestinian-Jordanian community has been marked by misguided approaches to coexistence and integration. Determined to uphold the integration of the majority Palestinian population into Jordanian society as a success to be envied by its regional cohorts, Jordan and its inhabitants have nonetheless struggled to sustain the existing Jordanian identity alongside a burgeoning Palestinian one. As Jordanian society endeavours to preserve this indigenous entity, so, too, has it traversed extremes, the most notable being the 'Jordan First' campaign.[2] On the one hand welcomed as a proactive approach towards enhanced national unity, the Jordan First initiative equally has been perceived as an ultimatum, as it does not request, but rather demands that those in possession of multiple identities choose one: either the Jordanian or Palestinian identity. Emphasizing the issue of loyalty, it has prompted, among other questions, 'Who said Jordan *wasn't* first?'

In the case of Jordan and Palestine, a common culture and history should be conducive towards a symbiotic identity, since 'Jordan is linked to Palestine by a national relationship and a national unity forged by history and culture from earliest times'.[3] As a diasporic community, the Palestinians in Jordan have established an identity within a framework that is unique to a population forcefully displaced. To cope with the fragmentation of the present, the community seeks to return to the past, a memory sculpted 'by "legends and landscapes", stories of golden ages, enduring traditions, heroic deeds and dramatic destinies located in promised homelands with hallowed seats and scenery'.[4] In the Palestinian-Jordanian instance, they reside in a country ruefully close to the 'hallowed seats and scenery' and regularly encounter people from the homeland. Stoked by fresh tales of 'heroic deeds' in addition to updates on the demise of the towns and villages they once knew, the Palestinian identity retains its potency.

Jordan's array of multiple identities has enabled not only the Palestinian and Jordanian identity to endure simultaneously, but also a hybrid identity to emerge. A juxtaposition of Palestinian and Jordanian hybridity has given rise to 'the Palestinian-Jordanian identity'. According to Nasser, identity is organized around two aspects: the *synchronic* and the *diachronic*. The synchronic dimension can be applied to the contemporary Jordanian identity through examples of who the Jordanians are, with the focus on their locale and identification with the regional (Arab) and the universal (Islamic) collective.[5] Equally, the synchronic evokes the 1960s boundaries of Jordanian identity and their links to Arabs and Muslims.[6] Although seemingly similar, the diachronic dimension addresses the historical evolution of the nation, commencing with the Arabs' ancient history and culminating with the demarcation of Jordan from the Islamic and Arab collectives, giving rise to a separate entity in modern times.

Particularly evident in the context of regional progress, Jordan shares with Palestine legacies of the British and French Mandate that juxtaposed distinct ethnic/national groups within one state, or separated the same national group into different states. For Iraq and Jordan, their imposed leaders served colonial, rather than popular interests. In turn, the nascent states were compelled to fashion a national identity from the fusion of ethnic, tribal and religious components in the new environment. Unlike Egypt, Iran or Syria, Jordan lacked a cohesive identity or history, defined as it was by boundaries set by the colonial powers, a formal title, a ruling dynasty, patronage from the former rulers and a diverse population.[7] In common with its neighbours, Jordan was, and continues to be, distinctly non-homogenous and comprises numerous ethnic, religious, cultural and linguistic minorities in addition to the Palestinians, including Circassians, Chechens, Iraqis and Syrians. It has, however, made a concerted effort towards evolving a national identity that reflects its heterogeneity, a feat that remains elusive to the states in the wider region.

Loyalty and Identity: *Qawmiyya* and *Wataniyya*

Whether the identity of an individual connotes loyalty towards Arab nationalism (*al-qawmiyya*) or a nationalism based on state sovereignty (*al-wataniyya*) presents an ideological question that is integral to an analysis of the Palestinian-Jordanian dynamic. Although the debate surrounding *al-qawmiyya* and *al-wataniyya* has been previously applied to the cases of Egypt and Iraq, it is also relevant to the case of the Palestinians in Jordan. The ideological clash that first took place between Nasir and Qasim realized the nineteenth-century debate between the German and Anglo-French schools,[8] in which the former associated the Arab world's *al-qawmiyya* with the oneness of the people (*volk*), united under a unifying language and a continuous historical experience. Though political and geographical divisions might have separated members of the nations, the boundaries were disregarded due to their artificial nature and deemed irrelevant to the definition of *al-qawmiyya*.[9] In contrast, the Anglo-French school embraced *al-wataniyya*, a nationalism built through state institutions within 'a geographically limited space, even if the citizens were to speak different languages and/or profess different ethnicities'.[10] In the case of the Palestinian identity, *al-qawmiyya* could be regarded as the dominant ideology, since language and historical experience united the Palestinian people. Conversely, the Jordanian state could be considered a proponent of *al-wataniyya*.

Analogous to Qasim's demonstration of Iraq's political independence through the 'Iraq First' aphorism, in times of uncertainty Jordan has called on the slogan 'Jordan First' to unite the population, regardless of ethnic origin or faith. Just as Qasim's slogan of 'Iraq First' presented a quandary to the nationalist (*qawmi*) hopes for Arab unity, so too has the 'Jordan First' campaign drawn mixed responses. Unlike the Iraqi case, in which 'the euphoric *qawmiyeen* (nationalists) watched, aggrieved and dumbfounded, as the Arab nationalist march, seemingly so near to its ultimate goal of Arab unity, came against the roadblock of the "Iraq First" *wataniyya*',[11] the Jordanian maxim has not presented a substantial obstacle to Palestinian unity in Jordan.

For Arab nationalists, the 'cherished *qawmiyya*' represented a means to execute a relentless assault on state sovereignty, a revolutionary 'crusade against "artificial" political boundaries' that one day would witness the realization of Arab nationalism's ultimate goal of a unified Arab nation-state.[12] Of course, the similarities between the efforts of the Arab nationalist movement and those of the Palestinian movement have been lucidly exhibited. Just as the Arab nationalist movement sought to conduct a relentless assault on state sovereignty in order to establish a unified Arab nation-state, so too did the forays of the Palestinian *fedayeen* during Black September in Jordan symbolize a concerted effort to establish a proxy Palestinian state within the Kingdom. Thus, as the Arab nationalist movement waned, *al-qawmiyya* continued to thrive within the Palestinian movement, epitomizing a parallel struggle for a Palestinian state. In the years following 1967, 'it was *Arab statism* not *Arab nationalism* that defined the post-1967 era, *wataniyya* not *qawmiyya* that determined political relations among the Arab states.'[13] By the end of the twentieth century, *al-qawmiyya* had declined an acknowledgement of cultural proximity that at best established vague general parameters for political action.[14] Conversely, the Palestinian-Jordanian identity had embraced both the *al-qawmiyya* of the Palestinian movement and a smattering of Jordanian *al-wataniyya*. In turn, a hybrid ideology has emerged that enabled the Palestinian-Jordanians to retain their longing for Palestinian statehood while demonstrating individual belonging (*intima'*) to Jordan, thereby facilitating integration within Jordanian society.

Qabila: Everlasting, Ever-present

Jordan is our father and the tribes are our mothers.[15]

As hosts, the Jordanian community represents an intriguing case: small in number, Jordanians have maintained a strong grip on the reins of power through a system that has been at once lauded and condemned as defensive and discriminatory, credited with facilitating the professional and ethnic divide between Palestinians and Jordanians in the private and public sector. All the while, the Jordanian regime has retained the capacity to determine the legal and political destiny of the Palestinian population resident in the Kingdom. Having roamed the Jordan valley since the seventeenth century, the Bedouin tribes have dominated the region and its foothills. Sharing many qualities with the camel-herding Bedouin clans (the Beni Sahkr, Huwitat, Beni Hassan and Rwalla)[16] they engaged in long-distance migrations. The altitudinous and ecological diversity of the Jordan Valley proved fitting for goat and sheep herding and until the 1950s the Adwan, Abbad, Ghazawia, Mashalhah and Balawna tribes moved with their flocks from the hills in the summer to the valley in the winter and spring, scattering grain crops on the fertile soil of the Jordan River's alluvial bed as they advanced.[17] By 1900, tribal Bedouins were engaging in the sedentarization process and while the process of sedentarization would be facilitated by government measures, by the early years of the twentieth century the Bedouin were touched by the most fundamental impulses of man: desire and envy. When the nomadic tribes first encountered the cultivators with their techniques for reaping the land and maintaining a steady livelihood, they pillaged their crops with grazing and robbery. This was to be short-lived, however, as the clans began to discard their previous perceptions of villagers as unenterprising and cowardly, and instead developed an appreciation of the virtues of cultivation and residing in one area. In turn, the clans adopted the skills of the settled villagers and abandoned the peripatetic life.

While life had previously entailed raising livestock in the harsh environment of Jordan's scrubland, the tribes progressed from raiders to the raided, as one tribe departing from the desert was quickly replaced by another, until almost all had integrated into or established settled communities. Although relations between Bedouin and villagers were initially characterized by squabbles and mutual loathing, villagers soon developed a rapport with the newly settled Bedouin as association guaranteed protection, both from raids and internal disequilibrium. Enacted through social channels, association took form through marriage as the tribe, who previously would have been aghast at such a union, now renounced village prejudices and adapted their system of authority in accordance with their new lifestyle. In the past, the Bedouin acknowledged the authority of a supreme chief on account of his capacity for leadership, as opposed to descent; as the tribe moved as a single unit there was little conflict between individuals or families since all were engaged in the common struggle for water and sustenance. Once settled, the natural order of authority – that is, survival of the fittest, rather than sanguine-based selection – crumbled as the tribe began to own and till the land, resulting in a series of minor chiefs whose arbitrary jurisdiction over their subjects proved conducive to renewed squabbling.[18] Where once major concerns arose from clashes with other tribes or a lack of resources, village life presented a new collection of quandaries comprising power and cooperation. As the tribal ties loosened, the Bedouin forged a bond that would survive the raids and characterize the early period of interaction between the Bedouin and villagers, and endure into politics long after the tribal system had waned.

The process of bonding was gradual, yet perceptible. Primarily, the Bedouin tribes had previously identified themselves in terms of the tribe and its opposition; that is, the Arab tribes of the Arab Peninsula are defined in opposition to non-Arabs. Secondly, among the Arab tribes identities are delineated according to social status, kinship, economic status and religion. Within the tribe, social hierarchies are ordered according to genealogy, enabling certain members to garner more respect than others.[19] While kinship affords a means to link with common ancestors and the past, it is difference rather than similarity that determines their sense of individual identity within and between tribes.[20] This has been demonstrated through the act of joke-telling in villages: while in 1960 villagers would commonly share jokes about other villages in their vicinity to illustrate their stereotypical attributes – such as ignorance, stubbornness or naïveté – by 1986, the villagers had transferred their jesting to villages outside the district.[21] As Antoun discerns, 'Too many ties had been forged – educational, occupational, marital – with villagers within the district to permit such joking.'[22] In a country fashioned by colonialism, the term 'indigenous' when applied to the Jordanian population could be regarded as contrived. Yet in the context of identity it is apt, capturing a population settled in the territory of Jordan. And indigenous though it may be, the Jordanian identity is not monolithic, for both tribes and tribalism (*ashariyya*) have proven crucial to the evolution of the state, though 'the definition of tribe and tribalism is not clearly delineated and its application is obscured, particularly as an analytical term'.[23] In a discourse pertaining to the Palestinian-Jordanian identity, it is essential to define the concept of 'tribes' and 'tribalism' in the Jordanian state.

With adaptability constituting a dominant characteristic, 'tribalism' can be defined as a culture, incorporating customs and characteristics; as an element of national identity; or as a definitive indicator of one's ethnic background. The assertion that an individual born into a tribal community is imbued with an awareness of their tribal identity from birth is worthy of further consideration. For Huntington, 'A new baby may have elements of an identity at birth in terms of a name, sex, parentage, and citizenship. These do not, however, become part of his or her identity until the baby becomes conscious of them and defines itself in terms of them.'[24] If it is considered that identity 'refers to the images of individuality and distinctiveness ("selfhood") held and projected by an actor and formed (and modified over time) through relations with significant "others"'[25] it gains added significance. As people engage with others, they have little option but to define themselves in relation to those others – in this case the tribe or the community – and identify their similarities with and difference from those others.

For Lewis, an ancestral affiliation is established from the outset through the triad of consanguinity, geography and religion, which enable 'the family, the clan, the tribe, [to develop] into the ethnic nation'.[26] The significance of bloodlines has been noted for its ability to tenaciously bond members of a group while effectively excluding outsiders. The allegiance of a tribal member, in this context Bedouin, is principally to his immediate kin, emanating into ever wider spheres of social contact. The nature of consanguinity is perhaps best captured by the Arabic maxim 'me against my brothers, my brothers and me against our cousins, my cousins, my brothers and me against the rest of the world.'[27] Yet the tendency to bond and disassociate according to consanguinity is not just a tribal phenomena. On an international level, it is evident in the French and German context, as 'their national identity loses salience in relation to their European identity [...] when there emerges a broader sense of difference between "us" and "them", [such as] between the European and the Japanese identities.'[28] This is closely followed by geography, which accelerates the evolution of tribal identity by binding the individual to a place. However, while the village, province and country can provide a geographical affiliation, this does not necessarily coincide with the primary element, consanguinity.[29] Lastly, religion is ambiguous in the formation of national identity, as '[f]or many, religion is the only loyalty that transcends local and immediate bonds'.[30] As such, religion can either unify or transcend the above elements within the tribal community, just as it would in the Palestinian-Jordanian community.

The notion of a lasting tribal identity infusing the individual from birth is questionable, since identities, both tribal and non-tribal, remain malleable throughout life or, as Amin Maalouf construes it, untameable: the 'wild beast of identity'.[31] This is in accordance with Lewis' components, the varying nature of which enables identities to adapt according to their surroundings over time. Just as tribal society progresses, so too must the definition of tribalism change. No longer captured neatly in the confines of the three dependable points, it has broadened to embrace roles as a genealogical unit, a coping mechanism, a means to reinterpret tradition, and as a force to unite or separate ethnic from national identities.[32] Unlike the Palestinian identity, which retains a focus on the realization of Palestine as a viable state, the Jordanian identity strives to legitimize the presence of the ethnic Jordanian populace as the host, owners and leaders of the Kingdom.

As such, it remains fluid, reflecting the needs of its leaders and their objectives at any given time.

The relationship nurtured between the Hashemite regime and the tribes has enabled 'tribalism' to evolve towards a formidable national entity and a means by which Jordo-Jordanians can confidently assert their personal identity. While tribalism satisfies the nationalist aspirations of the Jordanian population, it also holds an allure for non-Jordanian minorities. As the Jordanian tribes maintain a stronghold on the public and military sector, additional families, clans and individuals who identify themselves as being of tribal origin 'create a tribe'[33] with the intention of discarding their minority status and accessing resources previously monopolized by Jordanian parties. Most notably, this has been achieved by the Circassian community, who despite their political importance[34] remain lost amidst the plethora of identities and national groups in Jordan.[35] Just as the Circassian community and Jordanian tribes tout the nation's history as evidence of their inherent right to be considered the indigenous children of Jordan's terrain, the notion of 'tribal' has evolved to exude valour, courage and moral virtue in the present. Conversely, it has also become the object of derision, perceived as a hindrance to the progress of society.[36]

Tribalism has been widely defined within a Western framework and tribes are identified as organic, coherent, internally closed systems that eventually succumb to 'a unified evolutionary process occurring in a coordinated way like parts of a growing body'.[37] The organic aspect extends further to nationalist and tribal discourse, creating a dichotomy between the past and present. Consistently portrayed as romantic warriors eking out a livelihood from Jordan's harsh land, the reality is quite different: engaging in political and social activities, many Bedouin have swapped tents for offices, and their traditional dress for the business suits. The Bedouin of today are, in effect, participating and excelling in every aspect of national life, while the idealized past has become merely a barrier to development.

The absorption of tribal communities into the city and their methods of integration are by no means unique: in his observations of late 1960s Iraq, al-Wardi commented that in the cities modernization was superficial, and that many city-dwellers were Bedouin for whom 'the trappings of modernity, such as Western clothing, simply camouflaged deeply ingrained tribal values'.[38] While on the one hand tribal culture is utilized to assert Jordanian identity, simultaneously it endures within 'the trappings of modernity', disproving the adage that 'the clothes maketh the man'. This transformation can be attributed to the greater access to power granted to the tribes through centralization and state control, which is conducive to tribalism executing a shift 'from a reliance on kinsmen to a reliance on patrons'.[39] By retaining elements of the tribal system, such as the granting of favours and utilization of influence (*wasta*), the tribal communities eased themselves into the state apparatus and established economic and political networks. In contrast, just as a vast number of Bedouin have adjusted to excel in the pecuniary-driven corporate realm, the commercial Bedouin endures. Twenty years since Layne's observation, the tribal gimmick is employed with gusto in the vast hotels of the capital, with Jordanians nestling amidst isolated islands of cushions, *nargeileh*, coffee pots and shoe-shining implements that infuse visiting tourists with a sense of the 'real Jordan'.

The dichotomy between sedentarized and pastoral Bedouin resonates linguistically in the terms *hadarī*, 'pertaining to settlement'; *'ashā'rī*, denoting tribal; and *badawī*, 'pertaining to pastoral nomadism'.[40] *Hadarī* and *'ashā'rī* are often adopted as antonyms by Western-educated scholars and non-tribal Jordanians, while the application of the term *badawī* to nomadism in Jordan has been contested by Young, who argues that a number of the families who identify themselves as *badu* and keep livestock are not nomadic, but reside in 'lavish villas'.[41] Given the status of the Bedouin in Jordanian society, the primary definitions of 'tribe' and 'tribalism' – *hadarī* and *'ashā'rī* – become less awkward in their union. With the majority of rural people in the Kingdom being both *hadarī* (settled) and *'ashā'rī* (tribal), only 3 per cent remain nomadic, a trifle compared to the 97 per cent residing in the urban environment.[42] If the concepts of *hadarī* and *'ashā'rī* were initially disparate, they have since merged to reveal little division. This is particularly tangible in Amman, where many workers from the tribal villages relocate to the capital in search of employment. For one respondent, originally from Salt, the one-hour trip home is eagerly anticipated after almost a week of long shifts. Working from eight until six during the day in an administrative post at the government, swiftly followed by a night shift at a downtown hotel from seven until seven the following morning, Omar remains in Salt from Thursday evening until Sunday morning. Holding no permanent residence in Amman, despite residing in the city for more than ten years, he demonstrates Lewis' hypotheses regarding geographical and consanguineous affinities, as the individual opts to return to his geo-familial locale. The tribal population of Jordan, though they may be predominantly based in the towns and cities, take pride in their patrilineal descent and can recite lengthy genealogies as a means to accentuate their Jordanian identity and attachment to the country.

Regarded as the foundation of the Jordanian state, the tribes are firmly linked to Jordan's past. The socio-political role of the Bedouin tribes during the inception of Transjordan in 1921 has remained a poignant moment in Jordanian history, a point sustained by the tribal background of the monarchy. Following the British delineation of the country from its regional neighbours, state-building commenced with the recognition of Transjordan as an autonomous entity in 1923. With its foundation steadfastly entrenched in the tribal structures, the loyalty of the population to the government was guaranteed and tribe-based identities were unified (for the external observer at least) through the moniker 'Transjordanian', thereby establishing national interests as a priority over regional markers.[43] By constituting the foundation of the regime, both in terms of support and manpower in the military and state bureaucracy, the tribes assumed an influential role within the Jordanian authority, protecting its members through access to the informal channels of redress and respite when required.[44] In this respect, the Jordanian community mirrors that of the Palestinian-Jordanian, albeit the Palestinian-Jordanian community exercises its kinship through the private sector, since this is the sector in which the community is dominant.

Tribalism's presence in the Jordanian public sector has drawn strong criticism from Palestinian and Jordanian quarters alike, in the belief that traditional customs hold little applicability to contemporary social and political conduct. It also has been contended that the

endurance of activities such as honour killings amidst the sedentarized
tribal community are detrimental to social progress. Despite vocalization against the ubiquity of tribalism, the monarchy has remained
adherent to the status quo. The predicament climaxed in 1985 when
King Hussein wrote to Prime Minister Ahmad 'Ubaydat; the corre-
spondence was subsequently published in all the daily newspapers.[45]
Chastising dissenters who had denigrated tribal tradition, Hussein
proudly expounded his own tribal heritage:

> I have noticed that some articles have been directed against the
> tribal life, its norms and traditions. I would like to repeat to
> you what I told a meeting of tribal heads recently, that 'I am
> al-Hussein from Hashem and Quraish, the noblest Arab tribe of
> Mecca, which was honoured by God and into which was born
> the Prophet Mohammad'. Therefore, whatever harms our tribes
> in Jordan is considered harmful to us [...] and will continue so
> forever.[46]

The outburst would be neither the last expression of the ruling family's tribal identity, nor an end to the debate. The competing efforts to
promote 'tribalization' and 'detribalization' throughout the 1970s and
1980s gave way to a schism between the traditionalists calling for an
endurance of the status quo and the reformists, both of whom were
dominated by sedentarized Jordanians.

By turns defined as a unifying force for good, or a dire impediment to progress, tribal custom in contemporary Jordan's legal and
political system has divided Jordanian society. Surviving as the tribal
mode of conflict resolution, 'tribal law' (al-qānūn al-'ashā'rī) has provided an unwritten code of procedures accentuating intermediaries
and intermediation: wasta, delegations (jahas), truce ('atwa) and final
reconciliation and peace-making (sulha).[47] At best tribalism denotes
a 'persistent social and political force bringing together people for
many different purposes, and doing so in the context of many different, competing or alternative principles of alignment.'[48] Accordingly,
it has been regarded less as an 'ethnic chauvinism, whereby one tribal
group uses its economic, social or political position without regard

for other groups in the country'[49] and rather a unifying element in contemporary Jordanian society.

An aspect of tribal custom that continues to gather national and international condemnation is honour crimes. Despite the endeavours of human rights organizations and Queen Rania to abolish the practice of honour killing, the government and judiciary permits the practice through the leniency of the applied sentences.[50] Adherence to traditions in Jordanian society is equally evident in the nationalist discourse. Akin to its neighbours, Jordan was forged from fragments of the decaying Ottoman Empire and lacked a unique identity. The active discrimination in the employment sector exercised by the Jordanian community can be viewed less as prejudice and more a concerted effort to assert themselves through tradition. As a minority in their homeland, their status indubitably prompts the incentive to be heard, felt and respected.

The Lesser-Known Invader

The Palestinians were given passports by Abdullah I, not by the Jordanians. All of them are strangers and invaders to our country.[51]

The role of King Abdullah I in the creation of the Jordanian state remains a point of contention in the Jordanian nationalist interpretation of history. The contrast between the nationalist narrative and that which is chronicled through contemporary academic publications is stark. Since the former is promulgated by the Jordanian National Movement (JNM)[52] and a number of historians seemingly rewriting history in a bid to breathe life into the ethnic Jordanian identity, the course of domestic Palestinian-Jordanian relations is not without its obstacles. The representation of historical events from a heavily Jordanian perspective commences early and from eighth grade and above children are instructed on the benignly dominant role of Jordan in the Palestine-Israel conflict, while a subtle distinction between Jordanians and Palestinian-Jordanians intimates the notion of 'other' through nuances within the historical texts. Having glossed over the Ottoman period, the narrative slows to exude detail in the extreme as Abdullah enters and the Great Arab Revolt (1936–1939) is accorded 'repeated and increasingly detailed descriptions of [its] goals and achievements'.[53] From 1948 onwards, Jordan assumes a central role in the events unfolding in Palestine-Israel, as a host and heroine: 'when Jordan entered the Palestine war in 1948, the Jordanian army was able to save many Palestinian villages and towns from Zionist occupation, preeminent among them, Jerusalem.'[54] The tendency to avoid key points (Abdullah's negotiations with the Zionists; that 250,000 Palestinians displaced from the West Bank into the East Bank during the 1967 War were Jordanian citizens)[55] and deemphasize others (Jordan's annexation of the West Bank in 1950) are understood by Brand as a promotion of the 'Palestinian-Jordanian unity' – a trend that ostensibly endures through the current concept of 'Jordan First'.

Despite endeavours to intensify the Jordanian fortitude and presence in the shaping of the post-1948 region and her role in the Palestinian-Israeli discourse, resistance to the narrative remains – from within. Working from documents filed during the British Mandate and publications of the period, the JNM argues that Amir Abdullah I's expedition into Jordan was an imperialistic sojourn: that the legacy of which has survived to the present is due to Western and Israeli support. As al-Abbadi notes,

> Abdullah declared, 'first, I am coming on an invasion visit to Jordan' and second, 'Jordan is for Arabs, not for Jordanians'. Most of the land was confiscated from the hands of the Jordanians within the first 25 years. He then called people from Syria, Hijaz and Palestine; they came and he gave them passports, nationality and identity. Their allegiance and love was to him, not to Jordan or the Jordanians.[56]

From the outset, both the monarchy and the Palestinian community, regardless of the longevity of their residence in the Kingdom, are perceived as de facto squatters, in turn setting the agenda for a schism between the two communities. The interpretation of Jordanian history in recent years promotes this aspect to an outnumbered Jordanian populace, eager to embrace a version of history that would clarify the status quo. Equally, the distribution of the findings has facilitated a pan-generational breakdown in relations, as witnessed during my visit to the University of Yarmouk. When a group of students queried the subject of my research, their response to 'Palestinians in Jordan' came not without bitterness: 'Palestinians? Why not study Jordanians?' Naturally, once queried regarding their origins they announced with pride, 'Jordanian! *Only* Jordanian!' and 'Jordan is for the Jordanians – not the Palestinians!' While such patriotism in the present generation is not remarkable, it was more alarming to observe the prevalence and nature of it, bordering as it was on hostility. The following year the sentiment had grown and the JNM now appeals to a receptive audience. As the wave of revolutionary unrest unfurled across the region, Jordan was not exempt; neither was the JNM above utilizing the strife as a means to undermine the regime. Following the violent clashes on 25 March 2011 in which 81 protesters were arrested, the JNM website featured large-scale images of Jordanians with gauze-bound foreheads, wounded and prone in tents under the headline, 'Pictures from the Crime Scene [...] Committed by King Abdullah II and his Thuggish Regime: Friday, March 25, 2011.'[57] The protests were sparked by socio-economic issues, but the utilization of the images by the JNM was pure propaganda: the images invoke a brutality that undermines Abdullah's calls for national unity and in this manner the JNM foments further societal division along lines of Palestinians and Jordanians, pro-Hashemites and anti-monarchists, rich and poor and 'us' against 'them'.

The ethos of the JNM[58] demonstrates scant understanding of the Palestinian-Jordanian community. The reality that just as the JNM seeks to shake off the Hashemite yoke, so too do the Palestinians strive for a liberated Palestine. Al-Abbadi's conjecture that 'We [the Jordanians] suffered 3,000 years of invasion from the Greeks to the Hashemites; we like liberation, we like to be free'[59] bears a close resemblance to the sentiments of their Palestinian counterparts. There is little doubt that liberation is desired, but the question remains whether the future Jordanian state – to be established by 2016, according to al-Abbadi – will have its roots in a homogenous past, or a heteroge-neous future. The reality is that population displacement and move-ment is a global phenomenon and it is essential that the nationalist movement acknowledge this factor. While the JNM contends that the non-Jordanian community[60] weakens state resources, their eco-nomic contribution cannot be ignored. Should the future comprise a radicalized 'Jordan First' agenda in which non-Jordanian communities become isolated, it would be to the detriment of the Jordanian state and liberation would fade from a positive venture towards a homog-enous and repressive pseudo-state. History created a Kingdom that has existed because, not in spite, of its rich socio-cultural milieu. And though it was crafted by imperialists for the few with political influ-ence to realize their nationalist aspirations, to create a state for Jordo-Jordanians would not be progress: rather, it would be an alternative source of intervention seeking to satisfy the same politico-nationalist desires.

Nationalism as a Defence Mechanism

We reject the premise that a Palestinian-Jordanian is Jordanian. We come from the premise that a Palestinian-Jordanian is Palestinian.[61]

The origins of Jordanian nationalism can be traced to five events: the Battle of Karameh (1968), Black September (1970–1971), the introduc-tion of the tenet 'Jordan is Palestine' (*al-watan al-badil*) (1981)[62] and the Intifadas of 1988 and 2000. The events of 1948 and 1967 altered the course of Jordan as it absorbed influxes of refugees that trans-formed the Kingdom both socially and economically, positively and negatively. Yet they were not conducive to a Jordanian nationalism. Though the establishment of Israel and the diaspora that followed pro-vided the foundations, Jordan's blend of nationalisms arose from the Transjordanian and tribal-based identities that bear the marks of the aforementioned crises and became manifest in the rhetoric of national-ism in the Kingdom.

The Palestinian diaspora infused ideology into the politics of the state, prompting an imbalance in the Jordanian political sphere as well as providing a catalyst for Transjordanian nationalism. The 'aggrieved and highly vocal Palestinians added weight and a sense of urgency to the rudimentary Transjordanian opposition'[63] and rendered the need for institutions more pressing. For certain Palestinian-Jordanians, their presence is a blessing, for: 'before the Palestinians arrived, Jordan was nothing. Before we [the Palestinians] came, there were only tribes, milk, *mansaf* and grazing. There were no structures.'[64] Recurrent themes in the Jordanian nationalist discourse bear similarities to the calls of indigenous populations the world over: namely the scarcity of jobs, issues of loyalty and the implications of the minority communities (or in the context of Jordan, the majority) on the regional and international image of the host country.

The dichotomy between Palestinians and East Bank Jordanians has been acknowledged as a 'nation-threatening cleavage'[65] in Jordanian society. Although many are considered *de jure* Jordanian citizens, the desire for a homeland of their own kept the Palestinian refugees from forging a sense of Jordanian national identity, rendering Jordan forever the host state and never the homeland.[66] At worst, Jordan has been perceived as an impediment to the achievement of an independent Palestine, as oppositional forces in the region surmise that the host could provide an ideal alternative. The conditions endured by Palestinians in the refugee camps of Jordan are not only deplorable, but conducive to a widening of the schism between Palestinians and Jordanians. The justification offered by the Jordanian authorities forms the crux of Palestinian resentment towards Jordan: should the state prove a comfortable alternative, it would be regarded as an alternative homeland for the Palestinians. Ergo, by compelling Palestinian refugees to dwell in lamentable conditions, the Jordanian government (so it reasons) maintains the sense of Palestine, sustains the desire of the Palestinians to return to their homeland, and keeps world attention focused on the position of Jordan as a 'temporary' homeland. Granted that refugees have dwelled in the camps for three generations, or more, since 1948, this reasoning is emblematic of the Jordanian desire to retain 'Jordan for the Jordanians'.

Just as the events of Black September can be regarded as a turning point in Jordanian-Palestinian domestic relations, so too, can the war of 1967. The loss of the West Bank added impetus to the Jordanian nationalist movement, which flourished throughout the 1970s. The defeat and loss of territory set in motion a process that prompted Jordanians to reconsider the state of their national identity, a redefinition of previously accepted ideologies and the obliteration of the revered ideal of Arab unity.[67] The loss of the West Bank rankled not only in territorial terms, for the Kingdom's nascent identity and nationalism had been infused with military pride. Following King Hussein's 1957 crackdown on political parties, a vacuum emerged that would be filled by a Hashemite-oriented form of Jordanian nationalism. Uniting Transjordanians and Palestinians with the king at the centre, as opposed to the previous polarization that had prevailed during the period 1955–1957, Hashemitism emphasized two pride-inducing elements by which to rally the population: first, Jordan's position as the custodian of the holy shrines in East Jerusalem, and second, its supporting role alongside Palestinian combatants in defence of said shrines against the Israeli military endeavours to capture them during the 1948 war.

A Jordan comprising both the East and West Bank represented a successful prototype of Arab unity during a time of longing for regional unanimity. That Jordan held the longest lines of confrontation with Israel[68] appealed to Transjordanians, given their strong links with the army. For the Palestinian-Jordanians, particularly those experiencing Israeli hostility in the West Bank, the concepts were less pride- than fear-inspiring. The defeat in 1967 not only realized their concerns, but confirmed their conviction that Jordan alone could not defend the West Bank.[69] While certain Palestinian-Jordanians followed Hashemite rhetoric and developed a bond to the Kingdom in its hour of loss, a simultaneous dichotomy between the Palestinian-Jordanian and Jordanian identity emerged as the foundations of future Jordanian and Transjordanian nationalism held little allure for the Palestinian community in their hour of disappointment and defeat.

The loss prompted a lack of confidence in the Jordanian state's ability to protect the Palestinians and strengthened independent

Palestinian organizations, bestowing a confidence that would lead to the events of September 1970. As the Palestinian identity emerged stronger and more determined, so too did it stimulate the growth of a faltering yet cohesive Jordanian identity that would mature into a multifaceted monolith:

> based on east-Jordanian tribal and Islamic values, loyalty to the royal family and to the king's army, and more pertinently, cleansed of Palestinian, pan-Arab and progressive ideologies. This rather bitter redefinition of political community – particularist, isolationist, anachronistic – was replete with ironies, coming as it did from the family that launched the Arab revolt.[70]

The fortified Jordanian identity mirrored the flurry of nationalist activities in the neighbouring states, the most notable being the establishment of a government-sponsored one-party system, the Jordanian National Union (JNU) (*al-ittihad al-watani al-urdunni*) in September 1971. Initially intended to provide a manageable channel for the political aspirations of a wide spectrum of the population, it proved ineffective and was dissolved five years later.[71] Despite the failure of the JNU to provide a unified Transjordanian movement, the 1974 Arab Summit in Rabat supplied an expedient catalyst for Jordanian nationalism with the transfer of Palestinian representation to the PLO. A notable repercussion of the Summit manifested as assertions of unity between Palestinians and Jordanians were cast aside and a moral rationale for a clear separation between Jordanian and Palestinian identities was fostered. The Rabat decision enabled 'Those Palestinians who had PLO leanings [to] now openly and legitimately declare them. For Hussein, Rabat legitimised the exclusion [...] of the more radical amongst his Palestinian population.'[72] In doing so, the way was now clear for the burgeoning Jordanization process to forge ahead, to reinforce the Jordanian identity and nourish its nationalism.

It is essential to distinguish between Jordanian and Transjordanian nationalism: the evolution of nationalist sentiments in Jordan is unique in its diversity. While Jordanian nationalists draw support from advocates of the pan-Jordanian identity and Palestinian-Jordanian integration, in addition to being resolute Arabists and Islamists, theirs is a voice silenced by that of the favoured discourse of the government, Transjordanian nationalism. Preferred in times of diplomatic progress, such as the 1994 Israel-Jordan Peace Treaty, Transjordanian nationalism leapt to the fore of state politics. The titles 'Jordanian' and 'Transjordanian' are frequently substituted for each other, raising the question of whether the title is merely a semantic attribute subject to historical reference. It is not: 'Transjordanian' denotes the period prior to 1970 and the process of Jordanization, while 'Jordanian' indicates contemporary Jordan. Given its tribal foundations, it is not implausible to suggest that the titles signify a variance according to ideology, with proponents of Transjordanian nationalism favouring a traditional, tribal-influenced method of governance and legislature amidst their endeavours to promote the interests of the Jordo-Jordanian population. Alternatively, Jordanian nationalism can be viewed as a progressive force that encompasses all Jordanian citizens, regardless of origins, through its promotion of the interests of the population, all the while seeking to modernize the more traditional aspects of the state system.

Since 1970, Transjordanian nationalism has produced three groups: the pragmatics, the tribe-based and the radicals.[73] The first group comprises individuals of the pragmatic orientation and emerged within the boundaries of the state with leaders and advocates originating from within the Transjordanian ruling elite. A number of political parties are affiliated to this group, the foremost of which, Al-Ahd, can be perceived as the unofficial mouthpiece of the state in its tireless promotion of state policies. On the issue of the Palestinian-Jordanian community in Jordan its leader, Abdul-Hadi al-Majali, a Member of Parliament and former minister, was forthright in his expression of their fate. Contrary to embracing his 'Palestinian brothers,' he argues that,

> For the West Bankers, wherever they are in the diaspora, they should practice their political rights on Palestinian territory [...] He who chooses to remain Jordanian, though it is preferable that he practices his political rights in his country, Palestine. [...] He has to apply to become Jordanian. In this way, the [Jordanian] identity and loyalty will be reaffirmed.[74]

Writing in 1999, Abu Odeh was critical of the stance of the party, con-
cluding that 'This group is not ideologically flexible. I think it is accurate to call it the pragmatic school [...] after all, it is associated with the
Transjordanian ruling élite and is state sponsored.'[75] In the years that
have passed since his study of the Palestinian-Jordanian relationship in
Jordan, Al-Ahd has not changed.

The tribe-based group grew within the boundaries of the tribal
system in the same manner as the army, since both the tribes and the
army occupy central roles in the Transjordanian identity. Although no
political party represents this school, it is represented by individuals in
the local press and others who are members of certain political parties.
The most active promulgator is Dr. Ahmad Owaid al-Abbadi, a tribal
historian and former police officer, who in November 1997 was elected
for a second time as a Member of Parliament. Amongst the first of the
Transjordanian groups to become apprehensive of the growing challenge posed to the Kingdom in the late 1960s by the Palestinians and
by the *fedayeen*, the group comprised the clans (*al-asha'ir*) motivated
by the prospect of a potential Palestinian ruler. The notion exuded a
nightmarish element for the group through the threat it posed to the
tribal character of Jordan. The events of Black September brought a
raw realization of the threat posed to their Kingdom to the Jordanian
people and though the act was perpetrated by a single group, the consequences of their actions rippled across society, prompting suspicion
of the wider Palestinian-Jordanian population. In the aftermath of
the incident, a tribal discourse ensued in response to the notion that
all citizens, Transjordanians and Palestinian-Jordanians alike, might
be equal and anonymous members of a Jordanian community.[76] It is
worth noting at this point that Abu Odeh utilizes the change in titles,
'Transjordanian' to 'Jordanian', to demonstrate the shift from tribal-
based concerns to an all-inclusive community that incorporates both
Transjordanians and Palestinian-Jordanians.

For the clan-based group, such a situation did not appeal. Perceiving
it as an erosion of the tribal power structure the group recuperated
from their loss of political standing through state assistance, whose
interests in strengthening its power base promoted an interest in tribal
affairs, and through Jordanian mass education and communications.[77]

The promotion of Jordanian history and culture through works such as *Al-Tarikh al-Hadari li-Sharq al-Urdun fi al-Asr al-Mamluki* (The Civilization History of Transjordan in the Mamluke Era [Fourteenth and Fifteenth Centuries]), by Youssef D. Ghawanmeh, a professor of Mamluk history at Yarmouk University[78] is an example of such endeavours: his list of notables who excelled in jurisprudence and religious knowledge in the cities where Islamic civilization thrived[79] indicates a yearning to depict Jordan as an ancient culture that has long contributed to regional development. It seemingly does not matter that the 'Transjordanian' state had been tangibly realized during the twentieth century at the whim of colonial powers.

Emerging from the Communist and Ba'ath parties, and the pan-Arab movement, the radical group comprised thwarted leftists who had departed from their parties in despair. Though not formally organized as a political body, since 1982 proponents of the group have assumed the title 'Jordanian National Youth Federation' and are considered the nucleus of the modern Jordanian National Movement, expressing their views through their newspaper, *al-Mithaq*. Led by Nahed Hattar, editor-in-chief of *al-Mithaq*, their ideology, oxymoronic though it may seem, blends radical leftist principles with a right-wing orientation. Far from advocating an all-encompassing policy applied equally to the Jordanian and Palestinian communities, Hattar's sentiments reflect anxiety about the status quo: 'The Jordanians are worried because of the increasing of the Palestinian political influence in Jordan; everyday they are more influential than before and in the end, this will lead us to a Palestinian state here in Jordan.'[80] On the issue of loyalty he believes the Palestinian-Jordanian community holds little patriotism for the host state, 'they are loyal to the Palestinian problem and this issue is not solved. Until now they did not obtain enough political privileges here in Jordan and that's why they are not worried. They are loyal to their cause – not to the state where they are living now.'[81] Thus, the fear that infused the Transjordanian nationalist movement during the late 1960s and fuelled its meteoric rise to the political nationalism of the state endures to the present day.

The same fear has spilled from the political arena and into direct expressions of hostility towards the Palestinian-Jordanian community.

Since 1971, Transjordanian aggression has been linked with the land –
that is, the East Bank from which it derives its name. The Palestinians
on the East Bank have become foreign residents who face an uncertain
future and exist merely under the auspices of the Transjordanians.[82]
The *muhajirin-ansar* (emigrant-supporters) schism reinforces the notion
that Transjordanians are the hosts and that the Palestinian-Jordanians
are the guests, indicating that 'the Palestinian guest is [...] a stranger
whose long visit has become irritating'.[83] Maintenance of the 13
Palestinian refugee camps reminds the population of the unique position of the Palestinians in Jordan – temporary, yet with an uncertain
end. The enduring role of 'host' has placed the Transjordanian movement in a position of power; despite their minority status they succeed
in perpetuating the cycle of discrimination in order to maintain that
power and in turn the security of their state and national identity
is ensured. The muted Palestinian-Jordanian response to the activities of the Transjordanian movement, and the failure of parliament
and the political parties to protest on their behalf, only encourages
Transjordanian nationalists to sustain their aggressive approach.

Palestine and the Concept of *al-Watan al-Badil*

> The lands of Palestine and Jordan cannot be defined in terms of
> precise geographical borders. But as an idea and inspiration they
> will survive as long as humanity.[84]

The greatest threat to the Jordanian identity in recent years is the
concept of Jordan as Palestine (*al-watan al-badil*). Employed as a tool
for strategic intents, political ends and as a unifying force within the
country, the steady movement of population from Palestine to Jordan
has stirred relations between the two communities. Introduced as a
constructive perception by King Hussein, the close ties between West
Bank towns such as Nablus and Hebron, and East Bank towns, such
as Salt and Karak, during the 1950s and 1960s prompted the monarch to quip that 'Jordan is Palestine and Palestine is Jordan'.[85] Carved
out of an area dominated by states such as Syria, Iraq and Egypt,

Jordan's consolidation did not come easily. As the Arab world adopted the Palestinian cause the pressure on Jordan to follow suit increased, despite its developing economy and expanding population following *al-Nakba*. Combined with the demands of the Zionist movement, the Jordanian regime confronted further instability in 1977 when the revisionist Likud party seized power in Israel with the slogan 'Jordan is Palestine'.[86] Although the Kingdom dreaded Israel more than the Palestinians, the prospect of a united effort between the two reinvigorated Jordanian nationalism in its assertion of national identity.

In spite of the Jordanian disengagement from the West Bank in 1988, the political links between the East and West Banks lingered as a reminder that geo-political severance does not eradicate the fact that Jordan and Palestine were one until the collapse of the British Mandate and the independence of Jordan in 1946. Predating Jordan's annexation of the West Bank following the 1948 Arab-Israeli War, it has historically been easier to travel from East to West across the Jordan River than from the southern to the northern areas of the East Bank.[87] Yet the axiom was to become emboldened when Ariel Sharon let fall the phrase 'Jordan is Palestine' in 1981, catalysing sentiments of suspicion, anxiety and bitterness among Jordanians. It can be contended that Sharon's utterance alone did not sow the seeds of animosity – rather it proved an accelerant to the rancour held since Black September.

Sharon's argument that the Palestinians did not need an independent state since they already had one, across the border to the east, denied Jordanian legitimacy to the restoration of authority in the West Bank and implied the eventual expulsion of an additional one million Palestinians into Jordan from the West Bank.[88] But Sharon was not alone in his view, as Moshe Dayan and Yigal Allon also rejected the Palestinians' connection to Palestine, intimating that their place was in Jordan.[89] As the Israeli right-wing contended that 'Jordan is Palestine' and the call for a transfer of Arabs out of Israel and the Occupied Territories into Jordan intensified, King Hussein announced the disengagement of Jordan from the West Bank in 1989. For the Jordanian regime, one move would simultaneously reduce the threat from both Israel and the Palestinians. Disengagement enabled the

PLO to declare a Palestinian state in November 1988[90] and by nurturing the possibility of a separate Palestinian entity, Jordan could focus on its own East Bank Jordanian national identity.[91] The assertions of an Israeli-facilitated takeover of the Kingdom on behalf of the Palestinians fuelled Jordanian nationalism and in 2004 the government launched the 'Jordan First' campaign.

Jordan and Palestine had been connected through administrative, economic and social affairs initiated by the British Mandate, as 'Transjordan was Palestine's twin. The culture of the two countries was virtually identical, and the movement of people from one side of the Jordan stream to the other was continuous and normally unrestricted.'[92] Historically, Transjordanian sentiments for the Arab cause in Palestine were strong and when trouble erupted in Palestine, the repercussions were immediately felt in Transjordan. With each outbreak of hostility, the involvement of Abdullah I in Palestine's affairs increased, uniting the two countries.[93] These sentiments persist in contemporary society. When asked where he came from, Ahmed, a taxi driver born in Jordan to a Palestinian family, initially responded 'Jordan'. When asked whether he was originally from Jordan or Palestine, his response altered marginally and he laughed 'They are twins! Jordan and Palestine are one!' This was reiterated by Mustafa, a salesman from Irbid. When asked where he was from, he primarily responded '*Urdun*', yet when presented with the distinguishing question of 'Jordan or Palestine?' he merely raised one finger and said in English, 'One. They are one.'

The notion that 'Jordan is Palestine' can be interpreted in a plethora of ways, politically, culturally and historically. The belief that the Palestinian-Jordanians constitute the dominant community in the Kingdom – eclipsing even the indigenous Jordanian population – is accepted both within and outside the Kingdom. Yet the assertion continues to rouse heated contention. For proponents of Jordanian nationalism, the figures supporting the Palestinian majority are regarded as a ploy by the government to control the JNM. In contrast, certain Palestinian-Jordanian observers perceive it as a means to secure extra state financial assistance in the name of the Palestinian refugees inhabiting Jordan's 13 camps. As al-Abbadi argues, 'The Palestinians in Jordan are not more than 40 per cent and the others are Transjordanians. They say we are nothing, so this means we are not men, we have no children, we are impotent and we are unable even to make our women pregnant. This is shameful.'[94] This view is not unique. During his tenure as Prime Minister of Jordan, Abdulsalam al-Majali commented in a Jordanian daily that assertions of a Palestinian-Jordanian majority in the country are 'absolutely incorrect [...] It lacks evidence, figures, and statistics [...] When the first Palestinian emigration occurred (1948), we and the Arabs inflated the number of refugees [...] for purely political and propaganda purposes. [...] Since then an accurate census for those refugees has not been conducted.'[95] In addition to political and propaganda purposes, there are economic incentives. There is little doubt that the visible Palestinian refugee presence in Jordan has proven a magnet for financial aid from world organizations and NGOs, which has provided a much-needed boost to a frequently flailing economy.

Yet the notion that 'Jordan is Palestine' transcends present day tensions, holding its roots in the Old Testament. According to al-Abbadi,

Sharon said that from the Talmud, which states that Jordan is part of Palestine. For this you have to go back to the time of the Old Testament and to Exodus. The Torah conception – is that Jordan is Eastern Palestine. But Jordan, never ever in its whole history, was a Palestinian land and Palestine never ever was a Jordanian land.[96]

In contrast to the historico-religious argument, critics perceive the utilization of the concept as a solution to the present difficulties in Palestine as no more than a ruse that will serve the interests of the Israeli state at the expense of Jordanian territorial integrity:

When he [Sharon] says it from his own intelligence and ideology; we [Jordanians] feel it is a real threat for two reasons: first, that Jordan will be finished as a name and identity; and second, the new status – as an alternative to our state – means that we will be finished as a people, which is a real threat.[97]

Al-Abbadi's disparagement of the religious basis for Sharon's assertion must be regarded within the context of the concerns of the JNM,
which predominantly reside with the legitimacy of the tribes of Jordan
to retain their position as the enduring inhabitants of Jordan's terrain.
To ensure this does not occur, Jordanian society practises a process
of isolation vis-à-vis the Palestinian-Jordanian presence in Jordanian
national institutions, such as the army, government and intelligence
services. As Rantawi elaborates:

> There is an approach in the government that does not make
> it easy to integrate and fulfil the citizenship concept, before
> solving the Palestinian problem. The main approach adopted
> by the government in the last few years was that the Palestine
> issue should be kept within certain limits. And there are many
> excuses to do that. Sometimes, we don't want to give the
> impression that Jordan is Palestine, as this will facilitate the
> Israeli solution of the Palestinian problem outside of Palestine,
> in Jordan.[98]

Significantly, Rantawi reiterates that 'Jordan is Jordan. Palestine is
Palestine. If there is a problem it should be solved in Palestine, not
Jordan.'[99] Far from welcoming the prospect of a 'new Palestine' in
Jordan, the Palestinian-Jordanians want a solution, not a replacement.
This reality must be acknowledged and embraced by the Jordanians if
a cohesive society is to flourish in the Kingdom.

In the assertion that 'Jordan is Palestine', Sharon found Jordan's
Achilles' heel. Had the Kingdom been as cohesive as portrayed in its
international image, the Palestinian influx and ensuing aspersions
would not have impacted upon it. From its inception, Jordanian nationalism identified a significant adversary in the Palestinian presence in
Jordan and as a consequence the 'Jordan is Palestine' maxim presented
practical quandaries that are addressed by the nationalist movement.
Underlying this endeavour is the absence of a Jordanian 'master narrative that could serve as a glue for national cohesiveness.'[100] The concerted efforts of the JNM to chronicle Jordan's history are another
endeavour to save the 'occupied' homeland. Yet it is not to the past

that Jordanians should look to save their country, but to the future, as Rantawi concludes:

> We grow up with the theory that Israel believes the Palestinian issue should be solved in Jordan: Jordan is Palestine. This theory makes people – both Jordanian and Palestinian – concerned, from different angles, but we reach the same conclusion: we have to defend this country. For the Palestinian because his country is occupied; for the Jordanian because he wants to defend his identity.[101]

The notion that 'Jordan is Palestine' will remain empty, providing the Jordanian and Palestinian-Jordanian communities integrate and acknowledge their fears for the future. For the Jordanians, the prospect of losing their land amidst a population tsunami endures as an impediment to integration and equality within the Kingdom. For the Palestinian-Jordanians, the loss of their homeland continues, but they are willing to collaborate in ensuring that history does not repeat itself in the host state.

Jordan First: Saving the Nation, Destroying Cohesion

In recent years, Jordanian nationalism has been asserted through the 'Jordan First' campaign. Viewed as a question of loyalty posed to the Palestinian-Jordanian community, and as an endeavour to promote the economy through a cohesive population, upon its initiation King Abdullah II could not have foreseen the mixed reaction it would inspire. From the outset, the Hashemite regime was weathering contempt from a number of assailants. The Bedouin subjects were incensed by the increasing naturalization of Palestinians and in November 2002 the Kingdom endured the worst violence in 32 years during the Ma'an riots that signified a decline in support for the monarchy by the East Bank Jordanians, customarily the support base for the Hashemites. The regime's response to the riots through the army was heavy-handed and in contrast to the events of Black September. While Hussein's use of tanks and artillery in 1970 inspired the Jordanian population to rally round, the use of force against East Bankers strained relations between the monarchy and the East Bank.

Tribal anger reached its zenith when Abdullah II opted to suspend the elections and dissolve parliament, which previously provided an outlet for tribal tensions and rule by decree. As a means to soothe pressures, the king commenced the 'Jordan First' campaign with a desire to end domestic Palestinian-Jordanian rivalries and forge a national identity based on the Kingdom, rather than kinship. Emphasizing investment in education, health and communications, it also pledged to fight poverty and unemployment, enhance public freedom, accountability and transparency, and alter the status of women in society, or at least how they are perceived.[102] In addition, the program included a proposal to decentralize Amman's political control and rezone the state into northern, central and southern governorates that would further enfranchise Jordan's Palestinian majority and strengthen their Jordanian identity.[103] That the Palestinians in Jordan have regarded the king and his wife – a Palestinian from the West Bank city of Tulkarm – positively, inspired hopes of a warm reception towards the reform. However, Jordanian reactions have been less than cordial, with the East Bank publication *Shihan* heralding the campaign as 'Gazans First'. The East Bank columnist, Fahed Fanek, quipped, 'If we're not doing enough to keep the West Bank Palestinian, we should at least keep Jordan Jordanian. The slogan "Jordanians First" would be better.'[104] Wholesome or wily, its success remains ambiguous. As the billboards remain raised around the country emblazoned with 'Jordan First' slogans, the mood of the country has soured, rather than sweetened.

Inextricably linked since its launch to the mercurial Palestinian-Jordanian relationship, certain observers believe that 'Jordan First' should be regarded as a response to a number of problems. Dr. Abdul Baset al-Athanmeh, an economist at the University of Yarmouk, points to the mass influx of Iraqis since the beginning of the second Gulf War as an incentive for the regime's move:

> There was a rapid growth from the Iraqi population, so the pressure on infrastructure, public institutions and services

increased and there was severe competition to gain benefits from these services. Thus, the 'Jordan First' campaign believed that Jordanian people should be first politically, socially and economically. 'Jordan First' does not imply that we want to get rid of our commitments to the Palestinian cause; 'Jordan First' is a political address for the insider, while the outside policy stays as it is.[105]

According to Dr. Ibrahim Hejoj, senior poverty advisor at UNRWA, the slogan has 'become a dual concept. It leads the country economically and is a reform process that transcends tribal lines. It espouses that everything must be for Jordan, and that regardless of background, resources must be pooled for the betterment of the nation for all citizens.'[106] However, '[despite being] still part of the nationalist campaign, it is not felt greatly. Society has become more open, but restrictions have increased. Crack downs on nationalist and Islamist movements have become a priority. King Abdullah wants to open society and invest in tourism and open up the economy to the world.'[107]

That 'Jordan First' has been hailed amidst the Palestinian-Jordanian community is questionable. In contrast to Hejoj's assertion that the Jordanian nationalist sentiment 'is not felt greatly', many feel the program is an escalation in the tensions between Jordanian nationalists and the Palestinian-Jordanian community. Dr. Labib Kamhawi, a former professor of political science at the University of Jordan, is cynical of the intentions of the slogan:

It is insensitive. I ask myself 'why Jordan first? Who said Jordan second?' Nobody ever said Jordan was second. But if 'Jordan First' means we must forget everything else, this isn't correct. If 'Jordan First' means we have to forget Palestine and forget any links with Palestine, this is wrong.[108]

Whether the move was directed at Palestinian-Jordanians alone, or whether it encompasses other migrant groups hosted by the state, such as Iraqis and Egyptians, the question prompted an unequivocal response: 'They have no rights in Jordan; they could be kicked out at anytime – they are just visitors. "Jordan First" is directed to

Jordanians. Maybe it was directed a little towards the Muslim movement, but again, the Muslim movement never questioned Jordan as
a political entity.'[109] Thus, 'Jordan First' has fared little better among
the Palestinian-Jordanians and failed to allay concerns that the campaign could fail to dismantle the existing discriminatory system.

Conclusion

The Jordanian identity is in the throes of a renaissance. Just as the
cultural revival draws the attention of non-Jordanians to a heritage
that has been overshadowed by the tragedy of Palestinian history, the
concerted effort to reclaim Jordan for the Jordanians exposes a challenge to the integration that Jordan has promoted. Initiatives such as
'Jordan First' commenced with an optimistic economic objective to
unite all communities and observe the flourishing outcome. Yet the
implementation saw discrimination brought in that culminated in a
cool reception from the Palestinian-Jordanian community.

Jordan's demographic factor complicates the Palestinian-Jordanian
dynamic. The Jordanian government flits between accentuating the
unity between Palestinian and Jordanians as equal citizens in one
nation-state, and privileging a local Transjordanian identity. During
periods of hostility, the Transjordanian identity was emphasized and
government debate and polices shifted in its favour. In recent years,
this stance has gained permanence as the state has relocated its por-
trayal of the national image to suit the circumstances. When necessary, Jordan becomes the 'large extended family', while during periods
of crisis the media produces images of Jordan as the small, beleaguered
tribe.[110] By focusing on the virtues of the *'asha'ir*, the regime has reinforced the salience of tribal affiliation to the East Bank identity.[111]

The implications of an ongoing process of discrimination, whether
it is 'positive' or not, bodes ill for future Palestinian-Jordanian relations. As the Palestinian-Jordanians sustain aspirations of Palestinian
statehood while demonstrating loyalty and patriotism to Jordan, the
Jordanian identity is evolving from a personal quality into a defensive strategy. Spurred on by 'Jordan is Palestine' and memories of
Black September, the Transjordanian nationalist is edging the country

towards the end of Jordan's position as a state untouched by conflict in the region. Ironically, the future tribulations were predicted by al-Abbadi:

> I don't believe it will exceed 2010 to have problems in Jordan; maybe just before that, maybe just after. We, the tribes, used to be very close supporters of the Hashemites; we are now against, *against* the Hashemites. [...] Jordan is coming towards a very bad collapse and multiple civil wars: Iraqi-Iraqi, Palestinian-Palestinian, and Jordanian-Jordanian. It is coming: today, tomorrow, but I don't believe it will exceed 2010.[112]

As 2011 witnessed further unrest in Jordan, al-Abbadi's prophecy – though out by one year – bears poignancy. The Transjordanian identity must broaden and accept the integration of non-Jordanians. When quizzed why the JNM ideology continues to fight the presence of non-Jordanians while pointing to Britain as an example of successful integration, al-Abbadi responded that the government should be for the Jordanians, just as the country was for the Jordanians. The notion of enhanced participation for the Palestinian-Jordanians in the public sector was unacceptable. As the number of supporters for al-Abbadi's movement continue to soar globally[113] via the Internet, the prospects for the Transjordanian identity being used for positive ends, such as emphasizing the country's culture and pre-state history, dwindle as the nationalist behemoth continues to emerge.

4

THE PALESTINIAN-
JORDANIAN MAJORITY

Similar to their Jordanian counterparts, the Palestinian-Jordanians
have forged their identity as a means of survival both within and
external to the homeland. While in the Occupied Territories and Gaza
the Palestinian identity endeavours to thwart the dominant Israeli
presence, so too can parallels be drawn with the Jordanian effort to
assert their own national identity over non-Jordanian communities.
As opposed to perceiving the influx as positive, Jordanians consider
themselves marginalized and in turn accentuate their identity to sustain foundations of ethnic and territorial legitimacy. Equally, in the
diaspora the Palestinian identity gains an added purpose as the 'homeland' is sustained through education, cultural traditions and community activities. In pursuing these lines, Palestinians ensure that the
national narrative continues and the land is remembered by subsequent generations residing in the diasporic communities. That both
identities share similar objectives – Palestinian-Jordanians to regain
their country; Jordanians to retain their state – demonstrates a common ground between the two communities that ironically hampers
cohesion all the same.

Since the Palestinian community flowed into Jordan in 1948
and settled into the host state, schisms have arisen both amidst the
existing Jordanian population and within the resident Palestinian
community. The diaspora community comprises two categories of

Palestinians: those of the inside, *Felistenio al-Dakhil*, and the refugees, *Felistenio al-Shatat* or *al-Kharij*.[1] Despite the perceived dichotomy, the two groups remain united in their commitment to the national narrative as a means to revive Palestine for the next generation through life stories, documentation and oral narratives. While the events of 1948 can be regarded as the foundation for the Palestinian national narrative, additional sites of Palestinian collective memories also serve as an incentive to maintain the struggle from afar. The 1967 Six-Day War, Black September, Land Day (*Yawm al-Ird*, an annual commemoration since 30 March 1976), the Sabra and Shatila massacre in Lebanon (September 1982), the Intifadas of 1987–1993 and 2000–2005 and the Gaza War (2008–2009) all emphasize a heritage steeped in conflict. Al-Nakba, however, remains the foundation of Palestinian collective memory, irrevocably altering the course of Palestinian society and representing the defining moment in the history of the Palestinian people.[2] In turn, manifestations of the contemporary Palestinian identity are traceable to al-Nakba and the enduring popularity of the national narrative ensures that the 'obsession with places, from general topography to details of the tiniest street, would [...] preoccupy them, with Palestine travelling around the shoulders of its children.'[3] The notion of Palestine as a weight to be borne by subsequent generations is perceptible in the visual culture through the works of artists such as Sliman Mansour (*Jamal al-Mohamel*, or *Camel of Hardships*, 1973) and the political cartoons of Naji Al-Ali, for whom the reality of 'being Palestinian' was as much a physical and emotional struggle as a legal and national one.

A Question of Identity

Conceived in exile, the Palestinian-Jordanian identity comprises both a collective and a singular identity shaped by an individual's socio-economic status and socio-cultural experiences. Within the community an individual seeks to redefine his or her identity in the context of the constructed group and its objectives. Thus, if the basis for the primary feature of the group disappears, perhaps having achieved the objective it was created for, the existence of the group is threatened, unless it constructs another cause to motivate its members.[4] In the case of the Palestinian-Jordanians the cause – the attainment of Palestine – endures, while new motivations reconsolidate group identity through significant events (Black September, the Intifadas and the Gaza strikes). Accordingly, the Iraq War that commenced on 20 March 2003 has reinforced the Palestinian identity as those residing in Iraq once more confront conflict, flee and lose their homes and professions for the hastily established camps on the al-Karama border between Jordan and Iraq, pertinently known as 'the No-Man's Land' Camp. In doing so, for many Palestinians history is repeating itself, creating another act in the national narrative.

The environment in which one resides bears a significant influence on self-perception, both in terms of in-group and extraneous relations, including the political authorities of the host state. Should an individual enter a social situation in which he or she is perceived as the stranger who does not belong, it is plausible that the individual would proceed to consider themselves within that context.[5] Ergo, if an individual is unwelcome within a state for extended periods of time, he or she adapts to the imposed role of 'unwanted person(s)' and considers themselves socially marginalized. For Palestinians and Palestinian-Jordanians, the political rhetoric that reiterates that Palestinians are not Jordanian, and in turn should seek full rights in Palestine, lends potency to the Palestinian identity as the sense of belonging is once more undermined. Likewise, ancestry provides a crucial means by which kinship is maintained and while political alliances can prove tenuous, and religion a source of persecution, kinsmen can be relied upon for loyalty and afford the ultimate refuge.[6] Disputes and schisms, though inevitable among kinsmen, are negotiated by the Palestinian community as they work towards a common national objective.

To ascribe an identity, one must 'belong' and in turn the two concepts are intertwined, both in the diaspora and/or the homeland. Governed by an emotional attachment to the land, belonging facilitates the construction of hybrid identities, unified by a hyphen and constructed in the third space.[7] Not restricted by an attachment to one land, second and third generation Palestinians nurture a sense of belonging in more than one host-state, reformulating the notion to become multifaceted through belonging to the country of one's childhood, one's parents and grandparents and the current nation of residence. Yet while hybridity juxtaposes ethnic identities, belonging is less precise as 'one's sense of belonging and communities of belonging are constructed in the swirl of often seemingly contradictory forces',[8] a melange that Migdal acknowledges as conducive to 'a world of multiple types of boundaries overlapping one another [producing] numerous mental maps [and] many different forms of belonging'.[9] Likewise, Croucher advances the complexities through a constructivist approach that attributes belonging to the collision of multiple identities comprising individuals holding an 'emotional and a material need to belong' that is sated by 'an array of socio-cultural, political, and administrative groups, including families, churches, schools, ethnic groups, nations, and states'.[10] Nevertheless, the flaw with such definitions resides in the perceived passivity of both the individuals sustaining the identity and the elements influencing the extent of belonging. Rather, one must acknowledge the impact of the emotional drive to belong – be it in the host state or a constructed homeland – and the obstacles presented by the array of external factors, as opposed to the assumption that the input of state mechanisms is wholly positive. In the context of the Palestinian-Jordanian community, the absence of affirmation by the state regarding their 'belonging' to the Jordanian nation spurs the endurance of hyphenism: forever in-between, the ties to the Palestinian homeland remain tenacious and reinforced for the duration that full rights (and in turn comprehensive integration) are elusive and anti-Palestinian sentiments pervade. Although diminished, this does not denote an absence of belonging; as Hall notes, belonging can exist to manifold degrees:

> Such people retain strong links with their places of origin and their traditions, but they are without the illusion of a return to the past. They are obliged to come to terms with the new cultures they inhabit, without simply assimilating to them and losing their identities completely. They bear upon them traces of the particular cultures, traditions, languages, and histories by

which they were shaped. The difference is that they are not and
will never be unified in the old sense because they are irrevocably the product of several interlocking histories and cultures,
belonging at one and the same time to several 'homes' (and to no
one particular 'home').[11]

The significance of Hall's observation resides in the 'obligation to come
to terms' with the new environment, be it cultural or – one might add
– national. In turn, Palestinians in Jordan actively belong both to the
nation in which they reside and the one of the past: the latter being
a natural inclination imparted through pan-generational narratives,
while the former emerges as a subconscious obligation, an acceptance
of the status quo.

The multiple sentiments of belonging can be expanded further
through Foucault's heterotopology: in addition to the scenarios outlined by the five heterotopias[12] the constructed homeland can be redefined. Commencing with Foucault's definition of utopia, parallels can
be drawn with the reconstruction of Palestine through oral narrative,
as 'Utopias are sites with no real place. They are sites that have a general relation of direct or inverted analogy with the real space of Society.
They present society itself in a perfected form.'[13] Thus, through not
only oral narrative, but also cultural expressions such as art, poetry
and literature, pre-1948 Palestine is recounted as a land of bountiful
orchards, fertile and peaceful; post-1948 the landscape changed: the
orchards, like the people, become vulnerable; the land is synonymous
with sadness, loss and struggle. The dual discourse – pre-1948 'fertile'
Palestine and post-1948 'bloodied' Palestine – can be captured within
the counter-sites, 'a kind of effectively enacted utopia in which the
real sites, all the other real sites that can be found within the culture,
are simultaneously represented, contested, and inverted'[14] – in this
instance, with the sustenance of Palestine in Jordan, and a simultaneous 'belonging' to both. In turn, the two sites (Palestine and Jordan)
counter each other, as 'their role is to create a space that is other,
another real space, as perfect, as meticulous, as well arranged as ours
is messy, ill constructed, and jumbled.'[15] The diaspora is reality: hec-
tic, problematic, the homeland sullied by occupation and struggle; the

alternate site is Palestine, remembered. Recounted through cultural artefacts and oral narratives, it creates an alternate space of belonging; one might go even further to distinguish between physical and emotional belonging, for in the case of the Palestinians, though they have a physical belonging to Jordan in the diaspora, their emotional belonging to Palestine is not diminished.

The concept of diaspora originated from an imperialistic hegemonizing notion of ethnicity towards 'a necessary heterogeneity and diversity; by a conception of 'identity' which lives with and through, not despite, difference [...] constantly producing and reproducing themselves anew, through transformations and difference.'[16] The transformation is particularly tangible in the hybrid identity nurtured by the Palestinian-Jordanian community. The hybrid identity discourse has evolved since its inception as an element of postcolonial theory. In the context of cultural development, the term 'hybrid' bears links with nineteenth-century colonialist exploits; yet over the course of the twentieth century it has become an analytical means to understand the emergence of new identities, societies and ideologies. A significant feature of hybridity in the identity context is its ability to morph according to individual characteristics. As a result, hybrid identities are among the hardest to comprehend since '[t]here is no single, or correct, concept of hybridity: it changes as it repeats, but it also repeats as it changes.'[17] As a concept, hybridity has assumed a key position in cultural criticism and postcolonial studies, as well as cultural appropriation and contestation in the context of borders and the ideal of the cosmopolitan. Alternatively – a notion prevalent in early identity discourse – hybridity can denote 'contamination' to promulgators of the essentialist notion of pure origins.[18] As shall be demonstrated shortly, for ultra-Jordanian nationalists this is particularly resonant, perceiving as they do the Palestinian community as a foreign presence.

With globalization, hybridity has emerged as a means to reflect the relationship between the 'local' and the 'global', while defining hybridity itself has become an altogether more complex task, as '[t]his interpretation of identity as hybrid is a direct challenge to earlier quasi-scientific claims that hybrids were sterile, physically weak, mentally inferior and morally confused'.[19] The assertion that a flow of

individuals non-indigenous to the region could prompt the proliferation of essentialist sentiments has been contended, since emphasizing
the 'hybridity of modern indigenous existence, charges of essentialism as indigenous peoples assert their identities are themselves essentializing, positing in contemporary existence a descent from racially/
ethnically pure past.'[20] In the context of the Palestinian-Jordanian
dynamic, the notion that indigenous communities – in this case, ethnic Jordanians – endorse essentialization, denotes a sanctioning of an
alternative essentialization through the assumption that indigenous
groups default to such mechanisms due to inherent racially and/or
ethnically pure backgrounds.

As a bridge between cultures and nationalities, the theory of
hybridity excels where others have failed to become a 'multi-purpose
globalizing identity kit'.[21] Following that, identity is not the combination, accumulation, fusion or synthesis of various elements; hybridity
is no longer restricted to an acknowledgement of difference. Its 'unity'
is not found in the sum of its parts, but the product of the process
of opening a 'third space' within which other elements convene and
adjust each other, creating the hybrid identity.[22] In doing so, a 'vague
and undetermined place created by the emotional residue of an unnat-
ural boundary [and] [p]eople who inhabit both realities [...] are forced
to live in the interface between the two.'[23] Equally, it becomes 'neither
the negative result of partial definition nor the triumphal synthesis of
opposites.'[24] The bridge and the third space are demonstrated – quite
literally – through the hyphen. Composed of the reconciliation between
the apparent and the obscure, be it linguistically or culturally, the
hyphen juxtaposes two identities, creating a new one that encompasses
both, yet negates neither. In the context of the Palestinian-Jordanian,
identity respondents – particularly of the younger generation – demonstrate the ability to absorb aspects from their Jordanian environs
and merge them with the Palestinian identity, adding the hyphen and
creating a bridge between the two, similar, cultures.

Yet there remains a point of contention within hybridity discourse:
synthesis. On the one hand, hybridity can be synonymous with synthesis, also known as syncretism, since it 'is not best understood in terms
of locations and roots but more as hybrid and creolized cultural routes

in global space. [...] They are the syncretic and hybridized products of interactions across space.'[25] The contention resides in its association with other traditional movements:

> Occasional mention will be made of the terms *syncretism* [...] to designate processes of *hybridization*. I prefer this last term because it includes diverse intercultural mixtures [...] and it permits the inclusion of the modern forms of hybridization better than does 'syncretism,' a term that almost always refers to religious fusions or traditional symbolic movements.[26]

The debate that hybridization is the mixing of that which is already a hybrid is dubious, since it removes the fusion – or hyphen – that makes it possible to discern between two cultural backgrounds that give rise to hybrid identities. If one subscribes to this theory, it would be impossible to perceive the Palestinian-Jordanian identity as a hybrid, since both the Palestinian and Jordanian identities are hybrids, thereby reducing the Palestinian-Jordanian entity to a banality. To do so would be troublesome on two levels: primarily, the virtue of hybrid identities resides in the fusion across cultures and borders to forge new identities that capture the best of both cultures – that is, Palestinian and Jordanian. The Palestinian identity can be regarded as a hybrid due to its history as a port down the centuries; equally, the Jordanian identity can be viewed as a hybrid due to the vast number of migrants from Syria, Arabia and the Hijaz that settled in the territory among the Bedouin tribes. That the majority of Jordanian respondents do not demonstrate affinity with these prior cultures or countries indicates that an identity can be distilled into two components, reinforcing the hyphen identity or, third space.

Yet a flaw in hybridity remains in its impermanence and complexity, characterized by the hybrid identity's ability to be 'not only double-voiced and double-accented [...] but also double-languaged; for in it there are not only [...] two individual consciousnesses, two voices, two accents, as there are [...] socio-linguistic, consciousnesses, two epochs [...] that come together and consciously fight it out.'[27] In the context of diasporic hybrid identities, matters become further

convoluted. The appearance of multiculturalism and intellectual popularity that furnishes hybridity with its allure dissipates to reveal the
reality of the migrant's horizon, one that is replete with experiences
of itinerancy, ghettoization and illegality. Accordingly, displacement
becomes not only more common, but a more complex experience and
phenomena, both for the individual and the researcher alike.[28] Lastly,
as identities by their very nature 'are neither pure nor fixed but formed
at the intersections of age, class, gender, race and nation'[29] hybridity
emerges as more than a theory of national identities – such as Jordanian-
Palestinian – but as something that is unique to the individual with
the aforementioned elements customizing the hybrid identity. In the
case of diasporic identities such as the Palestinian-Jordanian identity,
such factors can influence individual identities without obscuring the
overriding common traits that unite the Palestinian-Jordanian community through their origins and aspirations to return to, or witness,
the establishment of an independent Palestinian state.

Language and Identity in Jordan

Despite the geographical proximity of Jordan and Palestine, differences
in dialect have emerged between Palestinians and Jordanians, providing
distinguishing aspects within their respective identities. Synonymous
with the wider region, variants in terms of language, religion, customs,
values and historical experiences contribute towards a complex cultural
mosaic. The Middle East, incorporating Iran and Turkey, is characterized by the reality that half of the population of the region is non-Arab.
Nonetheless, 12 of the 16 countries are Arab states and unified by Islam
and its sectarian variations. Yet it is language that provides a means to
differentiate between groups.[30] Language is central to both state and
nationalist discourse, for 'language is the soul and the life of the nation;
history is its memory and its cognizance.'[31] The link between a common
language and shared history cannot be underestimated in the formation of a nation, and in the context of the Palestinian identity the subtle
dialectal transformation, and one might even venture exchange, differentiates it from other Arab identities of the region, for whom Arabic
provides a shared trait.[32] And while the Palestinian dialect provides a

variant between ethnic Jordanians and Palestinian-Jordanians, the two dialects are similar. In addition to the traditional family links between Nablus and Salt and between Hebron and Karak, frequent contact is maintained through marriages and trade and the two groups – Hebron and Nablus on the one side and Salt and Karak on the other – share a dialect, possibly a result of the high consumption by East Jordanians of Palestinian publications and media broadcasts.[33]

Most tangibly, the two dialects differ on the letter *qaf* [q], as Jordanians 'define their own as well as others' linguistic behaviour by a variant of [Q]. [...] The most common way of describing somebody's speech, or the speech of a certain social group is by referring to them as speakers of [g], speakers of [ʔ] or speakers of [q].'[34] This observation was reiterated by interviewees, some of whom promoted their enunciation as an indicator of their identity. An additional variant emerges from [*kh*]: Khalil, a 45-year-old taxi driver, has a Jordanian mother and a Palestinian father, yet when asked his name he emphasized the vernacular variation through the Jordanian pronunciation of his name with a gruff '*gh*' (rendering the sound '*ghalil*'), while the Palestinian speaker, he observed, uses the brusque '*k*', enunciating '*kalil*'. When asked which he preferred, Khalil pronounced the Palestinian version, despite being born and raised in Jordan.[35]

The linguistic variances within Jordan are discernible as: Madani, Bedouin and Fallahi, all of which bear historical and political connotations.[36] Characterized by the emblematic [ʔ], the Madani variety emerged among the Palestinians and Syrians entering the Kingdom in the 1920s and early 1930s, though the number of speakers from this background failed to pose a substantial challenge to the dominant presence of the Bedouins.[37] Spoken chiefly in the large urban hubs of Jordan, it is particularly popular among women, as responses towards the Madani dialect declare it 'soft', 'pretty' and 'effeminate'.

The second form, Bedouin, is denoted by the emblematic [g] and provides the prevalent dialect for the majority of Jordanians. Prior to the influx of Palestinian refugees into Jordan in 1948 and 1967, the Bedouin variety was predominant in a country that lacked an urban centre. Regarded as the most 'masculine' of the three dialects, it is widely used in the Levant and exhibits [g] speech in the region as a whole. While in Jordan it has become an ethnic indicator, the Bedouin [g] is also native to a number of Palestinians, notably those who originate from the Negev area or the villages around Hebron in Palestine.[38] The Bedouin variety gains further regard due to its proximity to standard Arabic, a point drawn upon by Jordanians invoking the Bedouin role as arbiter in linguistic quarrels among grammarians. The reverence held by Jordanians for the Bedouin dialect is traceable to the deep-rooted nature of Bedouin Arabic, which emerged during the fourteenth century when Ibn Khaldoun noted the speech of the Bedouins was less remote than that of the sedentary population from the 'original Arabic language'.[39] Bearing the linguistic kudos, contemporary Jordanians are reinvigorating their heritage to consolidate the national identity and in the process language becomes central to their historic-territorial narrative.

Representing the preponderance of Palestinian-Jordanians, Fellahi is a direct product of the flow of Palestinians into the country in the aftermath of the 1948 and 1967 wars with Israel, and its speakers, formerly residents of the rural Palestine and northern Hebron, currently dwell in large urban centres, including Amman, Zarqa and Irbid.[40] Similar to Madani, the Fallahi dialect is considered a result of Palestinian displacement and is regarded at times disdainfully by the Jordanian population, for whom the dialects – Madani and Fallahi – with their distinguishable [ʔ] and [k] are 'alien', in contrast to the Bedouin dialect, which is deemed 'indigenous'.[41] As a recent addition, the Fallahi dialect has become stigmatized in Jordan, yet it is this very linguistic stigmatization that enables the Palestinian identity to thrive, as Mazen, a hotelier originally from Gaza, elaborates:

The accent is different between Palestinians and Jordanians. It is in your blood and your upbringing. People from Hebron speak with a Hebron accent; people from Gaza speak with a Gazan accent, so you can tell where people are from just by their accent. In many parts of Palestine we would say *ulli* – which means 'tell me', but a Jordanian would say *qulli*. There is an evident difference between the accents of Jordanians and Palestinians in many words.[42]

While the Fallahi dialect maintains the Palestinian accent in Jordan, linguistic dichotomies emerge along both gender and political lines, as the fresher Fallahi accent remains sandwiched between the indigenous Bedouin and integrated Madani dialects. Speakers of Fallahi, meanwhile, increasingly opt for an alternative to their native vernacular, with female speakers favouring the Madani variety, possibly due to its perceived effeminacy, and the males Bedouin, due to its 'masculine' tone. At this point it is worth noting the significance of 'code-switching'. Frequently employed by Palestinians in Jordan as a means to assimilate into a variety of social and professional situations, code-switching allows the native dialect to be applied in the home and with contemporaries, while the Bedouin/Madani varieties are used during interactions with Jordanian compatriots. While the trend of female code-switching to the Madani variety continues from a pre-1967 trend among West Bank Palestinians, the code-switching of [g] rarely occurred amidst male speakers on the West Bank.[43] The absence of code-switching between male Palestinians in the West Bank and Jordan prior to 1967 can be traced to the sociopolitical climate: within the time frame 1967–1971, Jordan underwent a series of changes with an influx of 175,000 Palestinian refugees following the 1967 Six-Day War, swiftly proceeded by Black September in 1970, the legacy of which survives almost 40 years on.

In the aftermath of Black September, Palestinian-Jordanian relations began to dissolve amidst heightened tensions and young Palestinian-Jordanian males actively sought linguistic assimilation:

I remember how this shift coincided, for young males, with the conclusion of the September 1970 confrontations. [...] I recall how some of my Palestinian male friends started to use [g] in speaking with Jordanians. This was particularly noticeable in routine exchanges between the Fallahi students and the soldiers who operated the Sports City (al-Madīna al-Riyādiyya) checkpoint between the town centre and the university. One soldier [...] used to joke with us, for he could tell from the name, from the place of birth on the card, and the poor rendition of Bedouin speech that the 'gifted' switcher (mawhūb) was not an indigenous [g] speaker.[44]

That male speakers prior to 1967 saw little cause to abridge their Fallahi accents indicates a confidence in their origins and the absence of the pressure that would be later applied by the 'Jordanization' movement to modify mannerisms and dialects. Although Suleiman omits the impetus behind the change, his observation that after six centuries Palestinian males suddenly realized that Madani and Fallahi dialects were no longer 'desirable' or 'masculine' indicates a political nuance underlying the shift.[45]

Similar to the cultural exchange, the linguistic infusion flowed both ways with the Palestinian dialect having perhaps a greater impact on the Jordanian through the channels of education and business, than vice-versa. As the majority of Palestinians entered Jordan educated and politicized, there was a considerable expansion in the number of schools and educational institutions in the Kingdom, since 'Most teachers in these schools were Palestinians because of their higher level of education. [...] The dialectal influences of Palestinian teachers are likely to have had some effect on their Trans-jordanian pupils.'[46] It is ironic, then, that as the Palestinian dialects imbued the Jordanian, the Palestinian-Jordanians are compelled to adapt their dialect to integrate with the host state and promote solidarity.

As an aside, it is worth noting the term *'Beljīkī'.*[47] Literally translated as 'Belgian', the term is associated with Black September, yet bears multiple definitions ranging from a positive soubriquet to a national insult. Explanations for the phrase are as multitudinous as the degrees of interpretation: while the most functional pertains to the Belgian-manufactured boots and fatigues worn by the Palestinian guerrillas – which distinguished them from the U.S.-equipped Jordanian army[48] – the negative utilizes the epithet to denote the denationalization of the Palestinians as advocated by certain Jordanian ultra-nationalists. Despite calling for the removal of Palestinians from the Kingdom – the most notable instance during a demonstration in which the slogan *bidnā nihkī al-makhshūf, falastīnī mā bidnā nshūf*[49] was shouted – when queried on the term, prominent Jordanian nationalist Ahmad Oweidi al-Abbadi feigned ignorance, before conceding that *'Beljīkī* means Palestinians who are coming to Jordan. I don't know where it came from, but it is very cheeky and a bad term.'[50] Yet the term also bears folk-linguistic roots, as evinced by a member of the Jordanian National Movement Committee: 'The Palestinians are not originally from the region and came from places like Bosnia, Crete and Belgium. [...] Others will talk about Palestinians being a legacy of the Crusades.'[51] Just as controversial, the second avers that 'the Belgians are a mix of many races, German, French and Dutch, like the Palestinians. The implication being that the Palestinians are "mongrels".'[52] Another member ventured that 'The French look down on the Belgians the way the Jordanians look down on the Palestinians.'[53] Additional interpretations suggest political and militaristic origins:

> *Beljīkī* is a corruption of Bolshevik, a term used against [some Palestinian guerrilla groups] in government propaganda in 1970–1 in the army newspaper, *al-Aqsa* which began publication in mid 1969. *Beljīkī* also is from the acronyms BLJ, in turn derived from the Arabic *min barra li-juwwa*, meaning 'from outside to inside'. Lastly, *Beljīkī* was coined by Muhammad Rasoul Kaylani, Head of the Jordanian *mukhābarāt* at the time, who wished to avoid alerting Palestinians to the fact that he was speaking about them.[54]

Despite the controversial definitions outlined above, many Palestinians adopt the term as a positive appellation that implies a higher socio-cultural status than that of the East Jordanians, evidenced, they say, by their contributions to both the scholarly and business sector. The adoption of the term and its conversion to a favourable one is not uncommon:

> A more recent strategy observed among ethnic and other disad-vantaged groups has been to 'honour' the stigma, to render it as a positive value, and, thereby, to destigmatize it. Perhaps the most powerful and innovative use of this tactic lay in the assertion by black militants in the United States in the late 1960s, that 'Black is Beautiful!'[55]

What has become a term of ambiguity reflects the extremes of nation-alism within the country; though not mainstream, the schism remains significant and pervasive enough for Palestinians to utilize it in the linguistic war of words.

The introduction of the Madani and Fallahi dialects into the Jordanian daily vernacular links to the region's politics. The Arab-Israeli wars of 1948 and 1967 prompted the surge of Palestinian speakers into the Kingdom, with the majority migrating out of necessity. In turn, the dialects presented a challenge to the existing mono-dialectalism. Conceived in conflict, the Jordanian nation-state identity prior to 1948 lacked a cultural centre comparable to Beirut, Jerusalem or Damascus; forged by the British from the spoils of World War I, the emergence of [g] as a linguistic emblem of the country is associated with this event, and the subsequent conflicts in which the Palestinians and Palestine featured have kindled the desire to emphasize the Jordanian identity.

Poignantly the Palestinian rejoinder to the term *Beljīkī* has failed to catch on, emphasizing the dichotomy between the Palestinian-Jordanian and Jordanian communities along lines of 'position and hierarchy', reflected in the allocation of employment opportunities in government, the military, the security services and the parliament. Despite the introduction of the Palestinian-concocted term *gāradina* – a folk neologism stemming from Bedouin *gird*, literally 'ape' or 'monkey' – in reference to the Jordanians, the moniker floundered, in part due to the offensive nature of the term and diminished lexical subtlety in comparison with the Jordanian version.[56] The term *Beljīkī* denigrates the Palestinians as a group denoting political inferiority; that its usage has survived to the present day, while the Palestinian counterpart is virtually unknown, indicates an enduring linguistic imbalance.

Whether the language of Jordan would have evolved in the absence of the Palestinian influx is a hypothetical, the counter to which is whether the Palestinian identity would have strengthened in the absence of the events of 1948 and beyond. One could argue that it would have been inevitable since the variant [g] distinguishes Jordanians from the dialects of Lebanon, Syria and Palestine, while the variant [ʔ] would have remained socio-politically dominant at the level of nation-state politics.[57] Likewise, the utilization of 'code-switching' provides a manifestation of hybridism within the Palestinian-Jordanian identities. By assessing which dialect commands the most positive responses, individuals deploy the variant accordingly to gain acceptance with the ingroup – or in the context of the Palestinian-Jordanians, the Jordanians who determine their political and civil rights in the Kingdom. In turn, the dialect provides an insight into the Palestinian identity in the diaspora and the dynamic between the Palestinian-Jordanian and Jordanian community, with each group endeavouring to integrate or isolate the other and retain or gain a stake in the power of the state.

The Palestinian-Jordanian Identity

These people want to go back to their country. For the Palestinians, Palestine is their own door, their own village, or their own place in Haifa or Jaffa. They belong to that place.[58]

Of the Jordanian, Palestinian and Palestinian-Jordanian identities, the Palestinian identity fluctuates from an indefinable entity harboured by an individual to a response to their assimilation (or lack thereof) within Jordanian political and civil society. In the course of fieldwork, the task of defining the Palestinian identity drew polemic responses: while certain Palestinian-Jordanians were unsure in their articulation of the Palestinian identity, the Jordanian perception demonstrated a heightened awareness, not just of the potency of the Palestinian identity, but also the concerns it induces for the future of Palestinian-Jordanian relations within the Kingdom.

Amidst Jordo-Jordanian respondents, the Palestinian identity elicited caution and/or admiration. For Jordanian ultra-nationalists, the assertion of an alternative national identity to that of the Kingdoms presents a challenge as it 'rises high against Jordanian nationalism and is clear in the newspapers and the media. None of the Palestinians has loyalty to Jordan. This is the reality.'[59] Although a controversial figure in the Jordanian political scene,[60] al-Abbadi is not alone in his view; yet a substantial number of Jordo-Jordanians regard the sustenance of a Palestinian identity in Jordan as admirable, as Tareq al-Masarwa, a columnist for the national newspaper *Al-Rai*, explains:

I respect all those who say they are Palestinian, but living in Jordan. Why should we impose Jordan on their aspirations? It has to do with your identity and country; I respect those Palestinians who say 'I am Palestinian and I live in Jordan' because this is their reality. It may not be fulfilled in the near future, maybe it will take 200 years to return to Palestine, but this is their aspiration.[61]

Jameel Momany, editor of *El-Fajer* newspaper, echoes al-Masarwa:

I feel for the Palestinians: they are our brothers. If there is a problem with the Palestinians, it is as though there is a problem with me, because there is no difference between Palestinians and Jordanians. The Palestinian is like any person in the world. The difference is in the mind.[62]

For many Jordanian respondents, the Palestinian identity and evidence of Palestinian nationalism in Jordan does not pose a threat to that of Palestinian-Jordanian demands for increased political rights. While al-Abbadi blends issues of national identity, loyalty and enhanced political rights into a melange of territorial anxieties, the preponderance of Jordo-Jordanian respondents distinguish between calls for enhanced political participation and the rights of an individual to assert their national identity in the Kingdom. As such, Jordo-Jordanians acknowledge the Palestinian identity in Jordan, while observing the evolution of Palestinian nationalism within the Kingdom.

In recent years, the schisms wrought by Palestinian and Jordanian nationalism have manifested through violent protest at football games. Since the late 1980s, al-Wihdat has drawn supporters predominantly of Palestinian origin; established in 1956 by UNRWA and sharing its name with the Amman-based refugee camp, from 2009 clashes with the Jordanian-favoured rival, al-Faisali, intensified with police beating Palestinian supporters and firing teargas. The role of al-Wihdat as an expression of Palestinian nationalism can be traced back to the events of Black September: the suspicions that have endured almost 40 years on have resulted in a disdain for overt 'Palestinianess' and as a consequence, the opportunity to support a team synonymous with the homeland holds allure. That the vein of expression is sport is not unusual; as Amara observes, in the Arab world sport has been appropriated for socio-political ends:

> sport at the level of popular culture (sport for all) and high performance has been 'captured' by nationalist/political interests [...] In politico-social terms, the over-political manipulation of sport has turned sports arena (particularly football stadia) into a space for youth to express their frustrations and their dissatisfaction (sometimes with violence) with Arab states' policies.[63]

In the aftermath of the events in Qweismeh on 13 December 2010, the fusion of sport and politics was openly acknowledged by Jordanian and Palestinian-Jordanian bloggers alike, including Muhammad, for whom 'It is no longer sports at all, but purely political'.[64] The Jordanian blogger, Naseem, similarly noted the link between football and societal divisions:

> Faisali and Wehdat football games are not mere football games but rather an arena where elements of honor, national identity, origin and roots all seep in. And it is as divisive as one can imagine when it comes to these elements; you are either a fan of one team or the other. In other words, you are either pro-Jordanian or pro-Palestinian; to be a member of one camp is to proclaim yourself the antagonist of the other.[65]

Although a small number of Palestinian-Jordanians have played for al-Faisali, in the aftermath of the violence the notion of enforced incorporation of players of Palestinian origin into the team, and Jordanians likewise into al-Wihdat, was proposed in a bid to quell the nationalist tensions between the teams and their supporters. Should football cease to represent a potent source for nationalistic expression in the Kingdom, the question of the next alternative outlet would invariable arise.

Removed from sport, within the Palestinian-Jordanian community reactions are divided between camp residents and members of the elite.

According to Ibrahim Hejoj, Senior Poverty Advisor at UNRWA, the Palestinian identity is equally strong among the wealthy Palestinians in Jordan with many Palestinians investing in the Arab Bank due to its Palestinian roots.[66] Yet the hardship confronted by residents of the Palestinian refugee camps undoubtedly shapes their identity. For Majed, a Palestinian businessman, the struggle for Palestine accentuates the Palestinian identity, since 'It's good to struggle. Life is good when you have to fight; when life is easy, it is neither interesting nor good.'[67] His stoicism emphasizes the difficulties confronted by camp residents and reinforces the urgency of their plight in a manner that strengthens their identity. In a visit to the Rusaifa camp, conversations with female respondents often turned towards memories of Palestine; perceptions of Palestine for the generation born out of Palestine and activities that maintain a sense of Palestinianess.

Just as socio-economic differences affect the Palestinian identity in the diaspora, so too can those differences strengthen or weaken an individual's identity. While Fadi, a shop owner in downtown Amman, and his brother were born to Palestinian parents in Jordan, his brother's relocation to the United States commenced a decline in his affinity for Jordan and Palestine. Employed by NASA in 1986, Fadi's brother married and settled in California, enjoying a comfortable life. However, he no longer wishes to hear about the economic and ideological struggles confronting his homeland, nor does he wish to visit Palestine or Jordan.

For Palestinians in Jordan, however, Palestine remains an important part of their lives. In the current political climate, Palestinian-Jordanians from all echelons of society experience discrimination and abrogation of their rights as citizens, whether it is through the denial of full schooling for their children – as in the case of Palestinians from Gaza dwelling in Jordan – or under the electoral law that is roundly denounced due to its exclusionary clauses. A point of consensus among Jordanians of Palestinian origin remains that the discriminatory practices by the Jordanian government strengthen the Palestinian identity and acts against their endeavour to minimize future conflict in the Kingdom along lines of ethnic Jordanian and Palestinian origin. According to Labib Kamhawi, the impact of the discriminatory practices on the Palestinian identity in Jordan cannot be underestimated:

> The Palestinians never forget Palestine and the Jordanians of Palestinian origin never look at themselves as being any different from other Jordanians. But nobody wants to listen to the logic in this argument, because the *raison d'être* behind the discrimination is a matter of gains and losses. When you are pushed into a corner, you are forced to realise that you are a different person and the Palestinians and the Jordanians of Palestinian origin have become more aware of their identity, because they have been pushed into this situation.[68]

In turn, the Palestinian identity is evolving as opposed to dwindling, while the absence of equality for Jordanian citizens of Palestinian origin enhances marginalization and impedes integration and full cohesion in contemporary society.

The Political and Cultural Role of National Costume

> Many young girls have started wearing the *sharahi*, the Islamic dress. I feel bad, because it is not our heritage. My enemy is not only Sharon; it is Sharon on one side and the *sharahi* dress on the other.[69]

Since 1948, the Palestinian identity has manifested itself tangibly through cultural artefacts that sustain the past for subsequent generations in the diaspora as an expression of political and religious sentiments and the aspiration to return to the city or town of origin. From the marked increase in the adoption of the black and white keffiyeh by Palestinian youth in Jordan in the aftermath of Black September, to the recent rise in religious slogans embroidered onto cushions and dresses, costume provides an indicator of an individual's identity from the outset. And it is not restricted to costumes: across the socio-economic spectrum the homes of Palestinian-Jordanians exude a reminder of the

past and in certain cases correlate to the degree of attachment felt by
the individual. In contrast, in Jordanian abodes a tangible assertion of
Jordanianess through crafts was absent, a point that can be attributed
to the unique predicament of the Palestinians, both within and outside
of Jordan.

The Political and Cultural Role of the Keffiyeh

Opinion differs markedly on the origins of the keffiyeh's colours: from
the assertion that the red-and-white keffiyeh denotes Jordanian and
the black-and-white Palestinian, to the notion that the colours are the
legacy of the British military presence. On the streets of Amman, one
will commonly observe uniform numbers of Palestinians sporting a
'Jordanian' keffiyeh and Jordanians donning a symbolic 'Palestinian'
one. When quizzed, the response recalls a bygone era, when Jordan
and Palestine were one land and the red and black-and-white keffiyeh shared by the two groups. Although those who perceive little difference are predominantly amidst the older generation (those of 60
years and above), the notion of unity is filtering down to the middle and younger age group. In addition to nationalistic reasoning, a
further socio-economic dimension designates the black-and-white as
a 'proletariat' or 'rural' keffiyeh and the red-and-white as the 'royal'
keffiyeh. As a symbolic link with the land, the association of the black-
and-white scarf with Palestine transcends socio-economic environs by
recalling 'discourses of Palestine and its imagined, memorialised landscape. [...] representing Arafat as both peasant and fighter, [it] sits like
a crown on the Dome of the Rock in Jerusalem, the glorious throne
of all Palestine.'[70] Through its association with the *fellahin* and rural
areas of Palestine, the keffiyeh starkly contrasted with the city-dweller's
fez and during the 1930s it emerged as the symbol of Palestinian
nationalism, adopted by Palestinians in support of Grand Mufti Amin
al-Husayni during the Arab revolt of 1936–1939. Although the British
endeavoured to ban the scarf in Jenin through the threat of jail, they
ultimately failed and the penalty was revoked.

By the 1950s, the scarf gained an added political weight as a trib-
ute to the populism of Nasser, a potent symbol of opposition to the

monarchical structure of the Kingdom. Over 40 years later, the black-
and-white keffiyeh has remained emblematic of struggle and a herald
of impending resistance to regimes. In 2005, the Iranian authorities
commenced a crackdown on the donning of the Palestinian keffiyeh
by the Ahwazi Arab minority who were utilizing officially sanctioned
religious festivals to protest against the Iranian regime's policy of ethnic cleansing in Khuzestan. In defiance of the regime, the Ahwazi
promoted symbols of Arab cultural identity, notably through the
keffiyeh and *dishdasha*, flying the Ahwaz national flag and perform-
ing Arab cultural plays in the streets. The restrictions peaked during the November Eid al-Fitr demonstrations when the Governor
General, Heyat Mojadam, decreed that all those wearing the keffiyeh
be arrested. According to one youth detained during the protests, the
prosecutor, Farhadi Rad, argued that the wearing of the keffiyeh was
a 'political statement' that indicated support for secessionism.[71]

If the symbolism of the keffiyeh in Jordan seems ambiguous,
it assumes added complexities in the Iranian case. From adorning
the backs of Iranians during the 1979 Revolution, to providing 'the
sacred defence' for Iranian soldiers in the 1980–1988 war with Iraq,
it is worn by the very figures the youth strive against: Iran's supreme
leader, Ayatollah Ali Khamenei, President Mahmoud Ahmadinejad
and the Basij militia uniform.[72] Yet the utilization of the keffiyeh by
the regime has not passed without criticism: during a ceremony to
celebrate the arrival of the Cyrus Cylinder on loan to Tehran from the
British Museum in 2010, Ahmadinejad garlanded two actors, dressed
as an Achaemenid soldier and a member of the Basij respectively,
with kuffiyat. For the Iranian Students News Agency (ISNA), the
scarf provided 'the symbol of the resistance and honor of the Iranian
people'; for young Iranians, the appropriation by the regime lacked
the very honour it proclaimed. For Andishe, an Iranian blogger, the
gesture was misguided cultural reference: 'How can one mix two very
different symbols that go against each other? [The] keffiyeh is the
symbol of bloodshed, war, and terrorism in Palestine and Lebanon.
[The] keffiyeh is the symbol of the Palestinians. Look at what Cyrus
the Great and the Iranian civilization have to say and look at what
Ahmadinejad and *Velayar Faghih* (the rule of the Supreme Jurist) have

to say.'[73] Despite being used by the regime, Iranian youth are reclaiming the keffiyeh's heritage as the indicator of resistance and from
rap artists to the Ahwazi community, it is experiencing a sartorial
counter-resurgence. Moreover, it is worth noting that the kuffiyat
used by the Basiji differ from the Palestinian version, with larger,
black checks for the men and green versions for the female paramili-
tary members. Nevertheless, in the Iranian instance it is the keffiyeh's
synonymy with resistance, rather than the colours, that is of import
for both the regime and its detractors.

The censure of the keffiyeh is not restricted to the Middle East and
Iran: in 2002 the *Columbia Spectator* columnist, Adam B. Kushner,
advocated a ban on the Palestinian keffiyeh at university graduation
ceremonies on the basis that it represents a 'dogmatic symbolism'
that provides little opportunity for those who disagree with the pro-
Palestinian stance to respond with their arguments.[74] Kushner's assertion received a tepid welcome: critics indicated that speech through
symbols like the keffiyeh holds a unique virtue as the keffiyeh exhibits support for the Palestinian cause and invites discourse on Middle
Eastern affairs in a more subtle manner than vocally. Moreover, 'to
ask that all of these [gender and cultural expressions] be muted in the
name of drawing students together for graduation is absurd; to advocate that pro-Palestinian politics in particular be muted is to apply
an absurd principle unequally.'[75] In 2008, the TV cooking show host
Rachael Ray unwittingly resurrected the debate through a Dunkin'
Donuts campaign in which she promoted latte while wearing a black-
and-white keffiyeh. When the Republican journalist Michelle Malkin
denounced the garment as 'jihadi chic' and 'a regular adornment of
Muslim terrorists' linked to a 'murderous Palestinian jihad'[76] the
controversy escalated and Dunkin' Donuts pulled the commercial.
For Malkin and fellow conservatives, it constituted a victory as 'an
American company show[ed] sensitivity to the concerns of Americans
opposed to Islamic jihad and its apologists.'[77] For those of a non-right-
wing disposition, it breathed life into misconceptions, prejudices and
bigotry surrounding the Middle East and its inhabitants, lending credence to the notion that a scarf can pose a threat to American society
through a (misconstrued) link to the Palestinian cause.

Returning to Jordan, a more urbane interpretation indicates less tribal, political origins and more one borne of practicality. According to Widad Kawar, a collector of Palestinian costumes and artefacts, the black-and-white version was used by all Arabs prior to the British Mandate, while the red-and-white keffiyeh emerged from military necessity:

> It was always black-and-white for not just Bedouins, but all Arabs, in Palestine and elsewhere. The first red-and-white version came from Manchester; when the British were here they ordered for the Jordanian military red-and-white as they wanted the army to be different. It was suggested by Glubb, because the Bedouins at that time wore black-and-white. The men liked it, so it stopped being only for the army.[78]

Indeed, not only did Glubb Pasha equip the Jordanians, but also his Palestinian soldiers, and to distinguish between the two he outfitted the West Bank Palestinians in black-and-white kuffiyat and East Jordanians in red-and-white.[79] In the process, the seeds were sown of a politically loaded and nationalistically potent scarf.

Within Jordan, the popularity of the red-and-white keffiyeh among Palestinians is noticeable. In the Gaza Camp near Jerash, where the Palestinian identity is keen amidst the dismal conditions – both in terms of milieu and political and civil rights – elderly men congregate on stoops topped by red-and-white kefiyyat; when I addressed this observation to my colleague, he shrugged, quipping, 'In 100 meters there will be four Palestinians wearing a red keffiyeh, because it was common for the army to wear the red keffiyeh and it was seen as a part of army dress.'[80] Thus, for the older generation, the keffiyeh lacks the distinct national symbolism with which it is now associated. Nevertheless, divisions pervade through the political nuances of the black-and-white keffiyeh and the red-and-white. On a societal level, it is believed that Transjordanian urban males promote their Jordanianess through the red-and-white keffiyeh 'as an assertion of national pride'[81] – a move that has proved a sartorial catalyst as 'Palestinian Jordanians followed suit by wearing the black-and-white keffiyeh [and] those among them seeking assimilation wore the red-and-white keffiyeh.'[82] Kawar, however, maintains it has become purely a matter of fashion:

> Today the keffiyeh is 'supposed' to be red for Jordanians and black for Palestinians. Now they are green, mauve, pink and yellow. They started to make them in Syria for table-tops and now we have them of all colours for fashion. Women wear them as a shawl; men don't wear the coloured ones – only red and black.[83]

The emergence in recent years of the green-and-white keffiyeh has prompted associations with the Palestinian Islamist group, Hamas, and by virtue of its status as a banned political group, bearers of the green scarf could court politico-religious controversy. But keffiyeh vendors in Amman remain sceptical and adopt a pragmatic approach, reasoning it is merely another variant on the popular accessory and that in terms of sales, it falls far behind its red and black cohorts. Whether due to the nature of Jordan's relationship with Hamas or the enduring preference of the black-and-white as a symbol of the Palestinian struggle, the majority of respondents dispelled the notion of a Hamas version in support of Kawar's fashion-oriented theory. The association can be further disparaged by the lack of Hamas officials donning the scarf: perceiving the garment as a secular, nationalistic symbol favoured by Fatah, they are to be seen with a green band around the forehead. A more credible explanation retaining the religious nuance sans a political undertone follows that green denotes one's religious identity; ergo, green being the colour synonymous with Islam, it becomes linked to a wider, non-political Islamic identity.

The political significance of the keffiyeh cannot be underestimated: during the 1970–1971, skirmishes between Palestinians and Jordanians, also known as Black September, a simultaneous upsurge in popularity of the red-and-white keffiyeh occurred among Jordo-Jordanians:

> As a witness to events of this kind at the time, I can report how some Jordanian male students at the University of Jordan started to wear this head cover in an ostentatious display of their Jordanian identity and anti-Palestinian credentials. Palestinians

who, before 1970, would sometimes wear the black-chequered *kufiyya* (imitating Yasser Arafat) stopped doing so.[84]

Although Suleiman's account stops short of explaining why there was a downturn in the number of Palestinians sporting the black-and-white kuffiyat, it is possible that in a period of heightened inter-communal tensions regulated by the Jordanian security services (*mukhabarat*), it was prudent to avoid overt displays of Palestinian identity.

The socio-religious role of the garment in contemporary Arab society enables the keffiyeh to at times transcend the political. In her study of male veiling, Fadwa El Guindi demonstrates the keffiyeh's role as a 'male veil' that reinforces the exclusivity of rank, kinship status and behaviour. At the same time, it offers a hint of an element of power and autonomy in its function as a vehicle for resistance.[85] During a visit to the university campus in Cairo, El Guindi observed the socio-religious application of the keffiyeh:

> While I was with women students in the women's lounge, a man knocked on the door. The women scrambled for their *hijabs* and *qina's* (face masks). Moments of confusion and tension passed, after which the man knocked again on the door. I looked out of the door and saw a man in a *gallabiyya* (an ankle-length white, unfitted gown with long sleeves). He pulled his *kufiyya* (head shawl) over his face and entered very cautiously, literally rubbing against the wall trying not to look in the direction of the women until he reached a curtain diagonally hung in the corner of the room.[86]

Once ensconced behind the curtain, the man engaged in a discussion concerning Mawdudi with the women, during which:

> It was the man who both face-veiled when with women and sat behind the *hijab* (curtain). His shadow showed him lifting the *kufiyya* off his face and letting it down to his shoulders, but keeping it on his head. [...] After about thirty-five minutes, he excused himself, and went through a ritualized exit, similar to his entry.[87]

El Guindi's case demonstrates the versatility of the keffiyeh and the parallels to be drawn between the red-and-white keffiyeh and Jordanian nationalist sentiments through its evocation of rank, (tribal) kinship and power. This was further evidenced during interviews with the Jordanian National Movement committee, with all present sporting head garments of the red-and-white hue. Conversely, by donning the black-and-white keffiyeh, wearers invoke notions of resistance and, in particular, Palestinian resistance through the reinforcement of its synonymy with Palestine.

For many Palestinians and non-Palestinians, the keffiyeh provides a means to express disdain for repression and injustice: from militant resistance fighters in Iraq, Indonesian independence fighters and Nicaraguan revolutionaries, the keffiyeh has become deeply associated with Palestine and struggle. The PLO in the Occupied Territories and Lebanon, Syria, Jordan and Egypt fuelled its iconic rise through political posters and imagery, more so in Jordan and Lebanon during the 1960s and 1970s where the Palestinians and Arafat wielded significant power.[88] In terms of visual culture, the works of Palestinian political cartoonist Naji Al-Ali, featuring the loyal Handala, are suffused with elements of the keffiyeh: as a shroud cast upon a prone, bullet-riddle figure (male and female versions), a sketch of Palestine filled with the chequered pattern, or an injured man, head wrapped in a keffiyeh and hands clawing at a soil whose parched cracks bring the semblance closer to the black-and-white cheques. Similarly, alternative images portray Palestinian figures wrapped in kefiyyat ploughing the earth with picks that double as Kalashnikovs, and the phrase 'The land belongs to those who liberate it'.[89] The assertion that along with the linguistic aspects of identity '[t]he nationalized *keffiyeh/shmagh* [...] became corporeal and verbal performances that guarantee national identity. Affirming both publicly became part of the daily rituals of staging Transjordanianess and Palestinianess'[90] rings true: as multifaceted as the Palestinian identity itself, the keffiyeh stands as a fashion statement, a political and/or religious symbol, an icon of the Palestinian movement and a means to sustain the defining markers of identity between the Palestinian-Jordanian and Jordanian community in Jordan.

A Cross-Cultural Fusion: Costume and the Palestinian-Jordanian Identity

Every dress has part of their own town and they carry it with them in the camps.[91]

Predominantly exhibited through women's dress, the Palestinian costume provides both a visual reminder of the splendour of a free Palestine and a means to unite the Palestinian community through embroidery and dress manufacturing, from the dusty camps of Rusaifa and Ba'qa to the bold mansions of Abdoun, where wives and mothers convert vast salons into fitting areas and private showrooms. Although for some a lucrative distraction, for many in the camps the dresses provide an emotional and pecuniary sustenance. On a sunny day in the refugee camps of Jordan, elderly women rest bare-foot on the dusty pavement; oblivious to the heat or the raucous children kicking footballs, they are intently absorbed in the tiny and intricate stitches that make the masterpiece that will ultimately hang in *al-balad*,[92] to be pawed by tourists enraptured by an ethnic bargain, oblivious to the miniscule profit to be made by the creator. Yet the dresses are more than cultural phenomena: similar to the keffiyeh, they represent resistance, remembrance, fusion and fashion over a period of almost 60 years, four generations and a ceaseless period of diaspora and occupation.

Although little remains from the decades of turmoil that marked the 1950s and 1960s, traditional costume began a renaissance through plainer designs thereafter. With limited access to locally woven goods or imported fabrics, costumes lost their ornate features and assumed a practical function. The distinction between attire for special occasions and everyday wear was lost, and the veils and elaborate headdresses became relics of a not so distant past. The move into the refugee camps eroded the traditions of regional styles; costumes became identifiable by general styles, such as the 'six branch'[93] and the *shawal*,[94] designed originally for Western markets. Recalling the shift that occurred in the camps, Kawar, then a student at the

American University of Beirut, observed the transformation upon her return in 1950 to Bethlehem:

> I found a great change in the life of the villages. When I returned after two years Bethlehem was full of refugees and there were camps around the town. The women that were so beautiful in embroidered dresses in the villages were now queuing for milk, queuing for flour, and living in tents.[95]

By 1987, the Intifada heralded a revival in Palestinian costume and the embroidered dress became a proclamation of Palestinian national and social consciousness. In the Occupied Territories, the wearing of traditional costume developed a more overt political function, and by wearing it one declared a social and political affiliation:

> In 1988 the Palestinian women started a dress with flags called 'the Intifada costume.' This made the Israelis mad, because a group of women could walk with the flag embroidered – you can't take it off! When they had the flag the Israeli would take it off their hands. But if you are wearing the dress, they could not take off the dress! They are political and they became very fashionable.[96]

The subtle display of nationalism evolved with the introduction of a new style of *shawal* dress, specifically designed to promote the Intifada. Considered to have originated in Hebron, the dress featured embroidery in the colours of the prohibited Palestinian flag, with motifs of the map of Palestine, the Al-Aqsa Mosque, guns and grenades, and the patterns of the keffiyeh worked into the structure of the *qabbeh* and the vertical skirt panels. Furthermore, inscriptions in both Arabic and English would feature the words 'Palestine', 'PLO', 'Abu Amar' (Yasser Arafat) and 'We shall return'. Interestingly, while the *thob* experienced a renaissance in Palestine among young women donning the costume for university, the revival in Jordan amongst the Palestinian community was muted: 'It wasn't very strong in Jordan to show that we are Palestinians. It is made there [Palestine] to show that they are

Palestinians, but I don't think they want to show it off here.'[97] Instead, an intriguing hybrid emerged from the camps, fusing the Palestinian and Jordanian identity with 'the Palestinian flag on one side and the Jordanian flag on the other. They never wore it for demonstrations or for everyday wear. It was non-reactionary, not strong enough.'[98] The hybrid design can be attributed to the duration of time spent in Jordan, relations with the Jordanian people – through marriage, for example – or a means to reaffirm their loyalty to both Jordan and Palestine, literally illustrating the notion that it is one land, one community traversing the two banks. As Kawar affirms: 'Most refugees come and go; sometimes they stay and get married here in Jordan, sometimes they disappear and get married in Palestine. So they came over from Palestine and made it in Jordan.'[99]

Despite the lesser popularity of the Intifada costume in Jordan, by the second Intifada in 2001 the costume's design infused several projects in the Kingdom as refugee embroidery groups incorporated the Intifada dress into their commission books, along with traditional Palestinian designs. The word 'Palestine' and 'Abu Amar' could also be regarded as a form of rudimentary branding, as from the mid-1980s onwards Israel commenced an appropriation of Palestinian culture and cuisine, with a palpable example being the postcard bearing the image of falafel skewered by an Israeli flag with the slogan 'Falafel – Israel's national snack'.[100] In response, embroidery projects introduced Palestinian symbols and inscriptions to ensure that the cultural and geographical origin could not be modified. Thus, the Intifada dresses serve a dual purpose that can be viewed to be most potent in the Occupied Territories: as a silent protest towards the Israelis, and a means to exhibit their heritage within the diaspora.

Produced in the refugee camps as a means of income, embroidery has become a source of engagement in the sustenance of Palestinian cultural heritage. For a population lacking a homeland, costume is a device through which a disjointed legacy could re-establish itself. No longer restricted to dresses, embroidery developed as a cultural form separate to costume in the late 1980s under the encouragement of NGOs to create new products, such as cushions, clocks and maps of

Palestine. In the camps of Jordan a diversity of goods is being produced, and not all are destined for the Western market. In the home
of Fatima, a refugee originally from New Abasan, but now residing
in Rusaifa, creating Palestinian dresses over the course of one a year
has resulted in piles of cloths embroidered with the same pattern:
the word Intifada, surrounded by flowers. Scattered throughout her
modest salon and adorning the walls, the fabrics feature intricately
painted maps of Palestine festooned with symbols and faces; even cut-
lery, pots and plates bear images etched and glazed to the outline of
Palestine. Sporting a dress from her own collection crafted with red
embroidery encircling the neck and cuffs, Fatima explained that she
was currently in the process of writing a book about her village in
the Gaza Strip, motivated by the need to educate the next generation
about the homeland. Fatima's enthusiasm for cultural awareness of
Palestine was tangible not only through her handicrafts, but also her
desire to ensure that the land is remembered. Due to the conditions
of the camps, the indeterminate fate of the Palestinians in Jordan and
the societies that maintain relations between Palestinians in Jordan
and their contemporaries in the Occupied Territories, the desire to do
more remains insatiable.

Outside of the home UNRWA centres and projects such as Jordan
River Designs focus on the production of quilts designed with dress
motifs and layout, while the Jordan Design and Trade Centre, part of
the Noor Foundation, produces traditionally woven carpets based on
dress motifs. In the poorer refugee camps, where access to external
Western funding is virtually unattainable, modestly wrought goods
are produced from embroidered panels cut from old dresses: 'branches'
of birds become cases for glasses and *qabbehs* morph into tea cosies. One
such shop that specializes in the sale of goods manufactured in the
camps is The Green Branch located in Jabal al-Weibdeh. The owner,
a Palestinian Christian woman originally from Bethlehem, promotes
the sale not only of cushions, dresses, wallets and bags produced from
old dresses in the camps of Jordan, but also statuettes carved in olive
wood to the image of Christ, the Virgin and the disciples, all of which
are crafted in the camps of Palestine. With a substantial proportion
of the revenue returning to the camps to assist in the manufacture of

such goods, the Palestinian community ensures that despite the lack of external aid an alternative assistance for camp residents is sustained through the tourist market and the Jordanian consumer.

The proximity of Jordan and Palestine has been conducive to exchanges and fusions in designs. Palestinian dress designers, such as Leila Jeryas in Amman, demonstrate the similarities through the *thob 'ub*, a double or long dress originating from Jericho and Salt. Additionally, the stitching has evolved; while the northern Jordanian stitch is fine and similar to lace-work, the Palestinian is an easier cross-stitch. Thus, in many areas of Jordan the original stitch has been abandoned in favour of the Palestinian, which is applied to the Jordanian dress, creating a new, cross-cultural costume. The pieces have merged to the extent that Kawar, an expert in both Palestinian and Jordanian dress, is confounded at the origins her pieces: 'The embroidering on the cushions, on the shawls makes it impossible to know which is Palestinian or Jordanian. They got mixed up in a kind of mergence.'[101] Equally, Bedouin weaving skills – considered the most dextrous in the Middle East – are integrating methods from Beit Sahor and Gaza.

The ongoing efforts of embroidery projects, cottage industries and collectors to uphold Palestinian traditional handicrafts occupy a significant role in the Palestinian identity in Jordan. That the two communities clash on a socio-political level is offset by a merging that cannot be denied through rhetoric; the crafts demonstrate that despite calls for 'Jordan First' and assertions that the Palestinians do not belong in Jordan, the Palestinians are more a part of the Jordanian heritage and contemporary society than is acknowledged. That the Intifada crafts of the Occupied Territories and Gaza are adapted in Jordan to incorporate the Jordanian flag indicates a loyalty both to the home and host-land. If this fusion can occur on the most subtle of levels – culturally – then the time has come to stop looking to the events of Black September, to ignore the Israeli whispers of *al-Watan al-Badil*;[102] rather, one must look to the future of Jordan as a cohesive society that incorporates Palestinians into the civil and political system, creating a fusion on a political and societal level akin to that of the cultural sphere.

Gender and the Palestinian Identity in Jordan

In certain cultures, gender is synonymous with sex – that is, the biological differences between males and females.[103] A fitting lexical example of this interchange can be found in the absence of a word for 'gender' in the Hebrew language. Instead, the term is expressed through the same word for 'sex': *min*, rendering gender indistinguishable as one word encompasses both. Despite the close association of the concept of gender with femininity, the notion of gender as a social, cultural and political aspect of human existence and behaviour has enabled 'the exploration of varieties of masculinity and femininity that are highly variable across cultures, time, and socio-political contexts'.[104] Through its incorporation of discourses and power relations, gender provides a means to view behaviours, social norms, systems of meanings, thought processes and the way women experience, understand and represent themselves.[105] In the process, alternative social relationships, including those which sustain unequal relations of power and privilege, become legible.

Whether organized collectively, individually or alongside their male counterparts, women have rallied both for issues concerning gender and women's rights, as well as social and political progress. In the context of the Palestinian struggle, the culmination of World War I initiated a new phase in women's activity and with the fall of the Ottoman Empire in 1922 Palestine assumed the yoke of the British Mandate, one whose foremost goal was the establishment of Israel. As the number of Jews entering Palestine swelled, the Palestinian national movement emerged and, concurrently, a Palestinian women's movement was established in 1929.[106] Initially the activities of the women's movement comprised protests alongside men – against the land sales to *olim*, the expulsion of peasants from the land and the ongoing immigration ('ascent' or *aliyah*) to Palestine/Israel – and their involvement was notable: of 120 Arabs slain by the British at nationalist protests in August 1929, nine were women.[107] Yet despite their presence, the extent of their involvement remains immeasurable due to incomplete early accounts.

The first women's conference held in Jerusalem in 1929 provided a significant turning point in the organization of women's resistance in

Palestine. Chaired by the wife of the Arab executive committee head, Musa Hatem al-Husseini, the preliminary meeting was attended by 200 women, many of whom were affluent or held political connections. While the conference reiterated the delegates' renunciation of the Balfour Declaration of 1917 and ongoing *aliyah*, it was the participants' post-conference antics that attracted notoriety as delegates took to the streets of Jerusalem in protest. In one instance, a number of women descended on the home of the British governor and, removing their veils, exclaimed, 'To serve our homeland we shall take off our veil!' before presenting a memorandum consisting their demands.[108] Aware of the growing threat to their state, the women of Palestine united in protest and to save their country. The conference provided a platform for an organized women's movement that vocalized the concerns of the female population, a means to express their opinions and act independent of their male cohorts.

The removal of the veil is symbolic: during the 1920s the Egyptian feminist and nationalist Huda Sha'rawi spurred debate upon her unveiling, a move that bore not just religious connotations, but also socio-cultural. As Khaf notes, the *hijab* was, and remains, a multilayered symbol:

The word *hijab* has always had two layers of meaning in Arabic: concealment and covering. The dominant meaning of *hijab* for most of Islamic history has been concealment, manifesting itself in face-veils and seclusion in regard to women. In the Twentieth Century [*sic*] the meaning of covering has slowly gained prominence and *hijab* has come to refer simply to certain garments rather than to the sequestration or masking of women. I lifted the *hijab*; I donned the *hijab* [...] Lifting the *hijab*: I removed the facial screen that I used to wear; I opened the curtain behind which the upper-class household secluded its ladies; I dislodged the barrier impeding women's access to public life. Donning the *hijab shari'i*: I ground my action in Islamic religion and Arabic culture; I claim the right to interpret that culture anew with authority and legitimacy; I offer a new symbiosis of tradition and modernity which gives women the autonomy, individuality,

and efficacy demanded by modernity yet enables them to benefit
from the advantages offered by tradition.[109]

From this dual perspective the *hijab* can be viewed as an emblematic
tool by Palestinian women – emerging to the fore, into the light, sar-
torially and politically – through the removal of the veil, and also in
a contemporary respect with the return to faith as noted in Chapter
6. The *hijab* is power: dependent on the woman's objective, it can be a
show of political or religious strength – and, more importantly, both.

Following the conference the women's national movement gathered
pace. According to Peteet, four significant periods distinguish the historical circumstances and the emergence of the women's movement
in the context of national struggle. Foremost, 1920–1929 witnessed
the surfacing of women's resistance through burgeoning opposition to
rising Zionism and the British Mandate. The period 1936–1939 was
characterized by revolts in Palestine and female members gained experience in militant politics, preparing them for the battles of 1947–1948.
Despite the national crises of 1948–1965, the women's movement frag-
mented, rather than flourished, in confronting the challenge for which
they had prepared as the Palestinians scattered throughout the Arab
world and became subjected to restrictions by Arab host governments.
The final period, 1965–1982, observed a cohesive women's movement
resurfacing under the middle class and elite, geared towards preparing
the women for national struggle; at the same time, it became formally
integrated into the national movement.[110] Significantly, the changes
occurring within the movement were not restricted to the Palestinian
territories; as the exodus of Palestinian refugees sought sanctuary in
neighbouring states, so too did the desire to resist the occupation –
albeit from afar – continue in the new environs.

A notable female figure in the Palestinian resistance movement
of Jordan, Khuzama Rasheed was the first female guerrilla leader of
the DFLP Political Office at its founding conference in August 1970.
Based in northern Jordan, Rasheed enabled the DFLP to become
'the first political group to include women in its Political Office'.[111]
Despite promoting a positive female presence in the resistance movement, Rasheed's decline was dispiriting, prompted by the relocation

of high-ranking partisans from Jordan to Syria without seeking her approval. Jaded, Rasheed left the DFLP to return to party head-quarters, where she continued to lead at a reduced level. The dominance of the male members of the movement had prevailed; while women strove to actively participate in the struggle, male leaders retained ultimate influence over the direction and level of involvement afforded to female partisans. Equality in battle, though evidenced at a grassroots level, was distinctly absent within the political organizations.

The disparity can be perceived further in the rhetoric promulgated by the movements, as the language and images evoke specific notions of masculinity and femininity with men portrayed as fighters and protectors ready to sacrifice their lives for their women, children and land; women, meanwhile, remain passive victims in need of masculine protection, occasionally smacking their cheeks and being 'thrilled' by male-led victories. The images of 'mothers [who] have wept for their sons' has been used to emphasize that the threat of 'violence' and 'terror' must be met with militaristic, masculine actions of 'defence' and 'sacrifice'.[112] These overtures were poignantly demonstrated during the 1987 Intifada, when leaflets distributed by four women's organizations on 1 October 1988 – in protest against the deportation of nine activists – addressed 'the heroic masses of our Palestinian people, the heroes of the great Intifada'. Noteworthy by its absence is the acknowledgement of women, with the exception of the following sentence: 'heroic masses of our people, your Intifada has reached the whole world [...] and Palestinian women have thrilled with joy.'[113] Overlooking the endeavours of the female partisans within the resistance, the organization's perception of female participation comprises 'thrilling' to their men's heroic feats of endurance undermines the role of women in the struggle and reinforces the stereotype of 'women' being a bystander, passive and unengaged in the country's demise.

On the contrary, Palestinian women before and after the Intifada of 1987 were as active as their male counterparts. From the 1920s, women in the West Bank organized watch committees to prevent looting, distributed emergency rations and on 26 October 1929, convened the Palestine Arab Women's Congress in Jerusalem. Although smaller women's organizations had existed since the turn of the century in Jaffa and Jerusalem, the Congress marked the entrance of women onto the political and national platform with 200 participants relocating gender participation from the local to the national.[114] In the immediate aftermath of the Congress the tenacity of the Palestinian women's movement was tested: having presented the petition to the British High Commissioner's wife, in line with Mandate etiquette, the British flatly refuted the demands. In 1933 'for the first time in history a Christian lady delivered a political speech from the pulpit of a mosque',[115] evoking rhetoric involving the Muslim and Christian conquerors of Jerusalem, before being succeeded by a speech by a Muslim lady beside Christ's tomb in the Holy Sepulchre.[116] Move forwards to the events of 1987 and beyond and the involvement of women transcended the political into the murkier realm of combat participation: suicide bombing and the preparation of Molotov cocktails occurred side-by-side with the more traditional role, as ascribed by Hamas, of fulfilling the roles of mothers who raise fighters and martyrs. The conflict had a profound impact on the position of Palestinian women in society, as Said observes:

> During the intifada [...] women came to the fore as equal partners in the struggle. They confronted Israelis (male) troops; they shared in decision-making; they were no longer left at home, or given menial tasks, but they did what the men did, without fear or complexes. Perhaps it would be still more accurate to say that because of the intifada, the role of men was altered, from being dominant to becoming equal.[117]

The women's committees evolved from their neighbourhood-watch roots of the 1920s to recorders of violations of human rights, with rape and sexual harassment by Israeli soldiers replacing looting and banditry as the most common injustice. In response, women participated with increasing vigour, 'joining street demonstrations, hurling stones and shouting at Israeli soldiers, or using their bodies as barricades to block the beatings and to stop the arrests of their children.'[118] From the passive bystanders to the vociferous objectors, Palestinian women have been a present and active force in the national struggle since the beginning – but not without overcoming great challenges.

The evolution of the women's movement was not smooth and allegations of continued male interference and inequality persisted to inspire disenchantment among members. While regional unrest disrupted activities within both the male and female Palestinian resistance movements, in the aftermath of the war, the remnants of the Palestinian Women's Union (PWU) and the Arab Women's Executive (AWE), established in 1921 and 1929 respectively, reassembled in Lebanon, Syria, Gaza and Jerusalem. In Jordan, however, political work was not tolerated and the word 'Palestinian' was deleted from the Palestinian Arab Women's Union and their work curtailed to relief and welfare.[119] At a local level, the politicization of women's groups resulted in disenchantment amongst members, as Rubenberg's interviews of Palestinian resistance members attests: 'The women are very selfish, very closed – competitive not cooperative – and they don't value you as an individual. You are evaluated according to the faction – if someone is with the DFLP and you are with the PFLP, that person looks down on you.'[120] Accordingly, elite women defined the context of political activities both before and during the Intifada and frequently continued to follow the direction of male political leaders.

As Rubenberg demonstrates, a significant flaw within the women's movement has been the tendency of organizations to become appendages of the main political factions, characterized by weakness and too factionalized to address male counterparts with the issue of gender inequality within the external context of a national struggle.[121] For Palestinian women in Jordan and Palestine seeking to express nationalism and participate in the resistance, the women's movement proved not only an extension of the male-dominated factions, but also rife with equal measures of competition, discrimination and disarray. While the challenge of gender equality might have been removed, it was replaced with one of a socio-economic nature, as women of low income and residents of the refugee camps were overlooked by those at the helm of the organizations, captivated as they were less by the struggle and more by the desire to accentuate their own social profiles.

In Jordan female participation continues the conventional manifestations of identity and national struggle and through the course
of interviews with Palestinian women residing in Jordan, certain
aspects evoke similar activities in Palestine. While in the West
Bank and Gaza rural and camp women participated in extensions
of gender roles, such as visiting families, knitting sweaters for pris-
oners and providing alternative education when schools were closed,
Palestinian-Jordanian women participate in publications, exhibitions,
political organizations, UNRWA and privately funded embroidery
projects. From the cottage industries of the refugee camps to the col-
lections held by Widad Kawar, the Palestinian identity is sustained
on a plethora of levels. Although Palestinian women settled in Jordan
cannot engage directly in the uprising, support for their counterparts
across the border is maintained through alternative, and no less significant, means.

The Historiography of the Common Past

The Israelis came from Nablus laughing: 'who wants to go for
a picnic to Amman?' – they could not imagine anyone would
come out of *Jordanian* territory and fight.[122]

National narrative and the recollection of key events, be they military or otherwise, forms a point of unity as well as conflict. It binds
communities in pride and remorse and is crucial to identity formation and sustenance, both at home and in the diaspora. In the Battle
of Karameh, one discovers not a point of shared recollection, but a
point of contention as differences emerge on the combat effectiveness
of the Palestinians, Jordanians and Israelis, the full extent of Israeli
goals involving Jordan as well as the Palestinians, and the extent to
which Jordan extended its military strength to assist the Palestinians.
Spilling into the international arena, accounts fall into three categories: supporters of the Palestinian narrative, advocates of a Jordanian
victory and an objective repertoire that encompasses the endeavours of
both parties, regardless of the fighting duration, total mortalities and

tales of derring-do. For the Palestinians, the events of 21 March 1968 had a profound effect on the people, for whom the despondence triggered by the 1967 War became synonymous with the loss of dignity, a loss reinforced by the ironic fact that the town's name, Karameh, translates as 'dignity'. As a result, the engagement between the Israelis and Palestinians became ingrained in the Arab psyche as 'the battle for dignity', which was lost in June 1967.[123] For Jordanians there remains little doubt that Karameh presented an opportunity for cooperation, as the Kingdom's forces reached into the Palestinian-populated town and plucked victory from the Israeli forces. As an adaptation of 'David and Goliath' for the twentieth century the Jordanian version recounts a sorry depiction of the Palestinians as they fled their dwellings, pausing only to hurl a stone.

That the confusion surrounding the events at Karameh proceeds into non-Jordanian and non-Palestinian authored literature is unsurprising, though the majority of publications reflect both sides. A notable case in which the author omits mention of the Jordanian forces entirely is Alejandro Pizarroso Quintero's *Nuevas guerras, vieja propaganda (de Vietnam a Irak)*. During a brief appraisal of the events at Karameh, Quintero notes the Palestinian presence:

> After the loss of the Six Day War Israel continued to practice incursions into towns and camps in Jordan, where the Palestinian resistance was organised. On the 21 March 1968 around Karameh 305 Palestinian guerrillas, instead of retreating, confronted 12,000 Israeli soldiers, 1,200 were killed and a great part of their artillery lost, obliging them [the Israelis] to retreat.[124]

Far from an example of cooperation between the Jordanian troops and Palestinian guerrillas, the victory was proved testament to the fortitude of the Palestinian resistance.[125] That Jordan is mentioned as a backdrop to the battle is notable, and the prevalence of such accounts is attributable to the early Palestinian desire to grasp any optimistic news in the aftermath of the Six-Day War. Arriving as a significant victory following years of upheaval and military losses, pride at the fortuitous turn of events minimized any chance that the Palestinians would allow the battle to become a feather in the military cap of Jordan.

The Battle of Karameh became highly symbolic for the Palestinian resistance movement due to the fast work of the Fatah propagandists: eager to seize control of the nascent PLO, the myths constructed around Karameh were welcomed by a Palestinian populace ready to believe that the skirmish was heroic and tragic, as opposed to dismal.[126] As details emerged of feats of luck and human endurance, Palestinian leaders contributed first-hand tales that would endure in the imagination of the refugees languishing in the camps for years to come. Khalil al-Wazir (Abu Jihad), a senior Palestinian leader, recounted that Palestinian fighters 'threw themselves at the Israeli tanks. Some climbed onto the tanks and put grenades inside them. Others had sticks of dynamite strapped to their bodies.'[127] That the events seem fantastical could cast doubt on al-Wazir's tale; certainly, it is highly unlikely that in light of the high number of Israeli forces present on the day of the battle, Palestinian guerrillas would have evaded enemy infantry and scaled the tanks, let alone entered them.[128] Further contradictions emerge when raconteurs emphasize that their forces punished 'Israeli arrogance' and humiliated the then Israeli Defence Minister, Moshe Dayan. At the height of his military career in 1968, Dayan was both the poster-boy of Israeli military might and the Palestinian nemesis, yet in the aftermath of the engagement at Karameh Dayan had not been suffering grave injuries incurred by plucky Palestinian guerrillas, but rather bed-ridden with injuries as a result of a cave-in at the Azur archaeological site.[129] Despite the disparities, the myth of Karameh proved crucial in developing Palestinian nationalism that had been suppressed during the 1950s and 1960s by the Transjordanian establishment. More crucially, the battle elevated the Palestinians from their doldrums and into a realm of heroism and feats of valour:

> Only Karameh was the antithesis of Refugee. The end of one road. The beginning of another. It brought to an end the Moatteren phase for the Palestinians and opened up the possibility where existential and political realities came together in an exquisitely aligned bond.[130]

At a time when the Palestinians were increasingly portrayed as help-less refugees, the battle afforded role models that symbolized cour-age, fortitude and reinvigorated the flagging morale that pervaded the Palestinian population following the Six-Day War.

Al-Wazir's narrative is not unusual and the equally admirable tales that relegate the involvement of Palestinian guerrillas to the back-ground are as popular among Jordanians. The response of Shaher Rawashdeh, a former major in the Jordanian army and present at the battle, was brief on Palestinian involvement: 'they were fighting for one hour in a small village. They killed some Israelis and then they withdrew and went south.'[131] When questioned whether the victory could be deemed a shared one Rawashdeh is unequivocal: 'No! Just Jordanian! Purely Jordanian, of course!'[132] In response to the final question concerning the emergence and endurance of narratives con-trary to the Jordanian perspective, the response was equally blunt: 'Those who say this have been ill-advised for a long time.'[133] Thus, just as contrary accounts issued by the Palestinians did not meet with patient ears then, nor do they now. Karameh ultimately proved to be a small reward that preceded an immense upheaval as the consequences of the Palestinian victory resonated in the Kingdom over the subse-quent ten years.

King Hussein's unease during Palestinian jubilation was well-founded as the increasing bluster of the *fedayeen* movement saw Palestinian guerrillas moving openly around the entire country, arms on display. Once the events of Karameh unfolded the perceived suc-cess of the guerrillas expanded within the Arab world, marginalizing the Jordanian dimension in terms of their military contribution and ability to safeguard their Jordanian interests. As the Jordanian army grew disquieted at the burgeoning military profile of the PLO's guer-rillas and the internal threat that they posed, the Kingdom was tense. Having created a 'state within a state', an attempt in February 1970 by the Jordanian government to curtail the powers of the PLO via decree escalated the situation, prompting an abrupt volte-face by Hussein. But it was too late: emboldened by their conquest at Karameh, the PFLP and DFLP proceeded to alter the course of Palestinian-host state relations, both in Jordan and Lebanon, through Black September, and in the process created a new, darker narrative that would overshadow the pride of Karameh.

Despite negative repercussions, the Battle of Karameh bore fruits for Fatah with 5,000 new members had signing up within 48 hours of the ceasefire.[134] Although Ali Hassan Salameh, an officer in Fatah, lowers the number of volunteers, the disparity between the initial number and the post-Karameh figure remains startling: 'Following the battle of Karameh, we were only 722. Suddenly, we were 3,000.'[135] Outside the region the triumph drew renewed support and established fresh networks of solidarity. Throughout Western Europe newspapers commenced new publications: *Resistencia* in Rome and Madrid; the *Free Palestine* magazine in London and the French *Comités de Solidarité*, the latter drawing a comparison between the Palestinian fighters and the French resistance movement. In West Germany *Resistentia* was followed by *Falastin al-Thaura* (Palestinian Revolution) in Bonn, *Palästina-Nachrichten* and *Freies Palästina*. As students pinned images of Palestinian *fedayeen* to their walls and the traditional keffiyeh was donned throughout Europe,[136] Fatah had excelled in thrusting the Palestinian cause into international consciousness. It was, however, a double-edged sword as equal numbers perceived the organization's activities during Black September in Jordan and at the 1972 Munich Olympics as barbaric, thus garnering support for the Israelis and sympathy for the Jordanian state.

Black September etched deeper scars into the relationship between the two communities and a noticeable sign of the enduring competition between Palestinian and Jordanian storytellers is perceptible in the history text books. A former history student of Palestinian origin, now in his 60s, 'Faisal' lamented the absent account of Palestinian participation in Jordanian school books: 'The government is trying to erase Palestinian endeavours from the history books. Why? To glorify Jordan and to make us look weak.' That the Jordanian government would rewrite history to portray itself both as protector and host indicates a desire to consolidate its own identity in spite of a burgeoning Palestinian one. Karameh assumes but one aspect of Palestinian identity in comparison to Black September, yet its role as a political milestone shared with the Jordanians renders it crucial in the application of othering in a domestic context.

The Silent Minorities: Chechen and Circassian Identities

Our problem is hundreds of years old. We are here 143 years already in Jordan. Everybody knows the Palestinians. No one knows us.[137]

While Palestinian-Jordanians comprise the majority of the Jordanian population and provide the most visible non-ethnic Jordanian element, the Circassian (Adyghe) and Chechen presence in the Kingdom eclipses the Palestinian-Jordanians with a record of longevity sustained by a significant role in the nations' development. Akin to their Palestinian counterparts, the Circassian and Chechen communities have maintained an identity and culture that has transcended generations since their arrival during the late nineteenth century. Arriving as refugees in Transjordan between 1878 and 1909 under the auspices of the Ottoman government,[138] the Circassians joined the Chechens who left the Karachay-Cherkess Autonomous Province in southern Russia during the Russian Tsar's occupation wars that raged between 1722 and 1917.[139] By the final battle in 1862, almost 1.5 million Circassians had been massacred, or died of exposure or starvation while fleeing into the mountain ranges; of the children that survived, the Russian soldiers retained them for target practice for their cannon shells.[140] Ten years later, the Circassian community entered Jordan and settled in Amman, Wadi Seer, Na'ur, Jerash, Sweileh, Zarqa and Azraq. Of the contemporary Circassian community, 90 per cent reside in the diaspora, scattered between Turkey and Jordan, with approximately 400,000 remaining in Russia and calls for an autonomous Circassia continue under the warning that an independent state would not pose a threat to Russia – but a divided one could.[141]

Fleeing Grozny in 1865, 50,000 Chechens entered Turkey, Syria and the Golan Heights, to be followed by a second wave in 1877 after the Chechen revolt against the Russians, then a third migration in 1901 during which settlements were established in Zarqa in 1902, Sweileh in 1905 and Al-Sukhna.[142] As Jordan emerged from the aftermath of World War II, the Chechen and Circassian communities asserted their presence in the new state, occupying key roles in the Jordanian government and security services. Similar to the Palestinian-Jordanians, they have maintained a separate identity through language, cultural events and narratives, while adopting a diverse approach to integration that contrasts with that of the Jordanian and Palestinian-Jordanian community.

Strongly contested over several centuries, the hostilities between the Ottomans and Tsarist Russia climaxed in the conquest of Chechnya in 1859 by the latter, initiating the migration of Chechens to neighbouring regions under Ottoman control, including Anatolia, Armenia and Azerbaijan.[143] Adapted from a Russian ethnonym pertaining to a lowland Chechen village, the 'Chechen' language constitutes a linguistic fusion of Russian, Kumyk – a variant of the Turkic language spoken in northern and eastern Caucasus – Arabic, Persian and Georgian.[144] Identifying themselves as *Nokhchi* – or *Nokhchuo* in the singular – the Chechen are Sunni Muslims of the Hanafi school, having converted between the seventeenth and nineteenth centuries. Since then, Islam has occupied a moderate yet central role in Chechen culture and ethnic identity, while the structure of society upholds principles of family and clan honour, deference to one's elders, hospitality, formal relations between families and clans, and courteous public and private behaviour.[145] These social values, shared by the Chechen and Jordanian communities, provided a pre-state foundation on which the monarchy could establish a close association – one that has enabled Chechen-Jordanians to become an inherent part of the Jordanian state.

The arrival of the Chechens in Jordan was preceded by the emergence of the nationalist-oriented Young Turks in the early twentieth century and the seizure of Anatolia, which prompted the Chechen diaspora to move deeper into the Ottoman Empire to parts of what would become Jordan, Syria and Iraq.[146] Ironically, while the Ottomans encouraged the Chechens to enter the empire as ballast against the encroaching Bedouin tribes of Arabia,[147] in later years the Chechen community would nurture strong loyalty to the Hashemite monarchy in spite of British opposition. In accordance with their religious path, *al-Naqshabandiyya*, they welcomed Emir Abdullah as a descendant of the Prophet Muhammad. Yet their allegiance to the leader can be viewed on a shrewder level: in return for their services and loyalty, Abdallah assured them of security and protection of their properties. The reciprocal nature of the relationship would ultimately extend to legislation and the Jordanian constitution through disproportionately high representation in the Chamber of Deputies, a legacy of the 1947 constitution and the subsequent 1952 amendment. In 1986, the Election Law redefined the practice of representing rural areas further through quotas for Christian, Chechen and Circassian minorities. Thus, the Chechen and Circassian community established their presence from the outset: by assisting the Emir during the early days of state formation, they consolidated their presence and secured favour with subsequent generations of the monarchy. In contrast to the Palestinians arriving from 1948 onwards, this favour has not been questioned due to the perceived modest behaviour of the Chechen and Circassian communities. While in recent years questions have been raised concerning support amidst the Chechen communities for leaders such as the late Dzhokbar Dudayev and successive Chechen militants, their muted displays of support within Jordan is perceived by both the Kingdom and the international community as more favourable than the activities of the PLO during the 1970s.

In the years preceding World War II, a fresh wave of Chechens arrived in Jordan. Following the demise of the Ottoman Empire and Russian sequestering of vast swathes of the Caucasus, the dilemma of Chechnya presented quandaries for the region. While in Europe the emergence of Nazism and Communism gained momentum, the Stalinist purges of the Soviet Army in the 1930s were succeeded by a war with Germany, which culminated in a Communist victory. Flushed with success, in 1944 the ruling Soviet authorities commenced a campaign of ethnic cleansing, compelling ethnic groups such as the Chechens to flee to Central Asia and towards the Middle East once more.[148] Settling in Zarqa (formerly known as Qasr Shabib), Al-Sukhna, Sweileh, Al-Azraq and Rusaifa, contemporary Chechens continue to dwell in the same areas their ancestors inhabited and are predominantly employed by the government, the army and the public services.[149] Due to the extent to which Chechen groups outside of the North Caucasus have been assimilated into the socio-political systems of their host states and the desire of various host governments to minimize the significance of the Chechen communities, an exact population figure is difficult to determine.[150] Nevertheless, speculative figures compiled during the 1990s suggest that the majority reside in Turkey (100,000), followed by Jordan (8,000), Egypt (5,000), Syria (4,000) and Iraq (2,500).[151] Affording equality and political rights, Jordan has developed an environment in which Chechen language, customs, traditions and significantly, their identity, flourish under full citizenship.

Coupled with the laissez-faire approach to politics, the Hashemite system of rule and the tribal composition of Jordanian society, one discovers separate Chechen and Circassian identities that have endured for more than a century. Similar to the Palestinian-Jordanians, the Chechens have established their own cultural centres, magazines and associations, the most notable being the Chechen Benevolent Association, founded in Zarqa in 1958 with branches in Sweileh, Al-Sukhna and Al-Azraq. Equally, the Association of the Friends of the Chechen Republic was established in 1989, the Chechen Women's Voluntary Society during the early 1980s, the Caucasian Club – the first Jordanian sports club – in 1932, and intellectual centres such as the Sultan Murad Centre for Chechen Studies, founded in Zarqa in 1994.[152] The centres also provide points of commemoration: for example, the Chechen Benevolent Association observes World Chechnya Day. In addition to centres and associations, the Chechen culture is sustained through clothing, pictures and marriage customs. Just as many Palestinian homes in Jordan hold pictures of both the Jordanian monarchy – usually King Hussein and/or King Abdullah II – and a figure from the Palestinian struggle, the Chechen community displays images of the Jordanian monarchy alongside Dudayev or the Sufi Imam Shamil.[153] Likewise, just as the Palestinian-Jordanian youth don the keffiyeh as a symbol of Palestine, young Chechens wear t-shirts with slogans calling for the liberation and independence of Chechnya.[154] In doing so, apparel for both the Palestinian-Jordanians and the Chechen Jordanians is indicative of the enduring struggle for the homeland lost 60 and 100 years ago, respectively.

Within the Circassian community, activities such as dance classes and communal meetings contribute towards a cohesive identity that exists within Jordanian society. Perceived as the 'silent diaspora', certain Circassians bristle at the attention lavished on the Palestinian-Jordanian predicament. Already resident in the area when King Abdullah I took power, the Circassians had been successful farmers and wealthy land-owners who, similar to the Chechens, worked closely with the king to forge the new nation. In turn, they have held the highest positions in government, including the office of prime minister. Perhaps the most politically renowned is the Al-Mufti family, of whom Saïd al Mufti served as prime minister.[155] Yet while the Chechen community sustains its ethnic identity through language, many Circassians do not speak the idiom of their forefathers and reflect sentiments more akin to those of the Palestinian-Jordanians through ripostes such as: 'I am Circassian, but my nationality is Jordanian', 'All of us consider our-selves Jordanian. This is our home' and 'We are truly Circassian and truly Jordanian. But a lot of Circassians want to go back'.[156] Replace 'Circassian' with 'Palestinian' and the resemblance is even starker.

While in the case of the Palestinian-Jordanian community the Palestinian culture and heritage is maintained through narrative, cus-toms, traditions and cultural events, the Chechen identity is predomi-nantly maintained through language. For third and fourth generation Jordanian Chechens, societal bilingualism has enabled them to express pride in their national origin and their Jordanian national identity.[157] The manner in which the language is maintained is also indicative of the nature of identity formation in the Chechen community. According to Dweik, while 96 per cent of respondents questioned exhibited a high knowledge of the ethnic language, 'the respondents' low proficiency in reading and writing Chechen reflects the oral method of acquiring the language, and underlines the fact that the Chechen language is mostly oral.'[158] Thus, the bond within the Chechen community is forged by the rule that members must speak Chechen to Chechens whenever possible, thereby safeguarding their identity, heritage and culture.

This undoubtedly necessitates both social and personal determina-tion: while the Chechen and Circassian communities are integrated in the Jordanian state, linguistic and cultural islands persist, thereby limiting the interaction of Chechens with Jordanian society and inten-sifying community ties. Secondly, the use of the Chechen language at home and in the community in daily interactions facilitates the endurance of the language. Thirdly, the positive attitude towards language and the homeland held by the Chechen Jordanians strengthens the community language position and facilitates its endurance. Fourthly, local community shops, sports clubs and community associations provide an environment in which Chechen is the dominant tongue, enabling the younger generation to be nurtured in an environment governed in Chechen. Lastly, Chechen reticence towards inter-ethnic marriages has preserved the language by ensuring that families have the same cultural background, which is conducive to opportunities to promote the language and culture maintenance, perhaps more so than in mixed marriages.[159] The role of language, then, provides the primary source of identity preservation within the Chechen and Circassian community.

The Chechen identity differs from their Palestinian and Circassian counterparts in Jordan in so far as Palestinian and Circassian identity is maintained through narratives, shared experiences, family ties in the homeland and associations and events. While the dialect provides a mutual feature among Palestinians, it is not strong enough to form a nuance that sustains the Palestinian identity to extent that the Chechen lexicon does for its speakers, owing to the linguistic commonality shared with the Jordanian population through the Arabic language. Accordingly, while the Chechen community enjoys an agreeable relationship with the host state in comparison to their Palestinian counterparts, it can be contended that they are simultaneously integrated into, and isolated from, Jordanian society to a greater extent.

Conclusion

A melange of Jordanian stoicism and Palestinian caprice, the Palestinian-Jordanian identity is in a constant flux, oscillating between the indefinable entity that the individual has harboured throughout life and a vociferous protest at their political predicament in contemporary Jordanian society. Likewise, the relationship between the Palestinian-Jordanian and ethnic Jordanian community is characterized by tensions arising from the tussle for dominance among the Palestinian majority and the Jordanian minority. Amidst the protagonists, the Chechen and Circassian community has rested quietly, enjoying prominent positions in the government and security services, while attracting little acknowledgement for their support of the Chechen cause.

The politico-historical dimension represents a hub of recollection and national narrative: through the Battle of Karameh substantial differences emerge from the Palestinian and Jordanian accounts, both of which indicate the efforts of both communities to rewrite history. In doing so, when the heroic role of David against Israel's Goliath is bestowed, it is invariably to the detriment of the other, who is undermined. As Jordan struggles to control the burgeoning Palestinian-Jordanian identity, historical accounts of triumphant feats are crucial to consolidate their position as a host state, as opposed to a temporary Palestinian state. The influence of Karameh on the Palestinian and Jordanian identities in Jordan has been substantial, though Black September can be viewed to have etched further profound scars on the Palestinian-Jordanian relationship. Karameh is but a small aspect of Palestinian identity in comparison to Black September, yet its legacy renders it a crucial juncture in terms of identity and perception of the 'other'.

Multifarious, the Palestinian-Jordanian identity is both discerned from and associated with the Jordanian identity through the linguistic element of the Palestinian-Jordanian identity. Dialect and language assume a crucial role equal to that of a political and cultural orientation and affords an insight into not only the maintenance of the Palestinian identity in the diaspora, but also the dynamic between the Palestinian-Jordanian and Jordanian community as each group endeavours to integrate or isolate the other, retain or gain a stake in the power of the state, all the while nurturing private national objectives. Yet while dialect provides a mutual feature among Palestinians it lacks potency to encapsulate and sustain the Palestinian identity to a similar extent as in the Chechen example. As a result, the Chechen community provides an apt example of identity preservation in the diaspora that does not come at the price of domestic stability, integration and social cohesion.

5

THE SOCIO-ECONOMICS
OF IDENTITY

To comprehend the Palestinian-Jordanian relationship, it is necessary to explore their position in the economic development of the Kingdom. A simultaneous downturn in economic circumstances while on the cusp of a new life in a country adopted during wartime bears repercussions on the evolution of identity, most notably within the following demographic groups: the elite, the middle class and the refugees. As previously observed, Palestinians in Jordan experience inequity differently to their ethnic Jordanian counterparts due to the legislative framework in place in the Kingdom. The dichotomy between the affluent Palestinian-Jordanians and the refugee inhabitants of the Gaza Camp near Jerash contributes to a varied approach to the preservation of the Palestinian identity. When dire, the conditions of the refugee camps are conducive to a greater awareness of 'being Palestinian', in comparison with contemporaries residing in the prosperous districts of Amman. Yet despite the pecuniary differences, concern is shared by both parties for the future of Palestine and concerted efforts to maintain their Palestinian heritage is sustained. In contrast, there remain Palestinian-Jordanians who advocate that full integration into the largely Jordanian-dominated elite – the bastion of upper government employees, magnates and high-ranking military officials – requires but one identity: Jordanian.

Since this pressure develops within an environment in which the majority of powerful positions are held by Jordanians, credence is accorded to the notion that wealthy Palestinian-Jordanians confront a quandary: to express or suppress their identity? Just as pecuniary assets signify boundaries of class, so too do the maintenance and expression of one's identity vary according to the needs and expectations of the individual and the environment in which they reside. To fully comprehend the nuances of this environment, the treble tiers of society must be explored: first, the elite, both as a social and economic entity; second, the rise, fall and prospects of the Jordanian middle class; and third, the Palestinian inhabitants of the refugee camps, some of whom fit aptly into the category of 'middle class', while others remain in the lower income bracket. In turn, the ambiguity that suffuses the socio-economic dimension will be clarified to present a clear analysis of the contemporary Palestinian-Jordanian identity.

The Jordanian Economy

The rentier state is a state of parasitic, decaying capitalism, and this circumstance cannot fail to influence all the socio-political conditions of the countries concerned.[1]

Through his poignant observation above, Lenin heralded an era that would be replete with states sustained by rentierism and semi-rentierism. Certainly, for a large proportion of Palestinian-Jordanians who arrived in the aftermath of the 1948 and 1967 Wars, the ensuing economic peaks and troughs contributed to their social standing and self-perception. Following the transfer of independence from the British Mandate to the fledgling Kingdom on 25 May 1946, the economic phenomenon of rentierism had a sustained impact on Jordanian society. On his accession to the throne in 1921, King Abdallah I ensured a monthly subsidy of £5,000 to be bestowed by the British Colonial Office through subsidies to the civil administration, Arab Legion and the Crown. By the mid-1920s, this figure gradually approached £100,000 per annum and £2 million by the mid-1940s.[2] The ensuing conflict in the region that would last for more than 60 years provided both an advantage and hindrance to the Jordanian economy. Just as the influx of Palestinian refugees applied a pecuniary pressure, so too did the aid directed at the refugees provide an alleviation, albeit brief. Nevertheless, criticism persisted from Palestinian sectors on the motivation of the 'poor cousin' of the Arab world to absorb refugees, particularly as the aid was recorded as official transfers, in spite of its non-governmental status.[3]

Rentierism, however, brings both boons and burdens in equal measure, the foremost being its influence on the state outlook towards domestic affairs. This is particularly significant as state autonomy is strengthened by its access to externally generated economic reserves.[4] Since revenues are predominantly dependent on sources other than taxes, the state is less constrained by the interests of domestic actors and coercion becomes less important, since political legitimacy is purchased through economic rewards. In such an environment, citizenship becomes a commodity as the individual cherishes it as an economic resource that facilitates employment, social welfare supports and other economic rewards to be distributed by the state.[5] The exclusion from employment of Palestinian refugees of Gazan origin due to the citizenship and passport laws only emphasizes the significance of legislation in defining the identity of the Palestinian refugees, holding as they do few privileges associated with Jordanian citizenship.

By the 1970s, Jordan had attained full rentier-statehood and its economy unflinchingly bore the scars of its dalliance. Rentierism had become as much a feature of the Kingdom as its monarchy. Since its inception, the Jordanian predilection for rentierism at the behest of the neighbouring Arab states had enabled it to become inextricably intertwined with the economic phenomenon. By the onset of the 1967 Six-Day War, Jordan had lost control of the West Bank and with it approximately one-third of the Kingdom's economy. At the same time, the already financially beleaguered state began to receive increasing levels of Arab economic and military aid, with foreign grants accounting for approximately 58 per cent of all government revenues between 1967 and 1972. Between 1973 and 1974 and between 1979 and 1980, increases in world oil prices contributed towards a six-fold increase in the Kingdom's GNP between 1980 and 1983, and confirmed Jordan's status as a rentier-state.[6] In addition to foreign assistance that was largely drawn from petrodollar sources, the remittances gathered from the expatriate earnings of Palestinian-Jordanians and Jordanians employed in the petroleum industry in the Gulf states stimulated a boom in the development of the public sector and the GDP. In the decade following 1973, worker's remittances peaked at approximately JD 475 million in 1984, constituting more than a quarter of Jordan's GDP. Furthermore, in 1978, members of the Arab League meeting in Baghdad pledged a ten-year period of financial support, including U.S. $1.25 billion per year for Jordan. Between 1973 and 1980, foreign assistance accounted for over 50 per cent of Jordanian government revenue, while government expenditures represented almost 70 per cent of the GDP.[7]

As the 1970s yielded 'the Years of Plenty',[8] the global upsurge in raw materials contributed considerably towards growth in both aid and remittances; moreover, the culmination of the civil war attracted Arab aid, while the Rabat Arab League assembly of 1974 and the Camp David talks and agreement (1978–1979) enhanced the influx of financial assistance.[9] The contribution to the aid economy by the United Nations agencies, especially the United Nations Relief and Works Agency for the Palestinian Refugees (UNRWA), also provides aid in kind to the Palestinians residing in Jordan, thereby easing the strain on the fragile Jordanian economy.

The 'Years of Plenty' were to prove finite and the 1980s brought forth a renewed barrage of war and economic misfortune. As the members of the Organization of the Petroleum Exporting Countries (OPEC) observed their oil earnings slump under reduced demand, the diminished revenues contributed to the curtailment of economic aid by almost 50 per cent from U.S. $9,585.7 million in 1980 to U.S. $4,978.3 million in 1983. By 1989, the levels had dwindled to U.S. $1,486.6 million.[10] As the decade drew to a close, the Jordanian economy crumbled in the face of ineffectual government responses to three major events: the Iran-Iraq War (1980–1988), the demise of the oil boom and the repudiation of Jordan's claim to sovereignty over the West Bank.[11] The outbreak of the Iran-Iraq War temporarily boosted the Jordanian economy through an increase in both economic assistance

and the opportunities for trade with Iraq in return for Jordanian loyalty. By 1984, however, the Iraqis entered a cash deficit as a result
of the war and Jordan was once more plunged into economic despair
amidst global contempt for their misplaced loyalty.

The drop in oil prices shocked the Jordanian economy. The
Kingdom's dependency on transfers from oil producers compelled her
to adapt to the reduction at the same time as the loss of an equal
source of hard currency in the form of worker's remittances.[12] As the
Intifada unfolded towards the end of 1987, it constituted a dominant
factor in Jordan's disengagement from the West Bank in 1989, for
pecuniary as well as political reasons. Dire economic circumstances
further hastened the move as the cost of supporting the West Bank in
conjunction with further political pressures prompted King Hussein
to formally sever legal and administrative ties on 31 July 1988. In
doing so, he saved the Jordanian economy U.S. $60 million annually
on salaries and development projects,[13] but raised permanent questions
concerning Jordan's stance vis-à-vis the Palestinians.

The disengagement provided scant economic respite and between
1987 and 1989 GNP decreased from U.S. $6,619 million to U.S. $3,673
million, annual inflation soared from 0.2 to 25.8 per cent and government debt escalated from U.S. $1 billion to U.S. $8.5 billion between
1981 and 1989. This was accompanied by a rise in unemployment by
16 to 20 per cent in 1991 at the peak of the Gulf War (1990–1991). By
the early 1990s the Kingdom had become the unfortunate holder of
the title of 'one of the most heavily indebted countries in the world'.[14]
As the 'Years of Plenty' dwindled, the foremost foundations of Jordan's
rentier economy, workers' remittances and petrodollar foreign aid, began
a steady descent from U.S. $2.3 billion in 1981 to U.S. $1.5 billion in
1987 as a growing number of expatriate workers returned to Jordan.[15]

Politically, Jordan fared just as disappointingly: initially lauded as a
political achievement – despite the ambivalent public response within
the Kingdom – disengagement was not without socio-economic dis-
advantages as Palestinian residents of both the East and West Bank
were uncertain whether their Jordanian citizenship would be rescinded
by the state. The atmosphere of anxiety was reflected in consumer
and investment confidence as domestic relations unfolded across the

Palestinian-dominated public sector in Amman and Palestinian capital commenced a steady outflow from Jordanian banks.[16] But just as one community drifted away, another emerged. In 1991, the Kingdom absorbed a wave of 300,000 expatriates as they fled Kuwait during the Gulf War and as the families resettled into their new lives in Jordan, adjusting to a new life that often depended on an income less ample than they were accustomed to, with only 7.5 per cent of Gulf returnees maintaining their previous level of income in the Gulf once in Jordan.[17] As the new residents adjusted to life in the host state, reactions were ambivalent, for many of the new generation continued to look towards Palestine as a homeland, while holding fast to the Gulf states as a secondary home. Compared with the decadent malls and ample entertainment of their former cities, the then less-developed Amman was found wanting and for some it would be many years before Jordan could be even tentatively called 'home'.[18]

In response to the rapid downturn in economic events, Prime Minister Zaid Rifa'i introduced tighter fiscal policies and ventured a policy of further borrowing sponsored by the International Monetary Fund (IMF) and a series of expansionary policies that reduced foreign exchange reserves.[19] During the 1970s and 1980s, Jordan had relied heavily on external borrowing and Arab aid to support fiscal as well as account deficits. As the effects of previous ill-advised polices and external events emerged, the state's influence over macroeconomic policy slackened, resulting in widening fiscal deficits and distributional conflicts.[20] The IMF's intervention to contain the economic crisis of the Kingdom enabled Jordan to obtain U.S. $273 million in standby credits, in exchange for an agreement of a five-year stabilization program with the IMF.[21] Nevertheless, the government's unpopular economic reforms, introduced in an endeavour to appease international lenders, drew protest at the imposed daily subsidies from both Jordanian and Palestinian citizens alike.

On 18 April 1989 public dissatisfaction climaxed and riots erupted in a plethora of regime strongholds, commencing in Ma'an and spreading rapidly to southern towns and villages.[22] By the time the unrest was contained, at least 11 people were dead and scores were injured of the estimated 2,000 participants.[23] Though a subsequent change in leadership stabilized the Kingdom, it was a momentary adjustment and the threat of unrest affected future attempts by the state and the international community to challenge socially explosive situations concerning subsidies and employment, most memorably during the Karak 'bread riots' in 1996.[24] The chain of events that commenced with Black September in 1970 and continued through the Iran-Iraq War brought a decline in aid, the outbreak of the first Gulf War, a decrease in remittances and a resultant upsurge in the population.

The events wreaked havoc upon the economy and redefined socio-economic divisions in Jordanian society. During the clashes between the Jordanian and Palestinian forces, a British economic journal observed that:

> Economic activity [...] was sharply curtailed (in June, 1970) [...] For over a week Amman, the country's only commercial centre of any importance, was paralysed as rival factions fought in the streets [...] Business activity has remained slack since then and is likely to continue so for the near future. In many respect it has been a depressing period for Jordan's economy.[25]

The Iran-Iraq War initially provided relief to the Jordanian economy through a series of soft loans and grants agreed upon with President Saddam Hussein to the sum of U.S. $189.2 million and U.S. $58.3 million respectively. The majority of the funds facilitated the restoration of the port at Aqaba and the road between Aqaba and Iraq, thereby serving both external and domestic interests.[26] Despite the financial injection, Jordan remained on shaky ground and the Jordanian-Iraqi arrangement soon floundered amidst fears of an Iranian invasion. In turn, an enhanced defence expenditure in the Gulf states and Kuwait prompted a vast redistribution of economic resources into the military sector that increased by U.S. $535 million in 1980–1981, U.S. $712 million in 1981–1982, and U.S. $833 million in 1982–1983, providing the largest increases in 30 years.[27]

By the end of the twentieth century, the Jordanian government had succeeded in implementing a number of initiatives to staunch the bleeding economy. Reduced government debt developed the macroeconomic circumstances of the Kingdom positively: a program of privatization was initiated under the supervision of the IMF; spending was reduced from the military budget and the post-1994 economic boycott of Israel was rescinded.[28] The decision of the government to raise taxes in 1996 as a result of further IMF needling on consumer subsidies prompted a renewed round of protest in Karak and other cities and towns. The biting economic reforms and the stalling of the peace process exacerbated the discontent of Jordanians of both East Bank and Palestinian origin. Sentiments of betrayal towards state acquiescence vis-à-vis the peace agreement, and resentment regarding the elite's perceived determination to 'use whatever means in its disposal in order to ensure its political survival'[29] fuelled the riots.

Yet the 1996 protest was stronger and, due to their vested interests, the response of the elite to send military units to control the demonstrations emphasized a new, defiant stance. Equally, whereas the demonstrators in 1989 differentiated between the fiscal sources of their discontent and their sentiments towards the monarchy (to whom they were loyal and uncritical) by 1996 the scepticism was less concealed and the intimate relationship between state, monarchy and elite bristled with barely concealed animosity. Finally, King Hussein's response reflected a shift in relations, as he steadfastly stood by Prime Minister Kabariti's implementation of the subsidies and reasoned the benefits of the structural adjustment program.[30] The line of argument pursued by the king only served to rub salt to the wounds of those most punished by the consumer subsidies, those of low income in the provinces. More crucially, the benefits of the economic structural adjustment program were widely believed to remain in the capital while the costs would be met by the poorer sections of society.

As the socio-economic gap widened and the elite crept closer to the government and monarchy, subsidies and the rising cost of living pushed the middle class towards the lower end of the economic spectrum. Rapidly, a unique evolution began to take place in the class sector. The identities of Palestinians, Palestinian-Jordanians and Jordanians from all socio-economic backgrounds evolved to accommodate the changing economic circumstances, with some forsaking their origins in a bid to be accepted, while others lucidly displayed their allegiance to their homeland through editorials and public displays, which had an impact on their progress through Jordanian society.

An Elite Perspective

For once Palestinians in the homeland build their state, there will be nothing '*Palestinian*' about them. They will be just another people with a state, now cut off from all that the name *Palestinian* has historically conferred on Palestinians everywhere.[31]

The Palestinian diaspora arrived in an economic maelstrom, with just as many who had lost their assets as those who retained them due to familial connections or having assistance from charities such as Caritas. The latter group signified the arrival of a new elite in Jordan, the Palestinian elite, comprising the traditional urban elite (mayor and municipal council members) and the professional elite (doctors, lawyers and engineers). The arrival of a communications elite (journalists and writers) and a business elite (made up of merchants and landowners) as well as members of the academic community and Islamic religious establishment[32] combined to make the Palestinian elite a truly diverse social category. With time, however, integration drew Palestinian families into the Jordanian elite, which had been previously characterized by the presence of high-ranking government and military officials, politicians and noble families. While in certain instances being one of the elite provided a satisfying status in society, others craved difference, whether driven by power or enhanced integration. For others, the achievement of progressive social integration and financial security arrived with a sacrifice: their very 'Palestinianess'.

It is interesting to note at this point that despite the predominance of Jordanians occupying the elite of contemporary Jordan, the origins of that elite can be traced to the neighbouring states, including Palestine, Syria and the Hijaz, a fact aptly illustrated by the Kingdom's first three Prime Ministers, who were all of Syrian origin.[33] When national identities come into play, origins are quickly overlooked, as the political analyst Dr Labib Kamhawi notes: 'There is no original population. You have Jordanians of Palestinian origin, of Syrian origin, Circassian origin, of Hijazi origin – all sorts of people. To us, this is a transit country connecting so many states together.'[34] The merging of the Palestinian into the Jordanian elite was a gradual process. Unlike their established cohorts, many Palestinians worked their way into the sphere of the privileged. As a member of the commercial and professional classes contributing to Jordan's economic development, they consolidated the new elite. Business-oriented entrepreneurs who invested in trade and finance, agriculture, and industry eventually became the prosperous owners of banks and businesses, while others attained high-ranking positions in government and as members of parliament.[35]

The elite in Jordan largely consists of ex-officials in the employ of the government as ministers and at times former high-ranking army officers, though they are very limited and their involvement is minimal due to retirement. In contrast to neighbouring Israel, where the elite is drawn from military circles into roles such as leaders of political parties and organizations, trade unions and women's organizations, in Jordan those who hold the power to influence the opinion of society retire to the pages of the daily newspapers, where they are no less influential:

> They are really shaping the public opinion and they represent our society through their columns, especially the daily columns. He [the columnist] has influence in society, he has his own presence and many ways to shape opinions and this is different to other Arab countries.[36]

The business sector equally holds a share in the power stakes in Jordanian society. Over the last ten years, privatization measures were accelerated and a fluid transition from the business to the government sector emerged as partnerships between businesses and government divisions became frequent and business owners entered the government as ministers. Including royal advisors, leading families, security chiefs and wealthy Palestinians, the elite has entered the royal circle in an endeavour to ensure access to influential positions and sate common interests.[37] The parliament and the Upper House have not been excluded from the shift and the universities have been drawn into the process, albeit to a lesser extent, as the cultural, social, political, economic and intellectual realities draw a minority from academia into the realms of the political elite.

The elite and middle class of Palestinian origin in Jordan differ not only in terms of socio-economic background, but their history with the Kingdom and to a degree their ideologies. Already comprising powerful families from Palestine who had enjoyed special relations with the monarchy, the elite differ from the middle class insofar as the middle class confronted the challenge of re-establishing their businesses in a new country. Prominent families such as the Nashashibis launched alliances with the monarchy and acknowledged the annexation of the West Bank by Jordan in 1950. In return, they achieved access to high positions in Jordanian society. For less affluent compatriots, access to such positions has been tainted with the bitterness of discrimination, as Ahmed, a resident of the Rusaifeh camp in Jordan, relates:

> You can feel it and touch it while you're going to have a job opportunity in the government. You will find that there are many people who are less qualified and though you are more qualified, they have a better chance of getting the job. Only because you are Palestinian.[38]

The Nashashibis represented one of the foremost families in the Palestinian community during the Mandate and progressed to appointments in the Jordanian Senate in the early years of the annexation, with five of the eight West Bank Arabs appointed to the Senate holding ties to the dynasty.[39] The dilemma of supporting Hashemite hegemony or continuing the fight for Palestinian independence weighed heavily on ruling families such as the 'Abd al-Hadi, Dajani, Tuqan, Jayyusi and Nusaybah.[40] The temptations of the Hashemite inner circle clouded the moral obligations set by identity and heritage: prosperity and influential positions in the Jordanian government guaranteed a continuation of the living standards they were accustomed to, but at what price? Certainly, the inevitable consequence of losing the opportunity to represent the Palestinian people would be provoking the antipathy of thousands of refugees in the camps and around Jordan, who relied on the dominant Palestinian families to support and promote their cause.

The struggle between moral and social aspirations was to be resolved outside the Palestinian aristocracies' control. In 1974, the Arab Summit Conference in Rabat approved the PLO, prompting the monarchy to reduce its support for the ruling families.[41] Funds, salaries, industrial and agricultural subsidies diminished, as did the support held by the Palestinian elite for their new benefactors, the Hashemites. By the mid-1970s, even the most fervent of monarchists openly promoted their support for the PLO and the creation of a separate Palestinian entity in the West Bank and Gaza. The elite were reunited with their Palestinian heritage in word and deed, but how far in terms of identity? The dual courtship of the ruling families kindles a sense of scepticism. The fickle manner in which the wave of public opinion was mastered denotes an awareness of their environment and perhaps that moral obligation or self-interest triumphed in the name of preservation. Despite the moral quandaries, a dual Palestinian-Jordanian identity was born. Characterized by insouciance towards the question of being Palestinian or Jordanian, the elite inhabit the affluent northwest of Amman, where Palestinians and Jordanians live side-by-side. The region of Jabal Amman is an apt example, where housing units are often joined and Jordanians and Palestinians of the upper economic stratum coexist within an equal society.[42]

That members of the Palestinian elite primarily opposed the monarchy and supported and engaged in opposition party activities reveals not only the complexities of the Palestinian identity, but also the presence of an additional pan-Arab or pan-Islamic nature.[43] Sub-identities within the Palestinian identity are not uncommon, though it is more perceptible in the camp environment where the call of *min an-nahr lil-bahr*, the liberation of Palestinians, by Islamic candidates appeals to Jordanians of Palestinian origin, presenting as it does a positive alternative to camp residents.[44] Fathi's observation that the continuation in Jordan of the traditional combination of kinship and lineage is in keeping with Tachau's theory that 'the more traditional the society, the more prominent is descent likely to be in the identification of the élite'[45] demonstrates how cultural conventions persist.

It is interesting to note that the Palestinian identity was potent enough among the proponents of the Hashemite establishment to experience the sting dealt by the brother of a former Prime Minister, 'Abd al-Hadi Majali, in a public speech in January 1977. Addressing the issue of Jordanian identity and the question of dual loyalty, Majali asserted that it may be for the best if Jordanians of Palestinian origin, particularly those who claimed to be the victims of discrimination, would realize their political rights in Palestine.[46] The darker side to this proclamation is that it vocalized the concerns of many Jordanians who would not be disappointed to see the Palestinians of Jordan 'repatriated' to Palestine, a detail not lost on the Palestinian-Jordanian elite.[47] And figures demonstrate that their fears are not unfounded: from 1989 the composition of the Jordanian parliament and cabinet has exhibited a reduced number of representatives of the Palestinian majority of the populace.[48] Despite a Palestinian-Jordanian presence within the ranks of government, the Jordanian Foreign Minister, His Excellency Nasser S. Judeh, maintains that 'Every system has its flaws [...] it's not as colourful and controversial as people make it out to be, to my mind. If there are flaws, certainly every government who comes in tries to fix them and no system's perfect.'[49] That the long arm of Jordanian patriotism affects even the Palestinian-Jordanian elite illustrates that the group, despite its affluence and connections, is not integrated and the sense of 'Palestinianess' prevails enough to recognize the affront.

A leading proponent of the Jordanian exclusivist movement, the counsellor for press and cultural affairs at the Jordan National Bank, Nahed Hattar, endures court cases and criticism to promulgate the notion of the 'true Jordanian'. A speculative concept in itself, Hattar expressed his perception of the nature of Jordanian society through the article '*Man Huwa al-Urduni?*'[50] or 'Who is Jordanian?'. Over ten years on, Hattar maintains his stance: that the Jordanians are concerned about the sizeable Palestinian-Jordanian community in Jordan and that this fear is likely to contribute towards the reduced number of Palestinian-Jordanians in positions of authority in Jordanian government:

> They [the Jordanians] said, 'we are the *real* people, we are the original people of this state; they [the Palestinians] did not come from Jordan: how can they rule? They still have their rights – it is not here – their rights are in Palestine.' This is the real issue.[51]

When asked whether the Palestinian identity was perceptibly stronger amongst the Palestinian-Jordanians of a lower income capacity than those residing in the upper echelons of Jordanian society, Hattar associated the 'higher class' and 'middle class' of Palestinian-Jordanians with 'the spirit of merging inside the society they are living'[52] as their attachment to the Palestinian society – their old society – is less so than those of a lower income and the refugees. His reasoning is equally based in the socio-economic and sentimental, since 'poor people are always more spiritually emotional and patriotic than the rich; that's why they are more likely to be involved in thinking of Palestine and going back home. The Palestinian people – they are refugees wherever they are going, they don't have a state and they have their Palestinian loyalty. They are not loyal to anyone.'[53] Such an approach is not limited to the Palestinian international community as the low income Jordanian would be less likely to leave his homeland, in comparison to the wealthier Jordanian, who will be more willing to relocate to another country in order to enhance his or her educational or professional opportunities.

Yet certain Palestinian-Jordanians perceive a degree of Machiavellianism over the representation and concealment of the Palestinian identity amongst members of the Palestinian-Jordanian elite:

> Some elite from the Jordanian communities believe that this is the way to keep benefits, privileges and advantages. Part of the Palestinian elite, they show off by raising these issues [Palestine] and it sometimes helps in elections and campaigns in particular.[54]

By contrast, 'on a grassroots level, I don't think that this is a major issue and there is a very great deal of integration and marriages between Jordanians and Palestinians.'[55] Certainly, the Jordanian elite's concern with social survival outranks that of their contemporaries in Yemen and Egypt. The motivation for such social vigilance resides in Jordan's state formation, since 'the lack of historical legitimacy for the Jordanian state has an unintended consequence; that is, the survival of the élite and the survival of the state have been strongly linked'.[56] Historically, the elite emanated from the political strata during a period in which political parties dominated Jordanian society. During the last 40 years, however, the emergency martial law was enacted and subsequently curtailed elite activities within society. Through the measure, the government aspired to consolidate its efforts to introduce a balance and enable an active and influential role for itself. Alas this was not to be the case and the measure had a limited impact on the exploits of the elite, Jordanian and Palestinian-Jordanian alike.

It is, however, imperative to distinguish between the attitudes of the Jordanian elite and the Palestinian-Jordanian elite. For the Jordanian elite, the question of Palestine has been contentious when considered alongside the prospect of political liberalization. Free elections and full political participation for the Palestinians would bestow a level of power that could challenge the existing Jordanian elite as the population, and hence the majority of Palestinian-Jordanian and Palestinian residents, continues to increase. To preclude a potential threat to the ruling elite and the core constituents of East Bankers, the elite orchestrated a process of liberalization, electoral rules and laws that would ensure a disproportionate distribution of seats, thereby intensifying the representation of the East Bank residents and rendering areas comprising a Palestinian majority largely under-represented.[57]

Although the relationship between the elite has seen ruptures along lines of the elite and the working classes, as well as the Jordanian and Palestinian-Jordanian populations, the 1970s provided a brief respite from the tensions. The buoyant economic climate and free enterprise system enhanced employment opportunities and Jordanian and Palestinian businessmen established joint enterprises, working side-by-side in the professions. In such an environment, the Palestinians cast aside their past frustrations with the Jordanian monopoly of political power, while the political elites of both communities 'substituted a new interest in economic advancement and material consumerism for past involvement in political activity'.[58] A clear correlation between the economic circumstances of the individual and their level of attachment to the concept of 'home' and, in turn, their identity, therefore exists:

> Those who live in the camps of course feel they are a part of their country [Palestine] more than those who live in Abdoun or Shmeisani. They have their businesses and live a luxury life. For the people of the Gaza Camp it's the worst because it's even difficult to find a job, travel, have proper documents, or to attend universities and schools. Those people are totally Palestinian. Those who have good businesses and are involved in the political life are even more integrated in the society and they are not the same, at all.[59]

An alternative perspective worthy of consideration is assets as a stimulus towards Jordanization. Rather than income representing the dividing factor, Palestinian-Jordanians of the middle- to high-income bracket do not gravitate towards community clusters, but opt to dwell in diverse areas that are indicative of advanced integration. Equally, when asked what could make their life easier in Jordan, low-income Palestinian-Jordanians responded: 'relatives in the security and government', since *wasta* and favours are perceived to ease life in Jordan substantially.[60] By no means limited to Jordan, the Kingdom's tribal structures assume an integral role in the endurance of *wasta* and family names locate an individual within a defined social framework, affording him or her a position in the societal hierarchy of tribal and family influences.[61] That over 65 per cent of Jordanian citizens would seek *wasta* when they need 'to get something done at a government office, a company of organisation' is testament to the prevalence of the concept in contemporary Jordanian society.[62] Thus, it is not money that kindles the progressive Jordanization of the middle- and high-income Jordanian-Palestinians, but rather a

stake in the power share of key Jordanian institutions. The greater
the power share, the more representation is enjoyed and integration
is conducive to admittance to a society in a more active and favourable manner. By contrast, the low-income population has little or
no representation from the camps in the institutions and not only
does this override their rights, but it also compounds the isolation
between the low-income areas and the Kingdom at large. That their
socio-economic circumstances offer a limited chance they will be
able to afford to leave the camp reinforces the Palestinian identity
within a strongly Palestinian environment in Jordan.

Yet even within the circles of the high-income elite, boundaries are
imposed that fortify the differences between the two communities. It
is worth noting that though certain individuals express a reluctance to
employ the term 'communities' in conjunction with a debate concerning the Palestinian-Jordanians and Jordanians, it is necessary nonetheless to distinguish, since an awareness of 'difference' endures. It would
be pusillanimous to shy away from such linguistic clarifications, particularly as the issue is less than conspicuous in Jordanian society, as
Kamhawi notes:

> Most of my friends are Jordanian and when they talk politics or
> about the government they address each other and they don't
> even look [at] us [Jordanians of Palestinian origin], because they
> believe that it is not our business. Although we are very good
> friends, and many times I say, 'listen guys, why are you talking
> like this? Maybe *I* want to become involved, what do you think?'
> and they respond 'Oh, of course! Of course!'[63]

The inadvertent exclusion of individuals from aspects of political discussion can, then, reinforce the sense of difference and thereafter enable the continuance of the individual's identity. As Kamhawi states,
the Palestinian identity is maintained in spite of discreet Jordanization
'by being Palestinians. Jordan is first, of course, but if this means
Jordan first and we have to forget everything else, this is not correct.
If Jordan first means we have to forget Palestine and forget any links
with Palestine, this is of course wrong.'[64] Just as the consequences of

subsisting in less adequate conditions on a lower income in the refugee camps can promote a heightened sense of Palestinian identity, so too can subtle social slurs such as those described by Kamhawi reinforce a sense of identity amongst the Palestinian-Jordanian elite.

The Mythical Middle Class

When considering the character of the middle class in Jordan, it is vital to distinguish between the socio-economic revolution that occurred in late nineteenth-century Europe, which gave rise to the new middle class, and the evolution of the class structure in contemporary Jordan. Arising from this uniqueness is an ambiguity that has fuelled views within the Jordanian middle class and elite that the middle class is diminishing, a victim of the turbulent economy. Yet others contend that it is ever present. The certainty with which views are expounded as well as the wealth of literature that supports the latter renders questionable whether the demise of the middle class is merely a by-product of the current economic climate. Droeber's study of young middle-class women affirms the notion of a middle class existing in contemporary Jordan, comprising professionals, the petty bourgeois and holders of executive or administrative positions in business and government agencies. Nevertheless, the middle class did not escape Jordan's integration into a world market economy unscathed, with shifting economic structures, burgeoning urbanization and the influx of a more urbanized Palestinian refugee population having a significant impact on the socio-economic environment.[65] The resultant social stratification affirms the notion that a middle class exists in Jordan and has created a significant role within the society as a whole, bridging the economic gap between those languishing in poverty and the elite.

As a means to apply a degree of order to the economic chaos of society, the categorization of 'elite', 'middle class' and 'lower income' is successful insofar as it distinguishes between groups of varying income levels. Yet when coupled with the capricious nature of the economy and the volatile political and military disposition of the region, these social classifications are rendered ineffective. When reviewed in conjunction with the affluent nature of the former expatriate refugees who fled the Gulf States, the middle class enters a state of flux that varies annually by profession, income level and origins. It is this fluid-ity that has prompted the notion that Jordan no longer holds a middle class. In its place exists a burgeoning elite that consumes the upper middle class into its lower echelons and a broadening lower-income bracket, which absorbs the lower middle class.

The phenomenon is by no means recent: according to the *Survey of Employment, Unemployment, and Poverty* carried out by the Department of Statistics in 1961 and 1991, the middle class initially comprised employ-ees in the professional technical, sales and clerical sectors. By 1991, a shift in criterion had emerged, as sales workers were re-categorized as 'working class', and professional technical and clerical workers were replaced by professionals, semi-professionals and clerks.[66] Nevertheless, the middle class is attributable to one of the following theories of emergence: primarily, that there is no middle class: in times of high unemployment, the lower-income group absorbs those residing in the lesser income section of the middle class, while the remainder joins the 'upper class', creating a socio-economic vacuum. Secondly, that the educational and professional backgrounds of those constituting the middle class is varied to the point of rendering an accurate classifica-tion unfeasible, since many of those deemed refugees are equal holders of certificates of higher education that would enable them to exist as both refugees and members of the middle class. Finally, that they do not constitute a class, but rather a category that is neither very rich, nor very poor, but struggling between the two extremes. Although for many the primary classification is the most plausible in contemporary society, it is more likely that a juxtaposition of the second and final category contributes to the formation of the contemporary Palestinian-Jordanian middle class. Thus their fluidity, manifested in their endeav-ours to avoid going lower, while striving to go higher, is conducive to an ambiguity that remains their most dominant characteristic.

In its role as a regional transit state, Jordan has absorbed both waves and trickles of refugees and migrants of varying economic backgrounds seeking opportunities in employment and education. Incorporating the aforementioned Gulf returnees, adjusting from a substantial income to a quintessential 'middle-class' society on a lesser wage, to the refugees trading their life under conflict in Palestine for one in the camps, the middle class has emerged from a society that is as economically dispa-rate as it is culturally diverse. By turns it fades, revives and assumes new guises, which to date have merged to create a void between the upper and lower echelons of Jordanian economic society.

There remains, however, a strong case for the existence of a middle class. According to Droeber, the middle class can be further deline-ated into 'upper' and 'lower' sectors, with similar traits that enable their living standards, education – predominantly beyond second-ary – and political outlooks to be comparable.[67] Furthermore, the universities assume a contributing role in the survival of the mid-dle classes, since their graduates are destined for careers in admin-istration, teaching, private business or in the health sector.[68] The phenomenon of the Jordanian student hungry for a position in the government and administration was recalled by Kamhawi, a former academic at the University of Jordan:

> It's a frame of mind. For them [the students], the only important subject is government and becoming something, a minister, an ambassador. They love it. It's in their blood. I would ask most of the Transjordanian students – 'what do you want to do?', they would respond: 'I want to work in the government'. None of them would say anything else.[69]

Equally, if the model of the middle class is applied to an analysis of Jordanian society, the schism between the two communities, Jordanian and Palestinian-Jordanian, becomes more tangible as graduates are primed in the university environment for a career in the administra-tion. Thus they 'form the potentially most loyal part of the popula-tion, an aim that is made explicit in the National Charter: education is meant to form the individual as an integrated human being [and] to develop the feeling of belongingness to an Arab *Umma*.'[70] Despite the utilization of education as a means to unite the country in employ-ment, the division between the Jordanian-dominated administration and the Palestinian-Jordanian-led business sector is ensured through a complex university admissions procedure that restricts applicants of Palestinian origin from attaining much coveted places:

> To curb the number of Palestinians from going to university in big numbers, there is an annual quota of students that the university can accept. They could accept for example 5,000. These are examples, not accurate percentages: five per cent for the sons and daughters of the armed forces; five per cent for the sons and daughters of the teachers; five per cent for the governorates; ten per cent for the royal endowment. Technically, they siphon off 50 per cent of the seats for institutions that are predominantly Transjordanian, so the Palestinians are kept away from 50 per cent.[71]

In turn, the process of *makrumat malakiyya* or 'privileges of the King' capitalizes on the absence of transparency and ensures the continuation of the 'affirmative action for Transjordanians at the expense of Palestinians' through the allocation of quotas to sectors dominated by Jordanians: the army, ministries and tribes.[72] The result is a divide between the public and private sectors of employment that provides 'a smart way to discriminate against possibility, because if you have clear and transparent competition each year maybe 80 per cent of the students at Jordan University would be of Palestinian origin.'[73]

Defining the middle class is no mean feat. Although it is possible to categorize according to income, occupation, living standards and education, the undercurrent of discrimination and the influential nature of the political and economic changes ranging through the Kingdom signifies that the middle class could only ever exist according to these factors. At most, the middle class could be a socio-economic category in a state of flux, or at worst, the result of classification-hungry surveys that seek to neatly capture Jordanian society within the confines of a predefined socio-economic framework. That it has existed, and will continue to exist, is indubitable. For the present, those jaded by the clear delineation between the communities along lines of ethnic origin believe that the middle class is fading as the groups occupying the opposing economic poles of Jordan consume the 'upper' and 'lower' middle classes. In contemporary Jordan, however, it is clear that the middle class exists, characterized by a diverse collection of refugees, camp inhabitants and urban Palestinian-Jordanian families.

The Palestinian middle class occupies a grey area of identity. Arriving in Jordan as small merchants and lower-level government employees, the group progressed to a level of economic success and integration, and whatever hostility existed on arrival has become less pronounced, except for those involved in the Palestinian movement.[74] For some, ties to their Palestinian background are maintained through assisting in the refugee camps. In a series of interviews conducted in 1995, predominantly with camp residents, Abdallah gauged reflections not only on religion, social activities and aspirations, but identity. Amidst those surveyed was 36-year-old Nadia, an activist and leader of the Women's Union in Jordan. Residing in a suburb of Amman, she grew up in the camps and continues to provide information on rights that the refugees may be unaware they are entitled to.[75] By returning to the camps, Nadia and others like her demonstrate a willingness to maintain the connection with their cultural background through relating shared experiences and history.

Ilham, a fellow respondent, echoed this sentiment. Although the interview was primarily aimed at Aida, a resident of the Jabal Hussein Camp in Amman, her friend was drawn into the conversation when Aida's sister questioned why, if Ilham has the means to not only leave the camp but also the country, does she remain? Ilham's response that 'it would be easier elsewhere [...] but as a Palestinian, I have to stay here and help those who need help in the camps'[76] reiterates the sense of moral obligation associated with being a Palestinian in another country. In neighbouring states, the desire to reconnect once economically established in the host count is equally evident.

Ruben's 1974 study of 'successful Palestinians' in the prosperous Ras Beirut area in Lebanon explored the remorse of middle-class Palestinians regarding the conditions of the refugees.[77] The treatment of Palestinians in Lebanon is by far the worst of all neighbouring states, with prejudice prevalent not only in the work place as in Jordan, but in society. Unlike their Palestinian-Jordanian counterparts, middle-class

Palestinians questioned had little or no contact with the refugees and never visited any of the six camps within half an hour of the city.[78] Those seeking involvement were often at a loss where to begin, such as Dr Jamil Hamdan, an engineering consultant of Palestinian origin. Brought up in Lebanon with little awareness of his Palestinian heritage, he became aware of the Palestinian situation during his doctorate in the United States. Back in Beirut, he worked with fellow engineers on a tutoring program for students in the camps. Unfortunately, the welcome was less than amicable and all but Hamdan and his acquaintance immediately quit.

Whether middle-class Palestinians naturalized into the host states become involved in camp life to reacquaint themselves with their identity, ease the circumstances of their fellow Palestinians or out of curiosity varies on a case-by-case basis. The matter of identity comes to the fore when other Palestinians are questioned on the motives of the middle class. A Palestinian sociologist pressed by Ruben expounded that, 'The middle class who take this approach need the camps to maintain their own sense of identity in the diaspora in the same way that American Jews need Israel.'[79] Thus the camps become comfort blankets for diasporic Palestinians, until the formation of a Palestinian state at an indeterminate point in the future.

Not all Palestinians seek connections through the refugee camps in the host country – some grasp insights through events such as family gatherings, parties and meetings. Dr Eugene Maklouf, a participant in Ruben's survey, stated that he meets friends from Haifa and they continue the same activities they enjoyed in Palestine 25 years ago.[80] The only mementos of his former life in Haifa are a pair of stockings, a knife and a picture album, and it is through these pictures that he maintains contact with Haifa by seeking out and writing to the individuals captured on film.

While Dr Maklouf and Dr Hamdan have integrated into Lebanese society and seek to retain their Palestinian identity through camp programmes, friends and vestiges of Palestine, others bear the trauma of their predecessors more strongly, at times manifesting through an aversion to Zionism and Israel. While certain middle-class Palestinians endeavour to differentiate between the Jewish faith and Zionism, for others it is impossible,[81] representing an alternate manifestation of the Palestinian identity in a host state.

Whether in Amman or Beirut, the middle classes are demonstrably capable of transforming the Palestinian identity to suit not only their new environment but also their lifestyle. By blending Jordanian characteristics with Palestinian cultural traditions, the capacity of each determines the strength of Palestinian identity in the individual. Certainly, it is challenging to categorize the middle class since the elite veers markedly between extremes of supporting the monarchy and promoting the Palestinian cause. The refugees, meanwhile, hold fast to aspects of the Palestinian identity and strive to incorporate it into daily routines so that it may never be lost. Despite the ambiguity of the middle-class Palestinians of Jordan, they are nevertheless the greatest example of the Palestinian-Jordanian identity in action.

A Homecoming (of Sorts)

Prior to the Gulf War (1990–1991), Jordan afforded a haven for refugees fleeing through, or to, the Middle East since the nineteenth century when the Chechens and Circassians settled in Amman after the armies of the Tsar seized control of their country. Since the inception of the state of Israel in 1948, thousands of Palestinians have fled to the Kingdom in search of a secure future amidst their fellow Palestinians, who constitute the majority of the population. The Lebanese Civil War (1975–1991) further added to the number of refugees seeking protection in Jordan and the subsequent wave of *émigrés* thus constituted one of the largest and most diverse groups to seek refuge in the Kingdom.[82] During the Gulf War, Kuwait expelled 300,000 Palestinians who had been living in the Gulf state since 1948. Over the ensuing decade, an estimated more than one million Iraqis entered Jordan, fleeing the police state tactics of Saddam Hussein's regime.[83] As a result, for those Palestinian-Jordanians born in Palestine, relocated to Jordan and expatriated to the Gulf, the final move back to Jordan yielded an additional aspect to their identity as Palestinian-Jordanians, resulting in a unique cocktail of perceptions that blends their diverse heritage and experiences.

With their roots in Palestine, experience of life in Jordan prior to their relocation to the Gulf state, and their forced return to the Kingdom due to the conflict, these refugees created a complex identity that is not only disparate to that of their Jordanian colleagues, but also the Palestinian-Jordanian community. By now accustomed to a high standard of living in the Gulf states, the Palestinians had formed denizen-like communities almost entirely Palestinian in origin.[84] The return to Jordan was to be financially and emotionally disheartening since the Palestinian community had nurtured a greater attachment towards their host state than that held by their by their Jordan-based counterparts. While some had succeeded in salvaging savings and assets which eased their passage into a new life in Jordan, for others finances were dwindling and they were confronted with not only a new life, but a new socio-economic standard.

For these families, the wealth to which they had grown accustomed was lost permanently as more than half of those returning to Jordan remained unemployed for more than 12 months since the outbreak of the Gulf Crisis. In a survey of 207 workers displaced by the initial Gulf War, 17 per cent reported they had been without a job for 10–12 months, while 7 per cent had accrued an annual income upwards of JD 20,000 prior to the outbreak of the conflict – a figure that dwindled to 4 per cent following the displacement.[85] In an alternate survey by Shteiwi on a sample of 1,000 individuals returning from the Gulf states, the results reflected a substantial alteration in the demographic structure of Jordan's class system. Notably, 19 per cent of returnees from the Gulf are business owners, 18 per cent are self-employed and 27 per cent are wage earners, all of whom were absorbed by the middle class.[86] In turn, integration enlarged the middle class and enabled it to become a recognized and active socio-economic group.

In addition to the pecuniary losses, for some the transition was another traumatic move prompted by conflict. The desolation of the flight of the Gulf returnees was evoked in a report by the Economic and Social Commission for Western Asia (ESCWA):

> The misery of these expatriates has not been limited to the loss
> of jobs, which represented the only income source for most of

them. It also has extended to the loss of savings, end-of-service remunerations, and assets. Tens of thousands of the repatriated expatriates have experienced a tortuous misery. Coming home has been no great consolation for most of them, as they can hardly hope to secure a source of income in a country that already has high unemployment.[87]

As the Jordanians of Palestinian origin returned to Jordan from the Gulf, scant solace was to be found as a much preferred destination remained distant and unattainable – Palestine. According to a survey conducted by Le Troquer and Hommery, more than half of returnees wished to return to Palestine eventually, though many of those aged 30 and under expressed desires to return to Kuwait or continue to a Western nation.[88]

This desire to return to Palestine was often influenced by the age of the respondent: of the 207 participants interviewed by Ahmed and Williams-Ahmed, 39 specified that Palestine would be their primary choice for employment. Of those, 15 were between 41 and 50 years of age, while 11 were between 31 and 40 years. On the basis of years of employment, 42 of the respondents returning from the Gulf stated that they would prefer to return to work in Palestine, while of those, 27 also had 16 years or more experience of working in the Gulf.[89]

The move to Jordan was also perceived as a matter of convenience as the passport offered stability in the aftermath of the expulsion from Kuwait, rather than forming a new basis for identity or belonging. While in Kuwait, the Palestinian-Jordanians rarely utilized the Jordanian consular services and kept visits to the Kingdom to a minimum. As a result, the return back to Jordan was tinged by insouciance and a reluctance to engage in the affairs of the country.[90]

It is evident, then, that the returnees retain a robust awareness of being Palestinian, though the difference between their Palestinian identity and that of the Jordan-based Palestinian-Jordanians creates an aspect of identity that is shared with the Jordanian refugees who fled the Gulf state, one that has been shaped by the combined experience of the flight from Kuwait.[91] Manifested in their abhorrence of the former Iraqi leader Saddam Hussein, the sentiment is compounded by their own experiences rather than observances through the media or accounts by friends and relatives. It is worth noting that the sentiment regarding a figure such as Hussein varies according to the experience and political climate of the time. Through informal observations during the course research for this book, a number of Jordanians of Palestinian origin demonstrated support for Hussein during the course of his trial. In each case, the respondent had neither visited Iraq nor Kuwait and had resided in Jordan if not for all, then at least the majority of his or her life.

This sentiment was echoed by a few Jordanians during a heated discussion between an Iraqi refugee from Babylon and a Jordanian from Jerash on the virtues and vices of Hussein, as the young Jordanian exclaimed, 'Even if King Abdullah would put a bullet in my head, I would say Saddam is good!' Whether this espousal was a consequence of the East-West dichotomy rampant during the U.S. and British military presence in the region – Hussein's courtroom dramatics amassed a soap-like daily following due to his defiant underdog antics – or the sincere ramblings of an individual devoted to the former Iraqi leader is difficult to discern in times of political upheaval.

Indeed, the relationship between Jordan and Iraq has been a cold economic and political arrangement, characterized by fits of loathing and intimacy since the thrones of Iraq and Transjordan were juxtaposed by the British in the aftermath of World War I. Notable periods of unity include from the onset of Baghdad's conflict with Tehran, even before the actual outbreak of war in the summer of 1980, through the 1989 Arab Cooperation Council; and on the outbreak of the preliminary Gulf War, when King Hussein endeavoured to portray solidarity in his speech shortly before the invasion of Kuwait. It is possible, then, that should a sincere championing exist, it is as a result of previous espousals and support for the neighbouring state. It is, however, clear that the Jordanian and Palestinian-Jordanian returnees are united through their shared experience of the invasion of Kuwait, the memory of which has been integral in shaping their outlook.

The sense of 'not belonging' is omnipresent and shared by the returnees in Lebanon, as Ruben's analysis noted the sentiments of the Palestinians who fled to Kuwait via Jordan to Lebanon. For one respondent, 'the sense of not belonging is terrible. We hold Kuwaiti citizenship and we live well in Beirut, but we don't belong anywhere. I feel like someone in a camp.'[92] Although the respondent was not a Gulf War returnee, her account is significant as it demonstrates that wealthy, secure Palestinians in neighbouring states still retain an ardent sense of Palestinian identity and continue to experience a disassociation with their environment akin to that of camp residents.

Tales from a Besmirched Haven

Usually a man lives in a certain place in the world, but for the Palestinian the place lives in the man.[93]

The subsequent return of 300,000 Jordanian citizens – 85 per cent of Palestinian origin – in the aftermath of the 1948 and 1967 Wars resolved itself into four groups, each distinct from the other in their political identity, ideology, aspirations and social standing.[94] The refugees of 1948 largely retained their Palestinian identity, while constituting the core of the Palestinian opposition to the Jordanian regime and the rapprochement it enjoyed with Israel. Mutual antipathy and empathy characterized the relationship between Israel and Jordan, as they strained through 80 years of conflict and three major wars to limp finally into the Jordanian-Israeli peace treaty of October 1994. The result, from the perspective of the Palestinian refugees of 1948, is that the future remains bleak: even if a Palestinian state should be formed on the West Bank, many would still be unable to return to their homes as the majority originate from what is now Israel.[95]

Similarly, the refugees of 1967 did not integrate into the East Bank and have actively sustained their Palestinian identity, though their opposition to the peace process has been staunch as they anticipate a return to the land of Palestine.[96] Despite the coolness of the refugees of 1967 towards the regime, in comparison with subsequent waves of Palestinians into the Kingdom, the Palestinian identity is stronger. As Sayigh notes, the Palestinian refugees are distinguished

by 'nationalism, class and refugee status [that] are inextricably intertwined [...] their weapons are what they have always been: refusal to
forget, anger and a remarkable capacity for collective survival.'[97]

Socio-economically polar opposites to the elite, the inhabitants of
Jordan's refugee camps inhabit varying environments, often defined
by the degree of rights accorded to the individual. While certain
families hold the capacity to work, drive and contribute towards
healthcare, for others this is an area fraught with restrictions. Similar
to the middle class, refugee camp residents do not constitute a uniform group as many hold certificates of higher education equal to
members of the middle class, yet have chosen to remain in the camps
to maintain their Palestinian identity. As Ismael, a Palestinian-
Jordanian translator remarked, 'In these zincos you may see two or
three masters certificates on the walls. This makes you proud for
they are showing their children the way of life.'[98] The diversity was
further evident in camps such as Marka, where white-washed and
green-shuttered houses stand side-by-side with semi-demolished
buildings, clothes lines drawn across. When considering the inhabitants of the refugee camps, it is integral that they are not reduced to
a single sweeping category.

According to Al-Saqour, there are four fundamental concepts of
poverty applicable to the case of the Palestinian inhabitants of the refugee camps. Primarily, 'basic needs' are those things that are necessary to preserve an individual's life at an acceptable level that protects
his or her dignity and ability to work and earn a sufficient income.
These needs include food and drink, clothes, adequate housing and
educational opportunities. Secondly, 'destitution' is the state in which
basic nutritional needs are not fulfilled and when the individual
does not consume the quantity of calories necessary to maintain life
(between 2,000 and 2,500 calories per person, per day). Consequently,
the dividing line between those who consume the minimum number
of calories and those who fail to do so is deemed the 'destitution
line'. Thirdly, 'absolute poverty' is characterized by the inability to
meet basic needs, both of a nutritional and non-nutritional nature,
establishing the dividing line between those who satisfy their needs
and those who cannot as 'the absolute poverty line'. Lastly, 'relative

poverty' is identified as the proportion of impoverished people in a society and their living standards in comparison to those of a more affluent nature in the same society.[99]

Despite the government's contention that the dire conditions provide an unorthodox contribution to the Palestinian cause, since the everlasting indeterminate state ensures the issue is not forgotten, calls for upgrading the camps are more pragmatically rebuked due to the substantial cost of full renovation and relocation. The costs are determined by land values, civil and building works and population distribution. The principal uncertainty arises from the population estimates, which in turn influence the cost of relocation, compensation and income restoration. Indeed, the estimated figures alone are enough to strike anxiety into a host government: the population stands at approximately 546,000 or 1.5 times that of the UNRWA estimate,[100] while relocation costs have been estimated at JD 3,000 per household displaced, including compensation for loss of assets and investments to restore income-earning opportunities. On the basis of the above approximations, the cost of fully upgrading the camps would be in the range of U.S. $300 million. Thus minimum upgrading would cost about U.S. $200 million and land regularization would cost about U.S. $65 million. The speculated total would be U.S. $255 million, the mid-point between full upgrading and minimum upgrading. If the land costs have been underestimated by 50 per cent, the cost would increase to U.S. $300 million. An increase in relocation costs of 20 per cent would result in a new cost total of U.S. $262 million. If both escalations occur, the total cost would be U.S. $312 million.[101]

The human costs are no less staggering: 15 per cent of existing households would be required to relocate during the process of renovation. Areas near and adjacent to the camps would require development to accommodate transitory households and additional social facilities would be required to improve the temporary environs. In sites upgraded under the government's programme, the residents would pay for infrastructure services associated with roadways less than eight feet wide. Within the camps, however, other cost-sharing arrangements would be developed, as the residents would be charged for the services they currently had or would have to contribute through 'sweat equity' to their development. They might, therefore, be unwilling to pay again.[102] Since these figures were estimated over ten years ago, it is probable that the costs and implications would be greater in contemporary Jordan and with such a colossal investment the government would tread carefully before embarking on a pecuniary venture that would bode ill for an already woeful economy.

Certain camps, such as al-Wihdat, have been absorbed by the sprawling downtown of Amman and display an amalgamation so perfect that one can no longer distinguish between the Palestinian refugee accommodation and those of the lower-income Jordanian dwellings. Nevertheless, others languish as desolate outposts, a blemish on Jordan's record of maximum integration and minimal intolerance. For the inhabitants of the Gaza Camp, restrictions on employment, healthcare and even the attainment of a driving licence reveal the life of a camp dweller to be not only one of extreme poverty, but also of profound frustration at the insufficient means by which it is anticipated they will improve their circumstances. It is within this harsh environment that the Palestinian identity is at its most spirited. Nevertheless, as the government articulates its desire to serve the long-term interests of the camp residents, its reasoning falls on cynical ears.

Remonstrations by the Jordanian government that the inhabitants cannot assume full citizenship rights, as it will thwart the attainment of a Palestinian state in the undetermined future, have served only to redefine the line between 'us' and 'them', Palestinian and Jordanian, respectively. As Rantawi observes, not only is there a dichotomy between Palestinians and Jordanians, but also between Palestinians of varying economic categories:

> It's completely different. For the people of Gaza Camp it is the worst, because it's difficult for them to find a job, to travel, to have proper documents, to attend universities, schools. Those people are totally Palestinian. Those who have good businesses, are involved in the political life are even more integrated in the [Jordanian] society and they are not the same, at all.[103]

As a new generation emerges, for whom Palestine is revived by an accomplished collection of raconteurs, including narrations replete with symbolic details unique to the village of the tale, Palestine is a real and viable home. Even for the children whose parents are a union of Jordanian and Palestinian, life in camps such as Gaza has ensured that only one identity will survive, as they include themselves in the exhortation, 'we are Palestinians'. As Kawar elucidates:

> If we speak to the children, even the babies who are half-Palestinians, they keep saying we are Palestinian, but they don't want to use it in confrontation. And they don't want to forget it. Often a five-year old child will tell you, 'I'm from that village in Palestine'.[104]

It is clear then that since 1948 the Palestinians have developed strategies to integrate and in doing so have constructed new Palestinian cultures and customs in exile.[105] Through the narrations of family members, vivid depictions of social life and relationships in home villages contribute towards a contrast with the misery of their current milieu. In turn, the children who have never experienced Palestine recount the tales of their former village and blame their parents for leaving the family home and fleeing to 'these bad places', as opposed to defending their land and heritage.[106]

When imagining the 'bad places' the new generation describes, one cannot but help recall Gaza Camp, for which the term is an apt depiction. Congested by donkeys pulling dusty children, they trundle through lanes replete with refuse and sewage that courses pungently along the sidewalks. Gaza, then, exists in stark contrast to fellow camps. Whereas the Rusaifa and al-Wihdat districts retain a degree of sanitation amidst the white-washed houses and clear roads, the Gaza Camp is a sorry case. It is a forgotten camp in which Palestinians languish like castaways on an island of *zincos* in an ocean of ripe Jordanian farmland, for within metres of leaving the arid lanes the pot-holes give way to tarmac flanked by grand houses bordered by bountiful orchards and pristine cars in driveways. Owned by the Jordanian landowners who let their land to the camp, it was impossible to overlook the stark disparity.

Due to the heightened security presence in the Gaza Camp, it was not possible to conduct interviews, though the Marka Camp held inhabitants willing to share their experiences. For 41-year-old Hisham, originally from Acre in the Gaza District, discrimination was borne out in a medical context. A few months previously, Hisham had begun to vomit blood as a result of a heart condition and was conveyed to the Islamic Hospital in Amman. Once there, medical staff refused to treat him due to his lack of Jordanian citizenship. Solely Palestinian, his status prevents contributions towards national insurance and healthcare schemes. As the hospital turned him towards the Palestinian embassy, Hisham refuted the measure as futile, as to gain assistance from the Palestinian embassy one must have *wasta*, which he lacked. That the issue of citizenship transcended that of human rights and moral obligations prompted Hisham to conclude that 'they would not even treat an injured dog that way. How could they treat a human being?'[107]

Hisham's case demonstrates the cyclical impact of the scarcity of healthcare needs and an individual's essential right to live. As the holder of a Jordanian two-year residency passport he cannot gain employment without a permit, gain access to reliable and affordable healthcare, obtain a driving licence or a *rakheb al-watani* – national insurance number.[108] These are but a few basic rights that Hisham, and others, are bereft of. Having come to Jordan in 1967 and resided in Marka Camp since 1969, Hisham was obliged to pay JD 7,000 for his operation. Unable to find the means himself, the community of the camp initiated a collection to finance the procedure. As we departed, he revealed that as he recovers he is ashamed to step out of his house due to the humbling extremes the people of his community went to in saving his life. During the course of the afternoon passed with Hisham and his family, other accounts emerged, some more horrifying, some less, though always unavoidable and in stark contrast to the image the Jordanian government promulgates to the populace.

If one was to scrutinize the home of a Palestinian or Palestinian-Jordanian respondent for clues to their Palestinian identity across all socio-economic levels, one would find varying representations. In the palatial abodes of the affluent, stirring portraits of women gazing out of open doors or windows towards the hills of Palestine adorn the walls of offices. There also would be crafts in the traditional Palestinian design, while in the refugee camps, one would find a paper poster of Jerusalem tacked to the wall, *musakhan* – the traditional Palestinian dish – being served with frequency and numerous pieces of cloth strewn around the abode with the words *Intifada* embroidered by a dedicated and steady hand. For each of these families, Palestine is alive. Yet it is within camps such as Gaza that the longing is most evident, as it is here that the people have lost the most and are reminded of this loss through the circumstances in which they exist. It is true, then, that the government's strategy is effective – the Palestinian cause is indeed being kept alive – but for these families, it is resonant only to them. Abandoned in their *zincos*, they can only speculate whether the move is keeping the cause alive for those with the influence to bring an end to the limbo and restore them to a full life, with rights, a home and a land.

The issue of identity versus socio-economic circumstances and the degree to which one impinges on the other is, then, problematic. Formal and informal discussions on the perception of the identity of oneself and others revealed that the majority of respondents considered the notion of 'more money, less identity' to be credible. Yet the endurance of Palestine in the lives of Palestinian-Jordanians of all economic levels was tangible, which suggests that exterior factors – occupation, area of residence, duration of residence, income level – bears little or no influence on the development and survival of the Palestinian identity in Jordan, as it moves from one generation to the next. The economic condition of a country remains pertinent to the evolution of the Palestinian identity, as it simultaneously reflects the influence of the passport and citizenship laws on an individual's social mobility, particularly in the case of refugee camp residents.

As socio-economic circumstances vary, it is apparent that the Palestinian identity is constant, while its manifestation varies. Amidst the affluent, the Christians largely retained a secure standard of living through the assistance of Christian organizations, such as Caritas. In addition, relatives also presented a means by which to avoid relocation to the refugee camps. For those who successfully traversed the Jordanian socio-economic network to the upper echelons, it often came at a price, as overt demonstrations of Palestinianess did not receive a warm reception during assimilation into Jordanian society. The divide between the public and the private sector established standards by which the Palestinian-Jordanian elite must abide during their assimilation, whether it is integration into social or professional circles. As Jordanian former Deputy Prime Minister, Dr Jawad Anani, notes:

> In times of bad economic performance, such feelings show and people get excited. They want to defend their own interests. They say, 'Okay, you can go to the private sector; you're Palestinian, Palestinians-Jordanian are dominant in the private sector, so stay there – run your own shops and companies, go and work in the Gulf and leave the those jobs to us, it is our responsibility to manage our own country.'[109]

This approach has not passed unnoticed by the Palestinian-Jordanian community and has been reflected by the consumers, as a number of Palestinians purposely shop in stores owned by fellow Palestinians, as opposed to Jordanians, in order to keep their microcosmic economy buoyant while encouraging a sense of unity.

The chameleonesque middle class merges with the elite and lower-income groups in times of economic strife and flourishes during fiscal surges. Yet, throughout, their Palestinian identity represents a median between the restrained elite and the overt expressions of identity by the refugees. Largely composed of the Gulf returnees holding triple identities, they have continued to provide an excellent example of integration, due to their favourable position with the regime. As a consequence, though it is possible to categorize according to income, occupation, living standards and education, the undercurrent of discrimination alongside the influential nature of the political and economic changes raging through the Kingdom signifies that the middle class could only ever exist according to these factors and could, on the one hand, be a erratic socio-economic category, or the result of surveys that endeavour to portray Jordanian society within the confines of a socio-economic framework.

It would be facile to conclude that the Palestinian identity exists in its purest form in the refugee camps, since respondents from the middle class and elite equally endorse the anguish associated with the loss of a homeland. Yet the question of whether individuals would leave Jordan should a Palestinian state be established in the near future drew defining responses. Ismael, originally from Battir, near Bethlehem, arrived in Jordan during the 1960s seeking employment in Amman and has remained since the outbreak of the 1967 War with his wife and nine children. Unable to return to Palestine due to border complications, his immediate response: 'If only we had a *taboun* [oven] in Palestine, we would leave everything in Jordan and return'[110] was delivered without hesitancy. For Judeh, however, it is not as straightforward:

I will tell you that most of them will not, because they've been here for four or five generations. They are not going to suddenly disengage and delve into the unknown. A lot of them lost their properties back in 1948 and 1967, so nobody's going to start from zero unless it was totally transparent and guaranteed.[111]

Through this question, it is perceptible how significant socio-economic circumstances are in relation to the endurance of Palestine in the memory and identity of the Palestinian-Jordanians. For the middle class and elite, who have worked fastidiously during the last 60 years to re-establish their lives, both economically and socially, the prospect of leaving behind friends, schools, jobs and a home is generally less appealing. For the inhabitants of the refugee camps, however, life never settled completely. They are merely a population anticipating the imminent arrival of their homeland, to which they would return to, regardless of the conditions.

6

FAITH, AFFILIATION AND INTEGRATION

Religion in the diaspora communities of Jordan is expressed sali-
ently, both in terms of political and social organization. Often overlooked in the context of the Palestinian diaspora, the Palestinian
Christians transcend the boundaries of religious and national identity to assimilate into Jordanian society. Drawing on concepts from
social anthropology and international relations, it is possible to trace
the nuances that compose the identity of the Palestinian Christians
who migrated to Jordan from Palestine during the Arab-Israeli conflict, from 1948 to the present day, while gathering an insight into
the inter-faith dynamic. As new religious movements emerge in the
capital, the existing structure of the Christian community in Jordan
is challenged by a generational dichotomy, as younger Christians are
attracted to the evangelical movements. Originating from the United
States, evangelical missionaries are predominantly based in Israel with
Jerusalem providing the hub of activity, with tentative forays over the
border into Jordan. As stout proponents of the Zionist ideology, the
concerns of the older generation become both religious and political,
for the evangelists represent a branch of Christianity espoused by the
American Cyrus Scofield during the nineteenth century. In Scofield's
view, Christ cannot return to earth until a number of conditions are in
place: that the Jews must return to Palestine, control must be gained
of Jerusalem and the temple rebuilt, before engaging in the final,

terminal battle: Armageddon. In this manner, each act taken by Israel is deemed to be orchestrated by God, and should be supported by humankind. That the Palestinian-Jordanian and Jordanian youth are drawn to such movements is, then, highly ironic and intriguing as it reveals the depth and versatility of identity.

Likewise, the emergence of groups touting radical Islam raises a fresh conundrum for Jordan's security. While Jordan has sustained a record of foiling Islamist threats, the onslaught of infiltration none-theless continues – even increases, given the abundance of individuals open to new interpretations of progress masquerading as faith-based activity. As the Muslim Brotherhood and its political wing, the Islamic Action Front (IAF), maintain their hard-earned places in national and municipal elections, support is steady, especially within the camps. Yet this is no mean feat, as recent municipal elections have demonstrated, with the IAF withdrawing amid claims of governmental fraud. In con-trast with the radical groups, the Muslim Brotherhood has endured as a source of education, assistance and hope for the inhabitants of the refugee camps. Through their activities and sustained support for the Palestinian cause, the connection between identity and religion becomes tangible. Thus, as shall be explored shortly, the Palestinian-Jordanian Christian and Muslim communities provide an insight into the dynamic between religion and identity and in turn the implica-tions this has for the future of the Palestinian-Jordanian community in Jordan.

Territorial Politicization

Jordan has long nurtured a profound connection with the Holy Land and is home to a number of important religious sites, most notably Mount Nebo, the early Christian pilgrimage site commemorating the place at which Moses saw the Promised Land, appointed Joshua as his successor, and was buried. Although Betty Jane Bailey and J. Martin Bailey have contended that most Jordanian Christians are of Palestinian origin, the Jordanian Christian community has existed on the land for centuries. According to Pierre Medebielle, archaeological evidence suggests that the Christian presence in the area dates back to the first century AD, although a cessation in Christian development occurred during the period of the first Muslim Caliphates (635–1100 AD). Nevertheless, the Christian faith was sustained by nomadic tribes, and the arrival of Western missionaries during the nineteenth century facilitated a return to the Catholic and Protestant churches. By the establishment of the Transjordanian state in 1921, the Orthodox Patriarchate was thriving with renewed gusto, as a report commissioned by the Mandate government of Palestine in 1926 demonstrated:

> When one descends to the plain of Jericho, crosses the Jordan, and ascends into the hill country of Moab, one is astonished to find oneself in the midst of a vigorous Christian community, with the bearing, manners, and the dress which one has always associated with the Arabs of the desert. They are proud of their Christian religion [...] and have not the least intention of abandoning it. To have preserved their community in being is an achievement in which the Patriarchate takes an active and perhaps legitimate pride.[1]

While the report estimated the Christian population at 20,000, Haddad expresses doubt over the plausibility of such a figure, arguing that the ease with which Christian tribes could name their kinsfolk in entirety indicates that they comprised small units, thereby rendering the estimation of 30,000 by F. G. Peake in 1931 'difficult to believe'.[2] Also clustered around the towns of Irbid, al-Mafraq, Jerash, Zarqa and El Hosun, the Christians residing in pre-war Transjordan were swiftly integrated into positions in the nascent state government, a realm in which they have continued to excel.

Despite the decline in Jordan's neighbouring states, the Palestinian Christian community remains notable for their success at the feat of integration within the new environment. Unlike the Arab Christians in neighbouring Muslim-majority states, they have never been threatened by the government, subjected to religious persecution or political oppression. That they have excelled both socially and economically has not passed unnoticed, as Prince El-Hassan bin Talal observed in 2001: 'Christians across the [Jordanian] region have done well, and any

minority that has a successful record is looked at with a certain degree
of envy.'³ Without doubt, while their economic, social and political
strength remains disproportionate to their actual size and has provided a source of envy for other minorities,⁴ to date, reactions to this
modus vivendi have been largely restrained, thus enabling Jordan to successfully blend the constituent communities of its multi-faith society
into a relatively peaceful coexistence.

Migration and Integration

With the emergence of Israel in the aftermath of the Palestine War of
1948–1949, the demographics of the Middle East were revolutionized,
setting in motion a chain of events that would suspend the region in
a permanent state of flux as communities flourished and faded and
populations moved both within and outside the surrounding states. As
the Arab armies retreated, an estimated 60,000 Palestinian Christians
fled their homes along the coast and from the Galilean highlands,
in addition to approximately half a million Muslim Palestinians.
Of the Christians, around half settled in Jordan, either in the West
Bank, which comprised the hubs of the Christian faith — Jerusalem,
Bethlehem and Ramallah — or in Amman, Karak, Salt, Ajloun and
Madaba to the east. With the exception of Madaba, which holds a
sizeable Latin Catholic congregation, the majority of Christian communities were Orthodox, with slighter minorities comprising Melkites
and Latin Catholics. For the more fortunate Christian Palestinians,
the flight was rendered less agonizing due to the avoidance of refugee
status through contacts in Lebanon. For the preponderance of Melkites
fleeing Palestine, this was the favoured option, and by 1951 approximately 10,000 Melkites had established themselves in and around
Beirut, in comparison to a mere 2,500 who relocated to Jordan.⁵

The proximity of Jordan to Palestine could be viewed as but one
incentive to relocate to the land-locked and economically nascent country. Already home to certain Christian Arab tribes, the Kingdom was
viewed as a haven in the region for Christians of all denominations,
including Greek Catholics, Roman Catholics, Protestants, Armenian
and Syrian Orthodox, and Assyrians. Estimates place the establishment

of the first Christian presence in Jordan in the first century AD, and the number of churches excavated by both foreign and local archaeologists has revealed a thriving community that has continuously inhabited Jordan as a result of conflict, predominantly in Palestine, Lebanon and the Caucasus. As the eighteenth century brought forth the ravages of a war spanning 75 years in northern Palestine and Lebanon's middle and southern regions, the Christians bore the yoke of poverty, obliged to pay crippling taxes and tributes exacted by the Ottoman army and its authorities.

However, as Jasussin notes, it was not only pecuniary matters that compelled the Christian population to flee their land – sexual honour, or *ird*, is the most cited reason for migration during this period and is aptly captured in the expression, '*bil-ird wala bil-Ard*' [sic] or 'better sacrifice the land than the chastity'.[6]

Despite efforts to portray the Jordanian rule as oppressive in contrast to the purportedly benevolent Israeli administration, the question remains as to why, if conditions were better in the fledgling state of Israel, did so many Palestinian Christians migrate across the border to Jordan? Had Israel been more cordial, perhaps the Christians would have chosen to remain during the 1967 exodus. Indeed, the 18 years between the establishment of the state of Israel and the 1967 War provided ample opportunity to evaluate the two regimes. Ultimately, the Palestinian Christians chose Jordan, because they had seen – and endured – Israeli policies during *al-Nakba*, in addition to the abuses meted out to the Christians of Galilee. Through such shared experiences both Christian and Muslim Palestinians were compelled to leave Palestine and seek refuge in neighbouring states.[7] Furthermore, they considered Israel responsible for the 1967 War, which incurred additional losses for the Palestinian community, including a further refugee crisis.[8]

The migration initiated in 1948 prompted not only a spectacular rise in the population of Jordan, but also ramifications for the society as a whole. In 1951 Jordan's mixed faith community was 93,500; ten years later it nudged 115,000, while in terms of the number of Christians migrating to Amman, the community has grown from 5,000 to 40,000 since 1948. Such an increase in the already populated urban hub has resulted in the decline of the Christian majorities in a number of West Bank villages, while the subsequent settlement of Muslim refugees in the formerly Christian towns on both the West and East Banks reduced remnants of the Christian presence. In total, it is estimated that between 1948 and the aftermath of the 1967 Arab-Israeli War, almost one million Palestinians entered Jordan and the effects upon the demographic and social composition of the Kingdom brought positive as well as negative developments.

It is worth noting at this point that according to statistics gathered in 1951, significant migration from the East Jordanian countryside had not occurred until the mass influx of Palestinians. This implies that the majority of individuals making the transition were not part of an inter-migration pattern; rather, the increase in urban population was driven by an influx of immigration to the Kingdom, with the greater majority of Christians in Amman and Zarqa arriving in 1948 or from Lebanon or Syria in search of better living conditions.[9]

Many Palestinians entering Jordan arrived educated, politicized and ambitious, which hastened the fledgling modernization of the political and economic echelons of Jordanian society. Similarly, the dynamic between the Christian churches and the Jordanian state witnessed a process of secularization that subsequently weakened the role of the churches as community leaders. In an effort to counteract this development, the churches honed a new image as the unifying agent within the urban community. To date, this has proved successful, as Jordanian churches continue to exert substantial social influence through education and the religious courts, which also has served to maintain a Christian identity within an Islamic state for both Palestinians and Jordanians alike.[10]

Despite the positive nature of such integration within the political arena and Andrea Pacini's observation that the 'Jordanian Christians are therefore well-integrated politically, which is always an important sign when measuring the extent of integration of a social component in the rest of society',[11] it is questionable whether the schism that pervades the employment sector between Jordanians of Palestinian origin and native Jordanians is more or less pronounced in the Christian context. Specifically, do Christian Palestinian-Jordanians enjoy a similar standard of opportunities and living to that of their ethnic Jordanian

Christian compatriots? Certainly, it can be asserted that Pacini is correct in her observation that 'a very high percentage of the Christian population belong to the middle to upper classes'. Indeed, it is the very presence of these churches that has enabled the Christians fleeing Palestine to maintain their standard of living – or even enhance it – through religious organizations, such as Caritas.

As the Palestinian refugee camps of Jordan dominate the fringes of the capital and the surrounding towns, it is apparent that the majority of inhabitants are non-Christian. Addressing this observation to a Christian respondent, herself a resident of the more affluent stratum of Jordanian society and an ardent advocate of the Palestinian identity, drew the following response:

> I think there are no Palestinian Christians living in Jordan in the camps. They can afford it: they have relatives that help them to come out from the beginning. In Lebanon there is, because there are many Christian villages in northern Palestine and they moved together out of the village. But here you have the churches. The churches help. You have world movements – Caritas. Now all the Christian Iraqis go to Caritas and they help them with schools and food. So they didn't stay in the camps.[12]

The ubiquitous presence of church groups provides reassurance to Christian migrants entering the Kingdom in times of conflict that perhaps is not entirely evident in the camps. Certainly, for many families displaced from a privileged position within Palestinian society, the assistance resettles them within a familiar environment in which the skills gathered – educational, political and pecuniary – can enable them to progress into realms of Jordanian society that are often more challenging for a non-Christian Palestinian-Jordanian applicant.

The Palestinian Christian Diaspora

The Arab Palestinian Christians are part and parcel of the Arab Palestinian nation. We have the same history, the same culture, the same habits and the same hopes.[13]

Prior to the inception of the Israeli state in 1948, Palestinian Christians, and those from the surrounding states, assumed dominant roles in the renaissance of the Middle East, *an-Nahda*. Over the course of the second half of the nineteenth century, the Christians of Lebanon and Syria experienced a cultural, political, economic and literary awakening inspired both by foreign Christian missionary activities and the pioneering observations of the Egyptian scholar, Sheikh Rifa'a Rafi' al-Tahtawi (1801–1873). An Islamic expert from al-Azhar University, al-Tahtawi resided in Paris over a five-year period between 1826 and 1831 at the behest of Mohamed Ali's government in his capacity as an Imam for the army cadets undergoing the study of military science in France. During his observations of Western sciences and educational methods, al-Tahtawi's interest shifted from mere spectatorship to an increasing affinity for French society, his reflections on which became immortalized in his book, *Takhlis Al-Ibriz fi Talkhis Bariz*, compiled upon his return to Egypt.[14]

In addition to his acclaimed publication, al-Tahtawi experienced a personal revolution, as his views evolved from those shaped by the conservative Islamic teachings at al-Azhar University towards a more liberal stance which advocated parliamentarism, women's education, and, to a degree, secularism.[15] Although al-Tahtawi studied the works of Montesquieu, Voltaire and Rousseau at length, the belief that his mediocre linguistic expertise would have hindered his comprehension and lessened the influence of the aforementioned works on his later views has proved an issue of contention.[16] However, when considered alongside his significant contribution to *an-Nahda*, al-Tahtawi's dubious grasp of the great works pales in comparison.

Nurtured in the shadow of colonial rule, *an-Nahda* endeavoured to achieve a political, social and cultural regeneration of Arab society through the implementation of a common Arab identity that would provide the foundation for a future unified Arab movement. With its emphasis on Arab identity, the notion afforded an ideological framework in which to construct a national independence through which both Muslims and Christians could contribute towards the modern state, with religious differences integrated into a unified 'Arab identity'.[17] The appeal of *an-Nahda* lay in its ability to incorporate a secular tone alongside one that considered Islam to be a principal feature of the nascent Arab identity. Once again, their exposure to Western liberal ideas in the preceding centuries enabled the Christians to exert a substantial influence on the various movements for national independence and cultural renaissance,[18] while on a political level, Christians participated in the majority of the secular and national political parties.[19] In addition, the new political culture provided a promising arena for Christians to exercise their ideologies freely, as the traditional social and political framework of the Muslim state, which had previously inhibited the aspirations of the Christian community in the region, began to wane.[20] Thus, revelling in the new age of relative religious tolerance and philosophical inquiry, Christian and Muslim communities throughout the Fertile Crescent united in their endeavours to realize the all-inclusive 'Arab identity'.

The renaissance that followed resonated through all sectors of Arab society and prompted contributions from Christians and Muslims alike, with Butrus al-Bustani (1819–1883) providing an eminent example. A Lebanese Maronite Christian, al-Bustani studied under American missionaries and converted to Protestantism. His aspiration to spread knowledge and appreciation of the Arabic language resulted in the creation of one of the greatest contributions to the Arabic language through the first modern Arabic dictionary, an epic 16-volume publication that was completed by his son, Jalil, in 1881.[21] Through his endeavours al-Bustani inspired 'the creation of modern Arabic expository prose, a language true to its past in grammar and idiom, but capable of expressing simply, precisely, and directly the concepts of modern thought.'[22] Similar to his predecessor, al-Tahtawi, al-Bustani promoted receptiveness to European scientific discoveries in the belief that only through a willingness to acquire modern knowledge would the Middle East recover its proper place in the world.[23]

For the Palestinian Christian community in Jordan, their involvement in *an-Nahda* inspired a religious acceptance that would survive the twentieth century. According to Prince El-Hassan bin Talal, the Jordanian ethos has been, and largely continues to be, conducive to the peaceful coexistence between the Muslim and Christian communities in the Kingdom. Accordingly, this feature can be traced to *an-Nahda*:

'this is a tradition [...] looking at the Sharif Husayn of Mecca's treatment of the Armenians in 1911; or the continuous references to the
Covenant of 'Umar when the Hashemites deal[t] with the churches,
the Orthodox Church, in particular.'[24] Thus, Jordan has historically
embraced a cornucopia of religions in her midst. Such benevolent
actions became further accentuated in the twentieth century, as:

> This respect has been renewed and extended thanks to
> An-Nahda, which is the basis of Hashemite political thinking.
> The Nahda movement is [...] a tradition to which Christians not
> only in Jordan but in other parts of the Fertile Crescent look
> with much admiration. The Nahda movement was very much a
> sharing of Arab Muslim and Christian identities in expressing
> a vision. The Ba'th have taken the slogan of 'a nation with an
> eternal message,' but it was very much an Arab Nahda slogan
> in the first place.[25]

Jordan's religious cohesion was further demonstrated in 2002 during a
visit by Pope John Paul II to the Kingdom. An auxiliary in the Latin-
rite Patriarchate of Jerusalem, which includes Jordan, Bishop Selim
Sayegh enthused: 'When the Pope spoke at the National Stadium;
maybe 400 Muslims came to see him. And the speech that the king
gave to welcome the Pope – you wouldn't have believed this was the
speech of a Muslim king!'[26] Despite the religious disparity between
Christian and Muslim Palestinians, history has demonstrated that the
Palestinian community has created a unity that has augmented its
ability to establish a formidable power base within the political arena,
a legacy that continues to the present day as members of the Christian
community excel shoulder-to-shoulder with their Muslim counterparts in the political arena of both Jordan and Palestine.

Following al-Nakba, the early political movements exuded a tolerance that enabled members of the Christian community not only
to partake in their activities, but also to assume esteemed roles as
leaders and promulgators of the causes that movements such as the
PLO and the Syrian Nationalist Party (PPS) espoused. As the remaining areas of the British administration, including Egypt, Palestine

and Transjordan, witnessed a flurry of activity amidst a population in the grip of feverish nationalist sentiments, the Christian community clamoured to actively support the independence movements. Jordan was not exempt from the spread of Ba'thist ideology, and similar to her neighbouring states, the Kingdom succumbed to the political awakening in Jordanian society.

The Ba'thist party attracted Christians and Muslims in equal measure and hastened the political mobilization of the Transjordanian Christians, which had thus far been limited.[27] Concurrently, opposition to the Ba'thist movement was presented by the PPS and a communist party officially banned by the Jordanian authorities, both of which promoted a strongly secularist agenda. The secularist nature of the movements appealed to the Christian community, who sought a means to hasten the progress of liberalization towards an outlook that would ultimately bring greater access to the privileged echelons of the government sector for members of the Christian community. As the majority of followers of the latter two movements were Christian, an unexpected turn of events saw their political aspirations militate against them in Muslim circles, as a simultaneous disparity and unity emerged between the Christian and Muslim community in Jordan.[28] From the Ba'thist organizations to the Palestinian movements, Christians both of Jordanian and Palestinian origin swarmed to enact their political convictions, nowhere more than in the Palestinian cause. Ultimately, this development would culminate in an unwavering schism between Jordanians of Palestinian origin and those of ethnic Jordanian background.

With the ambit of tension shifting from national to religious, and on towards political, the Palestinian cause presents an apt demonstration of unity in the face of disparity. Confronted with a common enemy, relations between the Christian communities and the Palestinian Arab national movement have survived as a partnership of convenience. Ambiguous since its inception, the Christians have identified with the movement's anti-Zionist ideologies, but have remained reserved and apprehensive on the role of Islam in the movement. While Daphne Tsimhoni asserts that 'As a result of this affiliation, the Christians have not been accepted by their Muslim countrymen as equal Arab nationalists',[29] reason counters that the ulterior factors cited in this article, such as economic disparities, shared experiences and mutual perceptions, occupy an equal, if not more significant, role in the isolation of the Palestinian Christian community.

Moreover, Tsimhoni's claim that 'Since 1967 the Arab Christians have usually identified themselves with the desire to remove Israeli rule from the West Bank'[30] stirs debate, given the vast number of Palestinian Christians displaced during *al-Nakba* in 1948 and the extensive destruction of Christian communities and holy sites. As Wagner wryly observes, the 'uncritical reader will be impressed by the compassionate generosity of the Israelis in helping to rebuild the Church of the Holy Sepulchre and the Maronite vicarage [...] but these are veritable "drops in the bucket" in comparison to the land and population losses suffered by Palestinian Christians alone in 1948 and 1967.'[31] With little or no acknowledgement of the devastation, one could be mistaken in the belief that the Palestinian Christian community experienced little of the first 19 years of the Israeli occupation that has shaped the political consciousness of their Muslim counterparts and as such would have been inevitably doomed from the outset in their endeavour to assimilate into the nationalist movement.

On the contrary, the Palestinian Christians swiftly established themselves in the Palestinian nationalist movement, particularly in the leadership of the PLO. The first major involvement of Christians in Palestinian nationalism occurred at the 'Christians for Palestine' conference, held in Beirut in the summer of 1969. Among the speakers were Yasser Arafat, George Habash, Kamal Nasser, and a contingent of Lebanese Arabists who introduced the secular democratic vision for Palestine into the churches.[32] Primarily supported by the World Student Christian Federation (WSCF) and the Antiochian Orthodox Church, the architect and promulgator of the movement was the Director of the WSCF Office in Beirut, Gabriel Habib, a former member of the Orthodox Youth Movement in Lebanon and a law student at the American University in Beirut. Having been deeply influenced by Arab nationalism during his student years through Bishop Georges Khodr, Habib proceeded to become the founding general secretary of the Middle East Council of Churches in 1974, though he never lost the vision of juxtaposing Christian support for a secular democratic movement within the Arab states.[33]

Equally, George Habash, who was born in Lydda to Greek Orthodox parents, created the Popular Front for the Liberation of Palestine (PFLP) in 1967, following the decline of the Arab Nationalist Movement (ANM). Established in 1951 in Jordan, the ANM was the brainchild of Habash and Wadi Haddad, a fellow Greek Orthodox Christian from Safad. The pair had founded a clinic in Amman that provided free healthcare and literacy campaigns for the Palestinian refugees in the city and the surrounding camps. Due to the extensive contact between the two doctors and their patients, the membership of the movement extended across the social spectrum, comprising teachers and doctors, in addition to a large number of refugees.[34] As al-Khatib observes: 'the presence of so many doctors in the leadership structure played an enormous role in garnering supporters [...] because they earned the trust with their medical work, above and beyond their political activities.'[35] After his implication in the 1957 coup and subsequent conviction in absentia, Habash fled to Syria in 1958, and subsequently to Beirut in 1961, whereupon he began the reorganization of the ANM in 1964. In 1967, following the events of the Six-Day War, disillusion with Nasserism had become tangible and prompted the transformation of the Palestinian ANM into the PFLP, which sought to radicalize Arab nationalism through an infusion of 'Marxism-Leninism, Maoism, Che Guevarism, Regis Debrayism, and Giappism'[36] As the movement progressed, the foundations were laid for actions that would shake Jordanian society to the core and sear an association between the Kingdom and the Palestinian cause into the minds of global observers.

As a plethora of organizations dedicated to the Palestinian cause congregated in Jordan in the aftermath of the Six-Day War, the Jordanian monarch began to react to the unsettling atmosphere pervading the Kingdom. By 1970, the various groups were operating in Jordan with scant regard for the authorities and had established their own administrative networks in the refugee camps, which functioned in a manner that suggested they considered themselves to be exempt from the jurisdiction of the Jordanian state.[37] The pressure reached its zenith when a daring act of defiance by Habash's PFLP culminated in the hijacking of four civilian airliners in September 1970. Landing the three planes in an area of Jordan that the PFLP defined as 'liberated territory', the Jordanian army was powerless to intervene.[38] The audacious actions of the PFLP drew the full ire of the king, and in the summer of 1971, Hussein ordered the army's final drive to expel the guerrillas out of their remaining Jordanian bases in Ajloun and Jerash. During the ensuing four days of fierce fighting, approximately 1,000 guerrillas were killed or wounded, and an additional 2,300 were captured. The conflict commenced a spiral of violence and retribution that would continue under the guidance of a new movement, Black September, a motley group comprising, amongst others, members from the PFLP and As-Sa'iqa.[39]

Although the proportion of Christian PFLP members to non-Christian members is unknown, it could be ventured that the leaders, as Christians, exuded an allure that enabled the PFLP to transcend the boundaries of religion during its establishment and residence in the Kingdom. In doing so, it constructed an organization that draws from both the Christian and Muslim communities, from both within and outside the camps. Conversely, it could be contended that given the low proportion of Christians in the Palestinian refugee camps of Jordan, the number of Christians active in the PFLP could be comparatively fewer.

In 1988, the Intifada once more confirmed the unity of Christian and Muslim Palestinians while confronting the occupation. While certain estimates disclose a disparity in the number of fatalities – five Christians were killed during the first year of the Intifada, out of a total of 410 mortalities[40] – others reveal an equal effort undertaken by both sides. The Zoilean notion that 'the relatively small number of Christians killed also indicated their low involvement in acts of violence',[41] remains implausible, particularly when one notes the similar, and in some cases identical, experiences shared by Muslim and Christian Palestinians during the Intifada. Whether Christian Palestinians would be any less vehement in their opposition to the occupation of their land is a point ably dealt with by Bernard Sabella:

'Christians in the West Bank and Gaza Strip actively participated in [the 1988 Intifada]; some became martyrs; others were imprisoned and still others had to hide from Israeli pursuit. Christian communities reacted collectively as they pressed, like other Palestinians, for an end of the occupation.'[42] Thus, the prominent role that Christians assumed at all levels of the Palestinian cause is affirmed once more, as from the leadership of the PFLP to the grassroots, both in Palestine and in Jordan, Palestinians reacted as a unified body, Christian and Muslim alike, with a higher degree of Christian participation documented in Palestine-Israel.[43]

The Role of Religion

The role of religion in the lives of the contemporary Palestinian-Jordanians residing in the Kingdom is substantial, both in terms of their surroundings – Christian homes are frequently aglow with religious icons alongside depictions of Palestine through maps and/or artwork – as well as their social activities. The juxtaposition between politics and religion and its link to Palestine is equally strong. During the course of an interview with Mary and Yacoub Joury, both of whom are originally from Jerusalem but resettled in Jordan in 1983 following a globetrotting career with the Jordanian government, the expression of divided sentiments was peppered with comments such as: 'Palestine is our home, but Jordan welcomed us.' As Christians, Mary and Yacoub maintained a place for religion and Palestine to coexist in their lives in Jordan:

> It's a very painful thing. We can't detach ourselves from what's happening in Palestine. After the Jordanian-Israeli peace agreement a friend of mine organized a women's group to go there to the religious places and we visited the religious places in Jerusalem; we always keep in contact with our family there. We call once a week, maybe more and through the internet, so we're very close.[44]

When questioned on the relevance of religion to the Palestinian cause – both in Jordan and Palestine – Yacoub asserted that religion had attained a higher priority since the invasions of Iraq and Afghanistan, as the conflict and atmosphere of uncertainty drove people towards religion in search of solace and guidance. Viewing the increasing religiosity as a natural progression, Yacoub continued:

> Religion becomes an escape and there is nothing unnatural about it. They [the Palestinians] thought that liberation could come through religion and if anything it's getting stronger and this is the natural reaction. I keep saying that the moment the occupation ends, whether it's in Palestine or Iraq, the whole outlook will change. People will live a normal life; they don't have to become anxious about their means of livelihood and they will *live*. This is what is happening today. Everything is based on religion on account of a reaction to what has happened in the Western world against Islam.[45]

Although there has been a marked increase in the movement towards Islam, when asked whether the Christian faith has observed a similar rise in adherents during the first and second Intifada and the recent Israeli onslaught, Yacoub responded in muted tones that a similar escalation was not discernible:

> As Orthodox Christians the only thing that bothers us now is that we don't have an Arab Patriarch! I don't see any fundamentalism in the various Christian denominations, whether in Palestine or in Jordan that have followed the path at this stage.[46]

Perhaps there is little need for exclusive Christian organizations in the Palestinian struggle since the existing organizations, including those which hold Islamic values austerely at their core, exercise a level of religious tolerance that enables its members to overlook the significance of faith in favour of loyalty to Palestine. As Mary surmised:

> I think it is an excellent relationship and always has been. The Palestinians have always been the most secular and the

movement has been very secular in its thinking; even now, you find that Hamas want Christians in the cabinet and they've always included the Christians. We are part and parcel of the issue itself, Palestine.[47]

From *an-Nahda* to the Intifada, the involvement of Palestinian Christians can be traced in the political evolution of the region, and in the case of the Palestinian movement in Jordan, Lebanon and Palestine. Despite their deep attachment to Palestine and affiliation to the Palestinian movement in its various guises, the Palestinian Christians of Jordan have successfully assimilated into Jordanian society and enjoyed diverse careers in the government and private sector. By excelling alongside their Jordanian and Palestinian-Jordanian counterparts, regardless of faith, they have created a community that is entirely unique in its ability to integrate into a new society with minimal sectarian divergence.

Political Aspects of Integration

Within the arena of governmental politics, the Christian population of Jordan has enjoyed a salient role in the government due to a clause within the first Election Law, introduced in 1928, which afforded a degree of over-representation to minorities, including Christians, Circassians and Bedouins. A subsequent electoral law, promulgated a year after full independence was granted in May 1946, guaranteed the Christian contingent four seats in the 18-member Council of Representatives, the Kingdom's single elected representative body. That the members of the Senate comprised a number of dignitaries appointed directly by the monarch enabled a substantial number of Christians to garner additional posts and develop a niche that would be preserved for future Christian candidates. In 1949, a further 20 seats were added to the Council, three of which were destined to be occupied by Christians, bringing the total to seven Christian representatives drawn from the districts of Amman, Salt, Irbid, Karak, Jerusalem, Ramallah and Bethlehem.[48] Often of the Greek Orthodox denomination, Christians have attained posts as high as Minister of

Foreign Affairs, held by Antun Atallah in 1963–1964 and 1970, and Minister of Justice, held by Sim'an Dawud in the cabinet of Sa'd Jum'a in 1967, while yet others have prevailed in the Ministry of Finance.[49]

In 1986 the Election Law redefined the practice of representing rural areas to the utmost through the inclusion of quotas for Christian, Chechen and Circassian minorities, in addition to certain Bedouin tribes. Through a further series of amendments in 1989, the Christian community received 11.25 per cent of the seats despite composing merely 6 per cent of the general population.[50] That such a dispensation is bestowed upon a community has not gone without criticism, though the move has been defended by Prince El-Hassan bin Talal, patron of the Royal Institute for Interfaith Studies established in 1994 in Amman, as a form of proportional representation:

> I also advocate an intelligent system of proportional represen-
> tation, which I believe exists to a very large extent in Jordan.
> Maybe it is even overstated in Jordan, where Christians have
> more seats in parliament than their population entitles them
> to. The fact is, the Jordanian parliament represents Christians
> in a – I won't say a generous manner – but in a correct
> manner.[51]

Members of the Christian community of Jordan have equally thrived in the Foreign Service, with Anastas Hannaniya, Ambassador to Great Britain in 1959, and Antun Nabir, First Secretary to Washington in 1963, as prominent examples. Within the top ranks of the military the Christian presence was particularly tangible in 1967, with three Greek Orthodox brothers – Colonel Ibrahim Ya'qub Ayyub, Brigadier General Najib Ya'qub Ayyub and Major Tawfiq Ya'qub Ayyub – occupying the positions of Director of Military Intelligence of the Army General Staff, Chief of the Royal Signals and Commander of the Jordanian Coast Guard, respectively.

It is worth noting at this point that many of the Christians mentioned – including the Ayyub brothers – were of East Bank origin.

Since the events of Black September, the issue of loyalty vis-à-vis the Palestinian-Jordanian community has played a significant role in the appointment of Palestinian-Jordanians to positions of power within the Jordanian administration, irrespective of religious ties. Indeed, during the reign of King Hussein, it was from the Palestinian communities that the anti-monarchy recruits were drawn, with the movement being characterized by Christian leadership.[52] The process of integration for the Palestinian Christians into Jordanian society is, then, multifaceted. While Christians in general encounter minimal discrimination in Jordan, it is as Palestinians that individuals confront obstacles. Thus, in instances of inequity, it is less faith-based and more often motivated by nationalist identities, depending on whether the individuals concerned are Palestinian, Palestinian-Jordanian or Jordanian. On the one hand, as Christians a privileged position is bestowed upon them by right of the electoral laws that have been in force since 1928. Yet on the other hand, differentiation persists due to their origins and questions of their loyalty. As Bishop Sayegh comments, everyday divisions continue to be manifest between the Christian and Muslim communities in Jordan: 'if you go to a job, and you are the best candidate, because your name is George, they will give the job to someone else whose name is Mohammed. Or you run a grocery store, and if these people know that you are a Christian, they do not buy from your store.'[53] As Jordan progresses, the view that discrimination occurs according to origin is disputed, as certain individuals avow its existence vehemently, while others dismiss it as an urban myth. Apropos of the Palestinian Christian identity, such a division can only enhance the kaleidoscope of self-perception, while at the same time revealing a simultaneous disparity and unity between the Christian and Muslim Jordanians of Palestinian origin.

The Prism of Identity

I have been, as an Arab, as a Palestinian, and as a Christian, trapped since I was born [...] we have been defined by others, by Westerners. Our voice was never sought, was never heard, and was never articulated [...] The challenge we face is how to make our voices heard, our conceptions and practices articulated.[54]

In parts of the wider Middle East region, the Christian community has been compelled to choose between a religious identity and a national identity, though in most cases a compromise has been wrought through the juxtaposition of a religious and ethnic/national identity. Since the accession of King Abdullah I in 1921, the Christians in Jordan have benefited from a hospitable environment. Yet the assassination of the king in 1951 in the Old City of Jerusalem provoked not only the discontents of the Muslim Palestinians, who were frustrated by the King's failure to oust the Zionists, but also an influx of Palestinian Christians who were drawn from the Israeli-occupied territories by the late king's record of religious tolerance.

For many Palestinians, the transition was not marked by disparity on the grounds of religion: originating from Palestine, their identity was foremost as Arabs and Palestinians migrating from Palestine, an Arab land. In light of Fasheh's observation in the above quote, it is of little surprise that participation in the Arab nationalist movement since 1921 comprised both Christian and Muslim Palestinians, with Christian leaders such as Naif Hawatmeh and George Habash assuming prominent roles within the PLO.[55] Within Jordan, the promulgation of the Ba'thist ideology found support amongst both Christians and Muslims, galvanizing the previously latent political engagement of the Jordanian Christians. On a political level, the Palestinians emerged from their perpetual struggle into a new life in Jordan with a sophisticated awareness of politics and nationalism that could not be quelled by King Abdullah I. Though the Hashemites vehemently sought to integrate the Palestinians into the Jordanian nation-state, the inexorable hope of Palestinian refugees of all economic levels that one day they would return to their homeland and create their own state rendered assurances of 'Jordan and Palestine were always one people and one country'[56] futile. Despite being ruled by the Kingdom for 19 years, the West Bank bore few signs of Jordanization, and the West Bankers viewed the Jordanians more as occupiers than as countrymen. Mostly disliking or fearing the Arab Legion, the disparity became immortalized through cultural expressions such as embroidery, costume and identity.

The religious nuance in the crafts has evolved more subtly, though it is gathering pace in Palestine. Widad Kawar, the foremost collector of Palestinian artefacts and costume, has observed the change in styles:

> If the lady came from Jerusalem, 'Jerusalem is ours' she writes and is correct! That is something nice. Now they have something else. Allahu Akbar [...] These are very interesting. I don't know if it is spreading because we are losing hope. Are they clinging to something? It is strange. In Palestine it is more, much more. They are so disappointed, so hopeless. They seek religion in Palestine.[57]

For the Palestinian Christians, it is more subtle. As opposed to a mosque or a bird, as adopted by the Muslims, a Christian cross is favoured. However, the incorporation of Christian symbols is a relatively recent phenomenon, as the Palestinian embroidery forum, Tatreez, affirms:

> Palestinian embroidery did not, with rare exceptions, include patterns with any religious symbols. [...] Because Christian minorities in Palestine have enjoyed essentially full societal partnership with the Moslem majority, Christian minorities did not find it necessary nor desirable to separate themselves from their Moslem brothers as did Christians in some other Arab countries, nor deliberately made themselves stand out as non-Moslems.[58]

As the popular adage used in Palestine during the twentieth century, 'Religion is for God, but the country is for everyone' (*Aldeenu Lillah Walwatan Liljamee'*), attests – and as has been discussed through this chapter – religion has offered little impetus for conflict between the Christian and Muslim Palestinian communities. The popularity of Christian symbols could, then, be perceived as an individual representation of faith, as opposed to a divisive element. Since faith continues to be a significant element in Palestinian and

Jordanian identity, it is not unanticipated that the surge in popularity of the 'Intifada costume' during the uprisings mirrored an increase in individual designs that comprised symbols of both Christian and Islamic origin.

According to Haddad, mutual negative perceptions on the basis of denomination continue to occur, further fragmenting the community. A significant example is the Protestant community, whose sermons are based on the Old Testament. Through references to the return of the Jews to the Promised Land, murmurs have emerged amidst the Muslim and Christian communities of a Protestant Christian conspiracy against the Arabs, Muslim and Christian alike. Although the Protestant churches endeavour to weather the backlash by portraying themselves as Arab national churches, its members continued to endure a degree of alienation, hatred and rejection. Whether this schism endures today is debatable, as the culture and language of the Palestinian and Jordanian communities can be perceived as a unifying element, bringing the people of the land together regardless of faith and denomination.

This was exceptionally apparent in the responses of a number of interviewees, who emphasized the unity between denominations and faiths. One Palestinian-Jordanian respondent professed, 'It does not matter whether you are Christian, Muslim, Catholic, Orthodox; we're all Palestinian.'[59] This was echoed by two more Palestinian-Jordanians, who proudly asserted that 'Palestinians are the only people who accept all religions. We would never ask what religion you are',[60] and 'There is no difference, because it is one religion, one culture, one history. It is not like Yugoslavia.'[61] Through such a snapshot of the Palestinian-Jordanian Christian-Muslim dynamic, it is evident that little has changed since Khoury noted in 1992 that 'there is no difference between Orthodox and Catholic, Armenian or Syrian, Coptic and Maronite, Lutheran and Anglican, for we are all one nation, Palestinian. Our destiny is one, our hope is one.'[62] Thus, while religion has provided the basis for numerous conflicts in the wider region, for the Christian Palestinians in Jordan it presents a lesser obstacle than that of national identity, in particular, for those of Palestinian origin.

However, a further dilemma remains that is slowly afflicting the entire Christian community in Jordan and is linked to the political and economic environment in which the Christians exist. That the Christian community in Jordan is gradually diminishing due to the evolution that brought it to the Kingdom can be viewed as an ironic development. By 2001, the estimated number of Christians in Jordan peaked at 120,000, a mere 5,000 more than in 1961. Emigration, both of Jordanian and Palestinian Christians alike, has prompted a 'brain-drain' to Western countries, with numerous Christians seeking career opportunities. As Dr. Mitri Raheb, Pastor of the Christmas Lutheran Church in Bethlehem observed, it has become a regional concern: 'The problem of Christian emigration is terrifying for the whole Christian community in the Middle East [...] The Holy Land will lose its sense of significance if there are no Christians there.'[63]

The motivation to emigrate has not been restricted to professional needs, however, with the rise of Islamism in the Kingdom acknowledged as a contributory factor to the 'Christian exodus'. The significance of Islamism as an impetus for emigration is debatable, particularly when considered alongside alternative incentives, such as financial motives, familial aspects, and Jordan's record as a placid and tolerant society. Though the trend has raised concerns, Prince El-Hassan bin Talal has maintained an optimistic view that rising Islamist sentiments represent 'one cause, but not the only one. Their leaving is a form of brain-drain – not wholly a bad thing, by the way, for better brain-drain than brain-in-the-drain [...] we're talking not only about a Christian community, but a talented community.'[64] When observed in a broader context, it is clear that the Christian community of Jordan is located within a wider migratory pattern unfolding across the region.

The implications of a talented community on the move are not entirely positive, however, as the vibrant Christian population might become susceptible to further reduction through consecutive emigration as families relocate to the destination of the primary *émigré*. This theory was substantiated by a survey conducted in the early 1990s, which discovered that as the size of the Christian community shrank, it became more probable that the remaining members would wish to emigrate, and in turn the viability of specific Christian communities was threatened. The constant movement of the Christian population also may hold critical repercussions for the region as a whole, since the decline or disappearance of indigenous Christian communities could reflect negatively not only on the communities themselves but also on the prospects of open, plural and civil societies in the region.[65] Moreover, the Christian nature of North and South American societies cannot be underestimated as an inducement to emigrate there, since the process of integration would be eased by the shared religious background.[66] Despite the cheerless implications of the observations, when regarded within the Jordanian context, it is unlikely that such a sequence of events could unfold. This is in part due to the extent to which the Christian community as a whole is entrenched in the foundations of Jordanian society, from the government – with Christian members of parliament such as Hazem Al Nasser, Tareq Khouri, and Raji Haddad, to name but a few – to the business sector, which provides a source of stability.

The schism within the employment sector between Palestinian-Jordanian and Jordanian applicants and employees has unwittingly given rise to a balance in which neither party prevails, but neither do they chafe. On a religious level, Jordan has successfully integrated its Christian community to the utmost. The point of failure resides in the inherent division along lines of national origin. Questions of loyalty according to Palestinian and Jordanian origins have presented more contention than the rise of Islamism in recent years, and will doubtless continue to do so. This is not to say that the wave of Islamic fundamentalism, to be discussed shortly, will not cause anxiety amongst the Christian communities of the region. The sense of insecurity will prevail, but also will vary in levels of intensity from one state to the next. As George noted in 2005: 'Even the Christian minorities of Syria and Jordan, whose physical security is not an issue, have been shrinking through emigration. Of those that remain, the wealthier are hedging their bets.'[67]

Whether the Christian community of Jordan will survive the current trend of emigration is unknown, but the outlook is promising. The record of the Christian population in the region has been one of stability and influence that has endured over the centuries to become one of the world's oldest Christian communities. For Palestinian Christians, the move has been eased by economic assistance from the church organizations, while their disproportionate political representation has provided a means of access to the more privileged echelons of Jordanian society. Concurrently, the Palestinian-Jordanian Christians encounter hindrances in their progress in government careers due to their origins. In this manner, their position in Jordanian society as Palestinian-Jordanian Christians is a double-edged sword. As Christians, they are officially guaranteed an enhanced political role; as Palestinian-Jordanians, they are unofficially discriminated against. Perhaps most admirable, however, is the ability of the Palestinian-Jordanian Christians to maintain their Palestinian identity and nurture an attachment to Palestine throughout the process of integration. Whether it is through the arts, costume or meetings within the community, the Palestinian-Jordanian Christians have sustained a vibrant and precious heritage that will be inherited by the next generation, regardless of whether they remain in Jordan, Palestine or North America.

Political Islam in Jordan

Since its inception Jordan has encountered Islamic groups, from the sometime friend and nemesis the Jordanian Muslim Brotherhood (al-Ikhwan al-Muslimun), to the more recent radical Islamist factions led by Abu Musab al-Zarqawi and Isam Mohammad Tahir al-Barqawi, also known as Abu Muhammad al-Maqdisi. Moving through periods of cohesion and hostility with the government, the Muslim Brotherhood and its political branch the Islamic Action Front (IAF; Jabhat al-'Amal al-Islami) has been an enduring feature of the country's political agenda. Whether scaling new heights of confrontation during the 1989 and 1995 election fiascos or representing the political and social desires of both the Palestinian-Jordanian and Jordanian population, a degree of the Muslim Brotherhood's success can be attributed to its ability to appeal to multiple aspects of society. The emergence of radical groups during the late 1970s and early 1980s in Jordan sated the disillusioned amongst the more diverse political clientele, while remaining distinct on the belief systems of its members. Far from marginalizing the existent Muslim Brotherhood, the new groups have contributed a new dimension to state-Islamist relations and redefined the role of the Muslim Brotherhood within the Jordanian context.

Founded in 1945 under the auspices of King Abdullah I, the Muslim Brotherhood was officially recognized as a 'social and charity organization' and thus able to escape the dismantling of Jordan's political parties in 1957.[68] In reality, however, the organization had been utilized by the monarchy as a counterweight to the elements of Nasser's pan-Arabism which were threatening to destabilize the regime.[69] Monarchical protection continued to bear fruits after 14 years, when the Muslim Brotherhood placed its own survival and relations with the monarchy above the cause of Palestinian liberation by supporting the regime during Black September.[70] Despite strong support for an all-Arab Palestine, the Muslim Brotherhood nevertheless opted to withdraw support for Palestinian guerrillas in the stand-off with the regime in order to preserve their bases in the East Bank. While the decision ruptured the Brotherhood, the discord did not prevent those in favour of regime-relations prevailing.[71] The organization's influence was particularly tangible in the universities with faculties for Islamic studies in Amman, Irbid and Zarqa. Indeed, between 1995 and 1996 the Islamic movement nurtured a potent presence within Jordan's universities and student organizations, with students actively participating in Muslim Brotherhood rallies throughout the kingdom.[72] Having established itself in the district of Amman, Zarqa and Irbid, the movement continued to access the student body as well as a plethora of refugee camps discontent at their under-representation.

Galvanized by the national-territorial-ethnic nuance and the high level of contact between members of the Brotherhood and the inhabitants of the refugee camps, the Palestinian-Jordanian community began to pay heed to the movement's ideology.[73] Yet the impact of the events which occurred at the peak of the courtship between the Muslim Brotherhood and the Palestinian-Jordanian populace during the 1980s cannot be overlooked. Following the ousting of the PLO from Lebanon in 1982, Palestinian-Jordanians sensed Arab reticence in spite of Israeli determination. The outbreak of the 1987 Intifada breathed not only new life into Palestinian nationalism, but infused it with a desire for more action and tangible support that the Brotherhood readily supplied in political abundance, both in Palestine through Hamas (*Harakat al-Muqawama al-Islamiyya*) and in Jordan through the IAF. Moreover, the Iranian Revolution during the late 1970s and early 1980s prompted a 'new Islamic manifestation' that granted 'the appearance of an amorphous but very real movement back to Islam by many people from all levels of society'.[74] Manifested through an increased donning of Islamic dress, an upsurge in mosque attendance, and a fevered boom in mosque construction, the environment became ripe for a hike in the Brotherhood's popularity.

Although established in 1945, it was not until the Palestinian influx that the Muslim Brotherhood emerged as an organized socio-political force in Jordan. In the 1950s, Palestinians arrived with a heightened political awareness, surpassing that of the resident Transjordanians, and proceeded to revolutionize the political discourse. In this manner, they facilitated the growth of Palestinian nationalism, which would hasten the development of Jordanian Islamist cohesion and political consciousness.[75] Likewise, Muslim Brotherhood deputies reflected the movement's leadership, comprised as it was of well-educated professionals and academics holding postgraduate degrees from Western universities.[76] Yearning to establish a pure Islamic society rooted in *shari'a*, the movement advocated that their objectives be enacted within a controlled framework through the education of the individual and society, preaching the virtues of an Islamic government, while methodically disseminating the Islamic message through mosques, publications, posters, newsletters and the press.[77] To date, these tactics have proved fruitful and enduring, notably in institutions of higher education in the capital where individuals distributing brightly coloured cards comprising prayers and excerpts from the *Quran* idle outside the university gates. While the pamphlet distributors may not be working directly on behalf of the Muslim Brotherhood, they provide examples of the manner in which the Brotherhood's ideologies are disseminated.

The integration of the Palestinian-Jordanians into the Jordanian Muslim Brotherhood has been smooth in comparison to their progress through the political ranks, which has been marked by discrimination. Recognizing the urgency of the Palestinian issue the Muslim Brotherhood purposely offers significant representation to the Palestinian-Jordanians. In three election campaigns through the 1990s, between two and three out of seven members – roughly 40 per cent – of the Muslim Brotherhood executive committee were Palestinian in origin.[78] Similarly, 50 Palestinians were elected to the 120-member IAF Shura Council in December 1997, while four Palestinians out of 13 – 30 per cent – made up the executive committee.[79] The role of the IAF as a conduit for Palestinian representation in parliament has been notable: seven Palestinians out of 22 delegates – 32 per cent – entered parliament in the first national elections in 1989, while in the 1993 elections eight Palestinians out of 17 – a worthy 50 per cent – were voted in. Conversely, the significance of the Palestinian electorate was demonstrated during the parliamentary elections of November 1997, when voter turnout declined due to the boycott.[80] Strongest in the Palestinian refugee camps around Amman and Zarqa, the largest drop in turnout was recorded in these areas, indicating the significance of the Palestinian contingent in the Muslim Brotherhood support base.

The accord between the Palestinian and Jordanian members of the Jordanian Muslim Brotherhood has enabled little distinction to be made between ethnic background and political positions, whether of the dovish-pragmatic or hawkish-radical persuasion. Indeed, the senior figures of Palestinian origin within the movement have in the past been evenly distributed with a number under the hawkish wing (Mohammad Abu Zant, Hamam Sayyid, and Mohammad Abu Faris) and others within the dovish-pragmatic groups (Ishak Farhan, Hamza Mansour, Mohammad Awayda, and Mohamad al-Haj).[81] Due to their anti-Zionist stance and endorsement of Muslim unity in spite of foreign intervention, the Muslim Brotherhood has succeeded in maintaining the Palestinian vote. During the 1984 by-election, the advantage of promoting the Palestinian cause within its manifesto was noted by *al-Ra'y* newspaper, as refugees often chose ideological candidates in favour of those relying on kinship: '[P]art of the refugees voted in support for [*sic*] Leftist candidates and other supported candidates with a strong religious orientation.'[82] However, while individuals may opt for candidates with 'a strong religious orientation', it is not always indicative of the individual's own religious adherence. The process of voting by default ensures that the IAF and Muslim Brotherhood remains a dominant force on the Jordanian political agenda, as Kamhawi notes:

> I would say it would be a fair estimate to say anything between 16 to 20 percent of the population have religious tendencies that could be reflected in the polls, through the election of Muslim Brotherhood MPs. Beyond that, it is by default: if you want to vote against the government, the only force is the Muslim Brotherhood force because the government cannot suppress it. It is a protest vote.[83]

The prominence of Palestine in the agenda of the Brotherhood has gained a substantial amount of support from otherwise non-religious individuals. This was tangible in the case of respondents who were non-practicing Muslims, but nonetheless voted for the Muslim Brotherhood. Jamil, a 32-year-old hotel receptionist and resident of the Jabal al-Hussein camp, elaborated:

> I'm not religious at all, but they are approachable and care for the people. A member of parliament normally just sits in the government – a member of the Muslim Brotherhood is different: if you go to his door, he will invite you inside, any time.[84]

The appeal on a grassroots level is clearly the secret of the Muslim Brotherhood and the IAF's success, though it rankles liberals who perceive the Muslim Brotherhood's Islamic base as undemocratic. Rantawi attributes their success to a niche in Jordan's political ideologies: 'With the absence of other trends – nationalists, leftists, democrats and liberals – they succeed to fulfil the gap. Also, the Muslim Brotherhood is more capable in providing services to the poorer areas.'[85] Significantly, the discontent amidst the camp population concerning the absence of effective representation presents a political limitation which the Brotherhood smoothly acknowledges:

> When you know that you are not represented in the government, you look for alternatives and the Muslim Brotherhood is the one. The policies adopted by the government to tackle this representation issue are irresponsible because problems with the reforms affect the liberal or the democrat more than the Islamist movement, because they have their own ways to reach out to the communities, to the grassroots.[86]

As the Islamic element of the movement engages people in a manner that liberalism, or democracy, cannot, the Brotherhood courts a degree of controversy:

> You cannot prevent people from going to the mosque, nor can you prevent a seminar in the Wihdat camp. Who loses? The democrat, the liberal in those communities, because they are absent while the Muslim Brotherhood is there. The mosque is not a place where I can talk about gender, empowering women, democratization, secularization or liberalization. For them it's the proper place to convince the public of their discourse.[87]

While the incorporation of Palestine into the Islamist agenda garners success for the IAF and the Muslim Brotherhood, it is little more than an electoral gimmick. To date, little actual progress has resulted from slogans such as 'Islam is the Solution', which proposes Islam as the solution to Jordanian and Palestinian political, economic and social afflictions. Certainly, the value of Palestine as a political commodity is high: in 1989 the Brotherhood met the campaign with customary gusto, perceiving participation in the elections as an opportunity to expand its socio-political influence. Yet it cannot be denied that the Muslim Brotherhood as a social organization does much in Jordanian society to alleviate social and economic woes. From opening its first school in the 1950s to the establishment of the Islamic Center Charity Society (ICCS) in 1963, which organizes the movement's charity activities, the Muslim Brotherhood has proven invaluable to the Palestinian-Jordanian and Jordanian communities alike. Since its foundation it has built an extensive network of voluntary and charity institutions beyond the ICCS with vast resources and capabilities.[88] This is so pronounced that within recent years the movement has been speculated to hold an estimated 200 million JD in resources, making it a major competitor of all social organizations, including the General Union of Voluntary Societies, the Noor al-Hussein Foundation, and the Queen Alia Fund for Voluntary Social Work.[89] While the virtues of such endeavours merit commendation, it is the political progress of the movement that cuts an uncertain figure as its roots, steeped in Islamic tradition that advocates patience and ardent struggle, prevent it from committing to direct action, a limitation exploited by radical groups that whet the appetites of the battle-hungry young.

More recently, the Brotherhood has attracted criticism on the progress of the Palestine issue and its tempestuous affair with the Jordanian monarchy, which has enabled the movement to remain a permanent fixture on the political scene. A significant outcome of the Muslim Brotherhood's hesitancy has been the emergence of independent Islamic movements in Jordan, including the Islamic Jihad Movement Bayt al-Maqdas (*Harakat al-Jihad al-Islami Bayt al-Maqdas*), The Islamic Army, The Islamic Revolutionary Army and Hamas. Although many of the aforementioned groups have their roots in Palestine, their association with Jordan is maintained by former supporters of the Muslim Brotherhood, who wish to adopt a proactive, Islamist approach to the Palestinian struggle. Jordan, providing a suitable geographical base from which to launch strikes into Israel, has yielded a high number of adherents to the causes of each faction and a link has been forged between Jordan and Palestine through the Islamic groups.

For Hamas, the weakness of the Brotherhood has proved a boon: during the 1987 Intifada the Jordanian Muslim Brotherhood maintained close ties to Hamas, since its emergence from the Palestinian

wing of the Muslim Brotherhood in Gaza. Between 1948 and 1967
the Palestinian division engaged in an organizationally symbiotic relationship with the Jordanian Muslim Brotherhood by sharing office
space and members, with each branch governed by a separate general
overseer.[90] When Jordan lost control of the West Bank in 1967, the
West Bank branch of the Muslim Brotherhood edged towards the
Gazan office and though ties endured to the Jordanian movement, it
ultimately provided limited support for the Palestinian cause.[91] By
the 1988 Intifada, Palestinians in Jordan and Palestine had grown
weary of the arduous track charted under the Muslim Brotherhood
and welcomed the emergence of Hamas and its strident objective of
armed resistance.

Despite being embraced by Hamas, the Palestinian Muslim
Brotherhood remained organizationally linked to the Jordanian
Muslim Brotherhood and Hamas continues to be incorporated with
the Muslim Brotherhood directorate in Amman.[92] The ties between
the government and the Muslim Brotherhood have enabled Hamas
to maintain limited cordial relations with the Jordanian government.
Certainly, the relationship has been tempestuous: while the government has periodically cautioned the Brotherhood to contain Hamas
activities in Jordan, it has also demonstrated support for Palestinian
Islamists, notably through negotiations for the release of Sheikh
Ahmad Yassin, the then spiritual leader of Hamas.[93] With mercurial gestures such as these, it is unsurprising that ambiguity suffuses
questions of the Brotherhood's influence vis-à-vis governmental and
monarchical resistance.

All the same, the notion that the Muslim Brotherhood is a puppet
of the Jordanian government is gradually losing credence. As Hattar
observes, the Brotherhood in Jordan serves as a proxy for Palestinians
who would vote for Hamas, had the option been available. In doing
so, it has cloven the movement in two with a contingent favoured by
ethnic Jordanians and another by Palestinians:

The Islamic movement in Jordan and Hamas is one and the
same. The Jordanian side of Brotherhood is not for Hamas, but
for al-Qaeda. That's why when there is an election here in Jordan

all the Palestinians give their vote to the Islamic figures supporting Hamas. The Jordanian law is not a harsh one, but legally
it is forbidden that you will be a member of Hamas. That's why
it is possible for anyone in Jordan to say 'yes' to Hamas as a
movement, but not to be a member.[94]

Further schisms within the movement are perceptible through the
Palestinian refugees of 1948 and 1967. As prominent members of
Palestinian origin within the Jordanian Muslim Brotherhood and the
IAF, they have failed to present a cohesive bloc. This dichotomy has
manifested in the extremist voices of the movement often being refugees of 1967, proving that the direction of the movement vis-à-vis
Palestine is a dilemma divided along inter-Palestinian lines, as opposed
to a Jordanian-Palestinian dichotomy.[95] Yet the Muslim Brotherhood
is divided along both lines: the organization's tendency to acquiesce
with the Jordanian government in times of conflict with Palestinian
movements, such as Black September and during the suspension of
the al-Nabulsi government in 1957, divides those of Palestinian and
Jordanian origin. When coupled with the absence of cohesion in the
inter-Palestinian relationship in Jordan and the vain posturing by the
Muslim Brotherhood on the Palestine issue, the aforementioned weaknesses become cracks in an already fragile relationship.

   In terms of internal politics, the Muslim Brotherhood has been a
strong critical voice in the Electoral Law reform debate. Perceived by
many as an ineffective and unjust mechanism of governance, any hopes
of change to the electoral law expressed by respondents in 2006 and
2007 were to be dashed over the ensuing years. It is significant then
that the bulk of the Brotherhood's support base in the refugee camps
is composed of those who have the most to lose in terms of representation under the legislation. This is even more pronounced given the
Brotherhood's vociferous support of reform:

   The Muslim Brotherhood is against one man, one vote because
   this is against their interests. Each group has different views on
   it. Some want percentages – like the Israeli system. Some nationalists want the country to be one constituency, while others want

a bi-system, i.e. you vote for one local MP and one national MP.
Up until now they have not been able to come up with a new
law because the hidden goal remains to prevent the Palestinians
from prevailing in parliament.[96]

Alternatively, this call for reform could be regarded as a ruse to safeguard the interests of the Brotherhood and the IAF in future elections,
for while the rise of Islamist groups in society and politics represents
a challenge, the Brotherhood is supporting the most urgent causes of
its electorate: under-representation and Palestine. Yet it is on Palestine
that they stand to lose the most as the new generation, rankled by
years of inertia and longing for a proactive stance, are being sated by
contemporary movements such as the Islamic Jihad Movement in
Palestine, Hizbollah Palestine and Bayt al-Maqdas.

The (Re-)emergence of Radical Political Islam in Jordan

The rise of radical Islamist groups in Jordan affords an insight into the
socio-political future of the Kingdom. Since the 2005 bombings, the
country has maintained a reputation as an 'oasis of calm' in a turbulent region, yet with the highest percentage of Palestinian refugees,
the influence of manifold Islamist groups could alter Jordan's peaceful
status. The Amman attacks demonstrated that even the intelligence
services confronted a complex degree of organization in their attempts
to identify and counter the Jihadist threat. In the case of the unknown
Iraqi suicide bombers dispatched to enact the triple bomb attack in
2005, they were aided by the ability to move unnoticed within the
country. The flow of Iraqis into the country currently outnumbers
those being deported back to Iraq, creating a steady and inscrutable
exchange through the border. In this manner, the perpetrators could
liaise with the contact resident, Abu Musa al-Zarqawi, who in turn
had numerous resources at his disposal.

The culmination of the Six-Day War spurred the early ideologies
of radical Islam to their ascent as a powerful extra-political force in
Jordan and the wider region. The Arab loss imbued Saudi Islamism
with an aura of high respectability and prominence as the increase in

Saudi Arabia's strategic, political and economic influence accrued from the 1970s oil boom bolstered the appeal of radical Islam in Jordanian society. Beleaguered by economic deprivation, soaring unemployment and limited social mobility, elements of Jordanian society aspired to scale similar dizzying heights of affluence and piety to their Saudi brothers.[97] As well as the success of the Iranian Revolution, the 1979 Soviet invasion and subsequent occupation of Afghanistan not only contributed towards the internationalization of radical Islam, but enabled Jordanian Mujahedeen to receive military training in a strict ideological framework. Incorporating the ideologies of the founding father of jihadism, Sayyid Qutb, the course also included the thoughts of his protégées Abdullah Azzam, Dr. Ayman al-Zawahiri and Sheikh Omar Abdul Rahman. The culmination of training coincided with the end of the first Gulf War, the exodus from which boosted the Jordanian population by an additional 10 per cent as Palestinian-Jordanians and Jordanians alike streamed into the Kingdom from Kuwait. The massive surge, coupled with a rapid drop in the remittances that had previously buoyed the country's economy, wrought dire political economic and social consequences.

Hit most severely was Zarqa, host to 160,000 of the 250,000 returnees. Devoid of tribal structure and rife with despondency amidst rising poverty, the ideologies of Salafi jihadists found fertile ground as the inhabitants sought a new identity and a common cause to unite their uprooted community.[98] Already perceived as a caustic blend of despondence and militancy, Zarqa first secured infamy during the 1990s after 500 men journeyed to Afghanistan, shortly to be joined by Zarqawi.[99] The new Islamist movement was emerging fast with a ready supply of followers in the camps, yet the Muslim Brotherhood retained an advantage: time. The camps' inhabitants had grown accustomed to the Brotherhood's presence through charitable works; for all the religio-nationalist pledges of the nascent movements, the tangible evidence of the Brotherhood's assistance could not be overlooked. Nevertheless, the onslaught of new groups from Jordan and Palestine presented a steeper challenge. While the Muslim Brotherhood has maintained a slow-but-sure approach to Palestine, the quick-fix proactive mentality of recent groups has presented an attractive alternative for those languishing in *zincos* with little or no healthcare and a bleak future awaiting their children.

And it was on the basis of the Brotherhood's lack of action that a number of groups emerged. Established in the early 1980s by Dr Fathi Shqaqi and Sheikh Abdel Aziz Uda in Gaza and Palestine, the Jihad Movement in Palestine, also known as the Shqaqi Faction, strives for a liberated Palestine. Attracting support from Iran, Syria and Hizbollah in Lebanon, the movement received financial resources, weapons, fighting *matériel* and training in Syrian camps, and Hizbollah and Iranian Revolutionary Guard camps in Lebanon. While the Jihad Movement actively directed operations in the West Bank, Gaza Strip, Jordan and Lebanon, significant attacks occurred at the Beit Lid Junction in 1995 and the Dizengoff Center in 1996. Although the movement has attempted to expand within Jordan, the security forces foiled attempts to establish bases in the Kingdom. While the faction increased efforts to court support by using forged papers to enter Jordan from Syria, their endeavours proved fruitless after the security services laid ambushes along the Syrian lines and ousted existing members from within the Kingdom.[100] The 1994 peace treaty between Jordan and Israel motivated members to increase their onslaught on Jordan, both in terms of using Jordanian territory as a base for Israeli incursions and plotting sabotage against key figures in the Jordanian administration.[101] The success of the Jordanian security services in thwarting the efforts of the Shqaqi Faction limits further analysis on the extent to which the movement has triumphed in acquiring new members. Given the urgency with which it enters the country and establishes bases, it can be inferred that the camps and poverty-stricken areas of Jordan are a potentially bountiful source of recruits.

In light of this frustration, Hizbollah Palestine was established by Ahmed Hassan Muhanna in 1993. Born in the Gaza Strip in 1951, Muhanna initially joined the Islamic Jihad Movement in Palestine and Bayt al-Maqdas before leaving Tamimi's group in 1990. With a focus on sabotage activity in Jordan against Jordanian and Western targets, the movement aimed to destabilize the Kingdom through attacks on the American embassy and American tourists, to be executed by locally recruited terrorists. Like the Shqaqi faction Hizbollah Palestine intended to fire missiles into Israel from Jordanian territory, conduct sabotage in the Aqaba-Eilat area and attack Jordanian military officers and members of the ruling family. Once more the Jordanian security services gathered intelligence to block several attempts at smuggling fighting *matériel*, including Katyusha rockets, hand grenades and light weapons, into the country from Syria between 1990 and 1993, when a number of the group's members were killed in a skirmish with the Jordanian army.[102] Although Tal refers to 'Jordan terrorists', as opposed to Palestinians, the movement would not discriminate between followers and the term 'Jordanian' comprises Palestinian-Jordanian and Jordanian members alike.

The Islamic Liberation Party (*Hizb al-Tahrir*) differs from the aforementioned groups, having assumed a prominent position in the Jordanian government during the period 1954–1956 and presented a reasonable Islamist challenge to the political wing of the Muslim Brotherhood. Founded in 1953 as the second Islamic party in Jordan and Palestine, it was governed by Sheikh Taqi Eddin Nabhani, a Palestinian from Nablus, and an East Bank Jordanian, Sheikh Ahmed ad-Dawur from Qalqiliya, with Nabhani as its head until his death in 1977.[103] Although repeatedly denied permission to operate legally in Jordan, the ILP secured the position of one candidate during the fourth parliament between 17 October 1954 and 26 June 1956.[104] It has been speculated that a dispute between Nabhani and the Jordanian leadership concerning Jordan's decision to align with the British fuelled their mutual enmity, in addition to the close relationship enjoyed by the Muslim Brotherhood and the Jordanian government.[105] Nabhani's disdain for Hussein's decision to call upon Britain and the United States for aid following the events of 1948 was palpable. Subsequently, and perhaps entirely as a result of the aforementioned events, he was suspected of involvement in Abdullah al-Tall's attempted coup in Jordan during the mid-1950s.[106]

Believing that the restoration of the Caliphate is the foremost desire of all Muslims, the Islamic Liberation Party (ILP) divides the world into *dar al-Islam* (the land of Islam) and *dar al-kufr* (the land of the unbelieving). Since *dar al-Islam* cannot be attained until a Muslim Caliph emerges to rule the country in accordance with Islamic *shari'a*, which can be accomplished through 'a new Islamic personality and mentality through intensive Islamic training',[107] the majority of the Arab world and beyond continues to dwell in *dar al-kufr*. In addition, the party believes that it is forbidden (*haram*) for a Muslim to participate in a non-Islamic movement and that capitalism and socialism are corrupt and contradictory to the nature of human beings.[108] In a statement provided by Nabhani, the group summarizes their ethos within the following dictum:

> *Hizb-ut Tahrir* is a political party and its ideology is Islam. Politics is its activity and Islam is its ideology, and it works together, among, and with the *Ummah* in order that she takes the re-establishment of Islam in life, state, and society as its vital issue, thereby leading her to establishing the *Khilafah* and returning to the *hukm* (rule) of Allah.[109]

Similar to the Muslim Brotherhood, a significant weakness of the ILP resides in its predilection for employing ideological means to argue with others, reserving 'other means' for the forthcoming Islamic state. Yet the ILP differs from the Muslim Brotherhood insofar as the Brotherhood is not averse to liaising with non-Islamic groups such as the leftist party, the PFLP, the DFLP and the Communist Party.

Aside from a lack of support by the Jordanian regime, the ILP was hamstrung from the outset in its endeavours to court Palestinian support with ideologies expressing limited concern for the Palestinian issue. Mirroring the views of its contemporaries in the sphere of Islamist groups, the ILP asserts that the establishment of the Islamic state must be a primary objective and that only once this has been achieved will the remaining matters addressing statehood be attended to.[110] Accordingly, far from seizing arms and resisting the occupation, the Palestinians in the Occupied Territories are advised to patiently await the coming of the Islamic state. The somewhat passive stance dates back to the Muslims in Mecca, who waited helplessly until the Prophet's army arrived from Medina. Perceiving the Palestinians to be in a similar situation, the party disapproves of all forms of resistance – including strikes and demonstrations – and did not participate in the Intifada of 1987 or 2000, since it was deemed 'an artificial creation by hostile, secular, national forces'.[111] As a final pledge, the ILP has rejected all compromises, all attempts to make a settlement in the region, and UN resolutions concerning the issue and the call for an independent Palestinian state in the West Bank and Gaza Strip.

Since the passing of Nabhani in 1977, the mantle of leadership fell upon Abdul-Qadeem Zalloum. Since Zalloum's death in 2003, the leadership has been held by Ata Abu-Rashta, under whom the group has been organized in a cellular manner with hubs located throughout Central Asia, Europe, Southeast Asia, Australia, the Middle East, India and Africa, with minor representatives in the Americas.[112] In contrast to advocating terror in these regions, the ILP has retained a stoic approach, as the leader of the party in Britain observes: 'The bottom line was that al-Qaida-style terrorist attacks were not practical and did not help the group to achieve their goals.'[113] Given the spate of attacks perpetrated by Jordanians inside the Kingdom and the attempted, and partially successful, events involving a number of doctors of Jordanian origin in Glasgow in July 2007, one could disregard the necessity to discern between the influence of divergent Islamist groups on the identity of Palestinian-Jordanians and Jordanians. While certain groups advocate a proactive approach in Palestine, this must be firmly distinguished from the Jihadist groups – working to free Palestine is a world away from venturing onto foreign territory to wreak havoc.

The rise of new Islamist groups in Jordan is, as is predominantly the case with the Palestinian identity, a delicate matter. While the Muslim Brotherhood has courted popularity in the Palestinian community due to its charitable endeavours and unstinting support of the Palestinian cause (albeit more often rhetorically), the similar stance of the ILP has prevented it from breaking free from the shackles of exclusion maintained by the cautious Jordanian government. Alternatively, the emergence of militant groups such as Hizbollah Palestine and the

Shqaqi Faction are merely starbursts in a galaxy of militias. Although each advocates a proactive course of action towards the liberation of Palestine, Salafi-oriented groups create a schism as they attract a pre-dominantly Jordanian following. Thus, the plethora of Islamist groups emerging and enduring in Jordan cannot be perceived as a mono-lithic bulwark of jihadism burgeoning within an otherwise peace-ful Kingdom, but rather as a collection of disparate groups united by an underlying theological foundation. Similar to Christianity, faith assumes a key role in providing a means by which the despondence of the Palestinian-Jordanian community can seek solace and action towards re-attaining their homeland, thereby ending their period in exile.

7

(CYBER-)PALESTINE AND THE QUEST FOR A NATIONAL IDENTITY

The blogosphere burst forth with renewed vigour three years after the term 'weblog' debuted in 1997 and the catalyst for the surge is attributable to four major events: the inception of easy-access and functional software, 9/11, the commencement of the U.S.-led war on Iraq in 2003 and the 2004 Tsunami. With its own blogs (*mudawwanat*) and blogosphere, Arab bloggers have continuously defied restrictions to provide insights from Iraq, Sudan, Syria, Saudi Arabia, Bahrain, Egypt and Lebanon, engaging in cyber-discourses on politics (domestic, regional and international), human rights and LGBT issues. While the Middle Eastern blogosphere has not reached the dizzying heights of millions just yet, they represent a potentially formidable force. With a focus on the Palestinian identity, this chapter will chart the utilization of blogs as a means of sustaining the notion of 'the Palestinian homeland' in the communities of the Middle East and the United States. Preliminary research of blogs constructed by Palestinians in the diaspora indicate that a cohesive bond can be developed between individuals, producing 'cyber-communities' that share memories, provide support, and promote cultural and historical awareness through the blogging medium. The bond between individuals engaged in these networks heightens in times of conflict, such as the Israeli invasion of Lebanon in 2006 and the Gaza conflict in 2009. In addition, social network sites such as Facebook and Twitter provide sources of activism, cyber-communal interaction and support both in times of conflict and peace, raising the cybersphere as a platform for cyber-communities that in turn represent the impact of regional developments on the national discourse.

Locating the Palestinian National Identity

Considering the variety of identities and sub-identities within the region, it is inevitable that the Palestinian identity comprises nuances that alter according to experience, political affiliation and country of residence. As Khalidi notes, the lack of exclusivity inherent in the Palestinian identity became immortalized by late nineteenth and early twentieth century intellectuals and politicians, who divided their affinities between 'the Ottoman Empire, their religion, Arabism, their homeland Palestine, their city or region, and their family, without feeling any contradiction, or sense of conflicting loyalty'.[1] Primarily characterized through the establishment of a boundary between the Arabs and the Turks – thus excluding Muslims who were not Arab, or Arabic-speaking from the embryonic identity – the coalescence of Arabic-speaking Muslims and Christians incorporated members of both religions in the national community.[2] The final facet of the process established the creation of boundaries between Palestinian and non-Palestinian Arabs, thereby excluding those Arabic speakers not associated with the demarcated territory of Palestine. As Greenstein notes, the primary and secondary aspects were invaluable to the process of identity formation, as without them no meaningful Arab national identity could have survived. The ultimate aspect is more unclear as the construction of a general pan-Arab identity continued even as a distinct Palestinian-Arab identity emerged, thus indicating a lack of dependence between the two identities. Inevitably, pressure between the two foci of the competing identities, in addition to the Islamic focus, presented a subject for debate and a struggle among Palestinian Arabs since its formation.[3]

During the early years of the Ottoman period, expressions of national identity demonstrated a flexibility that enabled multiple identities to co-exist without hastening the desire for independent statehood.[4] Yet a state of confusion has been engendered by the multiple identities of the Middle East, as Khashan observes: 'Today, the Arabs are at a loss. They suffer from a severe identity crisis. Nineteenth-century reformers disturbed the Arab mind by sowing distrust in the Ottoman Empire, without securing a tenable alternative to that religious state and to Islam which it embodied.'[5] As a consequence, the Arab identity that moved into the twentieth century was less one of formidable versatility and more the product of 'a disoriented and politically indecisive mind'.[6] In this manner, identities are regarded as politically dependent, as opposed to religiously so, since 'An ideological wave prevails for some time before it dissipates, only to be replaced by a completely different wave [...] Political ideologies often rise and fall depending on the international situation.'[7] However, such an assertion can be refuted; while identities are indubitably influenced by the political milieu in which the individual exists, the alternative factors active during the formulation of an identity are too multitudinous to overlook. Conflicts and political affiliations do, to an extent, assume a substantial role; yet religion, upbringing, education, environment and cultural awareness are more probable elements influencing the formation of an identity. As such, identity can be viewed as an influence on political behaviour; rather than political situations guiding the individual, political views and actions are determined by the origins and experiences of the individual and their self-perceptions.

Political situations and the views that arise from them can be linked to an elementary feature of identity: differentiation. A pertinent aspect of identity, it initiates comparisons that would ultimately define one group from another and inspire questions such as 'are the ways of our group better or worse than the ways of their group?'. In doing so, competition arises:

Group egotism leads to justification: Our ways are better than their ways. Since the members of the other group engage in a similar process, conflicting justifications lead to competition. We have to demonstrate the superiority of our ways to their ways. Competition leads to antagonism and the broadening of what may have started as the perception of narrow differences into more intense and fundamental ones. Stereotypes are created, the opponent is demonized, [and] the other is transmogrified into the enemy.[8]

Accordingly, the group's sense of self rises and falls with the fortunes of groups with which they identify. Thus, ethnocentrically, the group may prefer 'to be worse off absolutely but better off compared to someone they see as a rival rather than better off absolutely but not as well off as that rival.'[9] As the individual or group gradually distinguishes itself in terms of what it is or is not in comparison to the opposing group or individual, the need for self-esteem leads each to believe that they are superior.

Operating not only as a form of expression, identity also functions within socialization, cultural dissemination and population distribution, while also surrendering to geopolitical phenomena, environmental changes and group experiences. As an 'inherent property of mankind', loss of identity is conducive to social marginalization and political ineptitude in open and competitive societies. Furthermore, it has an 'unsurpassed influence on interpersonal relationships including socialization, the vehicle for cultural dissemination.'[10] Guided by population distribution, living in groups eventually creates distinct group values, while individuals of similar persuasions may opt to relocate to a new territory so that they can immerse themselves in shared values.[11] Identities are therefore shared by groups en masse while evolving according to social space and changes in the modes of production. Yet while the evolution seems infinite, the influence of culture enables a boundary to be established. As Zdzisław asserts, identity 'represents the multidimensional, integrated human [...] and cannot be reduced to a series of separate roles which an individual plays in various social groups and situations.'[12] Finally, identities can be viewed as realistic representations of cognitive realities at certain points in time, epitomizing group experiences, achievements and aspirations through specific social organizations.[13]

Conceived in the diaspora, the Palestinian-Jordanian identity comprises a group identity, which is shared collectively, and a singular identity that is shaped by the individual's personal status and experiences. Once in the group, the individual seeks to redefine his or her identity in the context of the constructed group and its objectives. Thus, if the basis for the primary feature of the group disappears, perhaps because it acquires the goal that it was created to achieve, the existence of the group is threatened, unless it can attain another cause to motivate its members.[14] In the case of the Palestinian-Jordanians, the cause – the attainment of Palestine – is enduring, while new motivations arise, consolidating their group identity through catastrophes such as Black September and the Intifada. More recently, the Iraq War reinforced the Palestinian identity as thousands of Palestinians residing in Iraq are confronting the daily threat of murder on the streets that they had come to call home. In the context of blogs, this is demonstrated when, in response to a post touching upon Palestinian documentary movies, commenter 'Wassim' reminds fellow readers that:

> Most of the Palestinian movies are talking about the Pals in Lebanon [...] or in West Bank, there are a lot of Palestinians away from the spot. For example the Pals in Iraq NOW, those ppl [people] who are living in hell and nobody cares, and maybe hell is much better than Iraq now.[15]

Once more forced to flee and relinquish their comfortable environment for hastily established camps on the border of Jordan, for many Palestinians history is merely repeating itself, creating another act in a Palestinian tragedy.

The environment in which an individual resides bears a significant influence on the self-perception of that individual, both in terms of in-group relations and those extraneous yet connected, such as the political authorities of the host state. Should the individual enter a new social situation in which he or she is perceived as the stranger who does not belong, it is plausible that the individual would consider themselves within that context.[16] Thus, if one is made to feel unwelcome within a state for extended periods of time, then the individual adapts to the imposed role of 'unwanted person(s)' and begins to consider themselves within that context. For the Palestinian-Jordanians, the rhetoric of those in political positions of Jordanian origin who persistently reiterate that the Palestinians are not Jordanian and therefore should seek full rights in Palestine adds potency to the Palestinian identity in the diaspora. Equally, ancestry provides a crucial means by which kinship is realized and maintained. While political alliances may be ambiguous, and religion a potential source of persecution, the kinsmen can be relied on for loyalty and assistance, thereby affording the ultimate refuge.[17] While disputes and schisms are inevitable among the kinsmen, the Palestinian diaspora community has transcended these pitfalls in progressing towards a common objective.

Hybrid Identities: Bridging the Cultural Divide

As Hall observes, the concept of diaspora has evolved from the former definition comprising an imperialistic hegemonizing notion of ethnicity, towards the recognition of 'a necessary heterogeneity and diversity; by a conception of "identity" which lives with and through, not despite, difference [...] constantly producing and reproducing themselves anew, through transformations and difference.'[18] The transformation is especially tangible in the hybrid identity nurtured by the Palestinian-Jordanian community. The discourse surrounding hybrid identities has evolved substantially since its inception as an element of postcolonial theory. The term 'hybrid' in relation to cultural development conceals a past checkered with calumnious nineteenth-century musings constructed to justify colonialist exploits. Yet over the course of the twentieth century, the arcane has been transformed into the analytical and provided a crucial means by which to understand the emergence of new identities, societies and their ideologies. A significant feature of hybridity in the context of identity is its ability to morph according to the requirements of the individual. Equally, this has resulted in hybrid identities being the hardest to comprehend, since 'There is no single, or correct, concept of hybridity: it changes as it repeats, but it also repeats as it changes.'[19] As a concept, hybridity has assumed a key position in cultural criticism and postcolonial studies, as well as cultural appropriation and contestation in the context of borders and the ideal of the cosmopolitan. Alternatively – a notion especially prevalent in early analyses – hybridity has been perceived to herald the threat of 'contamination' to promulgators of the essentialist notion of pure and authentic origins.[20]

Barker and Galasiński's contention that hybridization is the mixing of that which is already a hybrid is dubious,[21] since it removes the fusion, or hyphen, that makes it possible to discern between two cultural backgrounds that give rise to hybrid identities. If one subscribes to this theory, it would be impossible to perceive the Palestinian-Jordanian identity as a hybrid, since both the Palestinian and Jordanian identities are hybrids, thereby reducing the Palestinian-Jordanian entity to a mere banality. To do so would be troublesome on two levels: primarily, the beauty of hybrid identities lies in their fusion across cultures, borders and experience to meld new identities that capture the best of both cultures – that is, Palestinian and Jordanian. The Palestinian identity can be regarded as a hybrid due to its history as a port down the centuries; equally, the Jordanian identity can be viewed as a hybrid due to the vast number of migrants from Syria, Arabia and the Hijaz that settled in the territory among the Bedouin tribes. Thus, an identity is often distilled into two components, reinforcing the notion of a 'hyphen identity'.

Within an increasingly globalized world, hybridity has emerged as a means to reflect the relationship between the 'local' and the 'global' and defining hybridity itself has become an altogether more complex task, as Papastergiadis notes:

> [H]ybridity has become one of the most useful concepts for representing the meaning of cultural difference in identity. Self-image is formed in, not prior to, the process of interaction with others. This interpretation of identity as hybrid is a direct challenge to earlier quasi-scientific claims that hybrids were sterile, physically weak, mentally inferior and morally confused. [...] This stigma has now been converted into a positive gain.[22]

The assertion that an influx of individuals non-indigenous to the region could prompt the proliferation of essentialist sentiments is further speculated upon by Weaver, who contends that in emphasizing the 'hybridity of modern indigenous existence, charges of essentialism as indigenous peoples assert their identities are themselves essentializing, positing in contemporary existence a descent from racially/ethnically pure past.'[23] Thus, in accusing indigenous communities – in this case, ethnic Jordanians – of endorsing essentialization, as researchers we are sanctioning it in our own manner through the assumption that indigenous groups default to such mechanisms due to their inherently racially and/or ethnically pure past.

As noted previously, language assumes a pertinent role in the expression of identity and hybridity. In the case of the Palestinian diaspora, linguistic differences afford markers of an individual identity, as Roba, author of the blog andfaraway, observes in the post 'Language Survey':

> The linguistic survey has 15 words we use often in Jordan [...] if you are a Palestinian living in Jordan, try to choose the country that you think you picked most of your dialect from. [...] Being of mixed background and having lived in Saudi Arabia myself, I have my own hoard of words that most Jordanians do not use, such as '7assabet', 'bishweish', and 'Ja7ad'.[24]

Nevertheless, in the context of diasporic hybrid identities, matters become even more convoluted. The initial appearance of multiculturalism and intellectual popularity that furnishes hybridity with its allure rapidly dissipates to reveal the reality of the migrant's horizon, one that is replete with experiences of itinerancy, ghettoization and illegality. Accordingly, displacement becomes not only more common, but a more complex experience and phenomena, both for the individual and the researcher alike.[25] Lastly, as identities by their very nature 'are neither pure nor fixed but formed at the intersections of age, class, gender, race and nation',[26] hybridity emerges as more than a theory of national identities: as something unique to the individual with the aforementioned elements customizing the hybrid identity.

However, in the case of diasporic identities such as the Palestinian-Jordanian identity, such factors can influence individual identities without obscuring the overriding common traits that unite the Palestinian-Jordanian community through their origins and aspirations to return to, or witness, the establishment of an independent Palestine.

Taking it Global: Identity Online

O, wonder!
How many goodly creatures are there here!
How beauteous mankind is! O brave new world,
That has such people in't![27]

The rise of online social networks has not diminished interaction between individuals; rather, it has elevated it to a multi-contact level that facilitates discourse between not only individuals, but groups and communities. Identity, as a means to define oneself, has smoothly entered into the digital realm and is asserted through blogs, Tweets, fan pages and media clips. This cyberculture has become characterized by a technosociality that is alternately definable as 'a broad process of sociocultural construction set into motion in the wake of the new technologies'[28] and an indicator of 'the combination of materiality and immateriality, subject and object, sentientism and insentientism and intentionality and automation in networks'.[29] Yet the convergence of the tangible and social through the cyber medium not only facilitates the promulgation of social identity and practices within the cybersphere, but evolves beyond the customary boundaries inherent in daily personal interaction. For example, in the context of lesbian, gay, bisexual and transgender (LGBT) organizations in the Middle East such as Bekhsoos and Meem, activism and debate that would otherwise prove controversial or difficult to express or enact on a tangible level is rendered conveyable online. The availability of anonymity enables authors to publish opinions and personal anecdotes with impunity under pseudonyms that raise awareness and provide guidance on issues that remain taboo. Thus, Goffman's theory that identity is perpetually constrained and shaped by external factors is particularly resonant in the above context, since:

> Society established the means of categorizing persons and the complement of attributes felt to be ordinary and natural [...] We lean on these anticipations that we have, transforming them into normative expectations, into righteously presented demands. Typically, we do not become aware that we have made these demands or aware of what they are until an active question arises as to whether or not they will be fulfilled. It is then that we are likely to realize that all along we had been making certain assumptions [...] evidence can arise of his possessing an attribute that makes him different [...] he is thus reduced in our minds from a whole and usual person to a tainted, discounted one.[30]

While society may influence the expression of one's sexual identity in a non-cyber context, the virtue of the Internet resides in its ability to transcend the boundaries established by society. As Meyrowitz notes, 'Even when Goffman mentions electronic and other media [...] he seems to view their effects as unusual or amusing and, in most cases, as peripheral to the core of social action.'[31] Written in 1961 and 1986 respectively, both Goffman and Meyrowitz pre-date the evolution of the cybersphere, yet their theories remain pertinent insofar as the expression of identity continues to be influenced by social expectations and new media facilitates the circumvention of these expectations.

In the case of national identity, a facet emerges that can be regarded as contrary to the notion of the cybersphere providing a forum for expression that would otherwise be stifled. In the context of national identity, the Internet facilitates broader participation, building on the manifestations of national identity exercised in a day-to-day non-virtual social context.[32] In the case of the Palestinian identity, the geographically scattered circumstances arising from the diasporic nature of the community are reconciled through shared points of interest, including memories, commemorations, cookery, poetry,

current affairs, debates and activism, all of which draws together
Palestinians from Jordan, Lebanon, Syria, North America and Europe.
In this manner, Meyrowitz's notion of electronic media transcending
boundaries is applicable in a substantial, geographical sense: though
separated by continents, blogs bring individuals together as writers,
participants and readers. Nevertheless, the notion of blogs bringing
together communities is not without ambiguity, for:

> [C]ritics argue that these groups do not constitute real commu-
> nities. Something is missing [...] that makes these online groups
> pale substitutes for more traditional face-to-face communities.
> Others respond that not only are online communities real com-
> munities, but also that they have the potential to support face-to-
> face communities and help hold local communities together.[33]

In the context of this chapter, the notion of 'community' will be
applied in an online context; far from being a static entity 'community' is malleable, determined by the environment in which it
gathers individuals around a common objective, interest or origin.
That Palestine provides a rallying point through blogs imbues the
Palestinian community with a new, pliable dimension through which
the essence of 'community' is carried into the cybersphere retaining
features of familiarity. Indeed, Hawley's 1950 definition of community is still applicable, since cyber communities are of 'a size which
enables the inhabitants to have a diffuse familiarity with the everyday
life of the area'.[34] Accordingly, the online Palestinian community is
definable as a 'community' due to the familiarity shared by participants of not only the area, but also its shared points of culture, history
and social reference.

The multidimensionality of blogs is further enhanced through the
formulation of communities through 'metablognition'. A synthesis of
online and offline identities, metablognition enables the two identities
to be analysed within a cyber-framework, and with roots in metacognitive reflection – essentially, 'thinking about thinking'[35] – metablognition deploys blogs as a means to express and analyse identity through
the electronic medium. In recent years, metablognition has emerged

as a pedagogical tool, yet the rationale behind its utilization is equally applicable in the context of online identity expression:

> Blogging [...] offers students a chance to a) reflect on what they are writing and thinking as they write and think it, b) carry on writing about a topic over a sustained period of time, maybe a lifetime, c) engage readers and audience in a sustained conversation that then leads to further writing and thinking and d) synthesize disparate learning experiences and understand their collective relationship and relevance.[36]

To date, the cybersphere has been predominantly subject to discourse with a focus on social and virtual networks, as well as the public and private sphere.[37] The links between social networks are sustained by social agents – that is, individuals, groups, organizations and societies engaging in 'communicative (inter)actions'[38] – while media networks accentuate communication via symbols and information. Although network theory defines the framework within which individuals communicate, technosociality identifies the motivations and determinants in the expression of individual identities. Identity defines who we are on a national, cultural, religious, social, economic, political and sexual level: it is the ultimate indicator of our individualism and collectivism, schismatic and unifying by turns. To recognize the role of the cyber- and blogosphere in contemporary society, it is necessary to look beyond the structure of the web and transcend the debate on the public and private sphere. In order to reach the core of identity creation and manifestation, it is crucial that an understanding of the finer nuances that constitute the realm of electronic media as a social communicative tool is grasped. Accordingly, by applying the notion of metablognition and technosociality to an aggregation of blog posts on the subject of 'Palestine', the multi-dimensional facets of each blogger's interpretation of what it means to be a Palestinian, both in the diaspora and within Palestine, emerges. As shall be explored shortly, the manifestation of an online national identity is shaped by the blogger's socio-economic background, present milieu and gender – to name but a few variables.

Jordan and the New Cyber Generation

By virtue of its status as a network the blogosphere is a sprawl of information constantly updated by millions of users per second, with one blog created every half-second.[39] It is a boon then that blog aggregators such as Technorati and Google Blogs emerged to provide a swift and efficient means to direct readers to subjects of interest. Blog providers – also known as domain hosts – such as WordPress, Blogger, MoveableType and LiveJournal afford nascent and seasoned bloggers alike the opportunity to build websites in their entirety through the utilization of Cascading Style Sheets, known as CSS code, or through ready-made themes that allow the blogger to enter the title and content and strike 'publish'. According to the blog tracker Technorati's 2009 annual report, bloggers can be divided into three categories: 'hobbyists', 'part-timers' and 'self-employeds'. Of the first group, 72 per cent of respondents to the Technorati survey stated that their blogs generated fun rather than profits, while 53 per cent use the medium to express their 'personal musings'. Of the part-timers, representing 15 per cent of the survey, 75 per cent blog to share expertise, while 72 per cent endeavour to attract business clients. The final group, self-employeds, represent 9 per cent of the respondents and are the most professional, blogging 'full time for their own company or organization', while 70 per cent stated they own a company and blog about their business.[40] Demographically, two-thirds of bloggers are male and 60 per cent are aged between 18 and 44 years of age; educationally, 75 per cent have college degrees and 40 per cent hold graduate degrees. The statistics produced by Technorati provide a compelling overview of the figures guiding the blogosphere, but they are not conclusive; the survey, based on the blogging members of Technorati, depends on a degree of participation that could exclude regions such as the Middle East and Asia. To assume the statistics as fully representative of the blogosphere's demographic would ultimately promote ambiguity, particularly when a regional focus is required.

The rise of aggregators based in the Middle East, such as the Jordan-based iToot and Jordan Blogs, is an advantage then. For the founders

the startlingly quick rise of blogs in the region provided the impetus
to draw together the best and most topical bloggers:

> Across Arabia and all around the world, intelligent, passionate,
> interesting, funny, knowledgeable and courageous people are
> using the web to make their voices heard. It started with a few,
> then a few hundred. Now, thousands of them are taking to their
> keyboards and starting to write blogs, share their knowledge,
> pictures, opinions, emotions and life.[41]

As noted previously, the flaw within aggregators resides in their ability to reflect a select blogosphere. Based on blogs submitted, accepted
or rejected they provide a snapshot of the blogs deemed desirable, a
move that leads ultimately to resentment:

> Aggregators face a core problem [...] either they include eve-
> rything, which becomes overwhelming; or they select what to
> include, which builds new resentments among those excluded.
> JordanPlanet.net, one of the early innovators in Arab blog
> aggregation, shut down over disenchantment with its grow-
> ing roster, while JordanBlogs.net experienced a nasty spat in
> February 2007 over the deletion of several controversial blog-
> gers. The popular iToot aggregator has generated complaints
> from many bloggers not selected by its administrators, as well
> as from those who felt that it was biased towards liberal voices
> writing in Egypt.[42]

Placing the ambiguity of blog selection aside, aggregators such as iToot
afford an invaluable forum for English- and Arabic-language opinion. As the revolutions unfurl from Tunisia, through Egypt, Libya,
Yemen and Bahrain – with sporadic outbursts in Jordan – bloggers
such as Mona Eltahawy and Sandmonkey have provided swift and
comprehensive analyses through Twitter and their blogs. And they are
not alone: scroll down iToot home page and a plethora of fresh posts
(termed 'freshly pressed') represent views from the Gulf to Lebanon.
Comprising a breadth of perspectives bloggers seize the subject from a

serious angle, such as Chez Chiara's 'Whence Gaddafi is Getting His Mercenaries: His Influence in Subsaharan Africa' to the wry shots by Egyptian Chronicles' 'The Lions and the Cocaine Addict' and Qunfuz's 'Cockroach Rule'.

Jordan's home-grown aggregator has blossomed from an idea between four Amman-based friends to pool the most cutting-edge Jordanian blogs into a steady stream of blogging consciousness that affords an insight not only into recent events, but the impact and aspirations of the people involved at a social level. No longer background figures in news reports, protestors and citizens have a voice; and be it cogent, sardonic, pleading or incredulous, it is one that would otherwise have passed unobserved due to the deficiencies within 'international' aggregators such as Technorati. Jordan is at the forefront of a cyber-revolution of its own: it is utilizing the blogosphere not only to vocalize but to connect, transcending borders to unite bloggers in a common cause: freedom – be it of speech and expression, or from the shackles of the regimes that have curtailed progress for the past 30 years.

'The newest cyberjunkie fixation': Watwet

While iToot gathers Middle East-centric blogs, Tootcorp launched the Arab world's first Twitter rival in 2008 in Amman. In conjunction with the Jordanian telecommunications company network, Zain Group, Watwet utilizes free SMS and web-based media to provide a micro-blogging and social-networking service. The brainchild of Arab entrepreneur Kareen Arafat, the application 'blend[s] personal features of blogging with the easy access features of SMS to extend online relationships further'[43] through English and Arabic interfaces. With a target audience of university students and Jordanian youth, Watwet extends blogging to an accessible and interactive level:

> We focused our efforts locally, in areas that are less exposed to digital media in Jordan [...] We tried to give those people some meaning or purpose that drives them to blog; to voice

their views and problems and use social media to connect with those around them. And they found out that they began to express their lives differently and helped narrow the gap between the tech savvy class in society and those who are less advantaged.[44]

And keeping it local proved the key to Watwet's success: by observing status updates Watwet trended pertinent topics in a manner akin to Twitter's trend feed. The results were telling: as Jordanian bloggers and micro-bloggers discussed electricity power failures, politics and favourite spots for social gatherings in Jordan, so too did Watwet tailor the application to focus on Jordanian social issues, domestic politics and local events. Although launched within months of each other, Arafat dismissed notions of a Twitter-Watwet rivalry:[45] once more sustaining the idea of cyber-locality, the application provides an accompaniment to iToot; while the latter provides the extended blogging forums, the micro-blogs afford a means to access and interact with the authors and subjects raised. In 2009, Watwet went global and joined forces with Twitter to link user's accounts enabling 'watwets [to] become tweets and tweets [to] become watwets!'[46] Thus, through Watwet, micro-blogs facilitate social connections on a local level, while promoting notions of liberty, rights and hope in its capacity as an extension of the longer blogging format.

Just Press ... iKbis

Whatever Twitter can do, Watwet can do it too – and whatever YouTube does, so can iKbis (translates as the verb 'press'), albeit better, localized and levelled at users in the Middle East and North Africa (MENA) region. Launched in November 2006 iKbis is the oldest of Tootcorp's applications and provides a platform for 'passionate Arab video creators, big and small, professional and amateur, who want to reach millions of Arabs in the region with their original, creative, inspiring, entertaining and informative content.'[47] With links to Facebook, users create a brief profile on which their contributions are archived. At its core, iKbis is about media sharing: both registered and unregistered users have access to the clips that comprise entertainment, news, politics, sport, religion and spirituality and the broader 'random' – the commonality residing in the Arabic language. Just as iToot affords a glimpse into the opinions of Arab bloggers, iKbis provides a wealth of audio-visual resources. At the height of the revolutions, the streams of uploaded material are dominated by clips on 'The Importance of Forgiveness' and the more vitriolic 'Gaddafi: Who Are You?!' settled alongside translated episodes of Turkish telenovelas on 'forbidden love'.

But iKbis is not just a video aggregate – nor is it an Arabian version of YouTube. In an endeavour to consolidate its presence in a regional cybersphere that is 40 per cent dominated by YouTube, iKbis announced in January 2010 that it would launch specialized video shows and episodes, as well as a TV show that would high-light original videos of its users via syndication on several Arab satel-lite channels.[48] As well as a second season of its Ground Zero series, iKbis also proposed shows focusing on Do-It-Yourself (DIY), as well as Islamic and female-oriented shows.[49] The overall objective of iKbis extends beyond mere aggregation and towards a social, cultural and regional source of entertainment, education, activism and connection. And Jordan is proving once more that its centrality in the region is not just geographical, but expressed in terms of cyber-network connections.

Going Global: Zoofs

Tootcorp's most recent contribution to the realm of Jordan-based cyber-communication is Zoofs: fusing Twitter and YouTube the video-discovery tool ranks entries according to the current Twitter trends. The homepage is a veritable mosaic of clip thumbnails, coupled with a drop-down menu detailing the 15 categories, which vary between 'Autos & Vehicles' to 'Education' and 'Non-profits & Activism'. Founded by Ahmad Humeid, Andreas Pieper, George Akra, Kareem Arafat, Mazen Arafat, Monther Abu Sheikh and Wael Attili (all sea-soned, familiar figures on the Jordanian blogging circuit as founders of iToot, Watwet and iKbis, and members of Tootcorp) Zoofs veers away from the local and steps into the global with a broad, all-encompassing manifesto:

> Beware though! Make sure you allocate enough time for Zoofs as it is highly addictive. Zoofs is your destination for YouTube videos that are hot, fun to watch and truly up to date with what's happening in the world. These are the videos that people thought are worth sharing with the world.[50]

For Kareen Arafat, it is a conscious move from Jordan-based networks: 'Zoofs is the result of our strategy to have some departure from strictly regional localization of content to a broader audience.'[51] Global though it may be, a foray into the category of 'News & Politics' brings it back to the region with a plethora of clips focused on impending protests in Morocco and the deaths of civilians in the Bahrain protests. Nevertheless, subject as it is to Twitter trends the association with the MENA region is tenuous and in flux, for each hour brings global changes and so too do the interests change on Zoofs. It is iKbis for a world audience and more significantly, the first steps of Jordanian cyber-networks into the non-Arabia centric arena.

Saying it with Scribbles: Kharabeesh

Returning once more to Jordan, Kharabeesh is an online forum with an artistic flavour: if iKbis encourages individuals to submit clips, then Kharabeesh is for those who prefer their visuals with a jagged, animated edge. Kharabeesh is a unique online phenomena, the cartoon aggregate: though for the founders and their followers, the members are brought closer through the notion of online 'tribes' who shirk popular media, 'we are not interested in publishing our work on satellite channels and will not produce movies in private cinemas [...] We are not interested in TV productions and we will not come up with the next Toy Story movie. [...] if you want to build a working relationship with us, you must be the kind who loves the risk of becoming mad – like us.'[52] Irreverence is ever-present through the content of the site: in the days after the rambling speech by the Libyan leader

Muammar Qaddafi on 22 February 2011, members posted clips and sketches depicting the dictator as a finger-puppet and in the Looney-Tunes theme. And he is not alone: further clips featured the deposed Tunisian President, Zine El Abidine Ben Ali, and Egyptian former President Hosni Mubarak as t-shirt and baseball-capped marionettes dancing to Britney Spears' 'Baby One More Time', and Mubarak as a glue-sniffer chatting on the phone to Qaddafi.

In addition to the individual clips and sketches are ten cartoon series: Khat Ahmar is a two-minute socio-political commentary that addresses the contentious issues of the day, Khaffash provides the comedic element through its eponymous protagonist, a Bedouin tribe leader who returns to the desert from New York to discover he has a mysterious brain disease that renders him a quirky character, and e7sebha-sa7, who tackles family relationships, integrity and smoking (to name but a few quandaries) from a religious perspective. Located in Amman, the creators intend to expand throughout the Arab region, bringing their unique, satirical art to a wider viewership and, no doubt, inspiring creativity in an alternative medium of expression.

Jordan as a Nexus: Linking the Diaspora

In the context of identity, the Middle Eastern blogosphere provides shared points of reference. Given the strong Palestinian presence in Jordan, Palestine provides a rallying point for Palestinian and non-Palestinian bloggers alike. Indeed, a simple Google Blogs search of Arabic-language blogs between 2000 and 2010 yields 73,029 returns on the term 'Palestine', while in the past year alone 35,214 posts have addressed the country.[53] Ranging from cookery to conflict, writers frequently draw upon personal experiences, while historical events – as well as unfolding political developments – inspire a flurry of interest. In the case of blogger Roba, author of andfaraway, the yearly anniversary of al-Nakba[54] is marked with posts that are by turns imbued with criticism and/or sentiment. Born in Jordan to parents of Palestinian origin, raised in Saudi Arabia and once more resident in Amman in Jordan, Roba identifies with the three countries in equal measure. This is particularly perceptible in the post titled 'Roots and Homes', in which she utilizes images and words to trace where her father was born, her mother, herself, where she grew up and her current milieu. Throughout the post she contrasts her memories of the locations with her parents':

Nablus, Palestine, also known as Jabal Al-Nar, the mountain of fire. My memories of Nablus as a child are of stone walls, jasmines, tea with mint, and the smell of burnt pine wood. My dad's tales of Nablus are of cinemas, circuses, and family love. The box with old pictures from Nablus is full of photographs of vintage cars, people dressed in gorgeous clothes, staged studio shots, and children climbing trees.[55]

On her city of birth it is the childlike aspects of the city that are most evocative:

My memories of my childhood in Amman is of a little, tranquil town, with a lot of green and sharp blue skies. My memories are of ice cream, playing soccer outside, and the sweet plastic smell of floaters and sunscreen. They are of a small, uncrowded town, with the taste of Jabri's cake icing and the cool blueness of Slush Puppies.[56]

Fast forward a little over 20 years and the return to Jordan from Riyadh marks a change in perception as much as the urban environs:

The Amman of my childhood has dwindled to nothing but the taste of red popsicles. My experience in wholly different from my memories. My experience if off [sic] spending the days either sitting in the garden or at the various outeries that this city shyly provides. It is of Jordan University, our messy Syntax office where life is always bustling with energy, or the horribly crowded summer streets at night.

And there. You have it. The collection of cities that have shaped the way we grew up.[57]

Life in the diaspora is characterized not necessarily by continuous movement – for many Palestinians relocated and remained in Jordan since 1948 – but by the remoteness from the homeland. In 'Once Upon a Summer Day in Jeddah', Roba once more utilizes images to relate accounts of life in Palestine before *al-Nakba* and it is her reliance on black-and-white photographs that provides the most profound, realistic and tangible link to the past. Through the images she takes the power of words beyond mere memory and into education: she guides the reader into a period that the subsequent years and events of history have since obscured through their inhumanity. For her maternal family, the Dallals and Samaras, the move to Jeddah in the mid-twentieth century was to be permanent beyond expectations:

> Some of [my mother's] family started their lives there, becoming Saudi citizens and producing offspring that still calls the coastal city home. Others, like my great grandfather, ended their lives there, buried away from home, having spent the last few years of life unable to go back to Palestine. [...] The Dallals are from Haret Al-Yasmeeneh in Nablus, Palestine, while the Samaras are from Denabeh, a small village right off Toul Karem, also in Palestine. Only a small handful of Dallals remain in Nablus, while the rest are scattered in diaspora, centralized in Amman and Jeddah. There is a larger portion of Samaras living in Toul Karem, with a lot more living in the UK and Jordan.[58]

Beneath the text are 17 images from the Dallal and Samara family collection depicting two generations attending barbecues, parties and day trips. The images are happy, peaceful and reflect the early days in the diaspora sans the tragedy synonymous with the dislocation. Nevertheless, behind the smiles, the bottles of Pepsi and balloons the reality of being far from 'home' pervades and is exhibited through the images comprised within '58', a commemorative post addressing the 58th anniversary of *al-Nakba*:

> Today is the 58th anniversary of the Palestinian Nakbeh. I could have pasted a history lesson or shared the stories of others as

I have none, but then I decided that I will be more personal, perhaps a little too personal, with a little family history. These are portraits of my family's pre-1948 life in Palestine.[59]

That Roba pointedly avoids reiterating the events of 1948 is symbolic of her approach to the issue of Palestine: through her images she emphasizes that pre-diaspora life was a vibrant and gregarious one – in another post, 'Whatever happened to Cinema in Palestine? For one, Cinema Al-Assi',[60] we are informed of the 'grandiose weddings' and 'Nabulsi hot chicks in mini-skirts waiting to watch movies' – and despite her dearth of first-hand experiences, she regularly triumphs a strong, if not stoic approach to the issue. Particularly notable is the reluctance to endorse the 'victim-tag' that is frequently applied to Palestinians both within and external to Palestine.

In 'Palestine Movie Watch', the blogger reviews three Palestinian documentary movies, which she notes 'have been making me think about alternative ways of spreading awareness about the Palestinian case'.[61] Indeed, Roba's reviews are indicative of her positivist approach to the Palestine quandary, for scoring eight out of ten in response to Hani Abu Assad's *Ford Transit* (2002) she commends that the humour provides 'a colorful mosaic of the Palestinian case [...] all the while giving some insights and avoiding playing the "victim card"'.[62] In contrast, the 'victim card' scored Hicham Jurdi's *Sabra and Chatila: The Past Continues* a meagre three out of ten:

My partner and I did not like this movie much. The characters the director chose to interview were both shallow and too simple, perfect players for the 'evermore victims' card. Furthermore, Jurdi's plot was merely focusing on how the Palestinians of Chatila are hopeless victims of circumstances, who do not have any courage or strength to face all the abusive action, and how only fate makes them alive. Regardless of the amount of truth in Jurdi's stance, I really dislike this depreciation of the Palestinian identity into the choice of living as victims, in the helpless victim mentality.[63]

The final film, *Palestine Blues* by Nida Sinnokrot, scored eight out of
ten due to its proactive stance; indeed, as in many of Roba's posts, the
appeal of Palestine Blues resided in its call to

> choos[e] to stand up and fight, take action, and take control of
> our lives. [...] the characters crawl right into your heart, close
> enough to remind you of your own uncles, grandmothers, aunts,
> and neighbors. It portrayed Palestinians like I know them, peo-
> ple like my aunts and cousins, rather than suicide bombers and
> massacre victims.[64]

Through andfaraway Roba effectively constructs a Palestine of her own
perceptions – though she may frequently acknowledge that she lacks
personal experience of the country, she provides cogent and evocative
representations of the land and its society. Born in Amman, raised in
Riyadh, once more resident in Amman, she successfully blends her
multiple identities with neither one diminishing the other. In accordance with Hall's observation, her posts manifest the notion that identity can live 'with and through, not despite, difference [...] constantly
producing and reproducing themselves anew, through transformations
and difference.'[65] Thus, while generations have emerged since 1948,
the awareness and affinity with the homeland is equally strong and
transfers via the digital medium without losing its sense of urgency
and import.

Moving from the Middle East to the United States, the blogger Al-Falasteenyia[66] shirks the hybridity theory through her disdain for the hyphen: 'in the technical sense I guess I could best
[be] described as "Palestinian-American". But truth is, I hate being
hyphenated, so please don't use that term.' To return to the notion
of hybrid identities, the hyphen is the essential bridge between
two identities and by its virtue enables the two to coexist without
negation on either side. Yet while as a third-generation Palestinian
Al-Falasteenyia acknowledges that 'America is my home', she nonetheless holds fast to the land her great-grandparents left in 1948,
almost to the negation of one half of her dual identity: 'I hold no
other passport, but I do assert that "kul qloob il nas jinseeyaty fal

tosqatoo 3any jawaz il safr" (all of the people's hearts are my identity so rid of me this passport) [*sic*].'[67] Adorned with intricate Palestinian artwork, including works by the Palestinian cartoonist Naji Al Ali and interspersed with excerpts from the verses of Palestinian poets such as Mahmoud Darwish, her blog retains a sharp focus on Palestine and its people. Similar to Roba, Al-Falasteenyia advocates a stern approach – no victim card to be played here – and links the struggle to the wider need for humanity: 'I'm a great believer in justice, and I think the struggle for Palestine is part and parcel of the struggle for justice everywhere – whether we're talking about homelessness here in the States, racism in Brazil, or cooperate [*sic*] expansion in Africa.'[68] Thus the content of the blog follows a strong, humanitarian line as is evidenced through the site's Label Cloud, which comprises the most pertinent topics ordered in size according to their frequency of use. Of the largest font, and therefore most touched upon, are 'Gaza' (75 posts), 'activism' (29), 'human rights' (29), 'nakba' (53), 'Israel' (38), 'Iraq' (46) and 'Palestine' (66), while topics such as 'environment' (one), 'peace' (one), 'terrorism' (two) and 'Chile' (one) are among the least.

For Al-Falasteenyia, however, it is not the cultural aspects of the cause or her personal reflections – or those of her family – that are utilized to convey Palestine through the blog; rather, it is her perception of the events unfolding therein and her critique of the internal political dynamic. The most recent post after a hiatus of three months finds Al-Falasteenyia in pensive mood: she has been reflecting on a collection of scenarios that have inspired a bout of despondence:

all this stuff (the pa [Palestinian Authority] mess, the right of return, bds [Boycott, Divestment and Sanctions], the continued expulsion from Jerusalem, the countless massacres and their subsequent anniversaries, kidnappings, assassinations, empty declarations, settler violence, apartheid and colonial expansion) all of it brings us back to the beginning. The elephant in the room that Israel wants forgotten. It all started with one word – nakba.[69]

Having started her blog in 2004, Al-Falasteenyia appears to have reached a point of blog-fatigue: where her opening post sizzled with vehemence ('To all those who say Palestine does not exist; keep in mind that would be like saying America didn't exist until the white man colonized it') to the final entry's perplexed, and not a little despondent, conclusion that:

> I've been trying to step back in order to gain a better perspective on things. Also been thinking strategically about what I'm trying to do here. On one hand I feel myself compelled to comment on current events and hot news items as they come and go [...] but I've also noticed that I often feel compelled to discuss anniversaries (while being against the very idea of an 'anniversary' to begin with).[70]

Of particular note is the language: 'I feel myself compelled to comment ...' and 'I often feel myself compelled to discuss ...' denote a sense of obligation on the part of the author. Despite Al-Falasteenyia's third-generation status, she is imbued with a sense of urgency to act on behalf of the country her great-grandparents departed over 60 years previously. While for some – Palestinian and non-Palestinian alike – the politics of the region galvanizes on a humanitarian level, for Al-Falasteenyia it is personal: it is her family, her roots and ultimately, her land.

In contrast to Roba, Al-Falasteenyia directly associates herself with *al-Nakba*: while the former observes that 'I could have [...] shared the stories of others as I have none', the latter boldly states:

> I realize now that despite the passage of time, I am in fact a part of it [*al-Nakba*]. It's weird – I used to think that I had to be of a certain age, or at least have grey hair, in order to be associated with nakba.[71]

The Internet, she continues, has made it impossible not to act. Indeed, the passage of time has not quelled the need for activism and though resident in the United States, Al-Falasteenyia calls upon readers to use

Facebook, Twitter and blogs to keep the Palestinian struggle alive. In turn, not only is the Palestinian cause sustained through the digital medium, but also the Palestinian identity. Through Roba, it is manifest through a love of *akoob*,[72] *waraq enab*[73] and *zaatar* (thyme): of the latter she playfully observes 'In Saudi Arabia, Palestinians are derogatorily known as "Abu Zaatar". Why it is considered to be derogatory I never really understood.'[74] Political activism is less tangible, while Al-Falasteenyia focuses less on the cultural aspect and predominantly on the political and strategic. Thus while Al-Falasteenyia inspires action, Roba's entries fit snugly within the notion of metablognition, for she reflects on the writing and thoughts therein, the topic is sustained; she engages readers and the audience in debate through the comments section and ultimately facilitates a learning experience through words and images of Palestinian culture, history and language. However, that Roba pursues the personal nuances does not lessen the metablognitive qualities within Al-Falasteenyia, merely that the latter expresses her Palestinian identity through a third party – current affairs. While the former summons images from family archives and strives to portray ordinary Palestinians and life before *al-Nakba* as joyful, Al-Falasteenyia focuses on the present, for all its despondent legacy and ongoing injustices.

Both women are products of the diaspora, resplendent in their hybrid identities – though Al-Falasteenyia would doubtless beg to differ. Nevertheless, the Palestinian identity in the digital age has seized upon the new medium and intends to exploit it to the maximum. As Al-Falasteenyia notes,

> Am I really expected to surrender? To adopt the role of that jaded individual who shouts at the TV every time the news comes on? I used to wonder about such people. People who would talk about and wonder about the coming 'generation'. Our 'saviors'. Will they blame us? They should. Will they search for their homeland on a map only to find out that it has been erased? I did.[75]

Modern communication is providing the means to not only maintain the social and emotional connections to the homeland across the generations, but also to promote notions of liberty, rights and hope. It is sustained through a web of common history, shared objectives and an ardent determination to never, ever, forget the land of origin.

Conclusion

> Palestine is the cement that holds the Arab world together, or it is the explosive that blows it apart.[76]

Since the emergence of the cybersphere in 1998, the Middle East has blossomed as a hub of activism, critique, debate and defiance. Yet while the blogosphere is primarily regarded as a source of individual political expression, there has emerged a more conspicuous yet infinitely potent source of action: the 'collective'. Bringing together journalists (iToot), graphic designers (Kharabeesh), activists and bloggers, collectives comprising students and young professionals are working together online to enhance opportunities professionally and socially. From gender equality to professional networking, Jordan is central to the new, larger movement and remains at the fore of the rising collectives: from blog networks retaining a focus on all topics Middle Eastern to home-grown versions of YouTube and Twitter, a definitive organization is taking place. Once a multitude of disparate voices, the blogosphere is seizing the virtue of unity.

The Palestinian refugee community within the Middle East region currently stands at almost five million.[77] Globally, this figure nudges 11 million.[78] Amidst the mêlée of innovative mediums rests identity: whether that identity is political, cultural or social, sites such as iKbis, Kharabeesh, iToot, Watwet and Zoofs provide a platform to share and express. In an increasingly cyber-reliant age, a pan-generational shift towards the Internet as a social network is occurring and just as the Palestinian community has sustained their culture and territorial aspirations in the absence of technology, so too are they seizing the medium as a form of vocalization and galvanization. The sustenance of Palestine online transcends gender and religious divides; expressions of support, empathy, joy and vitriol emerge direct from the core of the individual onto the screen. Within this subjective freedom, individuals express 'their own private judgements, opinions, and recommendations',[79] thereby providing a veritable web of public opinion related to the state – in this instance, the state of Palestine. But the pressing question remains: is it truly Palestine, albeit in the guise of (Cyber-)Palestine? Undoubtedly, Palestine as a state to be (re)achieved has sculpted the identity of both the featured bloggers and the countless Palestinians residing in the diaspora. Equally, the existence of the Palestinians and their call for statehood renders it an entity to be addressed, both territorially and politically. Thus, in an environment in which the notion of community is relentlessly redefined according to the whims of its participants, the cyber- and blogosphere endures as a potent conduit for the expression of identity in the Palestinian diaspora. And on a broader level, a new form of Arab unity is arising from the ashes of the notion created by the dictators who have since fallen. It is one of common goals: freedom, equality and respect; it is one of activism: protests, campaigns and the spreading of awareness, and significantly, one of support. The revolutions herald a new era of pan-Arab cohesion – not from the regimes, but from the people. Social and cyber-networks are the tool of choice – and for the moment, Jordan is the hub of cyber-activism.

EPILOGUE

The Arab world is 'awakening'. The accepted term of reference is, however, inaccurate. To awaken, one must sleep and the Arab world was never sleeping – rather, it was simmering to the opportune point at which Arab society could challenge the socio-economic stagnation of the region. In the case of Egypt and Tunisia, the shift is visible in the clashes between protestors and military forces, the removal of leaders and the commencement of a new, no less arduous process of state-building that could incorporate previously repressed political elements. Jordan differs through her consistency in sustaining sporadic yet persistent outbursts that have occurred prior to, and more noticeably after, the 1998 Ma'an Riots. Jordanian civil activism is inspired by domestic trends (such as the price of food and commodities) and international developments, including the relinquishment of the West Bank by King Hussein in 1988, in solidarity with the Palestinian Intifada in 2000 (in which 203 marches and 73 demonstrations were held in the first week of October)[1] and the invasion of West Bank towns by Israeli forces in 2002. Whether it is slow marches to the Israeli embassy or the beating of a protestor by 16 police officers in July 2011, Jordan has a history of uprisings that the monarchy has endured, even exploiting political mobilization to gain favour amidst the population.[2] Yet Jordan remains in contrast with states in the MENA region that have been marked by dramatic transition. Tunisia witnessed the accession of the Islamist party Ennahda in October 2011, Libya the public demise of Colonel Muammar Gaddafi in the same month and the Assad regime has perpetuated deadly strikes against the Syrian populace.

One factor encompasses all the nuances discussed through the preceding chapters: socio-political schism. The division between the Jordanian-dominated military and government, and the Palestinian-Jordanian-led economic and business sector (not to mention the socio-economic divergences between the refugee camps and Jordanian urban areas) yields a mosaic of divergent interests. While Palestinian-Jordanians seek full integration and the rights that accompany citizenship, Jordanians campaign for reform in alternative sectors. The notion of divide and rule as originally applied by a British-imposed monarchy from Hijaz on Jordanian tribes and Palestinian refugees was – perhaps – valid until the emergence of the Arab Spring. Since February 2011, interests have converged between the communities on matters pertaining to electoral reform, economic security and political freedom. As yet, political activism has not reached the point of sustained violent protest, but it indicates a new direction for Jordanian unrest. Previously characterized by primordial nationalism (Palestinian-Jordanian versus Jordanian), the communities are uniting in the demand for equality, fairness and freedom for all.

Relations between the Hashemites and the Palestinian-Jordanian community have been chequered by violence, peace, integration, ostracism, equality and discrimination. Jordan projects the image of 'an oasis of peace' in a region afflicted by internal conflict; yet while it is akin to an oasis in the refuge it offers, it is more often a mirage, concealing inequality and human rights violations that pose a challenge to state stability. The disparities within the Palestinian-Jordanian community reveal microcosms replete with identities, narratives and aspirations shaped by socio-economic circumstances, but more often through shared historical experience. Just as a homeland is determined by its potential as a source of prosperity in accordance with the modernist theory,[3] in the Palestinian diaspora 'prosperity' is gauged through the attainability of civil rights and the claim to a homeland. Accordingly, material gains do not necessarily ease the longing for a nation for those who have attained financial success in the Kingdom, while the loss of Palestine is equally (if not more) resonant among Palestinians in the refugee camps. While nationality, citizenship and electoral legislation are constructed to strengthen ties between state and society, in Jordan the legal mechanism is a noose around the necks of low-income Palestinian-Jordanians. Similarly, calls for reform are routinely denied, disparaged or delayed, as in the case of the National Agenda and the National Centre for Human Rights draft law, the Temporary Information Systems Crimes Provisional Law of 2010, the Nationalists and Citizenship Law (Law No. 6 of 1954) and the amended Personal Status Law in 2001 (Law No. 82 of 2001).

The early acts of integration that enabled Palestinians to become members of the Jordanian military and develop a territorial bond allowed the state to exhibit a 'post-independence' territorial nationalism, bringing 'together often disparate ethnic populations and integrat[ing] them into a new political community replacing the old colonial state'.[4] Although security provided a primary source of cohesion, it also brought the downfall of the union. Preceding World War II, the majority of Palestinians arriving in Jordan did so willingly and prepared. After 1948, the impetus was one of survival rather than selection, as the Palestinians fled towards Jordan. Confronted with an increasing population, the Jordanian government discerned the need for restrictions on both nationality and citizenship, and commenced reforms in earnest. Between 1948 and the Intifada of 2002, Jordan pursued a policy of self-preservation, protecting resources from the influxes of refugees through their eastern and western borders. The events of Black September 1970 inspired a reflection on the predicament of the Kingdom as a host and protagonist in the Palestine-Israel conflict, compelling Jordanians to assess both the Palestinian-Jordanian domestic dynamic and the security of the Kingdom. The sting of the perceived betrayal by their 'Palestinian guests' has proved enduring and for contemporary Jordanians the event serves as a warning of the dangers of ill-placed loyalty. The actions of the resistance movement in 1970 continue to influence the civil rights of Palestinian-Jordanians, providing justification for the inequity that defines the experience of subsequent generations of Palestinians residing in Jordan. History has taught the country the risk of trust, yet history itself is equally untrustworthy – particularly when subject to political agendas.

Jordanian legislature has evolved from the Ottoman period to the present, yet the status quo of citizenship, nationality and gender equality in Jordan has proceeded with little or no positive change. What change has occurred has not been inspired by concern for the people; rather, urgent circumstances have placed security as the primary interest. And the Palestinians are not alone in the citizenship process as Iraqi and Sudanese applicants – to name but a few – negotiate a process that renders a service more onerous than that which is afforded to foreign/non-Arab applicants. Once citizenship is granted, there is little guarantee that full civil rights will follow and the imbalance between the rights of women and children under the Nationality Law is perpetuated. Reform, when enacted, is but a tentative victory. The progress rendered through the amendment of the Personal Status Law in 2001 (Law No. 82 of 2001) survived only nine years, for in April 2010 the Jordanian parliament reversed the changes. Rather than advancing, Jordanian law is regressing and progress towards a cohesive and equal society is impeded once more.

The identities of Jordan bind individuals to their history and origin, fracturing the monolithic 'Jordanian' identity into a kaleidoscope of major and minor *ethnies*. Incorporating Palestinian-Jordanians, Palestinians, ethnic Jordanians and Bedouin tribal Jordanians, in addition to the Chechen and Circassian communities, identity is augmented by faith. In turn, the Christian and Islamic identities distil into denominations and sects, including Orthodox and Catholic, Shi'ite and Sunni. While the Palestinian-Jordanian identity is a point of convergence, the relationship between the two communities cannot be comprehended from a solely Palestinian perspective. The Jordanian identity is in the throes of a renaissance, becoming a 'modern' ethnic identity, albeit introspective as it endeavours not to be subject in its evolution and absorption of new characteristics to each vacillation in the milieu of the community and individual. The cultural revival draws the attention of non-Jordanians to a rich and vibrant heritage that has been eclipsed by that of the Palestinian culture. Yet the parallel effort to reclaim Jordan for the Jordanians disrupts the process of integration that Jordan has otherwise proven successful at promoting, notably in the case of religious coexistence. Despite the initial promise of the 'Jordan First' campaign, the implementation of the slogan has inspired discrimination, resulting in a cool reception from its intended target demographic, the Palestinian-Jordanians.

Identity, though appearing as a positive means to define an individual, once collective can impede cohesion between the communities. Devoid of the rights accorded to Jordanian citizens, Palestinian children mature with the six attributes of the *ethnie*: a collective proper name, one or more differentiating elements of a common culture, a myth of common ancestry, shared historical memories, an association with a specific homeland and a sense of solidarity for significant sectors of the population.[5] The belief that to grant citizenship to children of Palestinian origin would prove unfavourable to the demography of Jordan is reminiscent of the edict 'Jordan for the Jordanians' and problematizes the objective of the legal restrictions. The impact of the citizenship and nationality legislation on Palestinian-Jordanian domestic relations is considerable, and in the interest of the longevity of state–society relations in the Kingdom less stringency and more equality could facilitate an integrated, collaborative and stable society.

Correlating mourning Palestine to disloyalty has prompted a transformation of the Jordanian identity from a cultural revitalization to a defensive strategy. The concept 'Jordan is Palestine' and memories of Black September have collectively induced a shift by nationalists towards a schism that threatens Jordanian stability. However, it must not be assumed that all Jordanians accept the aforementioned views, for many hold reasoned understandings. Efforts to distinguish between the Jordanian and Transjordanian identity reveal a plethora of perceptions and experiences, both positive and negative, as varied as those held by the Palestinian-Jordanian community. Yet it is the negative views that are of most concern, for to avoid future conflict in the Kingdom the Transjordanian identity must broaden and accept the integration of non-Jordanians.

In contrast, the Palestinian-Jordanian identity continuously morphs from the indefinable entity that an individual harbours through life to a tangible manifestation of a political predicament that is received as an addition to contemporary Jordanian society. As Jordanians and Palestinian-Jordanians seek dominance in the public and private sector, the Chechen and Circassian communities continue to assume prominent positions in the government and security services. The contrast between the Chechen and Circassian, and Palestinian-Jordanian, dynamic with the host state demonstrates the varied approach to state–society relations. With a substantially greater influx staggered over the decades, the Palestinian presence increased demand on the economy and resources of the Kingdom and spurred contempt amidst the population. The divergence in relations is particularly apparent in the absence of 'Jordan is Palestine'-exclusionist sentiments from rhetoric directed towards the Chechen and Circassian communities, while the Kingdom remains muted on Chechen and Circassian nationalism exhibited through attire, imagery and events.

When combined with socio-economic circumstances, identity strengthens connections to Palestine. Through formal and informal discussions on the perception of identity, the majority of respondents considered the notion of 'more money, less identity' to be credible. However, the endurance of Palestine in the lives of Palestinian-Jordanians of all economic levels was visible and suggests that extraneous factors such as occupation, area of residence, duration of residence and income level bear negligible influence on the development of national identity in Jordan. In terms of socio-economic identity, an apt example is provided by the middle classes of Jordan. A median between the self-possessed elite and the expressive identities within the refugee camps, the middle class is absorbed by the elite and low-income groups in times of economic strife with a fluidity that could herald its demise should the economy continue to squeeze the population into two categories. In recent years, the cost of living in Jordan has been affected not by the Palestinians, but by affluent Iraqi migrants. As regal homes flanked by Hummers become a customary sight in west Amman, the financial boon initially welcomed by businesses has lessened in appeal as the results of the injection into the economy are observed by Jordanians and Palestinian-Jordanians alike.

Faith, economics and identity complete the triangle of identity in the diaspora, each determining the strength and endurance of the other. If faith presents a threat to the host state while comforting the ostracized, economics influence the degree to which one desires a physical return to the homeland. As respondents reasoned, their lives are established in Jordan in terms of residence, occupations and the education of their children. For the inhabitants of the refugee camps, their lives have remained in Palestine since 1948. The significance of faith in the diaspora lies in the ability to sustain endurance. Yet equally it presents a challenge to the status quo and the presence of evangelical groups stirs concern parallel to that provoked by the Islamist presence in the Islamic context. Arriving from America via Israel, the spiritual leaders captivate younger members of the Latin, Orthodox and Copt congregations with discos and barbecues. But it is not the events that worry the established churches, but rather the ideological intentions. Eschewing traditional decorum that recommends dialogue between existing churches and representatives, Orthodox and Latin priests observe evangelical leaders imparting Zionist ideologies that contradict the essence of the Palestinian struggle. While the risk posed to the security of Jordan is negligible, it introduces an ambiguous element that could influence future expressions of the Palestinian diaspora identity.

As host to the world's largest Palestinian community, Jordanian concerns are not unfounded: Black September and the struggles in Lebanon proved that the course of coexistence does not run smooth. Jordan has excelled at balancing religion, ethnicity, politics and economy to the benefit of stability. Whether the legal infrastructure is to the benefit of the people remains questionable. To maintain stability the Kingdom must confront the issues that have been promised resolution through reforms. Jordanian reticence arises from two counter points: to grant full citizenship and rights would inundate the state with Palestinians holding Jordanian nationality; yet the spectre of Jordan as a proxy Palestinian state is a fate craved neither by the Palestinians nor the Jordanians. The withholding of rights is a craven move, but one made in the belief that should full rights be granted, it is unlikely that Israel would refrain from encouraging more Palestinians to enter Jordan and the resulting influx would economically and socially destabilize the country further.

The predicament of the Palestinians in Jordan is a symptom of a wider malaise. In comparison with regional counterparts the monarchy has courted the support of the population with oppositional voices

audible, but not necessarily visible. How far this is indicative of genuine support or the effectiveness of the *Mukhabarat* is open to discussion – certainly, the might of the *Mukhabarat* has guided the political
trajectory of the Kingdom in the (not so) distant past.[6] The question
that remains is whether the Hashemites can hold fast to power in the
years ahead. Abdullah has demonstrated a lack of the magnanimity
that characterized the reign of his father, most clearly seen in recent
years with the arbitrary withdrawal of Jordanian nationality from
approximately 2,700 citizens of Palestinian origin.[7] In cases in which
the father lost nationality, the children followed likewise – regardless
of being Jordanian by birth.

The omnipotence of the monarchy places the king in a position of
political and economic dominance. Responsible for the appointment of
the government (though not the lower house of parliament), Abdullah
perpetuates the imbalance through the allocation of funds to tribal
areas, rather than those holding a higher number of Jordanians of
Palestinian origin. Likewise, should reforms be applied, the military,
security and civil services – all strongholds of Jordanians of East Bank
origin – are generally exempted from compliance.[8] As much in touch
with civic oppression as he is out of touch with the country's collective
population, over the years Abdullah has ensured that mechanisms are
in place to avoid the fate that befell Tunisia's Zine El Abidine Ben
Ali and Egypt's Hosni Mubarak in 2011. Temporary laws are quick
to pass and swift to enforce, compelling protest organizers to gain
permission in advance and censorship to be applied to the press and
blogosphere under Article 11 of the Temporary Information Systems
Crimes Provisional Law of 2010.

Stringent and arbitrary in recent years, the restrictions have reached
political circles and loyalty to the regime provides little protection. In
2006, former parliament senator and permanent Jordanian representative to the United Nations, Adnan Abu-Odeh, was briefly detained on
charges of having insulted the king during a debate on Al Jazeera; the
following year the former legislator and leader of the JNM, Ahmad
Oweidi al-Abbadi, was sentenced to two years' imprisonment upon
accusing the royal family of corruption. While the charges resemble
each other the recipients do not: al-Abbadi is a long-term critic of the

monarchy and does not shy from speculation, while Abu-Odeh has been a powerful presence in Jordanian politics since 1970, as well as the Political Advisor to King Hussein during the years 1988–1991.

As the Arab Spring reaches the one-year mark, Jordan confronts two paths. Time is on her side: unrest has been isolated and is of the variety that Abdullah has experience of quelling. Should he look to Morocco and follow the example of King Mohammed VI through the reduction of monarchical powers via constitutional reform, Abdullah could ensure both the stability of Hashemite rule and the country. Alternatively, continuation of the status quo – extensive monarchical powers, limited democratic initiatives, civic oppression, arbitrary rescindment of nationality, absence of gender equality and inequity under the nationality and citizenship laws – will place the state in jeopardy and risk prolonged instability. Transjordan entered independence as a created state comprised of a plethora of communities and succeeded in building a nation. The capacity for security and cohesion exists and as the new century progresses, Jordan can endure as a site of refuge and security in the region, providing wisdom is applied at the appropriate juncture.

NOTES

Chapter 1

1. Machiavelli, Niccolò. *The Prince* (London: Penguin Books Ltd.) 2003. p. 9.
2. Rosenfeld, Maya. *Confronting the Occupation: Work, Education, and Political Activism of Palestinian Families in a Refugee Camp* (Stanford, CA: Stanford University Press) 2004. pp. 33–4.
3. Ibid. Cf. Mishal, Shaul. *West Bank/East Bank: The Palestinians in Jordan, 1949–1967* (New Haven; London: Yale University Press) 1978.
4. Rosenfeld: *Confronting the Occupation*, p. 33.
5. Abidi, Aqil Hyder Hasan. *Jordan: A Political Study 1948–1957* (Bombay; New York: Asia Publishing House) 1965. pp. 63–4. Cf. Day, Arthur R. *East Bank/West Bank: Jordan and the Prospects for Peace* (New York: Council on Foreign Relations) 1986. p. 58.
6. Mutawi, Samir A. *Jordan in the 1967 War* (Cambridge: Cambridge University Press) 1987. p. 41.
7. Abidi: *Jordan*, p. 170.
8. Pevety, D. 'The Arab refugee: a changing problem.' *Foreign Affairs*, Vol. 41. April 1963. Cited in Mutawi, Samir A. *Jordan in the 1967 War* (Cambridge: Cambridge University Press) 1987. pp. 40–1.
9. Yorke, Valerie. *Domestic Politics and Regional Security: Jordan, Syria and Israel: The End of an Era?* (Aldershot: Gower for the International Institute for Strategic Studies) 1988. pp. 36–7.
10. Robins, Philip. *A History of Jordan* (Cambridge: Cambridge University Press) 2004. p. 74.
11. Vatikiotis, P. J. *Politics and the Military in Jordan: A Study of the Arab Legion, 1921–1957* (London: Cass) 1967. p. 119.
12. Ibid., p. 62.

13. Cf. Jarvis, C. S. *Arab Command: The Biography of Lieutenant Colonel F. W. Peake Pasha* (London: Hutchinson) 1942. Cited in Robins: *A History of Jordan*, p. 32.

14. Cf. Lockhart, L. K. 'The Trans-Jordan frontier force.' *Journal of the Royal Artillery*, Vol. 56, April 1929. p. 80. Lockhart claimed that they were mostly 'fellahin' from the towns and villages of Palestine. Cited in Robins: *A History of Jordan*, p. 208.

15. Ibid., p. 32.

16. Milton-Edwards, Beverley and Peter Hinchcliffe. *Conflicts in the Middle East since 1945* (London: Routledge) 2001. pp. 26–7.

17. Vatikiotis: *Politics and the Military in Jordan*, p. 26.

18. Ibid., pp. 28–9.

19. See 'Qanun al-Haras al-Watani,' Law No. 7 for the Year 1950, signed on 17 January 1950, *Official Gazette*, No. 1010 (9 February 1950), pp. 71–2. The Law stipulated that all Jordanians between 20 and 40 years should serve (or be trained) up to 150 hours per annum. See Articles 2 and 3 of the Law. Cited in Massad, Joseph A. *Colonial Effects: The Making of National Identity in Jordan* (New York; Chichester: Columbia University Press) 2001. pp. 329.

20. Massad: *Colonial Effects*, p. 57.

21. Glubb, John Bagot. *A Soldier with the Arabs* (London: Hodder and Stoughton) 1957. p. 289. Cited in Massad: *Colonial Effects,* p. 204.

22. Vatikiotis: *Politics and the Military in Jordan*, p. 80.

23. Qibya is a Palestinian village located near the cease-fire line which separated Israel from Jordan before 1967. On 14–15 October 1953 the village was attacked by the Israeli 'Unit 101' commanded by Colonel Ariel Sharon. After the Israeli raid 69 men, women and children were found dead in Qibya. According to Shlaim, 'The Qibya massacre unleashed against Israel a storm of international protest of unprecedented severity in the country's short history.' Cf. Shlaim, Avi. *The Iron Wall: Israel and the Arab World* (London: Allen Lane, the Penguin Press) 2000. p. 91.

24. Plascov, Avi. *The Palestinian Refugees in Jordan, 1948–1957* (London: Cass) 1981. p. 93.

25. Mishal: *West Bank/East Bank*, p. 31.

26. *Filastin*, 9 January 1952. Quoted in Mishal: *West Bank/East Bank*, p. 31. The relationship between King Abdullah and the Jewish Agency was ambiguous at best. In his analysis of the link, Robins questions 'the nature of the secret diplomacy between Abdullah and the Jewish Agency in 1946, 1947 and 1948 [...] Did Abdullah sell the Arabs in Palestine short? How far was Transjordan responsible for the collective failure of the Arab side in the war?' Cf. Robins: *A History of Jordan*, p. 60. Having cultivated Abdullah

through the 1930s the Jewish Agency sought out the king soon after the culmination of the war and two meetings were conducted at Shuna in the Jordan Valley in 1946. Although Abdullah was confident in his actions, his wish to conceal the proceedings signifies that he knew others would view it differently. The clandestine relationship was inevitably conducive to mistrust among Palestinians thereafter.

27. Hurewitz, J. C. *Middle East Politics: The Military Dimension* (Boulder, CO: Westview Press) 1982. p. 315. Cited in Fathi, Schirin H. *Jordan: An Invented Nation? Tribe-State Dynamics and the Formation of National Identity* (Hamburg: Deutsches Orient-Institut) 1994. p. 135.

28. Fathi: *Jordan*, p. 136. Massad: *Colonial Effects*, p. 101.

29. Vatikiotis: *Politics and the Military in Jordan*, p. 111.

30. Ibid., pp. 118–20. Fathi: *Jordan*, p. 136.

31. Vatikiotis: *Politics and the Military in Jordan*, pp. 319–20.

32. The settled, urban population. Cited in Fathi: *Jordan*, p. 136.

33. Massad: *Colonial Effects*, p. 206.

34. Ibid.

35. Vatikiotis: *Politics and the Military in Jordan*, pp. 28–9.

36. Hammer, Juliane. *Palestinians Born in Exile: Diaspora and the Search for a Homeland* (Austin: University of Texas Press) 2005. p. 37.

37. Article 1. This Ordinance was promulgated as a Law in *The Official Gazette*, 193 (1 June 1928). In Seton, C. R. W. *Legislation of Transjordan, 1918–1930*. (London) 1931, pp. 373–6. Cited in Abidi: *Jordan*, p. 66.

38. The Passport Law of 1929 was published as a bill in *The Official Gazette*, 228 (16 May 1929) and was promulgated in *The Official Gazette*, 235 (16 August 1929). Cited in Abidi: *Jordan*, p. 66.

39. Ibid.

40. Day: *East Bank/West Bank*, p. 58

41. U.S. Committee for Refugees and Immigrants. *U.S. Committee for Refugees World Refugee Survey 2000 – Jordan*. 1 June 2000. Via: http://bit.ly/gewk2t [Accessed: 15 April 2011].

42. Ibid.

43. Gubser, Peter. *Jordan: Crossroads of Middle Eastern Events* (Boulder, CO: Westview Press; London: Croom Helm) 1983. pp. 16–17.

44. Amended Electoral Law, No. 54 (1949). Cited in Abidi: *Jordan,* p. 68.

45. Ibid.

46. Yorke: *Domestic Politics and Regional Security*, p. 36.

47. Lavergne, Marc. *La Jordanie* (Paris: Éditions Karthala) 1996. p. 136.

48. Vatikiotis: *Politics and the Military in Jordan*, pp. 48; 53–4.

49. Ibid., pp. 51–2.

50. Day: *East Bank/West Bank*, pp. 121–2; Ibrahim Othman, 'Political trends and new elites in Jordan', *PASSIA Workshop Eight: Political Trends and the New Elites* (PASSIA, Jerusalem) 4 November 1996.

51. Cohen, Amnon. *Political Parties in the West Bank Under the Hashemite Regime (1948–1967)* (Ithaca, New York: Cornell University Press) 1980. pp. 20, 251. Cited in Betty S. Anderson, *Nationalist Voices in Jordan: The Street and the State* (Austin: University of Texas Press) 2005. p. 4.

52. Rosenfeld, Maya. 'Power structure, agency, and family in a Palestinian refugee camp', *International Journal of Middle East Studies*, Vol. 34. No. 3. 2002. pp. 519–51.

53. Sela, Avrahim. *The Palestinian Ba'ath* (Jerusalem: The Magnes Press, Hebrew University) 1984; Amnon Cohen, *Political Parties in the West Bank Under the Hashemite Regime (1948–1967)* [In Hebrew] (Jerusalem: The Magnes Press, Hebrew University) 1980. Cited in Rosenfeld: *Confronting the Occupation*, p. 216.

54. Ibid.

55. Cleveland, William. *A History of the Modern Middle East* (Oxford: Westview Press) 2000. p. 349.

56. Hourani, Albert H. *A History of the Arab Peoples* (London: Faber and Faber) 1991. p. 412.

57. Ibid.

58. Interview conducted with Dr. Hazem Nussaibah, by Samir A. Mutawi. Cited in Mutawi: *Jordan in the 1967 War*, p. 56.

59. Ibid.

60. Shavit, Uriya. 'Out of Jordan', *Haaretz*. 28 May 2002.

61. Mutawi: *Jordan in the 1967 War*, p. 41.

62. Day: *East Bank/West Bank*, pp. 60–1.

63. Wilson, Rodney (ed.) *Politics and the Economy in Jordan* (School of Oriental and African Studies, Routledge) 1991. p. 175.

64. Mutawi: *Jordan in the 1967 War*, p. 172.

65. Gross Stein, Janice. 'War and society in the Middle East.' p. 227 in *International Relations of the Middle East*, Louise Fawcett (ed.) (Oxford: Oxford University Press) 2005. pp. 208–30.

66. Rosenfeld: *Confronting the Occupation*, p. 203.

67. Wallach, John and Janet Wallach. *Arafat: In the Eyes of the Beholder* (Toronto, Birch Lane Press) 1997. p. 295.

68. Rubin, Barry and Judith Colp Rubin. *Yasir Arafat: A Political Biography* (Oxford: Oxford University Press) 2003. p. 62.

69. Cobban, Helena. *The Palestinian Liberation Organisation: People, Power, and Politics* (Cambridge: Cambridge University Press) 1984. p. 48.

70. Text of testimony on 15 February 1973, broadcast on Radio Amman on 24 March 1973; *Washington Post*, 15 March 1973; Christopher Dobson, *Black September* (New York: Macmillan) 1974. pp. 11–21; U.S. Defense Intelligence Agency, *International Terrorism: A Compendium*, Vol. 2, *The Middle East*. 1979. Cited in Rubin and Colp Rubin: *Yasir Arafat*, p. 63.

71. Aburish, Saïd K. *Arafat: From Defender to Dictator* (London: Bloomsbury) 1999. p. 123.

72. Ibid.

73. Ibid., p. 124.

74. Wallach and Wallach: *Arafat*, p. 295.

75. Harris, William. *The Levant: A Fractured Mosaic* (Markus Weiner Publishers, Princeton) 2003. pp. 162–3.

76. Gubser: *Jordan*, pp. 109–10.

77. *25 Years of History, The Complete Collection of H.M. King Hussein Ben Talal's Speeches 1952–1977* (London: Samir Mutawi and Associates Publishing) 1979. [In Arabic]. Vol. 2. p. 365. Cited in Mutawi: *Jordan in the 1967 War*, p. 64.

78. Day: *East Bank/West Bank*, p. 124.

79. Gubser: *Jordan*, pp. 15–16.

80. Ibid.

81. Abidi: *Jordan*, p. 174.

82. Ibid.

83. Schulz and Hammer: *The Palestinian Diaspora*, p. 132.

84. Ibid.

85. Hass, Amira. *Drinking the Sea at Gaza: Days and Nights in a Land Under Siege* (New York: Henry Holt & Company) 1996. p. 174. Cited in Schulz and Hammer: *The Palestinian Diaspora*, p. 132.

86. Farah, Randa. 'Paradoxical and overlapping voices: the refugee-UNRWA relationship and Palestinian identity in Jordan', paper presented at the *CERMOC International Symposium, The Palestinian Refugees and UNRWA in Jordan, the West Bank and Gaza, 1949–1999*, Mövenpick Hotel, Dead Sea, Jordan, 31 August to 2 September 1999. Cited in Schulz and Hammer: *The Palestinian Diaspora*, p. 132.

87. UNESCO, 1994. Table 3.11. Rosenfeld: *Confronting the Occupation*, p. 124. Report of the Commissioner-General of the UNRWA in the Near East, 1 July 1966 to 30 June 1967, p. 60.

88. Rosenfeld: *Confronting the Occupation*, p. 124.

89. Reiter, Yitzhak. 'Higher education and sociopolitical transformation in Jordan', *British Journal of Middle Eastern Studies*, Vol. 29. No. 2. 2002. pp. 137–164.

90. Abidi: *Jordan*, pp. 172–3.

91. Kanovsky, Eliyahu. *Jordan's Economy: From Prosperity to Crisis* (Tel Aviv: Moshe Dayan Center for Middle Eastern and African Studies, Shiloah Institute, Tel Aviv University) 1989. pp. 43–4.

92. Jansen, Michael E. *The United States and the Palestinian People*, Issue 23. (Beirut: the Institute for Palestine Studies) 1970. p. 182.

93. Report of the Commissioner-General of the United Nations Relief and Works Agency for Palestine Refugees in the Near East, 1 July 1966–30 June 1967, G.A.O.R. (XXII): Supplement No. 13 (A/6713), p. 19, in Jansen: *The United States and the Palestinian People*, p. 183.

94. Smith, Pamela Ann. 'The Palestinian diaspora, 1948–1985', *Journal of Palestine Studies*, Issue 59. Spring 1986. p. 100.

95. In 1948 the Arab bank succeeded in transferring some of its funds, records and staff to Amman, where its adeptness at paying claims immediately earned it a good reputation and helped it to expand not only through-out the Arab world, but to include affiliates in Switzerland, Germany and Nigeria. Cf. Jansen, Michael E. *Dissonance in Zion* (London: Zed Books) 1986. p. 95.

96. Lughod estimates a 36 per cent drop between 1949 and 1979. Cited in Smith: 'The Palestinian diaspora'.

97. Ibid., p. 100.

98. Shiblak, Abbas. 'Residency status and civil rights of Palestinian refugees in Arab countries', *Journal of Palestine Studies*, Vol. 25. No. 3. Spring 1996. p. 43.

99. Sha'sha, Zayd J. 'The role of the private sector in Jordan's economy', in Wilson: *Politics and the Economy in Jordan*, pp. 79–89 (81).

100. Seccombe, Ian. 'Labour emigration policies and economic development in Jordan: from unemployment to labour shortage', in *The Economic Development of Jordan*, Adnan Badran and Bichara Khader (eds.) (London: Croom Helm) 1985. pp. 118–32.

101. Sabatello, Eitan. 'The missing age group: demography', in *The West Bank Data Project: A Summary of Israeli's Policies*, Meron Benvenisti (ed.) (Washington, DC and London, American Enterprise Institute for Public Policy Research) 1984. pp. 1–7. Cited in Rosenfeld: *Confronting the Occupation*, pp. 153–5.

102. Rosenfeld: *Confronting the Occupation*, p. 158.

103. Barakat, Halim I. 'The Palestinian refugees: an uprooted community seeking repatriation', *International Migration Review*, Vol. 7. No. 2. Summer 1973. p. 151.

104. Abidi: *Jordan*, p. 181.

105. Ibid., p. 180.

106. Yorke: *Domestic Politics and Regional Security*, p. 36.

107. Aruri, Naseer. *Jordan: A Study in Political Development 1921–1965* (The Hague: Martinius Nijhoff) 1972. pp. 50–69. Cited in Rosenfeld: *Confronting the Occupation*, p. 34.

108. Yorke: *Domestic Politics and Regional Security*, p. 42.

109. Ibid., p. 40.

110. Harris: *The Levant*, pp. 159–60.

111. Ibid.

112. *Economist Intelligence Unit Country Reports – Syria* (Aug. 2001); *Jordan* (Sept. 2001); *Lebanon* (Oct. 2001); and *Israel* (Oct. 2001). Cited in Harris: *The Levant*, pp. 153–4.

113. Abidi: *Jordan,* pp. 168–9.

114. Ibid., pp. 174–5.

115. Elian Kwaiter, P. *Al-Rahbaniyya al-Mukhlisiyya fi-Khidmat al-Nufus fi-Madinat al-Zarqa-al-Urdun* [The Salvatorians in the Service of the Souls in the City of al-Zarqa — The Hashemite Kingdom of Jordan] (Beirut: Publication of the Third Centennial Jubilee of the Salvatorian Brotherhood, 1997). Additional Arabic-language texts include: P. Hanna Sa'id Kildani, *Al-Masihiyya al-Mu'asira fi-al-'Urdun wa-Falastin* [Contemporary Christianity in Jordan and Palestine] (Amman: n.p., 1993); M.Y. Al-Shurman, *al-'Ulaqat al-Ijtima 'iyya Bayn al-Moslemin wa-al-Masihiyyin fi-al-Husn, Shamal al-Urdun* [Social Relations between Muslims and Christians in el-Husn, a Village in Northern Jordan]; and Sami Al-Nahhas, *Tasrikh Madaba al-Hadith* [The Modern History of Madaba] (Amman: al-Dar al-'Arabiyya lil-Nashr wal-Tawzi, 1987.

116. Wagner, Donald E. *Dying in the Land of Promise: Palestine and Palestinian Christianity from Pentecost to 2000* (London: Melisende Press) 2001.

117. Ateek, Naim, Cedar Duaybis, and Marla Schrader (eds.) *Jerusalem: What Makes for Peace?* (London: Melisende) 1997. pp. 132–4.

118. Valonges, Jean Pierre. *Vie et Mort des Chretiens d'Orient des Origines a nos Jours* (Paris, Fayard) 1994. p. 615. Cited in Haddad: *Christians in Jordan*, p. 12.

119. Tsimhoni, Daphne. *Christian Communities in Jerusalem and the West Bank Since 1948: An Historical Social and Political Study* (Westport: Praeger) 1993. pp. 20–5.

120. Ibid., p. 21.

121. Haddad: *Christians in Jordan*, p. 27.

122. Haddad, M. Y. *Arab Perspectives of Judaism: A Study of Image Formation in the Writings of Arab Authors 1948–1978* (New York: Shengold Publishers) 1984.

123. Haddad: *Christians in Jordan*, p. 27.

124. Haddad: *Christians in Jordan*, p. 41.

125. Schulz and Hammer: *Palestinians Born in Exile*, p. 86.

126. Day: *East Bank/West Bank*, p. 65.

127. Arzt, Donna. *Refugees Into Citizens* (New York: Council on Foreign Relations) 1997. p. 45. Cited in Smilansky, Gene. 'Palestinian refugee camps: graveyards of peace', *Yale Israel Journal*, No. 7. Summer 2005.

128. Sayigh, Yezid and Rosemary Sayigh. 'The politics of Palestinian exile', *Third World Quarterly*, Vol. 9. 1987. pp. 28–66. Cited in Schulz and Hammer: *Palestinians Born in Exile*, p. 13.

129. Gilan, Signe, Are Hovdenak and Rania Maktabi, Jon Pedersen and Dag Tuastad. 'Finding ways: Palestinian coping strategies in changing environments', *Report 177*. Oslo: FAFO. 1994. p. 40. Cited in Schulz and Hammer: *Palestinians Born in Exile*, p. 13.

130. Brand, Laurie A. 'Palestinians and Jordanians: a crisis of identity', *Journal of Palestine Studies*, Vol. 24. No. 4. Summer 1995.

131. Smith, Pamela Ann. 'The Palestinian diaspora, 1948–1985', *Journal of Palestine Studies*, Issue 59. Spring 1986.

132. Ibid.

133. Among them were members of the Nashashibi, Tuqan, Dajani, Abd al-Hadi, Jayyusi and Nusaybah families. Smith: 'The Palestinian diaspora, 1948–1985'.

134. Mishnah, Seder Nezikin, Tractate Avot, Chapter 1/14.

135. Wallach, John. *Arafat: in the Eyes of the Beholder* (London: Heinemann) 1997. p. 271.

136. Ibid., pp. 267–76.

137. Cf. Ibid., p. 273.

138. Italics not in the original text.

139. Ibid.

140. El Hussini, M. *Soviet–Egyptian Relations, 1945–1985* (London: Macmillan) 1987. p. 176. Cited in Gat, Moshe. 'Nasser and the Six Day War, 5 June 1967: A Premeditated Strategy or An Inexorable Drift to War?', *Israel Affairs*, Vol. 11. No. 4. October 2005. pp. 608–35.

141. de Châtel, Francesca. *Water Sheikhs and Dam Builders: Stories of People and Water in the Middle East* (New Brunswick, New Jersey: Transaction Publishers) 2007. pp. 115–17.

142. Gazit, Shlomo. 'Israel and the Palestinians: Fifty Years of Wars and Turning Points', *The ANNALS of the American Academy of Political and Social Science*, Vol. 555. No. 82. 1998. pp. 82–96.

143. Ibid.

144. Hechiche, Abdelwahab. 'Renaissance et déclin de la résistance palestini-enne' [Translated from French] *Politique étrangère* N°5, 38e année. 1973. pp. 597–620.

145. Wallach, John. *Arafat: in the Eyes of the Beholder* (London: Heinemann) 1997. p. 282.

146. Ibid. Interview conducted with Khaled al-Fahoum, a member of the PLO Executive Committee 1964–1965 and 1967–1969, by Wallach. p. 283.

147. Hechiche. 'Renaissance et déclin de la résistance palestinienne', *Politique étrangère* N°5, 38e. 1973.

148. Wallach: *Arafat*, p. 284.

149. Ajami, Fouad. 'The End of Pan-Arabism', *Foreign Affairs*, Vol. 57. No. 2. Winter 1978. pp. 355–73.

150. Chaliand, Gérard. 'Cahiers de l'Orient Contemporain 1967–1969', *Le Monde Diplomatique*. March 1969. Also by Chaliand, *La Résistance Palestinienne* (Paris: Seuil) 1970. pp. 87–8. Cited in Hechiche : 'Renaissance et déclin de la résistance palestinienne'.

151. Wallach: *Arafat*, p. 291.

152. Rubin, Barry and Judith Colp Rubin. *Yasir Arafat: A Political Biography* (Oxford: Oxford University Press) 2003. p. 135–40.

153. Heikel, M. *The Road to Ramadan* (New York: Ballantine Books) 1975. p. 94. Cited in: Astorino-Courtois, Allison. 'Clarifying decisions: assess-ing the impact of decision structures on foreign policy choices during the 1970 Jordanian Civil War', *International Studies Quarterly*, Vol. 42. No. 4. December 1998. pp. 733–54.

154. Astorino-Courtois. 'Clarifying Decisions', *International Studies Quarterly*, Vol. 42. No. 4. December 1998.

155. Ibid.

156. Seale, Patrick. *Abu Nidal: A Gun for Hire* (London: Random Century Group) 1992. p. 153.

157. Lunt, James. *Hussein of Jordan: Searching for a Just and Lasting Peace* (New York: William Morrow and Company, Inc.) 1989. pp. 142–143.

158. Hart, Alan. *Arafat* (London: Sidgwick & Jackson) 1984. p. 322.

159. Cf. Seale: *Abu Nidal*, p. 83; Lunt: *Hussein of Jordan*, p. 133.

160. Massad: *Colonial Effects*, p. 14.

161. Robins: *A History of Jordan*, p. 162.

162. Bligh, Alexander. 'The Jordanian army: between domestic and external challenges', *Middle East Review of International Affairs* (MERIA), Vol. 5. No. 2. June 2001.

163. Rosenfeld: 'Power structure, agency, and family in a Palestinian refugee camp', p. 173.

164. Ibid., p. 161; Massad: *Colonial Effects*, p. 260.
165. Melman, Yossi and Dan Raviv. *Behind the Uprising: Israelis, Jordanians, and Palestinians* (New York: Greenwood Press) 1989. p. 203.
166. Ibid.
167. Jarbawi, Ali. 'The triangle of conflict', *Foreign Policy*. No. 100, Autumn, 1995. p. 94.
168. Ibid., p. 95.
169. Ibid., p. 94.
170. Ibid., p. 96.
171. King Hussein of Jordan. 'Address to the Nation.' Amman, 31 July 1988. [Translated from the original Arabic.] *United Nations Information System on the Question of Palestine (UNISPAL)*. Via: http://bit.ly/jwcfXT [Accessed: 4 May 2011].
172. Robins: *A History of Jordan*, p. 164.
173. Peretz, Don. *Intifada: The Palestinian Uprising* (Boulder, CO: Westview Press) 1990. p. 109.
174. Mayor Elias Freij of Bethlehem, *New York Times*, 9 June 1988. Cited in Peretz : *Intifada*, p. 109.
175. Robins: *A History of Jordan*, p. 163.
176. Ibid., p. 164.
177. *The Times*. 'Husain seals peace deal in Israel.' 11 November 1994.
178. Cf. Naiman, Robert. 'No jubilee for the Middle East?', *Middle East Research and Information Project*. MERIP213. Vol. 19. Winter 1999; Palestine Facts, 'Israel-Jordan Peace Treaty, 1994.' 2005. Via: http://bit.ly/m2uXh3 [Accessed: 4 May 2011].
179. Plotkin, Lori. *Jordan-Israel Peace: Taking Stock, 1994–1997* (Washington, DC: Washington Institute for Near East Policy) May 1997.
180. Further gains included the regaining of rights over water and land in certain areas occupied by Israel since 1967, full recognition of Jordan's western borders by Israel, and official Likud support for the treaty. Thus Jordan was able to consolidate itself and to kill the Likud's idea of an alternative Palestinian home. Jarbawi: 'The triangle of conflict', pp. 104–5.
181. *The Telegraph*. 'Jordan seeks the path of least resistance between two rising conflicts.' 17 August 2002. Via: http://bit.ly/lhp6Vu [Accessed: 4 May 2011].
182. *Jordan Times*. 'Ma'an riots continue: King warns Jordan will not tolerate instigation of violence.' 22 February 1998.
183. Originally established as an offshoot of the Muslim Brotherhood in the early 1970s, the group has operated in several countries and been responsible for terrorist activity in places where they have a presence. The Takfiri ideology

emphasizes a withdrawal from modern society, seen as an anti-Islamic culture. The ideology of *Al-Takfir W'al Hijra* is considered a foundation for other global terrorist groups, deriving its popular form of Islamism from past influential leaders such as Sayyid Qutb and Shukri Mustafa.

184. Kamal, Sana. 'Ma'an erupts again', *Middle East International.* 8 February 2002. p. 13.
185. Ibid., p. 14.
186. Harris: *The Levant,* p. 163.
187. Ibid, p. 164.
188. Kepel, Gilles. *Jihad: The Trail of Political Islam* (London: I.B. Tauris) 2003. p. 332.
189. Bregman, Ahron. *Israel's Wars: A History since 1947* (London: Routledge) 2002. p. 215.
190. *The Sunday Telegraph.* 'Jordan cracks down amid fears of spreading Palestinian unrest.' 10 June 2001. Via: http://bit.ly/iTOv5R [Accessed: 4 May 2011].
191. Ibid.
192. Ibid.

Chapter 2

1. Sonbol, Amira El Azhary. *Women of Jordan: Islam, Labor and the Law* (Syracuse, New York: Syracuse University Press) 2003. p. 38.
2. Ibid.
3. 'Annual Report by His Britannic Majesty's Government on the Palestinian Administration, 1923.' Cited in Amawi, Abla. 'Gender and Citizenship in Jordan', in Joseph, Suad (ed.) *Gender and Citizenship in the Middle East* (Syracuse, New York: Syracuse University Press) 2000. pp. 160–1.
4. Also recognized as the House of Notables and the House of Deputies, respectively. For the purpose of clarity and consistency, the original terms shall be used throughout. *Source:* The Hashemite Kingdom of Jordan Government Online, The Legislative Branch. Via: http://bit.ly/cChIUK [Accessed: 10 February 2009].
5. Davis, Uri. *Citizenship and the State: A Comparative Study of Citizenship Legislation in Israel, Jordan, Palestine, Syria and Lebanon* (Reading: Ithaca Press) 1997. p. 67.
6. Cf. Jordan: The Official Site of the Jordanian e-Government. Via: http://bit.ly/grcKdZ [Accessed: 21 March 2011].
7. Article 28 (e), Cited in The Constitution of the Hashemite Kingdom of Jordan, Part One, 'The King and His Prerogatives', 1 January 1952.

8. Article 30, ibid.

9. Article 34–38, ibid.

10. Articles 31–33, ibid.

11. See Seton, C. R. W. *Legislation of Transjordan, 1918–1930*, c. 1931. Cited in Davis: *Citizenship and the State*, p. 63.

12. Amawi, 'Gender and Citizenship in Jordan', in Suad (ed.): *Gender and Citizenship in the Middle East*, pp. 160–162.

13. 'Report by His Britannic Majesty's Government on the Palestinian Administration, submitted to the Council of the League of Nations 1929', 143. Cited in Amawi: 'Gender and Citizenship in Jordan', in Joseph (ed.): *Gender and Citizenship in the Middle East*, pp. 160–1.

14. Jordanian Nationality Law No. 6 for 1954, *Official Gazette*, No. 171, p. 105, 16 Feb. 1954. Ibid.

15. Ibid. Article 3 (ii).

16. Jordanian, foreigner, Arab and *émigré*, respectively. Cited in Davis: *Citizenship and the State*, p. 70.

17. Article 2 of the Jordanian Nationality Law No. 6 for 1854, clauses (i) – (iv). Cited in Davis: *Citizenship and the State*, p. 70.

18. Article 2 (v) states that the expression 'loss of capacity' (*fuqdan al-ahaliyya*) means being limited, or insane, or disabled or loss of legal capacity. Clause (vi) advises that in all matters pertaining to the implementation of this law at 18 years of age, according to the Gregorian calendar. Cited in Davis: *Citizenship and the State*, p. 70.

19. Amawi: 'Gender and citizenship in Jordan', in *Gender and Citizenship in the Middle East*, Joseph (ed.), p. 162.

20. Ibid. In accordance with Article 75 of the Constitution.

21. At the time of the compilation of the report, access to Camp A was limited only to those refugees with valid identity documents. Cited in Refugees International, *Visual Mission: Refugee Camps in Jordan and in the 'No-man's Land' at the Iraq-Jordan Border*, August 2003.

22. Refugees International, Visual Mission: Refugee Camps in Jordan and in the 'No-man's Land' at the Iraq-Jordan Border, August 2003.

23. Davis: *Citizenship and the State*, p. 71.

24. Formulated on 5 April 1954. Cited in Davis: *Citizenship and the State*, p. 71.

25. Ibid.

26. Massad, Joseph A. *Colonial Effects: The Making of National Identity in Jordan* (New York; Chichester: Columbia University Press) 2001. p. 40.

27. Ibid.

28. Davis: *Citizenship and the State*, p. 71.

29. In 1945 as Transjordan, 1946 as the Hashemite Kingdom of Jordan.
30. Article 6, Agreement of 5 April 1954 on Provisions Regarding Citizenship Among Member States of the League of Arab States. Cf. Davis: *Citizenship and the State*, p. 71.
31. Cf. Article 14 of Law No. 6 of 1954 on Nationality (last amended 1987).
32. Ibid. 'A person who acquires Jordanian nationality shall be deemed to be a Jordanian in every respect, but he may not hold any political or diplomatic position or any public office prescribed by the Council of Ministers and may not become a member of the State Council for at least 10 years after acquiring Jordanian nationality. He shall be eligible for nomination to a municipal or village council or to trade union office only after a period of at least five years has elapsed as from his acquisition of Jordanian nationality.' Law No. 6 of 1954 on Nationality (last amended 1987) [Jordan], 1 January 1954. Via: http://bit.ly/hoKYz9 [Accessed: 21 March 2011].
33. Cf. Article 42 and 75, cited in The Constitution of the Hashemite Kingdom of Jordan, 1 January 1952.
34. Davis: *Citizenship and the State*, p. 71. See also: 'Any person who, not being Jewish, possessed Palestinian nationality before 15 May 1948 and was a regular resident in the Hashemite Kingdom of Jordan between 20 December 1949 and 16 February 1954.' Law No. 6 of 1954 on Nationality (last amended 1987) [Jordan], 1 January 1954. Via: http://bit.ly/hoKYz9 [Accessed: 21 March 2011].
35. Massad: *Colonial Effects*, p. 40.
36. *The National*. 'Jordan hits back over Jewish land claims.' 22 June 2009. Via: http://bit.ly/dPECav [Accessed: 21 March 2011].
37. *Ha'aretz*. 'Despite Jordan denial, workers insist Israel-owned factory was sweatshop.' 17 August 2009. Via: http://bit.ly/gqdt2k [Accessed: 21 March 2011].
38. Gelber, Yoav. *Israeli-Jordanian Dialogue, 1948–1953: Cooperation, Conspiracy, or Collusion?* (Brighton; Portland: Sussex Academic Press) 2004. p. 103.
39. Davis, Uri. 'Citizenship legislation in the Syrian Arab Republic', *Arab Studies Quarterly*. Winter 1996.
40. Plascov, Avi. *The Palestinian Refugees in Jordan, 1948–1957* (London: Cass) 1981. p. 44.
41. Ibid., p. 45.
42. See al-Jaridah al-Rasmiyyah, *The Official Gazette*, 1.2.50, No. 1009, p. 48. Cited in Plascov: *The Palestinian Refugees in Jordan 1948–1957*, p. 45.
43. Ibid.
44. Gelber: *Israeli-Jordanian Dialogue*, p. 106–7.

45. Amawi: 'Gender and citizenship in Jordan', in *Gender and Citizenship in the Middle East*, Joseph (ed.), pp. 161–4.
46. Sonbol: *Women of Jordan*, p. 51.
47. Article 26 of the Residency Law and Foreigners' Affairs. Sa'di Abdeen, Musoat al-Jaib lil-Tashira' wa al Qada wal-Figq, The Residency Law and Foreigner's Affairs, No. 24 for 1973. Dar al-jib lil Nashir wal-Tawzea, Amman, 1991. The Residency of Foreigners Law published in the *Official Gazette*, No. 2426, p. 1112, 16 June 1973. Latest amendments No. 10 for 1991 published in the *Official Gazette*, No. 3740, p. 73, 16 January 1991. Cited in Amawi: 'Gender and citizenship in Jordan', in *Gender and Citizenship in the Middle East*, Joseph (ed.), p. 162.
48. *The Jordan Times*. 'Officials prepare response to U.S. State Department allegations of government violation of basic human rights principles.' 9–10 March 2001.
49. Husseini, Rana. 'Women seek equal rights under Citizenship Law.' *The Jordan Times*. 28 December 2007. Via: http://bit.ly/fJQ30S [Accessed: 6 February 2011].
50. Under Article 9 all paternally Jordanian applicants will be considered citizens regardless of where they are born.
51. Jordanian Nationality Law, Article 10. Cited in *Gender and Citizenship*, Joseph (ed.), p. 162.
52. Amawi: 'Gender and citizenship in Jordan', in *Gender and Citizenship in the Middle East*, Joseph (ed.), p. 162.
53. Hijab, Nadia. *Women Are Citizens Too: The Laws of the State, the Lives of Women* (Regional Bureau for Arab States, United Nations Development Programme) 2002. p. 6. See also: Rita Giacaman, Islah Jad and Penny Johnson, 'For the public good? gender and social citizenship in Palestine', *Middle East Report*. No. 198. Vol. 26. No. 1. 1996. pp. 11–17; Haya Al-Mughni and Mary Ann Tretreault, 'Citizenship, gender and the politics of quasi states', in Joseph (ed.): *Gender and Citizenship in the Middle East*, pp. 237–61.
54. Amawi: 'Gender and citizenship in Jordan', in *Gender and Citizenship in the Middle East*, Joseph (ed.), p. 162. See also Altorki, Soraya. 'The concept and practice of citizenship in Saudi Arabia', in *Gender and Citizenship in the Middle East*, Joseph (ed.), pp. 215–37.
55. States regulate the rules by which one becomes a citizen, by which citizens pass citizenship on to their children and spouses, and by which citizens can lose citizenship. Hijab: *Women Are Citizens Too*, p. 5.
56. Ibid., p. 7
57. Amawi: 'Gender and citizenship in Jordan', in *Gender and Citizenship in the Middle East*, Joseph (ed.), p. 162.

58. Amawi: 'Gender and citizenship in Jordan', in *Gender and Citizenship in the Middle East*, Joseph (ed.), p. 164.

59. Jordanian Nationality Law, Article 13.

60. Amawi: 'Gender and citizenship in Jordan', in *Gender and Citizenship in the Middle East*, Joseph (ed.), p. 165.

61. Sonbol: *Women of Jordan*, pp. 39–40.

62. Khayyat, Abdul Aziz. 'Women in society: in Islam and Christianity.' Paper presented at the third Symposium in Cooperation with the Pontifical Council for Interreligious Dialogue (the Vatican), 24–26 June 1992, Rome, Italy. p. 8. Cited in Amawi: 'Gender and citizenship in Jordan', In Joseph (ed.): *Gender and Citizenship in the Middle East*.

63. Article 15(4) of CEDAW: 'States Parties shall accord to men and women the same rights with regard to the law relating to the movement of persons and the freedom to choose their residence and domicile.' For the full Convention, see Convention on the Elimination of Discrimination Against Women, 29th Session. 30 June–25 July 2003. Via: http://bit.ly/ijmwWf [Accessed: 22 March 2011]. Cf. *The Jordan Times*, 'Activists praise Cabinet decision to lift reservations.' 11 February 2009. Via: http://bit.ly/ik3PGg [Accessed: 22 March 2011].

64. Sonbol: *Women of Jordan*, p. 51.

65. Nasser, Lamis. 'Important policy measures and other initiatives to promote the implementation of CEDAW in Jordan', paper presented at a UNDP and UNICEF workshop on CEDAW, Amman, Jordan, August 1997.

66. Convention on the Elimination of Discrimination Against Women, 29th Session. 30 June–25 July 2003. Via: http://bit.ly/ijmwWf [Accessed: 22 March 2011].

67. Amawi: 'Gender and citizenship in Jordan', in *Gender and Citizenship in the Middle East*, Joseph (ed.), pp. 163–164.

68. Ibid.

69. Ibid.

70. Ibid., p. 164.

71. Ibid.

72. Cf. *Stop Honour Killings*, 'Punishment for honour crimes in Jordan stiffens, but incident rate continues to increase.' 1 February 2010. Via: http://bit.ly/eWmdI9 [Accessed: 22 March 2011].

73. Sonbol: *Women of Jordan*, p. 253.

74. Cf. Interview with Anis F. Kassim, international law expert and practicing lawyer in Jordan in *al-Majdal*. 'Palestinian Refugees in Jordan and the Revocation of Citizenship.' Forced Secondary Displacement: Palestinian Refugees in the Gaza Strip, Iraq, Jordan, and Libya. Winter

2010. Via: http://bit.ly/fzUgwJ. [Accessed: 30 March 2011]. Kassim further concludes that 'These procedures are being completely ignored when the citizenship of a Jordanian of Palestinian origin is revoked.'

75. Ibid.

76. *Human Rights Watch.* 'Jordan: Stop Withdrawing Nationality from Palestinian-Origin Citizens.' 1 February 2010. Via: http://bit.ly/fRWe1R [Accessed: 14 March 2011].

77. Interview with Dr Nabil Sharif by *Russia Today.* 'Iraqi and Palestinian refugees are our brothers – Jordanian Minister.' 5 August 2010. Via: http://bit.ly/dFP0Qv [Accessed: 20 March 2011].

78. Ibid.

79. Cf. *Stateless Again: Palestinian-Origin Jordanians Deprived of their Nationality.* Human Rights Watch. 31 January 2010. Via: http://bit.ly/9VTqz9 [Accessed: 14 March 2011].

80. *Arutz Sheva.* 'Jordan Revoking Citizenship En Masse, Fearing Influx of PA Arabs.' 21 July 2009. Via: http://bit.ly/RvnSz [Accessed: 24 March 2011].

81. *The Star.* 'Nationality in Limbo.' 13 July 2009. Via: http://bit.ly/fLcWUb [Accessed: 30 March 2011].

82. *UPI.* 'Abbas receives Jordanian Citizenship.' 9 February 2011. Via: http://bit.ly/gm9STA [Accessed: 26 March 2011].

83. The full version of the speech is available in *The Jordan Times,* 1 August 1988.

84. Lynch, Marc. *State Interests and Public Spheres: The International Politics of Jordan's Identity* (New York; Chichester: Columbia University Press) 1999. p. 222.

85. Cf. Dinker, Dan and Pinchas Inbari. 'Are there signs of a Jordanian-Palestinian reengagement?', *Jerusalem Issue Brief,* Vol. 5. No. 1. 19 July 2005; Oroub Al Abed, 'Palestinian Refugees in Jordan,' *Forced Migration Online.* 2004. Via: http://bit.ly/eTRJj3 [Accessed: 24 March 2011].

86. Robins, Philip. 'Shedding half a kingdom: Jordan's dismantling of ties with the West Bank', *Bulletin (British Society for Middle Eastern Studies),* Vol. 16. No. 2. 1989. pp. 162–75.

87. Ibid.

88. Ibid., p. 166.

89. For further information see: Israel 1948–1967: West Bank Annexed, Palestine Facts, (2005). Via: http://www.palestinefacts.org [Accessed: 6 March 2012].

90. Radio Amman, 3 May 1988. In Nevo, Joseph and Ilan Pappé, *Jordan in the Middle East: The Making of a Pivotal State, 1948–1988* (Ilford: Frank Cass) 1994. p. 217.

91. The 19th (Emergency) Session of the Palestine National Council, Algiers, 15 November 1988. Cited in Davis, Uri. 'Palestinian Refugees at the Crossroads of 1996 Permanent Status Negotiations', *Shaml Monograph* 1. 1995.

92. Robins: 'Shedding half a kingdom', p. 166.

93. Lunt, James. *Hussein of Jordan: A Political Biography* (London: MacMillan) 1989. pp. 254–5.

94. Al-Khazendar, Sami. *Jordan and the Palestine Question: The Role of Islamic and Left Forces in Foreign Policy-Making* (Reading: Ithaca Press) 1997. p. 60.

95. Lynch: *State Interests and Public Spheres*, p. 1.

96. Al-Khazendar: *Jordan and the Palestine Question*, p. 60.

97. Lynch: *State Interests and Public Spheres*, p. 95.

98. Goodwin-Gill, G. S. 'The Rights of Refugees and Stateless Persons: Problems of Stateless Persons and the Need for International Measures of Protection', paper presented to the World Congress on Human Rights, New Delhi, India, 10–15 December 1990, in Saksena, K. P. (ed.) *Human Rights Perspectives and Challenges (in 1990 and Beyond)* (New Delhi, Lancer Books) 1994. p. 386. See also Takkenberg, Lex. *The Status of Palestinian Refugees in International Law* (Oxford: Clarendon Press) 1998. p. 185.

99. Lunt: *Hussein of Jordan*, p. 235.

100. Hart, Alan. *Arafat: A Political Biography* (London: Sidgwick & Jackson) 1994. p. 491.

101. Ibid.

102. Ibid.

103. Lynch: *State Interests and Public Spheres*, p. 102.

104. Yusef al-Azam, MP and member of the Muslim Brotherhood, Minutes of the Jordanian Parliament, first meeting in the first regular session, 21 January 1984, p. 12. Cited in Al-Khazendar: *Jordan and the Palestine Question*. Also, in Al-Khazendar's personal interviews with other Muslim Brotherhood leaders, such as Abd al-Latif Arabiat and Isaac Farhan, the same attitude and beliefs were expressed.

105. Al-Khazendar: *Jordan and the Palestine Question*, p. 141.

106. Lynch: *State Interests and Public Spheres*, p. 235.

107. Al-Khazendar: *Jordan and the Palestine Question*, p. 107.

108. Lunt: *Hussein of Jordan*, p. 235.

109. Takkenberg: *The Status of Palestinian Refugees in International Law*, pp. 156–7.

110. Shehadeh, R. *The Declaration of Principles & the Legal System in the West Bank* (Jerusalem: Palestinian Academic Society for the Study of International Affairs) 1994. Cited in Takkenberg: *The Status of Palestinian Refugees in International Law*, p. 157.

111. For an English translation of the press conference, broadcast by Amman Television Service, see JPS 69 (Autumn 1988) 290, 293. Cited in Takkenberg: *The Status of Palestinian Refugees in International Law*, p. 157.

112. Takkenberg: *The Status of Palestinian Refugees in International Law*, p. 158.

113. Al Abed: *Palestinian Refugees in Jordan*, p. 7.

114. Ibid., p. 8.

115. Beinin, Joel and Lisa Hajjar. 'Primer on Palestine, Israel and the Arab-Israeli Conflict: A Primer', *Middle East Research and Information Project*. 2002.

116. Cf. Al Abed: *Palestinian Refugees in Jordan*, p. 17.

117. Ibid., pp. 9–11.

118. Lynch: *State Interests and Public Spheres*, p. 82.

119. Davis, Uri. *Crossing the Border (An Autobiography of an anti-Zionist Palestinian-Jew)* (London: Books & Books) 1995.

120. Takkenberg: *The Status of Palestinian Refugees in International Law*, p. 184.

121. Cf. Borthwick, Bruce. 'Water in Israeli-Jordanian Relations: From Conflict to the Danger of Ecological Disaster', *Israel Affairs*, Vol. 9. No. 3. 2003. pp. 165–86.

122. Nevo, Joseph. 'The Changing Identities of Jordan', *Israel Affairs*, Vol. 9. No. 3. Spring 2003. pp. 187–208.

123. Ibid. See also: 'Rich or poor, a million Iraqi refugees strain the hospitality of Jordan.' *The Guardian*. 24 January 2007. Via: http://bit.ly/f1sYJP [Accessed: 22 March 2011] and 'Iraqi Artists, Actors and Designers Try to Build New Lives in Jordan.' *The New York Times*. 23 March 2011. Via: http://nyti.ms/fp7yD6 [Accessed: 22 March 2011].

124. Chatelard, Géraldine. 'Jordan: A Refugee Haven', Country Profile. *Migration Information Source*. 2004. p. 5.

125. Ibid., p. 4.

126. Ibid., p. 6.

127. Ibid.

128. Chatelard, Géraldine. 'From one war to another. Iraqi emigration to Jordan', *ISIM Newsletter (Leiden)*, no. 13, December 2003. pp. 26–7.

129. Ibid., p. 7.

130. Ibid., p. 13.

131. Chatelard, Géraldine. 'Chrétiens en Jordanie: entre appartenance communautaire et identité nationale', *Les Cahiers de l'Orient*, No. 48. 1997. pp. 117–22.

132. Chatelard: 'From One War to Another', p. 14.

133. Ibid.

134. *Zakat*: annual alms tax or tithe of two plus percent levied on wealth and distributed to the poor. Cf. Esposito, John L. *Unholy War: Terror in the Name of Islam* (Oxford: Oxford University Press) 2002. p. 172.

135. Zaiotti, Ruben. 'Dealing with non-Palestinian Refugees in the Middle East: policies and practices in an uncertain environment', *International Journal of Refugee Law*, Vol. 18. No. 2. June 2006. pp. 333–53.

136. Ibid.

137. Ibid.

138. Ibid.

139. Ibid.

140. Ibid.

141. Davis, Uri. *Citizenship for Palestine Refugees and the Peace Process* (Shaml: Palestinian Diaspora and Refugee Centre. Monograph Series No 1, Ramallah) 1996.

142. Article IV of the Transjordan Nationality Law, 1928. Cited in Davis, Uri. *Palestinian Refugees at the Crossroads of 1996 Permanent Status Negotiations* (Shaml Monograph 1) 1996.

143. Non-Palestinian residents of the camp included Somalis, Sudanese, Palestinians, Tunisians, Egyptians, Iraqis, Eritrean, Mauritanian and Turkish refugees and at the start of the U.S.-led attack on Iraq, an estimated 1,000 Iraqis. *IRIN Middle East.* 'Iraqi refugees face bleak existence.' 26 February 2004. Via: http://bit.ly/eWij4n [Accessed: 25 March 2011].

144. For a comprehensive analysis of the Iraqi refugee community in Jordan, see Seeley, Nicholas. 'The politics of aid to Iraqi refugees in Jordan', *Middle East Report.* Issue 256. Vol. 40. Fall 2010.

145. Ibid.

146. *American Foreign Policy.* 'Iraqi refugees in Jordan: Why America should care.' 2001. Via: http://bit.ly/fGvIEa [Accessed: 20 March 2011].

147. *Human Rights Watch.* 'Backgrounder: Jordan.' April 2007.

148. *Washington Post.* 'Iraq, Jordan See Threat To Election From Iraq.' 8 December 2004. Via: http://wapo.st/f7Ao72 [Accessed: 2 April 2011].

149. *International Crisis Group.* 'Failed Responsibility: Iraqi Refugees in Syria, Jordan and Lebanon.' Crisis Group Middle East Report. No. 77, 10 July 2008.

150. Susser, Asher. *Jordan: Case Study of a Pivotal State* (Washington, DC: Washington Institute for Near East Policy) 2000. p. 46.

151. Ibid.

152. Ibid., p. 48.

153. Simons, Geoff. *The Scourging of Iraq: Sanctions, Law and Natural Justice* (Basingstoke: Macmillan Press) 1998. p. 73.

154. Ibid.

155. Ibid.

156. Ibid., p. 37. See also: Andrew Bennett, Joseph Lepgold and Danny Unger. *Friends in Need: Burden Sharing in the Gulf War* (Basingstoke: Macmillan Press) 1997. p. 325.

157. Zaiotti: 'Dealing with non-Palestinian refugees in the Middle East', p. 19.
158. Ibid.
159. Ibid.

Chapter 3

1. Quoted in Khashan, Hilal. *Arabs at the Crossroads: Political Identity and Nationalism* (Gainesville, FL: University Press of Florida) 2000. p. 8.
2. Nevertheless, it remains debatable how indigenous the Jordanian identity remains in light of its role as a transit country in both the past and present.
3. Cf. Hamid, R. (ed.) *Muqararat al-majlis al-watani al-filastini 1964–1974* [Resolutions of the PNCs 1964–1974] (Beirut: PLO Research Centre) 1975. p. 178. Cited in Gresh, Alain. *The PLO: The Struggle Within: Towards an Independent Palestinian State* (London: Zed) 1985. p. 112.
4. Daniels, S. *Fields of Vision: Landscape, Imagery and National Identity in England and the U.S.* (Cambridge: Polity Press) 1993. p. 5. Cited in Woodward, Kathryn. *Concepts of Identity and Difference* (London: Sage Publications) 1999. p. 18.
5. Nasser, Riad. *Palestinian Identity in Jordan and Israel: The Necessary 'Other' in the Making of a Nation* (New York: Routledge) 2005. p. 67.
6. Ibid., p. 68.
7. Kumaraswamy, P. R. 'Who am I?: the identity crisis in the Middle East', *Middle East Review of International Affairs*, Vol. 10. No. 1. March 2006. pp. 63–73.
8. Dawisha, Adeed. *Arab Nationalism in the Twentieth Century: From Triumph to Despair* (Princeton, NJ; Oxford: Princeton University Press) 2003. p. 219.
9. Ibid.
10. Ibid.
11. Ibid., p. 220.
12. Ibid., p. 245.
13. Ibid., p. 254.
14. Ibid., p. 281.
15. Dr. Ahmed Oweidi al-Abbadi, quoted in Abu Odeh, Adnan. *Jordanians, Palestinians, and the Hashemite Kingdom in the Middle East Peace Process* (Washington, DC: U.S. Institute of Peace Press) 1999. p. 243.
16. Layne, Linda A. 'The dialogics of tribal self-representation in Jordan', *American Ethnologist*, Vol. 16. Issue 1. February 1989. pp. 24–39.
17. Ibid., p. 25.

18. Kirkbride, Alec S. 'Changes in tribal life in Trans-Jordan', *Man*, Vol. 45. March–April 1945. pp. 40–41.
19. Nasser: *Palestinian Identity in Jordan and Israel*, p. 88.
20. Al-Kird, A., R. Abed al-Hadi and A. Jabir. *al-Hadarah al-Qadimah fi al-Sharq wa al-Kharb* [Ancient History in the East and West] (Amman: al-A'aqsa) 1967. Cf. A. Al-Sasi, J.A. Jawish and A. Taj al-Din, *Dirasat fi al-Tarikh al-Qadim lil-Wattan al-Arabi al-Kabir* [Studies in Ancient History of the Great Arab Motherland] (The Ministry of Education and Culture in Saudi Arabia) 1966. Cited in Nasser: *Palestinian Identity in Jordan and Israel*, p. 88.
21. Antoun, Richard T. 'Civil society, tribal process, and change in Jordan: An Anthropological View', *International Journal of Middle East Studies*, Vol. 32. No. 4. November 2002. p. 451.
22. Ibid.
23. Fathi, Schirin H. *Jordan, an Invented Nation?: Tribe-State Dynamics and the Formation of National Identity* (Hamburg: Deutsches Orient-Institut) 1994. p. 33.
24. Huntington, Samuel. *Who Are We? The Challenges to America's National Identity* (New York: Simon & Schuster) 2004. p. 21.
25. Ronald L. Jepperson, Alexander Wendt and Peter J. Katzenstein, 'Norms, identity, and culture in national security', in Katzenstein, Peter J. (ed.) *The Culture of National Security: Norms and Identity in World Politics* (New York: Columbia University Press) 1996. p. 59. Cited in Huntington: *Who Are We?*, pp. 21–2.
26. Lewis, Bernard. *The Multiple Identities of the Middle East* (London: Weidenfeld & Nicolson) 1999. p. 4.
27. Fathi: *Jordan*, p. 53.
28. Committee on International Relations, Group for the Advancement of Psychiatry. *Us and Them: The Psychology of Ethnonationalism* (New York: Brunner/Mazel, 1987), p. 115; Jonathan Mercer, 'Anarchy and identity', *International Organization*, Vol. 49. No. 2. Spring 1995. pp. 229–52.
29. Lewis: *The Multiple Identities of the Middle East*, p. 4.
30. Ibid.
31. Maalouf, Amin. *In the Name of Identity: Violence and the Need to Belong* (London: Penguin Books) 2003. p. 157.
32. Antoun, Richard T. 'Civil society, tribal process, and change in Jordan: An Anthropological View', *International Journal of Middle East Studies*, Vol. 32. No. 4. November 2002. p. 451.
33. Cf. 'Ethnicity and leadership: the Circassians in Jordan', by Seteney Shami. (Unpublished PhD Dissertation, University of California at Berkeley, 1982), p. 15. Cited in Fathi: *Jordan*, p. 38.

34. Similar to the Bedouin, they are renowned for their loyalty to the Hashemite regime.

35. Fathi: *Jordan*, p. 38.

36. Layne, Linda A. 'The dialogics of tribal self-representation in Jordan', *American Ethnologist*, Vol. 16. Issue 1. February 1989. pp. 24–39.

37. Ibid.

38. — '*Ali al-Wardi, Lamahat Ijtima'iya min Tarikh al-'Iraq al-Hadith, al-Jusi' al-Rabi', min 'Am 1914 ila 'Am 1918* [Sociological aspects of modern Iraqi history, volume four, 1914–1918] (London: Dar Kufan li al-Nashr, 1992), pp. 402–3. Cited in Dawisha, Adeed. *Arab Nationalism in the Twentieth Century: From Triumph to Despair* (Princeton, NJ: Princeton University Press) 2005. pp. 293–4.

39. Gellner, Ernest. 'Patrons and clients', in *Patrons and Clients in Mediterranean Societies*, Gellner, Ernest and John Waterbury (eds.) (London: Duckworth) 1977. pp. 2–3. Cited in Fathi: *Jordan*, pp. 36–7.

40. William Young in personal communication with Richard T. Antoun, 23 December 1998. Cited in Antoun: 'Civil society, tribal process, and change in Jordan: an anthropological view'. p 445.

41. Ibid.

42. Ibid., p. 446.

43. Abu Odeh, Adnan. *Jordanians, Palestinians, and the Hashemite Kingdom in the Middle East Peace Process* (Washington, DC: United States Institute of Peace Press) 1999. p. 237.

44. George, Alan. *Jordan: Living in the Crossfire* (London: Zed Books) 2005. p. 243.

45. Massad, Joseph A. *Colonial Effects: The Making of National Identity in Jordan* (New York; Chichester: Columbia University Press) 2001. p. 70.

46. *The Jordan Times*, 28 January 1985. Cited in Fathi: *Jordan*, p. 35.

47. As Antoun denotes, the process of tribal conflict resolution is based on the principle of collective responsibility on the part of a stipulated and limited set of patrilineal kinsmen. If one of a tribe's members is wronged, this set of kinsmen must either take revenge on the aggressor or seek and receive compensation. If one of the tribe's members commits a crime and prompts a revenge attack from the victim's group, the offenders must seek refuge and protection (*dakhl*) with a third party, arrange for truce and mediation, and pay compensation. For further details see Antoun: 'Civil Society, tribal process, and change in Jordan'. p. 446.

48. Bates, Daniel G. and Amal Rassam (eds.) *Peoples and Cultures of the Middle East* (Englewood Cliffs, NJ: Prentice-Hall) 1983. pp. 257–258.

49. Clay, J. W. 'Epilogue: the ethnic future of nations', *Third World Quarterly*, Vol. 11. No. 4. 1989. p. 225. Cited in Fathi: *Jordan*, p. 35.

50. *Middle East Online*. 'Queen Rania Condemns non-Islamic "honour killings".' September 30, 2003. *The Jordan Times*. 'Amendment to Article 340 on honour crimes faces opposition in parliament.' November 17, 1999.

51. Interview conducted with Dr. Ahmed Oweidi al-Abbadi by author, Amman, Jordan. 17 February 2007.

52. In the intervening years, relations between the Jordanian National Movement and the the monarchy and government worsened. The movement has been classified as 'illegal' and its leader, Dr. Oweidi al-Abbadi, was sentenced to three years in jail and fined 30 JD ($42) for disseminating damaging information concerning the Jordanian state to outside sources, via e-mail and the JNM website. *The Jordan Times*, 9 October 2007.

53. Brand, Laurie A. 'National narratives and migration discursive strategies of inclusion and exclusion in Jordan and Lebanon', *International Migration Review*, Vol. 44. Issue 1. Spring 2010. pp. 78–110.

54. Ibid.

55. Ibid.

56. *The Jordan Times*, 9 October 2007.

57. *Jordan National Movement*. 'March 25 Crime (Special).' Via: http://bit.ly/eowpI3 [Accessed: 12 April 2011].

58. That is, that the ethnic Jordanian populace is a victim of occupation akin to that of their Palestinian-Jordanian counterparts.

59. Ibid.

60. Comprising Iraqis, Palestinians, South-East Asians and Egyptians to name but a few.

61. Abdul-Hadi al-Majali, quoted in Abu Odeh: *Jordanians, Palestinians, and the Hashemite Kingdom*, p. 242.

62. Susser, Asher. 'Jordan – the maze of tribalism, Jordanianism, Palestinianism, and Islam', in *Challenges to the Cohesion of the Arab State*, Asher Susser (ed.) (The Moshe Dayan Center: Tel Aviv University) 2008. p. 105.

63. Wilson, M. C. *King Abdullah, Britain and the Making of Jordan* (Cambridge: Cambridge University Press) 1987. p. 199. Cited in Fathi: *Jordan*, p. 122.

64. Anonymous interview conducted by author, 31 January 2007. Amman.

65. Gubser, Peter. *Jordan: Crossroads of Middle Eastern Events* (Boulder, CO: Westview Press; London: Croom Helm) 1983. pp. 15–16.

66. Fathi: *Jordan*, p. 122.

67. Ibid., p. 212.

68. Abu Odeh: *Jordanians, Palestinians, and the Hashemite Kingdom*, p. 240.

69. Ibid.

70. M. C. Hudson. *Arab Politics – The Search for Legitimacy* (New Haven: Yale University Press, 1977), p. 210. Cited in Fathi: *Jordan*, p. 212.

71. Fathi: *Jordan*, p. 212.
72. Khoury, N.A. 'The National Consultative Council of Jordan: a study in legislative development', *International Journal of Middle East Studies*, Vol. 13. No. 4. 1981. p. 430. Cited in Fathi: *Jordan*, p. 214.
73. Abu Odeh: *Jordanians, Palestinians, and the Hashemite Kingdom*, p. 241.
74. Ibid.
75. Ibid.
76. Ibid., p. 245.
77. Ibid.
78. Ibid., p. 251.
79. Such as Cairo, Mecca, Jerusalem and Damascus, where the majority of such notables resided.
80. Interview conducted with Nahed Hattar by author, 20 February 2006. Amman.
81. Ibid.
82. Ibid., p. 257.
83. Ibid.
84. Mansfield, Peter. 'Jordan and Palestine', in *The Shaping of an Arab Statesman: Sharif Abd al-Hamid Sharaf and the Modern Arab World*, Patrick Seale (ed.) (London: Quartet Books) 1983. pp. 21–39.
85. Diker, Dan and Pinchas Inbari. 'Are there signs of a Jordanian-Palestinian reengagement?', *Jerusalem Issue Brief*, Vol. 5. No. 1. 19 July 2005.
86. Jarbawi, Ali. 'The triangle of conflict', *Foreign Policy*, No. 100. Autumn 1995. pp. 92–108.
87. Ibid.
88. Layne. 'The dialogics of tribal self-representation in Jordan', *American Ethnologist*, Vol. 16. Issue 1. February 1989. pp. 24–39. Cf.: Clinton Bailey, *Jordan's Palestinian Challenge 1948–1983: A Political History* (Boulder, CO: Westview Press) 1984; Sheila Ryan and Muhammad Hallaj, *Palestine Is, But Not In Jordan* (Belmont, MA: The Association of Arab-American University Graduates Press) 1983; Dean L. Brown, 'The land of Palestine: West Bank not East Bank', *Middle East Institute Problem Paper.* No. 23. 1982.
89. Bar-Tal, Daniel and Yona Teichmann. *Stereotypes and Prejudice in Conflict: Representations of Arabs in Israeli Jewish Society* (Cambridge: Cambridge University Press) 2005. p. 137.
90. Lucas, Russell E. *Jordan: Domestic Responses to External Challenges, 1988–2001* (Albany: State University of New York Press) 2005. p. 26.
91. Cf. John Roberts. 'Prospects for democracy in Jordan', *Arab Studies Quarterly*, Vol. 13. No. 3–4. Summer/Fall 1991. pp. 119–38; Marc Lynch, *State Interests and Public Spheres: The International Politics of Jordan's Identity* (New York: Columbia University Press) 1999; Joseph A. Massad, *Colonial Effects: The Making of National Identity in Jordan* (New York: Columbia University Press) 2001.

92. Salibi, Kamal S. *The Modern History of Jordan* (London: I.B.Tauris) 1993. p. 126.
93. Ibid.
94. Interview conducted with Dr. Ahmed Oweidi al-Abbadi by author, Amman, Jordan. 17 February 2007.
95. Abu Odeh: *Jordanians, Palestinians, and the Hashemite Kingdom*, p. 256.
96. Ibid.
97. Ibid.
98. Interview conducted with Oraib Rantawi by author, Amman, Jordan. 22 February 2006.
99. Ibid.
100. Abu Odeh: *Jordanians, Palestinians, and the Hashemite Kingdom*, p. 259.
101. Ibid.
102. *International Crisis Group.* 'The challenge of political reform: Jordanian democratisation and regional instability.' 8 October 2003. Via: http://bit.ly/hXnneS [Accessed: 5 April 2011].
103. Diker, Dan and Pinchas Inbari: 'Are there signs of a Jordanian-Palestinian reengagement?'.
104. *The Christian Science Monitor.* 'Jordan queen's decree stirs tempest over citizenship rights.' 17 December 2002. Via: http://bit.ly/gR6USJ [Accessed: 5 April 2011].
105. Interview conducted with Dr. Abdul Baset al-Athanmeh by author, Irbid, Jordan. 15 February 2007.
106. Interview conducted with Dr. Ibrahim Hejoj by author, Amman, Jordan. 2 March 2006.
107. Ibid.
108. Interview conducted with Dr. Labib Kamhawi by author, Amman, Jordan. 22 February 2006.
109. Ibid.
110. Farah, Randa. *Popular Memory and Reconstructions of Palestinians Identity – Al-Baq'a Refugee Camp, Jordan* (D.Phil. dissertation, Department of Anthropology, University of Toronto) 1999. Cited in al-Abed, Oroub. *Palestinian Refugees in Jordan*, Forced Migration Online Research Guide, February 2004. p. 15.
111. Brand, Laurie. 'Palestinians and Jordanians: a crisis of identity', *Journal of Palestine Studies*, Vol. 24. No. 4. Summer 1995. pp. 46–61.
112. Interview conducted with Dr. Ahmed Oweidi al-Abbadi by author, Amman, Jordan. 17 February 2007.

113. According to al-Abbadi and the JNM website, membership has soared from three in 2003 to tens of thousands in 2007, in locations as diverse as New York, Sydney and Berlin.

Chapter 4

1. Sa'di, Ahmad H. 'Catastrophe, Memory and Identity: Al-Nakbah as a Component of Palestinian Identity', *Israel Studies*, Vol. 7. No. 2. Summer 2002. pp. 175–98 (181). It is worth noting that Palestinian-Jordanian members of both the middle class and elite define themselves as refugees, despite their socio-economic status. Reasoning that the loss of the homeland rendered all Palestinians refugees in the host state, the term 'refugees' can encompass all Palestinians compelled to seek refuge in Jordan, regardless of social standing.
2. Ibid., p. 195.
3. Sanbar, Elias. 'Out of place, out of time', *Mediterranean Historical Reviews*. 16 (2001) pp. 87–94 (90). Cited in Sa'di: 'Catastrophe, memory and identity', pp. 193–4.
4. Huntington, Samuel. *Who Are We? The Challenges to America's National Identity* (New York: Simon & Schuster) 2004. p. 22.
5. Ibid.
6. Gulick, John. *The Middle East: An Anthropological Perspective* (Pacific Palisades, CA: Goodyear Pub. Co) 1976. p. 39.
7. Cf. Bhabha, Homi K. *The Location of Culture* (London: Routledge) 2009 and Bakhtin, Mikhail Mikhailovich. *The Dialogic Imagination: Four Essays* (Austin; London: University of Texas Press) 1981.
8. Migdal Joel S. 'Mental maps and virtual checkpoints: Struggles to construct and maintain state and social boundaries.' In Migdal, Joel S. (ed.) *Boundaries and Belonging: States and Societies in the Struggle to Shape Identities and Local Practices* (Cambridge: Cambridge University Press) 2004. p. 21.
9. Ibid., p. 23.
10. Croucher, Sheila L. *Globalization and Belonging: the Politics of Identity in a Changing World* (Oxford: Rowman & Littlefield) 2004. p. 40.
11. Hall, Stuart. 'The Question of Cultural Identity.' In *Readings in Contemporary Political Sociology*, Kate Nash (ed.) (Oxford: Blackwell) 2000. p. 118–19.
12. Foucault, Michel. 'Of other spaces', *Diacritics*, Vol. 16. No. 1. Spring 1986. pp. 22–7. Foucault's principles of heterotopology include: 1. A presence in all cultures; 2. A heterotopia can be shaped by society according to a

desired function; 3. The heterotopia can juxtapose a single space with several sites that are inherently incompatible; 4. Heterotopias are linked to 'slices in time', also known as 'heterochronies'; 5. Heterotopias 'always presuppose a system of opening and closing that both isolates them and makes them penetrable.'

13. Foucault: 'Of Other Spaces', p. 24.
14. Ibid.
15. Ibid., p. 27.
16. Hall, Stuart. 'Cultural identity and diaspora', in *Identity: Community, Culture, Difference*, John Rutherford (ed.) (London: Lawrence and Wishart) 1990. p. 58.
17. Young, Robert. *Colonial Desire: Hybridity in Theory, Culture, and Race* (London: Routledge) 1995. p. 27.
18. Brah, Avtar and Annie E. Coombes. *Hybridity and its Discontents: Politics, Science, Culture* (London: Routledge) 2000. p. 1.
19. Papastergiadis, Nikos. *The Turbulence of Migration: Globalization, Deterritorialization, and Hybridity* (Cambridge: Polity Press) 2000. p. 14.
20. Weaver, Jace. 'Indigenousness and Indigeneity.' In Schwarz, Henry and Sangeeta Ray (eds.) *A Companion to Postcolonial Studies* (Oxford: Blackwell) 2000. p. 226.
21. Papastergiadis: *The Turbulence of Migration*, p. 169.
22. Bhabha, Homi K. *The Location of Culture* (London: Routledge) 2005. p. 56.
23. Anzaldua, Gloria. 'Borderlands/La Frontera: The New Mestiza' (San Francisco: Spinsters/Aunt Lute) 1987. p. 37. Cited in Bhabha, Homi K. 'Culture's In-Between', in *Questions of Cultural Identity*, Stuart Hall and Paul du Gay (eds.) (London: SAGE) 1996. p. 92.
24. Papastergiadis: *The Turbulence of Migration*, p. 143.
25. Barker, Chris. *Cultural Studies: Theory and Practice* (London: SAGE) 2008. p. 424.
26. García Canclini, Néstor. *Hybrid Cultures: Strategies for Entering and Leaving Modernity* (Minneapolis, MN; London: University of Minnesota Press) 1995. p. 11. n. 1.
27. Bakhtin: *The Dialogic Imagination*, p. 360.
28. Papastergiadis: *The Turbulence of Migration*, p. 20.
29. Barker: *Cultural Studies*, p. 260.
30. Held, Colbert C. and John Cummings. *Middle East Patterns: Places, Peoples, and Politics* (Boulder, CO: Westview Press) 2006. p. 94.
31. *Al-Husri, Ma Hiya al-Qawmiya: Abhath wa Dirasat 'ala Dhaw'i al-Ahdath wa al-Nadhariyat* [What is Nationalism?: Enquiries and Studies in Light of Events and Theories] (Beirut: Dar al-'Ilm li al-Malayeen) 1963 p. 210. Cited

in Dawisha, Adeed. *Arab Nationalism in the Twentieth Century: From Triumph to Despair* (Princeton, NJ: Princeton University Press) 2003. p. 68.

32. Dawisha: *Arab Nationalism in the Twentieth Century*, p. 74.

33. Gubser, Peter. *Jordan: Crossroads of Middle Eastern Events* (Boulder, CO: Westview Press; London: Croom Helm) 1983. p. 16.

34. Al-Wer, Emam. Phonological variation in the speech of women from three urban areas in Jordan (Ph.D. thesis, University of Essex) 1991. p. 58. Cited in Suleiman, Yasir. *A War of Words: Language and Conflict in the Middle East* (Cambridge: Cambridge University Press) 2004. p. 98.

35. Interview conducted with Khalil by author, 16 February 2006. Amman, Jordan.

36. Suleiman: *A War of Words*, p. 102.

37. Sawaie, Mohammed. *Linguistic Variation and Speakers' Attitudes: A Sociolinguistic Study of Some Arabic Dialects* (Damascus: Al-Jafan & Al-Jabi) 1994. Cited in Suleiman: *A War of Words*, p. 102.

38. Shorrab, G. A. -E. -J. *Models of Socially Significant Linguistic Variation: The Case of Palestinian Arabic* (State University of New York at Buffalo: Dissertation Abstracts International 42:5109A) 1981. Cited in Suleiman: *A War of Words*, p. 105.

39. Ibn Khaldun. *The Muqaddimah: An Introduction to History*. Volume 3. Translated by Franz Rosenthal (Pantheon Books) 1958. p. 351. Cited in Suleiman: *A War of Words*, p. 105.

40. Ibid.

41. Al-Wer: Phonological variation in the speech of women from three urban areas in Jordan, p. 58. Cited in Suleiman: *A War of Words*, p. 103.

42. Interview conducted by author with Mazen Jibreel, 29 January 2006. Amman, Jordan.

43. Suleiman: *A War of Words*, pp. 113–14.

44. Ibid., p. 115.

45. For further information on the reactions of the Jordanian state towards research addressing politico-linguistic correlations, see Suleiman: *A War of Words*, pp. 123–4.

46. Sawaie: Linguistic variation and speakers' attitudes, p. 14. Cited in Suleiman: *A War of Words*, p. 102.

47. Alternative transliterations include: *beljik, baljikiyyah* and *baljikiyyih*.

48. Massad, Joseph A. *Colonial Effects: the Making of a National Identity in Jordan* (New York: Columbia University Press) 2001. p. 253.

49. Translation: 'We want to declare it openly: We do not want to see any Palestinians [in Jordan].'

50. Interview conducted with Ahmad Oweidi al-Abbadi by author, 17 February 2007. Amman, Jordan.

51. Interview conducted with anonymous JNMC member by author, 17 February 2007. Amman, Jordan.

52. Ibid.

53. Ibid.

54. Ibid.

55. Cohen, Anthony Paul. *The Symbolic Construction of Community* (London: Routledge) 2000. p. 60.

56. Suleiman: *A War of Words*, p. 118.

57. Ibid., p. 107.

58. Interview conducted with Tareq al-Masarwa by author, 3 March 2006. Amman, Jordan.

59. Interview conducted with Ahmad Oweidi Al Abbadi by the author, 17 February 2007. Amman, Jordan.

60. For further details, see International Freedom of Expression Exchange (IFEX). 'Jordan: Release Critic Charged with Slander Authorities Muzzling Opponents Despite New Law.' 23 May 2007. Via *IFEX*: http://bit.ly/ganWjo [Accessed: 8 March 2011]

61. Interview conducted with Tareq al-Masarwa by author, 3 March 2006. Amman, Jordan.

62. Interview conducted with Jameel Momany by author, 22 March 2006. Amman, Jordan.

63. Amara, Mahfoud. 'The importance of culture: Sport and development in the Arab world – Between tradition and modernity.' In Houlihan, Barrie and Mick Green (eds.) *Routledge Handbook of Sports Development* (London: Routledge). p. 124.

64. *7iber*. 'Jordan free voices: The identity of the match.' [Arabic] 13 December 2010. Via *7iber*: http://bit.ly/dSzTmI [Accessed: 12 March 2011].

65. Naseem. 'Chaotic football and the Palestinian Jordanian identity conversation.' 12 December 2010. Via *The Black Iris*: http://bit.ly/gJoHnH [Accessed: 12 March 2011].

66. Interview conducted with Ibrahim Hejoj by author, 24 January 2006. Amman, Jordan. The Arab Bank was founded by Abdulhamed Shoman (1890–1974) originally from Beit Hanina, Palestine. Cf. *The Indomitable Arab: The Life and Times of Abdulhamed Shoman* (London: Third World Center for Research and Publishing Ltd) 1984.

67. Interview conducted with Majed by author, 4 February 2006. Amman, Jordan.

68. Interview conducted with Labib Kamhawi by author, 22 February 2006. Amman, Jordan.

69. Interview conducted with Mrs. Widad Kawar by author, 25 March 2006. Amman, Jordan.

70. Ramadan, Adam. 'A Refugee landscape: Writing Palestinian national-isms in Lebanon', *ACME: An International E-Journal for Critical Geographies*, Vol. 8. No. 1. 2009. pp. 69–99. p. 80.

71. *Or Does It Explode*, 'Wear keffiyeh, get arrested'. 27 January 2006. Via *Or Does It Explode*: http://bit.ly/epu65L [Accessed 25 February 2006].

72. Tait, Robert. 'Iran's underground rap artists take to wearing symbol of Islamic Revolution,' *The Guardian*. 1 December 2008.

73. Esfandiari, Golnaz. 'Historic Cyrus cylinder called "A Stranger In Its Own Home"', 14 September 2010. *Persian Letters*, Radio Free Europe/Radio Free Liberty. Via: http://bit.ly/aIUFvw [Accessed: 16 September 2010].

74. *Columbia Spectator*. 'Kaffiyeh and gown.' 29 April 2002. Via *Columbia Spectator*: http://bit.ly/g3dcqa [Accessed: 8 March 2011].

75. Columbia Spectator, 3 May 2002.

76. Malkin, Michelle. 'Rachael Ray, Dunkin' Donuts, and the keffiyeh ker-fuffle', 28 May 2008. Via *Michelle Malkin*: http://bit.ly/6BfYD [Accessed: 20 September 2010].

77. *The Boston Globe*, 'Dunkin' Donuts yanks Rachael Ray ad', 27 May 2008. Via: http://bit.ly/XONTb [Accessed: 7 July 2010]

78. Interview conducted with Mrs. Widad Kawar by author, 25 March 2006. Amman, Jordan.

79. Swedenburg, Ted. *Memories of Revolt: The 1936–1939 Rebellion and the Palestinian National Past* (Fayetteville, AR: University of Arkansas Press) 1995. p. 35.

80. Interview conducted with Ismail Musallam by author, 26 March 2006. Gaza Camp, Jordan.

81. Massad: *Colonial Effects*, p. 250.

82. Ibid., p. 250.

83. Interview conducted with Mrs. Widad Kawar by author, 25 March 2006. Amman, Jordan.

84. Suleiman: *A War of Words*, pp. 119–20.

85. El Guindi, Fadwa. *Veil: Modesty, Privacy and Resistance* (Oxford: Berg Publishers) 2000. p. 118.

86. El Guindi: *Veil*, p. 118.

87. Ibid.

88. *The Daily Star*, 'Arafat immortalized keffiyeh as symbol of Palestine', 12 November 2004. Via: http://bit.ly/grBVY1 [Accessed: 5 July 2007].

89. Ibid.

90. Massad: *Colonial Effects*, p. 253.

91. Interview conducted with Mrs. Widad Kawar by author, 25 March 2006. Amman, Jordan.

92. The downtown district of Amman en route to the historic Roman theatre.

93. The '6 branch dress' style, named after the six vertical bands of embroidery that ran from waist to hem, emerged in the late 1960s.

94. The *shawal* was first produced in the camps in a pre-embroidered uncut form and made of heavy linen with the embroidery done straight onto the main fabric and sold with a fringed shawl worked in the same manner. Although originally developed for the foreign market the *shawal* became popular amongst women in Jordan and the Territories who wore it to represent a variety of Palestinian haute couture.

95. Interview conducted with Mrs. Widad Kawar by author, 25 March 2006. Amman, Jordan.

96. Ibid.

97. Ibid.

98. Ibid.

99. Ibid.

100. For an example, visit http://bit.ly/ijad7X, a collection of Israeli post-cards. Images by Anna 1112. 8 August 2008. [Accessed: 8 December 2008].

101. Ibid.

102. Cf. http://www.jordanispalestine.com and 'Is Jordan Palestine?' by Daniel Pipes and Adam Garfinkle. *Commentary Magazine*. October 1988.

103. Sharoni, Simona. *Gender and the Israeli-Palestinian Conflict: the Politics of Women's Resistance* (New York: Syracuse University Press) 1995. p. 14.

104. Ibid., p. 14.

105. Ibid., p. 15.

106. Cf. Jad, Islah. 'From Salons to the Popular Committees: Palestinian Women, 1919–1989', in Nasser, Jamal R. and Roger Heacock (eds.) *Intifada: Palestine at the Crossroads*, Jamal R. Nasser and Roger Heacock (eds.) (New York: Praeger) 1990. pp. 125–43. Also Ellen L. Fleischmann, 'The emergence of the Palestinian women's movement, 1929–39', *Journal of Palestine Studies*, Vol. 29. No. 3. Spring 2000, pp. 16–32.

107. Jad: 'From salons to the popular committees', p. 127.

108. Abu-Zu'bi, Nahla. *Family, Women and Social Change in the Middle East: The Palestinian Case* (Toronto: Scholar's Press) 1987. p. 21.

109. Kahf, Mohja. 'Huda Sha'rawi's "Mudhakkirati': The Memoirs of the First Lady of Arab Modernity", *Arab Studies Quarterly*, Vol. 20. 1998.

110. Peteet, Julie M. *Gender in Crisis: Women and the Palestinian Resistance Movement* (New York: Columbia University Press) 1991. pp. 42–3.

111. Hasso, Frances Susan. *Resistance, Repression, and Gender Politics in Occupied Palestine and Jordan* (Syracuse, NY: Syracuse University Press) 2005. p. 38.

112. Sharoni: *Gender and the Israeli-Palestinian Conflict*, p. 21, n. 22.

113. Jad: 'From salons to the popular committees', p. 133.

114. Palestinian Academic Society for the Study of International Affairs, Jerusalem. 'The women's movement in Jerusalem, 1920s to 1930s.' Via PASSIA: http://bit.ly/eKpwVu [Accessed: 13 March 2011]. See also Antonius, Soraya: 'Fighting on two fronts: Conversations with Palestinian women', *Journal of Palestine Studies*, Vol. 8. No. 3. Spring 1979. pp. 26–45.

115. Mogannam, Matiel E. T. *The Arab Woman and the Palestine Problem* (London: Herbert Joseph) 1937. p. 70. In Antonius: 'Fighting on Two Fronts', p. 27.

116. Ibid.

117. Said, Edward. 'Intifada and independence', *Social Text*, No. 22. Spring, 1989. pp. 23–39.

118. Haj, Samira. 'Palestinian women and patriarchal relations', *Signs*, Vol. 17. No. 4. Summer 1992. pp. 761–778.

119. Brand, Laurie A. *Palestinians in the Arab world: Institution Building and the Search for State* (New York; Guildford: Columbia University Press) 1988. p. 196.

120. Rubenberg, Cheryl A. *Palestinian Women: Patriarchy and Resistance in the West Bank* (London: Lynne Rienner Publishers) 2001. p. 217.

121. Ibid., p. 226.

122. Interview conducted with Mr. Shaher Rawashdeh by author, 26 February 2007. Amman, Jordan.

123. Dawisha: *Arab Nationalism in the Twentieth Century*, p. 258.

124. Original text: 'Tras la guerra de los Seis Días el ejército de Israel continuo practicando incursiones en poblados y campamentos de Jordania, donde se organizaba la resistencia palestina. El 21 de marzo de 1968 atacaron Karameh y 305 guerrilleros palestinas, en vez de replegarse, hicieron frente a los 12,000 hombres del ejército israelí, causándoles 1,200 bajas y pérdida de gran parte de material, lo que les obligó a la retarda.' In Pizarroso Quintero, Alejandro. *Nuevas guerras, vieja propaganda (de Vietnam a Irak)* (Universistat de Valencia) 2005. p. 242.

125. Original text: 'a pesar de su inferioridad numérica, de manera que aquella batalla se convertía desde entonces en un símbolo de la resistencia palestina.' Ibid.

126. Luttwak, Edward N. and Daniel Horowitz. *The Israeli Army, 1948–1973* (Cambridge, MA: Abt Books) 1983. p. 304.

127. Hart, Alan. *Arafat: Terrorist or Peacemaker?* (London: Sidgwick and Jackson) 1987. p. 259.

128. Terrill, W. Andrew. 'The political mythology of the battle of Karameh', *The Middle East Journal*, Vol. 55. No. 1. Winter 2001. p. 99.

129. Ibid., p. 101.

130. Turki, Fawaz. *The Disinherited: Journal of a Palestinian Exile* (New York: Monthly Review Press) 1974. p. 16.

131. Interview conducted with Mr. Shaher Rawashdeh by author, 26 February 2007. Amman, Jordan.

132. Interview conducted with Mr. Shaher Rawashdeh, Mr. Ali Mohammad al-Tahrawi, Sheikh Ahmad al-Arman, Sheikh Khaled al-Madi by author, 26 February 2007. Amman, Jordan.

133. Interview conducted with Mr. Shaher Rawashdeh by author, 26 February 2007. Amman, Jordan.

134. Picaudou, Nadine. *Les Palestiniens: Un siècle d'histoire* (Editions Complexe) 2003. p. 140.

135. Original text: 'Avant la bataille de Karameh, nous étions seulement 722. Soudain nous fûmes 3,000' In Picaudou: *Les Palestiniens*, p. 140.

136. Frangi, Abdallah. *The PLO and Palestine* (London: Zed Books) 1983. p. 112.

137. An interview with Ahmed Wumar by Martin Slackman, 'Shamil Shroukh, 16, in a traditional Circassian costume, says he does not speak the Circassian', *The New York Times*, August 10, 2006.

138. Lewis, Norman N. *Nomads and Settlers in Syria and Jordan, 1800–1980* (Cambridge: Cambridge University Press) 1987. p. 107.

139. Murad, T. 'Summary of the Chechen history' (unpublished paper) (Sultan Murad Center for Chechen Studies) 1994. Cited in Dweik, Bader S. 'Linguistic and cultural maintenances among the Chechens of Jordan', *Language, Culture and Curriculum*, Vol. 13. No. 2. 2000. pp. 186.

140. Mufti, Shauket (Habjoka). *Heroes and Emperors in Circassian History* (Beirut: Librairie du Liban). 1972. p. 250.

141. Ria Novosti, 'Circassians move to seek autonomy within Russia.' Via *RiaNovosti*, 6 June 2010: http://bit.ly/fD5GSp [Accessed: 15 December 2010].

142. Dweik, Bader S. 'Linguistic and cultural maintenances among the Chechens of Jordan', *Language, Culture and Curriculum*, Vol. 13. No. 2. 2000. p. 187.

143. Shishani, Murad Batal and Cerwyn Moore. 'Jordan and Chechnya – an unquestioned relationship.' *Prague Watchdog*. 28 December 2005. Via: http://bit.ly/eMvsr9 [Accessed: 8 March 2011].

144. Nichols, Johanna. 'Who are the Chechen?', *The Linguist*, 13 January, 1995. p. 1.

145. Ibid., p. 4.

146. Shishani and Moore: 'Jordan and Chechnya'.

147. Kailani, Wasfi. 'Chechens in the Middle East: Between original and host cultures', Caspian Studies Program. (Belfer Center for Science and

International Affairs) 2002. Cited in Shishani and Moore: 'Jordan and Chechnya'.

148. Conquest, Robert. *The Nation Killers: the Soviet Deportation of Nationalities* (London: Macmillan, 1970). Cited in Shishani and Moore: 'Jordan and Chechnya'.

149. Al-Bashayer, R. *Mujtama Ash-she-shan fil Urdon. Dirasa Jugraphia, Bashariya Wa Ijtima'iyya.* (MA thesis, College of Arts, Geography Department, The Lebanese University) 1997. Cited in Dweik: 'Linguistic and cultural maintenances among the Chechens of Jordan', p. 188.

150. Kailani: 'Chechens in the Middle East'.

151. Ibid.

152. Dweik: 'Linguistic and cultural maintenances among the Chechens of Jordan', p. 188.

153. Haddad, Mohanna and Wasfi Kailani. 'Chechen identity, culture, and citizenship in Jordan', in *Middle Eastern Minorities and Diasporas*, Moshe Maoz and Gabriel Sheffer (eds.) (Brighton; Portland, OR: Sussex Academic Press) 2002. p. 255.

154. Ibid.

155. Said Al-Mufti served as Prime Minister between the following dates: 12 April 1950 to 4 December 1950; 30 May 1955 to 15 December 1955; and 22 May 1956 to 1 July 1956.

156. *The New York Times.* 'Seeking Roots Beyond the Nation They Helped Establish', 10 August 2006. Via *The New York Times*: http://nyti.ms/gzcsyl [Accessed: 8 March 2011]

157. Dweik: 'Linguistic and cultural maintenances among the Chechens of Jordan', p. 193.

158. Ibid., p. 189.

159. Ibid., p. 193.

Chapter 5

1. Lenin, Vladimir Ilyich. *Imperialism: the Highest Stage of Capitalism: a Popular Outline* (London: Lawrence) 1934. p. 253.

2. Brynen, Rex. 'Economic crisis and post-rentier democratization in the Arab world: The case of Jordan', *Canadian Journal of Political Science*, Vol. 25. No. 1. March 1992. p. 78.

3. Hammad, Khalil Nayef. *Foreign Aid and Economic Development: The Case of Jordan* (PhD Thesis submitted to Southern Illinois University at Carbondale. University Microfilms International) 1981. p. 94.

NOTES 307

4. Skocpol, Theda. 'Rentier state and Shi'a Islam in the Iranian Revolution', *Theory and Society*, Vol. 11. 1982. p. 269. In the Iranian case, however, the increasing autonomy of the state appears to have come at the cost of societal alienation from the Shah's regime. Cited in Lucas, Russell E. *Institutions and the Politics of Survival in Jordan: Domestic Responses to External Challenges, 1988–2001* (Albany: State University of New York Press) 2005. pp. 73–4.
5. Lucas: *Institutions and the Politics of Survival in Jordan*, p. 74.
6. Brynen: 'Economic crisis and post-rentier democratization in the Arab world', pp. 78–9. In Lucas: *Institutions and the Politics of Survival in Jordan*, p. 20.
7. Brynen: 'Economic crisis and post-rentier democratization in the Arab world', p. 79.
8. Knowles, Warwick. *Jordan since 1989: A Study in Political Economy* (London: I.B.Tauris) 2005. p. 32.
9. Ibid.
10. Beblawi, H. *The Arab Gulf Economy in a Turbulent Age* (London: Croom Helm) 1984. p. 30. Cited in Knowles: *Jordan Since 1989*, p. 34.
11. Knowles: *Jordan since 1989*, p. 76.
12. Joffé, George. (ed.) *Jordan in Transition: 1990–2000* (London: Hurst & Company) 2002. p. 51.
13. Satloff, R.B. *The Politics of Change in the Middle East* (Boulder, CO: Westview) 1993. p. 134.
14. International Monetary Fund (October 1995), 'Jordan – Background Information on Selected Aspects of Adjustment and Growth Strategy', *IMF Staff Country Report No. 95/97* (Washington: IMF). p. 5. Cited in Knowles: *Jordan Since 1989*, p. 79.
15. Brynen: 'Economic crisis and post-rentier democratization in the Arab world', pp. 84–5.
16. Lucas: *Institutions and the Politics of Survival in Jordan*, p. 26.
17. Ahmed, H. and M. Williams. 'Consequences of displacement after the Gulf crises: A study of the responses of 207 displaced Palestinians and Jordanian workers', *Digest of Middle East Studies*, Winter 1993. See also Van Hear, Nicholas. 'Consequences of the forced mass repatriation of migrant communities: Recent case from West Africa and the Middle East', *Discussion Paper no. 38. United Nations Research Institute for Social Development.* November; 'Mass Flight in the Middle East: Involuntary Migration and the Gulf Conflict' in *Geography and Refugees: Patterns and Processes of Change*, R. Black and V. Robinson (eds.) (London: Bellhaven) 1992a, 1992b; 'The Return of Jordanian/Palestinian Nationals from Kuwait: Economic and Social Implications for Jordan', *United Nations Economic and Social Commission for West*

Asia, Mimeograph 1992; 'The Socio-Economic Characteristics of Jordanian Returnees' (Amman, Jordan: National Center for Educational Research and Development) July 1991, cited in *Peace and the Jordanian Economy* by The International Bank for Reconstruction and Development (Washington, DC: The World Bank) 1994. p. 36.

18. Information gathered during informal discussions with individuals in their early 20s, conducted in Amman, Jordan, between January and April 2006 by the author.

19. Satloff: *The Politics of Change in the Middle East*, p. 132.

20. Joffé: *Jordan in Transition*, p. 24

21. Knowles: *Jordan since 1989*, p. 72. Lucas: Institutions and the Politics of Survival in Jordan, p. 26.

22. George, Alan. *Jordan: Living in the Crossfire* (London: Zed Books) 2005. p. 38. Lucas: *Institutions and the Politics of Survival in Jordan*, p. 25.

23. *Summary of World Broadcasts* (SWB), Third Series, ME/0439, 20.04.89, p. i. Cited in Knowles: *Jordan Since 1989*, p. 94.

24. Saif, Ibrahim. 'Changing the Rules of the Game: Understanding the Reform Process in Jordan', *Global Development Network*. September 2005. p. 19. Al-Faqih, Abdullah Mohammed. *The Struggle for Liberalization and Democratization in Egypt, Jordan, and Yemen* (UMI Dissertation Services, Doctoral Thesis, Northeastern University, Boston, Massachusetts) 2003. p. 186.

25. Economist Intelligence Unit, *Quarterly Economic Review – The Arabian Peninsula and Jordan*. August 1970. p. 33. Cited in Kanovesky, E. (ed.), *Economic Development of Jordan* (Tel Aviv: University Publishing Projects) 1976. pp. 37–8.

26. Knowles: *Jordan since 1989*, p. 35.

27. Ibid. See also: Laurie A. Brand, *Jordan's Inter-Arab Relations: The Political Economy of Alliance Making* (New York; Chichester: Columbia University Press) 1994. p. 139.

28. Knowles: *Jordan since 1989*, p. 97.

29. Al-Faqih: *The Struggle for Liberalization and Democratization in Egypt, Jordan, and Yemen*, p. 186.

30. Lucas: *Institutions and the Politics of Survival in Jordan*, p. 98.

31. Turki: *Exile's Return*, p. 27.

32. Sahliyeh, Emile. 'The West Bank pragmatic élite: The uncertain future', *Journal of Palestine Studies*, Vol. 15. No. 4. Summer 1986. pp. 34–35.

33. Seale, Patrick (ed.) *The Shaping of an Arab Statesman: Sharif Abd al-Hamid Sharaf and the Modern Arab World* (London: Quartet) 1983, p. 28.

34. Interview conducted by the author with Dr Labib Kamhawi, 22 February 2006. Amman, Jordan.

35. Yorke, Valerie. *Domestic Politics and Regional Security: Jordan, Syria and Israel* (Gower: International Institute for Strategic Studies) 1988. p. 36.

36. Interview conducted by the author with Oraib Rantawi, 26 February 2006. Amman, Jordan.

37. Harris, William. *The Levant: A Fractured Mosaic* (Princeton, NJ: Markus Weiner Publishers) 2003. p. 164.

38. Interview conducted by the author with Ahmed (surname withheld), 7 March 2006. Rusaifa, Jordan.

39. Mishal, Shaul. *West Bank/East Bank: the Palestinians in Jordan, 1949–1967* (New Haven; London: Yale University Press) 1978. p. 41.

40. Smith, Pamela Ann. 'The Palestinian diaspora, 1948–1985', *Journal of Palestine Studies*, Issue 59. Spring 1986. p. 97.

41. Ibid., p. 104.

42. Gilen, Signe, Are Hovden Ak, Rania Maktab, Jon Pedersen and Dag Tuastad. *Finding Ways: Palestinian Coping Strategies in Changing Environments*, FAFO Report 177. 1994.

43. Mishal: *West Bank/East Bank*, p. 75.

44. Fathi, Schirin H. *Jordan, an Invented Nation?: Tribe-State Dynamics and the Formation of National Identity* (Hamburg: Deutsches Orient-Institut) 1994. p. 229.

45. Ibid., p. 29.

46. *Al-Ra'y*, 20 January 1997. See also: L. Tachau (ed.) *Political Élites and Political Development in the Middle East* (New York: Shenkman Publishing Company) 1976. pp. 16–17. Cited in Fathi: *Jordan*, p. 29

47. Nevo, Joseph. 'The Jordanian, Palestinian and the Jordanian-Palestinian identities', *4th Nordic Conference in Middle East Studies*. August 1998. p. 7.

48. Ibid., p. 8.

49. Interview conducted by the author with His Excellency Nasser S. Judeh, 15 March 2006. Amman, Jordan.

50. Hattar, Nahed. 'Man Huwa al-Urduni?' in *Al-Hadath*, 1 November 1995. p. 9. Cited in Massad, Joseph A. *Colonial Effects: the Making of National Identity in Jordan* (New York: Columbia University Press) 2001. p. 265.

51. Interview conducted by the author with Nahed Hattar, 20 February 2006. Amman, Jordan.

52. Ibid.

53. Ibid.

54. Interview conducted by the author with Oraib Rantawi, 22 February 2006. Amman, Jordan.

55. Ibid.

56. Al-Faqih: *The Struggle for Liberalization and Democratization in Egypt, Jordan, and Yemen*, p. 142.

57. Ibid., p. 146.

58. Yorke: *Domestic Politics and Regional Security*, p. 42.

59. Ibid.

60. Perhaps the most succinct definition of *wasta* is that given by Joffé: 'The Arab term for intercession on behalf of a friend, relative, business partner, etc.: describes informal personal relations with the purpose of mutual benefit. Whoever is in a position to grant privileges (scholarships, licences, permits, or other "favours" of all kinds) extends *wasta*, knowing that this may one day become a reciprocal relation when he is in need of "getting something done". Also, it is considered normal (in the sense of "according to the norm") to extend *wasta* to family members who can be helped. It is inherent in the nature of this kind of social relationships that loyalty is primarily to the small and informal group and/or to the family rather than to office, country or the constitution.' Cited in Joffé, George (ed.) *Jordan in Transition: 1990–2000* (London: Hurst and Company) 2002. p. 251.

61. Droeber, Julia. *Dreaming of Change: Young Middle-Class Women and Social Transformation in Jordan* (Leiden; Boston: Brill) 2005. p. 106.

62. Arab Archives Institute, *Al-wasta fi-l-Urdun*, 2000. Cited in Joffé: *Jordan in Transition*, p. 242.

63. Interview conducted by the author with Dr Labib Kamhawi, 22 February 2006. Amman, Jordan.

64. Ibid.

65. Droeber: *Dreaming of Change*, p. 29.

66. Shteiwi, Musa, 'Class structure and inequality in the city of Amman', in *Amman: Ville et Société*, Jean Hannoyer and Seteny Shami (eds.) (Beirut: Centre d'Études et des Recherches sur le Moyen-Orient Contemporain) 1996. pp. 405–25.

67. Droeber: *Dreaming of Change*, p. 32.

68. Ibid.

69. Interview conducted by the author with Dr Labib Kamhawi, 22 February 2006. Amman, Jordan.

70. Badr, Majid. *Al-ta'lim al-'ali fi al-urdun. Baina al-mas'uliyat al-hukumiya wa al-qita al-khass* (Amman: Markaz al-dirasat wa al-abhath 'an al-sharq al-awsat al-mu'asir) 1994. Cited in Droeber: *Dreaming of Change*, p. 32.

71. Interview conducted by the author with Dr Labib Kamhawi, 22 February 2006. Amman, Jordan.

72. Reiter, Yitzhak. 'Higher education and sociopolitical transformation in Jordan', *British Journal of Middle Eastern Studies*, Vol. 29. Issue 2. 2002. pp. 137–64.

73. Ibid.

74. Brand, Laurie A. 'Palestinians and Jordanians: A crisis of identity', *Journal of Palestine Studies*, Vol. 24. No. 4. Summer 1995. p. 49.
75. Abdullah, Stephanie Latte. 'Palestinian women in the camps of Jordan: Interviews', *Journal of Palestine Studies*, Vol. 24. No. 4. 1995. pp. 62–73.
76. Ibid., p. 69
77. Ruben, Trudy. 'What do the Palestinians want? Conversations in the diaspora: the middle class in Beirut', *The Christian Science Monitor.* 20 May 1974. p. 4.
78. Ibid., p. 5.
79. Ibid., p. 6.
80. Ibid.
81. Ibid., p. 8.
82. Nevo, Joseph. 'Changing identities in Jordan', *Israel Affairs*, Vol. 9. Issue 3. 2003. p. 199.
83. Ibid., p. 170.
84. Van Hear, Nicholas. *New Diasporas: The Mass Exodus: Dispersal and Regrouping of Migrant Communities* (London: UCL Press) 1998. p. 82.
85. Ahmed, Hisham H. and Mary A. Williams-Ahmed. 'The impact of the Gulf crisis on Jordan's economic Infrastructure: A study of the responses of 207 displaced Palestinian and Jordanian workers', *Arab Studies Quarterly*, Vol. 15. No. 4. Fall 1993. pp. 36–44.
86. Shteiwi: 'Class structure and inequality in the city of Amman', p. 419.
87. Economic and Social Commission for Western Asia (ESCWA). *The Impact of the Gulf Crisis on the Jordanian Economy* (Amman: ESCWA) 1991. p. iiif.
88. Le Troquer, Yann and Rozenn Hommery al-Oudat, 'From Kuwait to Jordan: the Palestinians' Third Exodus', *Journal of Palestine Studies*, Vol. 28. No. 4. Spring 1999. p. 48.
89. Ahmed and Williams-Ahmed. 'The impact of the Gulf crisis on Jordan's economic infrastructure: A study of the responses of 207 displaced Palestinian and Jordanian workers', *Arab Studies Quarterly*, Vol. 15. No. 4. Fall 1993. pp. 56–9.
90. Brand, Laurie A. 'Palestinians and Jordanians: A crisis of identity', *Journal of Palestine Studies*, Vol. 24. No. 4. Summer 1995. p. 49.
91. Ibid., p. 50.
92. Ruben. 'What do the Palestinians want? Conversations in the diaspora: the middle class in Beirut', p. 3.
93. Rubenstein, Danny. *The People of Nowhere: The Palestinian Version of Home* (New York: Times Books) 1991. p. 7.
94. Sayigh, Rosemary. 'Dis/Solving the "Refugee Problem"', *Middle East Research and Information Project* (Summer, 1998). See also: Joseph Nevo. 'The Jordanian, Palestinian and the Jordanian-Palestinian identities', *4th Nordic Conference in Middle East Studies*. August 1998. p. 6.

95. Nevo: 'The Jordanian, Palestinian and the Jordanian-Palestinian identities', p. 6.

96. Ibid.

97. Sayigh: 'Dis/Solving the "Refugee Problem"', p. 6.

98. Interview conducted by the author with Ismael Musallam, 11 March 2006. Amman, Jordan.

99. Al-Saqour, Mohammad. *The Poverty Line in Jordan*, cited in Kamel Abu Jaber, *Income Distribution in Jordan*, Buhbe Matthes and Mohamad Smadi (eds.) (Oxford: Westview Press) 1990. p. 114.

100. It must be noted that the figures cited originate from a World Bank Report compiled in 1994; later figures cite the Palestinian refugee population size in the Kingdom as follows: 1,766,057 or 34.5 per cent of the wider population by 1998 and 1,570,192 by 2000, with the highest proportion – 56 per cent – below the age of 25 years. For further details, see: Abu-Libdeh, Hasan. *Statistical Data on Palestinian Refugees: Prospects for Contribution to a Final Settlement* (Palestinian Central Bureau of Statistics) 2003. p. 2; *Registered Palestine Refugee Population by Age Group and by Field as of June, 2000*, Table III (published by UNRWA) 2000.

101. The International Bank for Reconstruction and Development. *Peace and the Jordanian Economy* (Washington, DC: The World Bank) 1994. p. 49.

102. Ibid., p. 48.

103. Interview conducted by the author with Oraib Rantawi, 22 February 2006. Amman, Jordan.

104. Interview conducted by the author with Mrs. Widad Kawar, 25 March 2006. Amman, Jordan.

105. Said, E.. *After the Last Sky: Palestinian Lives* (New York: Pantheon) 1986. Cited in Sawalha, Aseel. 'Identity, self and the other among Palestinian refugees in East Amman', in *Amman: Ville et Société*, Jean Hannoyer and Seteny Shami (eds.) (Entre d'Études et de Recherches sur le Moyen-Orient Contemporain (CERMOC), Beyrouth) 1996. pp. 345–59.

106. Sawalha: 'Identity, self and the other among Palestinian refugees in East Amman', p. 353.

107. Interview conducted by the author with Hisham (surname withheld), 15 March 2006. Amman, Jordan.

108. As a holder of the two-year residency passport, Hisham has no family book – which registers the civil status of the members of the family, including birth and marital status – and could only attain a crossing card granted by al-Mutaba'a wal-Tafteish – the inspection and follow-up department affiliated with the Ministry of the Interior in Jordan – for the purpose of family reunification, with a blue card. In addition, the two-year residency

passport requires workers to hold a work permit, university education fees to be charged according to foreign fees status, and ownership with the approval of a ministerial council. See Oroub Al-Abed, *Palestinian Refugees in Jordan*, Forced Migration Online Guide. February, 2004. p. 11.

109. Interview conducted by the author with Dr Jawad Anani, 9 March 2006. Amman, Jordan.

110. Interview conducted by the author with Ismael Musallam, 11 March 2006. Amman, Jordan.

111. Interview conducted by the author with His Excellency Nasser S. Judeh, 15 March 2006. Amman, Jordan.

Chapter 6

1. Bertram, Sir Anton, and J. W. A. Young. *The Orthodox Patriarchate of Jerusalem: Report of the Commission Appointed by the Government of Palestine to Inquire and Report upon Certain Controversies between the Orthodox Patriarchate of Jerusalem and the Arab Orthodox Community* (London: Humphrey Milford) 1926. pp. 108–9.

2. Peake, F. G. *The History of Jordan and Its Tribes* (Coral Gables: University of Miami Press) 1958. Cited in Haddad: *Christians in Jordan*, p. 10.

3. His Royal Highness Prince El-Hassan bin Talal, interviewed by Hilal Khashan and Daniel Pipes, 'Jordanian Christians are fully integrated', *Middle East Quarterly*, Vol. 8. No. 1. Winter 2001.

4. *The Daily Star*, 'Jordan's Christians may feel safe, but they are also leaving' (Friday, 17 December 2004). Via: http://bit.ly/929Fns [Accessed: 25 February 2009].

8. Betts, Robert Brenton. *Christians in the Arab East: A Political Study* (London: Society for Promoting Christian Knowledge) 1979.

9. Jasussin, P. A. *Les costumes des arabes dans les pays de Moab* (Le Coffle, 1908).

7. For a comprehensive account of the experiences of the Palestinian Christians in the nascent state of Israel, see Wagner, *Dying in the Land of Promise*, p. 160.

8. Ibid.

9. Kwaiter: Al-Rahbaniyya al-Mukhlisiyya fi-Khidmat al-Nufus fi-Madinat al-Zarqa-al-Urdun, p. 77.

10. Pacini, Andrea. *Christian Communities in the Arab Middle East: the Challenge of the Future* (Oxford: Clarendon Press; New York: Oxford University Press) 1998. pp. 264–6.

11. Ibid.

12. Interview conducted by the author with Mrs. Widad Kawar, 25 March 2006. Amman, Jordan.

13. Reverend Riah Abu al-Assal. Anders Strindberg. 'Forgotten Christians', *The American Conservative* (24 May 2004). Via: http://bit.ly/qFEZR [Accessed: 5 June 2010].

14. Alternative translations of the title include: 'The quintessence of Paris' (1834); 'The refinement of the gold in a comprehensive depiction of Paris' and the German translation, 'Ein Muslim entdeckt Europa (A Muslim Discovers Europe)' cited in 'France as a role model', by Barbara Winckler, 2005. Qantara. Via: http://bit.ly/aq9yI5 [Accessed: 12 September 2009].

15. Mursi Saad El-Din, 'Plain Talk', *Al-Ahram Weekly*, No. 757, August 25–30, 2005.

16. Winckler, Barbara. 'France as a role model', Qantara.de. Via: http://bit.ly/bl3O6f [Accessed: 12 May 2010].

17. Pacini: *Christian Communities in the Arab Middle East*, p. 11.

18. Ibid.

19. Makdissi, A. 'Les Chrétiens et la Renaissance Arabe' ['The Christians and the Arab Renaissance'], *Islamochristiana*, No. 14. 1988. pp. 107–26.

20. Pacini: *Christian Communities in the Arab Middle East*, p. 12.

21. Ammar, Prof. Hassan. 'El Idioma Árabe', *Revista Árabe* (18 July, 1999).

22. Heyd, Uriel. *The Foundations of Turkish Nationalism: The Life and Teachings of Ziya Gökalp* (London: Harvill Press) 1950. p. 108. Cited in Cleveland, William L. *A History of the Modern Middle East* (Oxford: Westview Press) 2000. p. 127.

23. Cleveland: *A History of the Modern Middle East*, p. 127.

24. Pipes, Daniel and Hilal Khashan. 'Interview with Prince El-Hassan bin Talal: "Jordanian Christians are fully integrated."' *Middle East Quarterly*, Winter 2011. Via: http://goo.gl/odHQJ [Accessed: 14 December 2011].

25. Khashan and Pipes, 'Jordanian Christians are fully integrated', *Middle East Quarterly*, Vol. 8. No. 1. Winter 2001.

26. Jubber, Nicholas. 'The Cross in the Crescent', *Catholic World Report* (January 2002), p. 2

27. Salibi, Kamal. *The Modern History of Jordan* (London: I.B.Tauris) 1993. p. 174.

28. Ibid.

29. Tsimhoni, Daphne. *Christian Communities in Jerusalem and the West Bank Since 1948: An Historical, Social, and Political Study* (London: Praeger) 1993.

30. Tsimhoni: *Christian Communities in Jerusalem and the West Bank Since 1948*, p. 12.

31. Wagner: *Dying in the Land of Promise*, p. 20.

32. Ibid., p. 201.

33. Ibid., p. 201.

34. Anderson, Betty S. *Nationalist Voices in Jordan: The Street and the State* (Austin: University of Texas Press) 2005.

35. Al-Khatib, Amin. *Tadhakkurat Amin al-Khatib* [The Memoirs of Amin al-Khatib], Salib Abd al-Jawad and Mu'awiyah Tahbub (eds.) No. 2 (Bir Zayt: Markaz Dirasat wa-Tawthiq al-Mujtama 'al-Filastini, Jami'at Bir Zayt) 1992. p. 32. Cited in Anderson: *Nationalist Voices in Jordan*, p. 139.

36. Vatikiotis, P. J. *Conflict in the Middle East* (London: Allen and Unwin) 1971.

37. Cleveland: *A History of the Modern Middle East*, p. 353.

38. Ibid.

39. Cooley, John K. *Green March, Black September: The Story of the Palestinian Arabs* (London: Cass) 1973. p. 132.

40. Tsimhoni: *Christian Communities in Jerusalem and the West Bank since 1948*, p. 168.

41. Interview by Tsimhoni with Dr. Geries Khoury, *Ma'ariv*, 16 September 1988; *Ha'aretz*, 8 November 1989; and *The New Yorker*, 13 February 1989, cited in Tsimhoni: *Christian Communities in Jerusalem and the West Bank since 1948*, p. 168.

42. Sabella, Bernard. 'Palestinian Christians: Challenges and hopes'. Via: http://bit.ly/bwA49N [Accessed: 16 June 2010].

43. For further details pertaining to the reaction in Jordan to the Intifada, see Lucas, Russell E. 'Deliberalization in Jordan', *Journal of Democracy*, Vol. 14. No. 1. 2003. pp. 137–44, and Nevo, Joseph. 'Jordan, the Palestinians, and the al-Aqsa Intifada', *Civil Wars*, Vol. 6. No. 3. Autumn 2003. pp. 70–85.

44. Interview conducted by the author with Mrs. Mary Joury, 15 April 2006. Amman, Jordan.

45. Interview conducted by the author with Mr. Yacoub Joury, 15 April 2006. Amman, Jordan.

46. Ibid.

47. Interview conducted by the author with Mrs. Mary Joury, 15 April 2006. Amman, Jordan.

48. Betts: *Christians in the Arab East*, p. 171.

49. Pacini: *Christian Communities in the Arab Middle East*, p. 266.

50. Robins, Philip. *A History of Jordan* (Cambridge: Cambridge University Press) 2004. p. 46.

51. Khashan and Pipes, 'Jordanian Christians are Fully Integrated', *Middle East Quarterly*, Winter 2001.

52. Betts: *Christians in the Arab East*, p. 172.

53. Jubber: 'The Cross in the Crescent', p. 8.

54. Fasheh, Munir. 'Reclaiming our identity and redefining ourselves', in *Faith and the Intifada: Palestinian Christian Voices*, Naim S. Ateek, Marc H. Ellis

and Rosemary Radford Ruether (eds.) (New York: Orbis Books) 1992. pp. 61–70.

55. Tsimhoni: *Christian Communities in Jerusalem and the West Bank since 1948*, p. 12.

56. *25 Years of History, The Complete Collection of H.M. King Hussein Ben Talal's Speeches 1952–1977* (London: Samir Mutawi and Associates Publishing) 1979 [in Arabic], Vol. 2, p. 365. Cited in Mutawi, Samir A. *Jordan in the 1967 War* (Cambridge: Cambridge University Press) 1987. p. 64.

57. Ibid.

58. 'An Overview of Palestinian Embroidery', *Tatreez*. Via: http://bit.ly/aOkijm [Accessed: 2 June 2009].

59. Informal interview by the author with anonymous respondent, April 2006. Amman, Jordan.

60. Ibid.

61. Ibid.

62. Khoury, Geries. 'The Palestinian Christian Identity', in *Faith and the Intifada* Ellis and Ruether (eds.), pp. 71–7.

63. *Christianity Today*, 2 October 1995, p. 34. Cited in Wagner: *Dying in the Land of Promise*, p. 20.

64. Khashan and Pipes: 'Jordanian Christians are fully integrated.'

65. Sabella: 'The emigration of Christian Arabs.' Cited in Pacini: *Christian Communities in the Arab Middle East*, p. 128.

66. For further information, see the survey conducted by Dr. Bernard Sabella in 1993 in the Greater Jerusalem area. The excerpt used in this paper was cited in Bernard Sabella, 'The emigration of Christian Arabs: Dimensions and causes of the phenomenon,' pp. 127–54. Cited in Pacini: *Christian Communities in the Arab Middle East*. In addition, Sabella's comparison of Palestinian Christian migration is equally informative, as shown in his article, 'Christian emigration: A comparison of the Jerusalem, Ramallah and Bethlehem areas', *People On the Move*, March 1992, p. 69.

67. George, Alan. *Jordan: Living in the Crossfire* (New York: Zed Books) 2005.

68. Harrigan, Jane and Hamed El-Said. 'Faith-Based organizations in the Arab World and sense of common good: Lessons from Jordan's Muslim Brotherhood Movement', Institute for International Comparative and Area Studies. 1995.

69. Tal, Nachman. *Radical Islam in Egypt and Jordan* (Brighton: Sussex Academic Press/Jaffee Center for Strategic Studies) 2005. p. 187.

70. Schwedler, Jillian. 'Don't blink: Jordan's economic opening and closing', *Middle East Report*. 3 July 2002. p. 200.

NOTES

317

71. Ibid., p. 67.
72. Tal: *Radical Islam in Egypt and Jordan*, p. 188.
73. Ibid., p. 198.
74. Day, Arthur R. *East Bank/West Bank: Jordan and the Prospects for Peace* (Council on Foreign Relations) 1986. p. 48.
75. Boulby, Marion. *The Muslim Brotherhood and the kings of Jordan, 1945–1993* (Atlanta, Ga.: Scholars Press) 1999. p. 15.
76. Ibid., p. 104.
77. Tal: *Radical Islam in Egypt and Jordan*, p. 187.
78. Tal: *Radical Islam in Egypt and Jordan*, p. 198.
79. Ibid.
80. Ibid.
81. Ibid., p. 199.
82. *al-Ra'y*, 25 July 1984. Cited in Boulby: *The Muslim Brotherhood*, p. 100.
83. Interview conducted with Dr Labib Kamhawi by the author, 22 February 2006. Amman, Jordan.
84. Informal interview conducted with Jamil by the author, 20 February 2006. Amman, Jordan.
85. Interview conducted with Oraib Rantawi by the author, 22 February 2006. Amman, Jordan.
86. Ibid.
87. Ibid.
88. Clark, Janine A. *Islam, Charity and Activism: Middle Class Networks and Social Welfare in Egypt, Jordan, and Yemen* (Bloomington: Indiana University Press) 2004. p. 87.
89. UNDP, United Nations Development Report 2000, New York: UNDP, 2000. p. 170. Cited in Clark: *Islam, Charity, and Activism*, p. 87.
90. Schwedler, Jillian. *Faith in Moderation: Islamist Parties in Jordan and Yemen* (Cambridge; New York: Cambridge University Press) 2006. p. 198.
91. Ibid.
92. Ibid., p. 199.
93. Ibid.
94. Interview conducted with Dr Nahed Hattar by the author, 20 February 2007. Amman, Jordan.
95. Schwedler: *Faith in Moderation*, p. 200.
96. Interview conducted with Dr Labib Kamhawi by the author, 22 February 2006. Amman, Jordan.
97. Boukhars, Anouar. 'The Challenge of Terrorism and Extremism in Jordan', *Strategic Insights*, Vol. 5. No. 4. April 2006. p. 2.
98. Baylouny, Anne. 'Jordan's new "political development" strategy', *Middle East Report*. No. 236. Fall 2005. pp. 40–3.

99. 'In 1999, after his release from prison, Zarqawi followed them. In December 2004, more than 300 fighters from the Zarqa area were said to be in Afghanistan, Iraq or Chechnya, and 63 reportedly were in jail, in the U.S. prison at Guantánamo in Cuba or in Jordan.' Ibid.

100. Tal: *Radical Islam in Egypt and Jordan*, p. 183.

101. Kurz, Anat and David Tal. 'Palestinian Islamic Jihad', in Anat Kurz (ed.), *Islamic Terror and Israel* (Tel Aviv: Papyrus and Jaffee Center for Strategic Studies, 1993). p. 119 [Hebrew]; conversation with an Arab academic, 23 July 1995. Cited in Tal: *Radical Islam in Egypt and Jordan*, p. 183.

102. Tal: *Radical Islam in Egypt and Jordan*, p. 184.

103. Haas, Marius. *Hussein's Königreich: Jordaniens Stellung im Nahen Osten* (München: Tuduv Buch) 1975. p. 101.

104. Al-Khazendar, Sami. *Jordan and the Palestine Question: The Role of Islamic and Left Forces in Foreign Policy-Making* (Reading: Ithaca Press) 1997. p. 41.

105. Fischbach, Michael R. *Encyclopaedia of the Palestinians* (Facts on File Publishing) 2001. Cited in 'Hizb ut-Tahrir: nihilism or realism?' by John Horton, *Journal of Middle Eastern Geopolitics*, Year II. Vol. I. Number 3. January–March 2006. p. 72.

106. Massad, Joseph A. *Colonial Effects: the Making of a National Identity in Jordan* (New York; Chichester: Columbia University Press) 2001. p. 166.

107. Original: 'eine neue islamische Persönlichkeit und Mentalität durch intensive islamische Ausbildung.' Cited in Haas: *Hussein's Königreich*, p. 101.

108. Barghouti, Iyad. 'The Islamists in Jordan and the Palestinian Occupied Territories', in *The Islamist Dilemma: the Political Role of Islamist Movements in the Contemporary Arab World* Laura Guazzone (ed.) (Reading: Ithaca Press) 1995. pp. 136–7.

109. An-Nabhani, Taquiddin. *The Methodology of Hizb-ut Tahrir for Change* (London: al-Khalifah Publications) 1999. Cited in Horton: 'Hizb ut-Tahrir', p. 78.

110. Barghouti: 'The Islamists in Jordan and the Palestinian Occupied Territories', p. 138.

111. Ibid.

112. For further information see: http://bit.ly/90FOBe [Accessed: 18 June 2010].

113. Horton: 'Hizb ut-Tahrir', p. 79.

Chapter 7

1. Khalidi, Rashid I. *Palestinian Identity: The Construction of Modern National Consciousness* (New York: Columbia University Press) 1997. p. 19.

2. Greenstein, Ran. *Genealogies of Conflict: Class, Identity and State in Palestine/Israel and South Africa* (Hanover, NH : Wesleyan University Press: University Press of New England) 1995. p. 74.

3. Ibid.

4. Sheehi, Stephen. *Foundations of Modern Arab Identity* (Gainesville, FL: University Press of Florida) 2004. p. 10.

5. Khashan, Hilal. *Arabs at the Crossroads: Political Identity and Nationalism* (Gainesville: University Press of Florida) 2000. p. 1.

6. Ibid.

7. Sa'dun, Hamadi. *Tajdid al-Hadith 'an al-Qawmiyya al-'Arabiyya wa al-Wihda* [Resuming Talk about Arab Nationalism and Unity] (Beirut: Markaz Dirasat al-Wihda al-'Arabiyya), p. 24. Cited in Khashan: *Arabs at the Crossroads*, p. 1.

8. Ibid., p. 26.

9. Ibid., pp. 25–6.

10. Khashan: *Arabs at the Crossroads*, p. 18.

11. Ibid.

12. Zdzisław, Mach. *Symbols, Conflict, and Identity: Essays in Political Anthropology* (Albany: State University of New York Press) 1993. p. 3.

13. Khashan: *Arabs at the Crossroads*, p. 18.

14. Huntington, Samuel P. *The Clash of Civilizations and the Remaking of World Order* (London: Free Press) 2002. p. 22.

15. Al-Assi, Roba. 'Palestinian Movie Watch', 30 July 2007, 02:11 p.m. Via andfaraway.net: http://bit.ly/1LRic2 [Accessed: 14 May 2010].

16. Ibid.

17. Gulick, John. *The Middle East: An Anthropological Perspective* (Santa Monica: Goodyear Publishing Co.) 1976. p. 39.

18. Hall, Stuart. 'Cultural Identity and Cinematic Representation', *Framework*, No. 36. 1989. p. 235.

19. Young, Robert. *Colonial Desire: Hybridity in Theory, Culture, and Race* (London: Routledge) 1995. p. 27.

20. Brah, Avtar and Annie E. Coombes (eds.). *Hybridity and Its Discontents: Politics, Science, Culture* (London: Routledge) 2000. p. 1.

21. Barker, Chris and Dariusz Galasiński. *Cultural Studies and Discourse Analysis: A Dialogue on Language and Identity* (London: SAGE) 2003. p. 159.

22. Papastergiadis, Nikos. *The Turbulence of Migration: Globalization, Deterritorialization and Hybridity* (Cambridge: Polity Press) 2007. p. 14.

23. Weaver, Jace. 'Indigenousness and Indigeneity', in Henry Schwarz, and Sangeeta Ray (eds.) *A Companion To Postcolonial Studies* (Oxford: Blackwell) 2000. p. 226.

24. Al-Assi, Roba. 'Language Survey', 21 August 2007, 11:07 a.m. Via andfaraway.net: http://bit.ly/bA8jX9 [Accessed: 14 May 2010].

25. Papastergiadis: *The Turbulence of Migration*, p. 20.

26. Barker, Chris. *Cultural studies: Theory and Practice* (London; Thousand Oaks, CA: SAGE) 2008. p. 260.

27. Shakespeare, William. *The Tempest*, Act V, scene I, lines 180–185 (London: The Arden Shakespeare) 2007. p. 275.

28. Escobar, Arturo. 'Welcome to Cyberia: Notes on the anthropology of cyberculture', in *Cyberfutures: Culture and Politics on the Information Superhighway*, Ziauddin Sardar, and Jerome R. Ravetz (eds.) (Washington Square, New York: New York University Press) 1996, pp. 111–12.

29. Brown, Sheila. 'The criminology of hybrids: Rethinking crime and law in technosocial networks', *Theoretical Criminology*, Vol. 10. No. 2. 2006. p. 230.

30. Goffman, Erving. *Stigma: Notes on the Management of Spoiled Identity* (London: Penguin). 1990. p. 12.

31. Meyrowitz, Joshua. *No Sense of Place: The Impact of Electronic Media on Social Behavior* (New York; Oxford: Oxford University Press). 1986. p. 345.

32. See Gandolfo, K. Luisa. 'The political and social identities of the Palestinian Christian diaspora in Jordan', *Middle East Journal*, Vol. 62. No. 3. 2008. pp. 437–55.

33. Kollock, Peter and Marc A. Smith. 'Communities in cyberspace', in *Communities in Cyberspace*, Marc A. Smith and Peter Kollock (eds.) (London; New York: Routledge) 2000. p. 16.

34. Hawley, A. H. *Human Ecology: A Theory of Community Structure* (New York: Ronald Press) 1950.

35. Fogarty, Robin. *How to Teach for Metacognitive Reflection* (Glenview, IL: Pearson Professional Development) 1994. p. vii.

36. 'Metablognition'. Via: Weblogg-ed Website: http://www.weblogg-ed.com/2004/04/27 [Accessed: 18 May 2010].

37. See Habermas, Jürgen. *The Structural Transformation of the Public Sphere: An Inquiry into a Category of the Bourgeois Society* (Oxford: Polity) 1989; Nancy Fraser, 'Rethinking the public sphere: A contribution to the critique of actually existing democracy', *Social Text*. No. 25/6. 1990. pp. 56–80; Nicholas Garnham, in 'The media and the public sphere' in *The Information Society Reader*, Nick Heap, Ray Thomas, Geoff Einon, Robin Mason and Hugh Mackay (eds.) (London: SAGE, Open University) 1995. pp. 165–85.

38. Van Dijk, Jan. *The Network Society: Social Aspects of New Media* (London: SAGE). p. 25.

39. CNET News. 'There's a blog born every half second.' 7 August 2010. Via CNET: http://bit.ly/2S1XZn [Accessed: 20 May 2010].

40. Technorati. *State of the Blogosphere 2009*. 19 October 2010. Via Technorati: http://bit.ly/39Fc9b [Accessed: 20 May 2010].

41. *iToot*. 'About Us'. Via *iToot*: http://www.iiToot.net/about [Accessed: 20 May 2010].

42. Lynch, Marc. 'Blogging the new Arab public', *Arab Media & Society*. February 2007. p. 23.

43. ICT Qatar. 'Entrepreneur spotlight: WatWet CEO Kareen Arafat.' Via: http://bit.ly/bfWv35 [Accessed: 24 February 2011].

44. Ibid.

45. Ibid.

46. Watwet Blog. 'Watwet integrates with Twitter.' 20 May 2009, 03:55 a.m. Via *Whatwet Blog*: http://bit.ly/eL4BZt [Accessed: 24 February 2011].

47. IKbis. 'Team'. Via *IKbis*: http://bit.ly/hA0ddj [Accessed: 24 February 2011].

48. Arab Crunch. 'iKbis to Syndicate its Videos to Several Arab Satellite TV Channels.' 14 January 2010. Via *Arab Crunch*: http://bit.ly/4zgFmQ [Accessed: 24 February 2011].

49. Ibid.

50. Zoofs. 'What is Zoofs?' 2010. Via *Zoofs*: http://zoofs.com/help/about [Accessed: 24 February 2011].

51. Al-Shagra, Ahmed. 'Tootcorp Launches First Twitter Based YouTube Ranking Service.' 4 May 2010. Via *The Next Web*: http://bit.ly/bAPUTS [Accessed: 24 February 2011].

52. For the original Arabic, visit: http://www.kharabeesh.com/about-us.

53. Google Blogs search conducted by the author on 21 May 2010 for the period 1 January 2000 to 21 May 2010. The secondary search incorporates the dates 21 May 2009 to 21 May 2010.

54. Translates as 'the catastrophe'. The term is applied to the 1948 anniversary of the birth of the state of Israel and the simultaneous death of Palestine.

55. Al-Assi, Roba. 'Roots and homes', 23 July 2008, 10:18 a.m. Via andfaraway. net: http://bit.ly/9j7Ap3 [Accessed: 14 May 2010].

56. Ibid.

57. Ibid.

58. Al-Assi, Roba. 'Once upon a summer day in Jeddah', 31 March 2010, 02:43 a.m. Via andfaraway.net: http://bit.ly/9Vbxn7 [Accessed: 24 May 2010].

59. Al-Assi, Roba. '58', 15 May 2006, 07:20 p.m. Via andfaraway.net: http://bit. ly/22g0Tf [Accessed: 24 May 2010].

60. Al-Assi, Roba. 'Whatever happened to cinema in Palestine? For one, Cinema Al-Assi.' 25 November 2008, 02:50 p.m. Via andfaraway.net: http://bit. ly/2Dajz9 [Accessed: 14 May 2010].

61. Al-Assi, Roba. 'Palestinian Movie Watch.' 30 July 2007, 02:11 p.m. Via andfaraway.net: http://bit.ly/1LRic2 [Accessed: 14 May 2010].

62. Ibid.

63. Ibid.

64. Ibid.

65. Hall: 'Cultural identity and cinematic representation', p. 235.

66. Palestinian, feminine noun.

67. Al-Falasteenyia. 'About: Who,' 16 May 2006. Via alfalasteenyia.blogspot. com: http://bit.ly/aKcY4j [Accessed: 24 May 2011].

68. Al-Falasteenyia. 'About: What', 16 May 2006. Via alfalasteenyia.blogspot. com: http://bit.ly/aKcY4j [Accessed: 24 May 2010].

69. Al-Falasteenyia. 'Palestine: where are we going?' 6 December 2009. Via alfalasteenyia.blogspot.com: http://bit.ly/711XnW [Accessed: 24 May 2010].

70. Ibid.

71. Al-Falasteenyia. 'Nakba forever', 2 August 2009. Via alfalasteenyia.blogspot. com: http://bit.ly/faLKP [Accessed: 25 May 2010].

72. '[Akoob] or *gundelia* in English, is a very thorny plant that is found in the more mountainous regions of Palestine for a few weeks each year. [...] The granddaddy of all things unnecessary.' Cited in 'Top Five Dishes that are just [...] so not worth the effort' by Roba Al-Assi, 15 March 2009, 01:21 a.m. Via andfaraway.net: http://bit.ly/XHmFC [Accessed: 25 May 2010].

73. *Warq enab*: 'basically a horrifyingly large amount of perfectly formed vine leaves, usually freshly picked from the garden, and then meticulously filled with rice.' Ibid.

74. Ibid.

75. Al-Falasteenyia. 'Nakba forever' 2 August 2009. Via alfalasteenyia.blogspot. com: http://bit.ly/faLKP [Accessed: 25 May 2010].

76. Yasser Arafat quoted by *TIME*. 'The Palestinians Become a Power.' 11 November 1974. Via *TIME*: http://bit.ly/5CNL64 [Accessed: 25 May 2010].

77. United Nations Relief and Works Agency, *UNRWA in Figures*. 31 December 2009. Via UNRWA: http://bit.ly/avtvya [Accessed: 26 May 2010]. Surveyed countries comprising registered refugees are: Jordan, Syria, Gaza, Lebanon, West Bank.

78. *Yedioth Ahronoth*. 'PA: 11 million Palestinians around the world.' 1 February 2010.

79. Hegel, Georg Wilhelm. Hegel's Philosophy of Right, sect. 316, p. 204. Cited in Habermas, Jürgen. *The Structural Transformation of the Public Sphere: An Inquiry into a Category of Bourgeois Society* (Oxford: Polity) 1989. p. 117.

Epilogue

1. Schwedler, Jillian. 'More than a mob: The dynamics of political demonstrations in Jordan', *Middle East Report*, No. 226. Spring 2003. pp. 18–23.
2. In 2001, Queen Rania headed a march in protest at the Israeli incursions. For a full account, see Schwedler: 'More Than a Mob', p. 18.
3. Cf. Nairn, Tom. *Break-up of Britain: Crisis and Neo-Nationalism, 1965–1975* (Edinburgh: Verso). 1977; and Michael Hechter, *Internal Colonialism: The Celtic Fringe in British National Development, 1536–1966* (Berkeley and Los Angeles: University of California Press) 1975. Cited in Smith, Anthony D. *Nationalism: Theory, Ideology, History* (Cambridge: Polity Press) 2001. p. 47.
4. Smith: *National Identity*.
5. Ibid., p. 21.
6. Susser, Asher. 'Jordan: Preserving domestic order in a setting of regional turmoil', *Middle East Brief.* No. 27. March 2008.
7. *Human Rights Watch.* 'Stateless again: Palestinian-origin Jordanians deprived of their nationality.' 2010.
8. Yom, Sean L. 'Jordan: Ten more years of autocracy', *Journal of Democracy*, Vol. 20. No. 4. October 2009. pp. 151–66.

BIBLIOGRAPHY

Abdullah, Stephenie Latte. 'Palestinian Women in the Camps of Jordan: Interviews', *Journal of Palestine Studies*, Vol. 24. No. 4. Summer 1995.

al-Abed, Oroub. *Palestinian Refugees in Jordan*. Forced Migration Online Research Guide, February 2004.

Abidi, Aqil Hyder Hasan. *Jordan: A Political Study 1948–1957* (Bombay and New York: Asia Publishing House) 1965.

Abu Jaber, Kamel, Matthes Buhbe, and Mohamad Smadi (eds.) *Income Distributions in Jordan* (Boulder, CO: Westview Press) 1990.

Abu-Libdeh, Hasan. *Statistical Data on Palestinian Refugees: Prospects for Contribution to a Final Settlement* (Palestinian Central Bureau of Statistics) 2003.

Abu Odeh, Adnan. *Jordanians, Palestinians, and the Hashemite Kingdom in the Middle East Peace Process* (Washington, DC: United States Institute of Peace Press) 1999.

Aburish, Saïd K. *Arafat: From Defender to Dictator* (London: Bloomsbury) 1999.

Abu-Zu'bi, Nahla. *Family, Women and Social Change in the Middle East: The Palestinian Case* (Toronto: Scholar's Press) 1987.

Ahmed, H. and M. Williams. 'Consequences of Displacement after the Gulf Crises: A Study of the Responses of 207 Displaced Palestinians and Jordanian Workers', *Digest of Middle East Studies*, Winter 1993.

Ahmed, Hisham H. and Mary A. Williams-Ahmed. 'The Impact of the Gulf Crisis on Jordan's Economic Infrastructure: A Study of the Responses of 207 Displaced Palestinian and Jordanian Workers', *Arab Studies Quarterly*, Vol. 15. No. 4. Fall 1993.

Ajami, Fouad. 'The End of Pan-Arabism', *Foreign Affairs*, Vol. 57. No. 2. Winter 1978.

Anderson, Betty S. *Nationalist Voices in Jordan: The Street and the State* (Austin: University of Texas Press) 2005.

Ammar, Hassan. 'El Idioma Árabe', *Revista Árabe*. 18 July 1999.

Amro, Rateb Mohammad. 'What went wrong in the Middle East peace process?: the Jordanian-Israeli relationship', in *The Search For Israeli-Arab Peace: Learning From The Past And Building Trust*, Edwin G. Corr, Joseph Ginat and Shaul M. Gabbay (eds.) (Brighton; Portland, OR: Sussex Academic Press) 2007.

Anderson, Betty S. *Nationalist Voices in Jordan: The Street and the State* (Austin: University of Texas Press) 2005.

Antoun, Richard T. 'Civil Society, Tribal Process, and Change in Jordan: An Anthropological View', *International Journal of Middle East Studies*, Vol. 32. No. 4. November 2002.

Anzaldua, Gloria. 'Borderlands/La Frontera: The New Mestiza' (San Francisco: Spinsters/Aunt Lute) 1987.

Astorino-Courtois. 'Clarifying Decisions', *International Studies Quarterly*, Vol. 42. No. 4. December 1998.

Ateek, Naim. Cedar Duaybis, and Marla Schrader (eds.) *Jerusalem: What Makes for Peace?* (London: Melisende) 1997.

Badran, Adnan and Bichara Khader (eds.) *The Economic Development of Jordan* (London: Croom Helm) 1985.

Bakhtin, Mikhail Mikhailovich. *The Dialogic Imagination: Four Essays* (Austin; London: University of Texas Press) 1981.

Barakat, Halim I. 'The Palestinian refugees: an uprooted community seeking repatriation', *International Migration Review*, Vol. 7. No. 2. Summer 1973.

Barghouti, Iyad. 'The Islamists in Jordan and the Palestinian Occupied Territories', in *The Islamist Dilemma: the Political Role of Islamist Movements in the Contemporary Arab World*, Laura Guazzone (ed.) (Reading: Ithaca Press) 1995.

Barker, Chris. *Cultural Studies: Theory and Practice* (London: SAGE) 2008.

Bar-Tal, Daniel and Yona Teichmann. *Stereotypes and Prejudice in Conflict: Representations of Arabs in Israeli Jewish Society* (Cambridge: Cambridge University Press) 2005.

Bates, Daniel G. and Amal Rassam (eds.) *Peoples and Cultures of the Middle East* (Englewood Cliffs, NJ: Prentice-Hall) 1983.

Baylouny, Anne. 'Jordan's New "Political Development" Strategy', *Middle East Report*, No. 236. Fall, 2005.

Bennett, Andrew and Joseph Lepgold, Danny Unger. *Friends in Need: Burden Sharing in the Gulf War* (Basingstoke: Macmillan Press) 1997.

Berger, John. *A Seventh Man: A Book of Images and Words about the Experience of Migrant Workers in Europe* (Harmondsworth: Penguin) 1975.

Bertram, Sir Anton, and J. W. A. Young. *The Orthodox Patriarchate of Jerusalem: Report of the Commission Appointed by the Government of Palestine to Inquire and Report upon Certain Controversies between the Orthodox Patriarchate of Jerusalem and the Arab Orthodox Community* (London: Humphrey Milford) 1926.

Betts, Robert Brenton. *Christians in the Arab East: A Political Study* (London: Society for Promoting Christian Knowledge) 1979

Bhabha, Homi K. *The Location of Culture* (London: Routledge) 2009.

Bligh, Alexander. 'The Jordanian Army: between Domestic and External Challenges', *Middle East Review of International Affairs* (MERIA), Vol. 5. No. 2. June 2001.

Boukhars, Anouar. 'The Challenge of Terrorism and Extremism in Jordan', *Strategic Insights*, Vol. 5. No. 4. April 2006.

Boulby, Marion. *The Muslim Brotherhood and the Kings of Jordan, 1945–1993* (Atlanta, Ga.: Scholars Press) 1999.

Brah, Avtar and Annie E. Coombes. *Hybridity and its Discontents: Politics, Science, Culture* (London: Routledge) 2000.

Brand, Laurie A. 'Palestinians and Jordanians: a Crisis of Identity', *Journal of Palestine Studies*, Vol. 24. No. 4. Summer 1995.

Brand, Laurie A. *Palestinians in the Arab World: Institution Building and the Search for State* (New York; Guildford: Columbia University Press) 1988.

Bregman, Ahron. *Israel's Wars: A History since 1947* (London: Routledge) 2002.

Brown, Sheila. 'The Criminology of Hybrids: Rethinking Crime and Law in Technosocial Networks', *Theoretical Criminology*, Vol. 10. No. 2. 2006.

Brynen, Rex. 'Economic Crisis and Post-Rentier Democratization in the Arab World: The Case of Jordan', *Canadian Journal of Political Science*, Vol. 25. No. 1. March 1992.

Clark, Janine A. *Islam, Charity and Activism: Middle Class Networks and Social Welfare in Egypt, Jordan, and Yemen* (Bloomington: Indiana University Press) 2004.

Cleveland, William. *A History of the Modern Middle East* (Oxford: Westview Press) 2000.

Cobban, Helena. *The Palestinian Liberation Organisation: People, Power, and Politics* (Cambridge: Cambridge University Press) 1984.

Cohen, Anthony Paul. *The Symbolic Construction of Community* (London: Routledge) 2000.

Cooley, John K. *Green March, Black September: The Story of the Palestinian Arabs* (London: Cass) 1973.

Committee on International Relations, Group for the Advancement of Psychiatry. *Us and Them: The Psychology of Ethnonationalism* (New York: Brunner/Mazel) 1987.

de Châtel, Francesca. *Water Sheikhs and Dam Builders: Stories of People and Water in the Middle East* (New Brunswick, New Jersey: Transaction Publishers) 2007.

Croucher, Sheila L. *Globalization and Belonging: the Politics of Identity in a Changing World* (Oxford: Rowman & Littlefield Publishers, Inc.) 2004.

Davis, Uri. *Citizenship for Palestine Refugees and the Peace Process* (Shaml: Palestinian Diaspora and Refugee Centre. Monograph Series No 1, Ramallah) 1996.

Dawisha, Adeed. *Arab Nationalism in the Twentieth Century: From Triumph to Despair* (Princeton, NJ; Oxford: Princeton University Press) 2003.

Day, Arthur R. *East Bank/West Bank: Jordan and the Prospects for Peace* (Council on Foreign Relations) 1986

Diker, Dan and Pinchas Inbari. 'Are There Signs of a Jordanian-Palestinian Reengagement?' *Jerusalem Issue Brief*, Vol. 5. No. 1. 19 July 2005.

Droeber, Julia. *Dreaming of Change: Young Middle-Class Women and Social Transformation in Jordan* (Boston: Brill) 2005.

Dweik, Bader S. 'Linguistic and Cultural Maintenances among the Chechens of Jordan', *Language, Culture and Curriculum*, Vol. 13. No. 2. 2000.

Economic and Social Commission for Western Asia (ESCWA). *The Impact of the Gulf Crisis on the Jordanian Economy* (Amman: ESCWA) 1991.

Escobar, Arturo. 'Welcome to Cyberia: Notes on the Anthropology of Cyberculture', in *Cyberfutures: Culture and Politics on the Information Superhighway*, Ziauddin Sardar and Jerome R. Ravetz (eds.) (Washington Square, New York: New York University Press) 1996.

al-Faqih, Abdullah Mohammed. *The Struggle for Liberalization and Democratization in Egypt, Jordan, and Yemen* (UMI Dissertation Services, Doctoral Thesis, Northeastern University, Boston, Massachusetts) 2003.

Fasheh, Munir. 'Reclaiming Our Identity and Redefining Ourselves', in *Faith and the Intifada: Palestinian Christian Voices*, by Naim S. Ateek, Marc H. Ellis and Rosemary Radford Ruether (eds.) (New York: Orbis Books) 1992.

Fathi, Schirin H. *Jordan: An Invented Nation? Tribe-State Dynamics and the Formation of National Identity* (Hamburg: Deutsches Orient-Institut) 1994.

Fleischmann, Ellen L. 'The Emergence of the Palestinian Women's Movement, 1929–39', *Journal of Palestine Studies*, Vol. 29. No. 3. Spring 2000.

Fogarty, Robin. *How to Teach for Metacognitive Reflection* (Glenview, IL: Pearson Professional Development) 1994.

Foucault, Michel. 'Of Other Spaces', *Diacritics*, Vol. 16. No. 1. Spring 1986.

Frangi, Abdallah. *The PLO and Palestine* (London: Zed Books) 1983.

Gandolfo, Luisa. 'The Political and Social Identities of the Palestinian Christian Diaspora in Jordan', *Middle East Journal*, Vol. 62. No. 3. 2008.

García Canclini, Néstor. *Hybrid Cultures: Strategies for Entering and Leaving Modernity* (Minneapolis, MN; London: University of Minnesota Press) 1995.

Gat, Moshe. 'Nasser and the Six Day War, 5 June 1967: A Premeditated Strategy or An Inexorable Drift to War?', *Israel Affairs*, Vol. 11. No. 4. October 2005.

Gazit, Shlomo. 'Israel and the Palestinians: Fifty Years of Wars and Turning Points', *The ANNALS of the American Academy of Political and Social Science*, Vol. 555. No. 82. 1998.

George, Alan. *Jordan: Living in the Crossfire* (London: Zed Books) 2005.

Gilen, Signe, Are Hovden Ak, Rania Maktab, Jon Pedersen and Dag Tuastad. *Finding Ways: Palestinian Coping Strategies in Changing Environments* (FAFO Report 177) 1994.

Goffman, Erving. *Stigma: Notes on the Management of Spoiled Identity* (London: Penguin) 1990.

Greenstein, Ran. *Genealogies of Conflict: Class, Identity and State in Palestine/Israel and South Africa* (Hanover, NH: Wesleyan University Press: University Press of New England) 1995.

Gresh, Alain. *The PLO: The Struggle Within: Towards an Independent Palestinian State* (London: Zed) 1985.

Gross Stein, Janice. 'War and society in the Middle East', in *International Relations of the Middle East*, Louise Fawcett (ed.) (Oxford: Oxford University Press) 2005. p. 277.

Gubser, Peter. *Jordan: Crossroads of Middle Eastern Events* (Boulder, CO: Westview Press; London: Croom Helm) 1983.

Gulick, John. *The Middle East: An Anthropological Perspective* (Pacific Palisades, CA: Goodyear Pub. Co) 1976.

Haas, Marius. *Hussein's Königreich: Jordaniens Stellung im Nahen Osten* (München: Tuduv Buch) 1975.

Habermas, Jürgen. *The Structural Transformation of the Public Sphere: An Inquiry into a Category of Bourgeois Society* (Oxford: Polity) 1989.

Haddad, M. Y. *Christians in Jordan: A Split Identity* (The Harry S. Truman Research Institute for the Advancement of Peace, The Hebrew University of Jerusalem) May 2001.

Haddad, M. Y. *Arab Perspectives of Judaism: A Study of Image Formation in the Writings of Arab Authors 1948–1978* (New York: Shengold Publishers) 1984.

Haj, Samira. 'Palestinian Women and Patriarchal Relations', *Signs*, Vol. 17. No. 4. Summer 1992.

Hall, Stuart. 'The Question of Cultural Identity', in *Readings in Contemporary Political Sociology*, Kate Nash (ed.) (Oxford: Blackwell) 2000.

Hall, Stuart. 'Cultural Identity and Cinematic Representation', *Framework*, No. 36. 1989.

Hammad, Khalil Nayef. *Foreign Aid and Economic Development: The Case of Jordan* (PhD Thesis submitted to Southern Illinois University at Carbondale: University Microfilms International) 1981.

Harrigan, Jane and Hamed El-Said. 'Faith-Based Organizations in the Arab World and Sense of Common Good: Lessons from Jordan's Muslim Brotherhood Movement', Institute for International Comparative and Area Studies. 1995.

Harris, William. *The Levant: A Fractured Mosaic* (Markus Weiner Publishers, Princeton) 2003.

Hart, Alan. *Arafat* (London: Sidgwick & Jackson) 1984.

Hasso, Frances Susan. *Resistance, Repression, and Gender Politics in Occupied Palestine and Jordan* (Syracuse, NY: Syracuse University Press) 2005.

Hawley, A. H. *Human Ecology: A Theory of Community Structure* (New York: Ronald Press) 1950.

Hechiche, Abdelwahab. 'Renaissance et déclin de la résistance palestinienne', [translated from French] *Politique étrangère*. N°5, 38e année. 1973.

Held, Colbert C. and John Cummings. *Middle East Patterns: Places, Peoples, and Politics* (Boulder, CO: Westview Press) 2006.

Horton, John. 'Hizb ut-Tahrir: Nihilism or Realism?', *Journal of Middle Eastern Geopolitics*, Year II. Vol. I. No. 3. January–March 2006.

Houlihan, Barry and Mick Green. *Routledge Handbook of Sports Development* (London: Routledge) 2010.

Hourani, Albert H. *A History of the Arab Peoples* (London: Faber and Faber) 1991.

Human Rights Watch. *Stateless Again: Palestinian-Origin Jordanians Deprived of their Nationality* (Human Rights Watch) 2010.

Huntington, Samuel. *Who Are We? The Challenges to America's National Identity* (New York: Simon & Schuster) 2004.

Jansen, Michael E. *The United States and the Palestinian People* (Beirut: the Institute for Palestine Studies) Issue 23. 1970.

Jarbawi, Ali. 'The Triangle of Conflict', *Foreign Policy*, No. 100. Autumn 1995.

Jasussin, P.A. *Les costumes des arabes dans les pays de Moab* (Le Coffle) 1908.

Joffé, George (ed.) *Jordan in Transition: 1990–2000* (London: Hurst & Company) 2002.

Jubber, Nicholas. 'The Cross in the Crescent', *Catholic World Report*. January 2002.

Kahf, Mohja. 'Huda Sha'rawi's "Mudhakkirati": The Memoirs of the First Lady of Arab Modernity', *Arab Studies Quarterly*, Vol. 20. 1998.

Kamal, Sana. 'Ma'an erupts again', *Middle East International*. 8 February 2002.

Kanovsky, Eliyahu. *Jordan's Economy: From Prosperity to Crisis* (Tel Aviv: Moshe Dayan Center for Middle Eastern and African Studies, Shiloah Institute, Tel Aviv University) 1989.

Kepel, Gilles. *Jihad: The Trail of Political Islam* (London: I.B.Tauris) 2003.

Khalidi, Rashid I. *Palestinian Identity: The Construction of Modern National Consciousness* (New York: Columbia University Press) 1997.

Khashan, Hilal. *Arabs at the Crossroads: Political Identity and Nationalism* (Gainesville, FL: University Press of Florida) 2000.

Khashan and Pipes. 'Jordanian Christians are Fully Integrated', *Middle East Quarterly*, Vol. 8. No. 1. Winter 2001.

Al-Khazendar, Sami. *Jordan and the Palestine Question: The Role of Islamic and Left Forces in Foreign Policy-Making* (Reading: Ithaca Press) 1997.

Kirkbride, Alec S. 'Changes in Tribal Life in Trans-Jordan', *Man*, Vol. 45. March–April 1945.

Knowles, Warwick. *Jordan since 1989: A Study in Political Economy* (London: I.B.Tauris) 2005.

Kollock, Peter and Marc A. Smith. 'Communities in Cyberspace', in *Communities in Cyberspace*, Marc A. Smith and Peter Kollock (eds.) (London; New York: Routledge) 2000.

Kumaraswamy, P. R. 'Who Am I?: The Identity Crisis in the Middle East', *Middle East Review of International Affairs*, Vol. 10. No. 1. March 2006.

Lavergne, Marc. *La Jordanie* (Paris: Éditions Karthala) 1996.

Layne, Linda A. 'The Dialogics of Tribal Self-Representation in Jordan', *American Ethnologist*, Vol. 16. Issue 1. February 1989.

Lenin, Vladimir Ilyich. *Imperialism: the Highest Stage of Capitalism: a Popular Outline* (London: Lawrence) 1934.

Le Troquer, Yann and Rozenn Hommery al-Oudat, 'From Kuwait to Jordan: the Palestinians Third Exodus', *Journal of Palestine Studies*, Vol. 28. No. 4. Spring 1999.

Lewis, Bernard. *The Multiple Identities of the Middle East* (London: Weidenfeld & Nicolson) 1999.

Lewis, Norman N. *Nomads and Settlers in Syria and Jordan, 1800–1980* (Cambridge: Cambridge University Press) 1987.

Lucas, Russell E. *Institutions and the Politics of Survival in Jordan: Domestic Responses to External Challenges, 1988–2001* (Albany: State University of New York Press) 2005.

Lucas, Russell E. 'Deliberalization in Jordan', *Journal of Democracy*, Vol. 14. No. 1. 2003.

Lunt, James. *Hussein of Jordan: Searching for a Just and Lasting Peace* (New York: William Morrow and Company, Inc.) 1989.

Luttwak, Edward N. and Daniel Horowitz. *The Israeli Army, 1948–1973* (Cambridge, MA: Abt Books) 1983.

Lynch, Marc. 'Blogging the New Arab Public', *Arab Media & Society*. February 2007.

Maalouf, Amin. *In the Name of Identity: Violence and the Need to Belong* (London: Penguin Books) 2003.

Machiavelli, Niccolò. *The Prince* (London: Penguin Books Ltd.) 2003.

Makdissi, A. 'Les Chrétiens et la Renaissance Arabe' ['The Christians and the Arab Renaissance'], *Islamochristiana*, No. 14. 1988.

Maoz, Moshe and Gabriel Sheffer. *Middle Eastern Minorities and Diasporas* (Brighton; Portland, Or.: Sussex Academic Press) 2002.

Massad, Joseph A. *Colonial Effects: The Making of National Identity in Jordan* (New York; Chichester: Columbia University Press) 2001.

Melman, Yossi and Dan Raviv. *Behind the Uprising: Israelis, Jordanians, and Palestinians* (New York: Greenwood Press) 1989.

Mercer, Jonathan. 'Anarchy and Identity', *International Organization*, Vol. 49. No. 2. Spring 1995.

Meyrowitz, Joshua. *No Sense of Place: The Impact of Electronic Media on Social Behavior* (New York; Oxford: Oxford University Press) 1986.

Migdal, Joel S. *Boundaries and Belonging: States and Societies in the Struggle to Shape Identities and Local Practices* (Cambridge: Cambridge University Press) 2004.

Milton-Edwards, Beverley and Peter Hinchcliffe. *Conflicts in the Middle East since 1945* (London: Routledge) 2001.

Mishal, Shaul. *West Bank/East Bank: the Palestinians in Jordan, 1949–1967* (New Haven; London: Yale University Press) 1978.

Mufti, Shauket (Habjoka). *Heroes and Emperors in Circassian History* (Beirut: Librairie du Liban) 1972.

Mutawi, Samir A. *Jordan in the 1967 War* (Cambridge: Cambridge University Press) 1987.

Nasser, Jamal R. and Roger Heacock. *Intifada: Palestine at the Crossroads* (New York: Praeger) 1990.

Nasser, Riad. *Palestinian Identity in Jordan and Israel: The Necessary 'Other' in the Making of a Nation* (New York: Routledge) 2005.

Nevo, Joseph. 'The Jordanian, Palestinian and the Jordanian-Palestinian Identities', 4th Nordic Conference in Middle East Studies. August 1998.

Nevo, Joseph. 'Jordan, the Palestinians, and the al-Aqsa Intifada', *Civil Wars*, Vol. 6. No. 3. Autumn 2003.

Pacini, Andrea. *Christian Communities in the Arab Middle East: the Challenge of the Future* (Oxford: Clarendon Press; New York: Oxford University Press) 1998.

Papastergiadis, Nikos. *The Turbulence of Migration: Globalization, Deterritorialization, and Hybridity* (Cambridge: Polity Press) 2000.

Peretz, Don. *Intifada: The Palestinian Uprising* (Boulder: Westview Press) 1990.

Peteet, Julie M. *Gender in Crisis: Women and the Palestinian Resistance Movement* (New York: Columbia University Press) 1991.

Picaudou, Nadine. *Les Palestiniens: Un siècle d'histoire* (Editions Complexe) 2003.

Plascov, Avi. *The Palestinian Refugees in Jordan, 1948–1957* (London: Cass) 1981.

Quintero, Alejandro Pizarroso. *Nuevas guerras, vieja propaganda (de Vietnam a Irak)* (Universsistat de Valencia) 2005.

Reiter, Yitzhak. 'Higher Education and Sociopolitical Transformation in Jordan', *British Journal of Middle Eastern Studies*, Vol. 29. Issue 2. 2002.

Robins, Philip. *A History of Jordan* (Cambridge: Cambridge University Press) 2004.

Rosenfeld, Maya. *Confronting the Occupation: Work, Education, and Political Activism of Palestinian Families in a Refugee Camp* (Stanford, CA: Stanford University Press) 2004.

Rosenfeld, Maya. 'Power Structure, Agency, and Family in a Palestinian Refugee Camp', *International Journal of Middle East Studies*, Vol. 34. Issue 3. 2002.

Ruben, Trudy. 'What Do the Palestinians Want? Conversations in the Diaspora: the Middle Class in Beirut', *Christian Science Monitor*. 20 May 1974.

Rubenberg, Cheryl A. *Palestinian Women: Patriarchy and Resistance in the West Bank* (London: Lynne Rienner Publishers) 2001.

Rubin, Barry and Judith Colp Rubin. *Yasir Arafat: A Political Biography* (Oxford: Oxford University Press) 2003.

Rutherford, John. *Identity: Community, Culture, Difference* (London: Lawrence and Wishart) 1990.

Sabella, Bernard. 'Christian Emigration: A Comparison of the Jerusalem, Ramallah and Bethlehem Areas', *People On the Move*, March 1992.

Sa'di, Ahmad H. 'Catastrophe, Memory and Identity: Al-Nakbah as a Component of Palestinian Identity', *Israel Studies*, Vol. 7. No. 2. Summer 2002.

Sahliyeh, Emile. 'The West Bank Pragmatic Élite: The Uncertain Future', *Journal of Palestine Studies*, Vol. 15. No. 4. Summer 1986.

Said, Edward. 'Intifada and Independence', *Social Text*, No. 22. Spring 1989.

Saif, Ibrahim. 'Changing the Rules of the Game: Understanding the Reform Process in Jordan', *Global Development Network*. September 2005.

Salibi, Kamal S. *The Modern History of Jordan* (London: I.B.Tauris) 1993.

Satloff, R. B., *The Politics of Change in the Middle East* (Boulder, CO: Westview) 1993.

Sayigh, Rosemary. 'Dis/Solving the "Refugee Problem"', Middle East Research and Information Project (Summer 1998).

Schwarz, Henry and Sangeeta Ray. *A Companion to Postcolonial Studies* (Oxford: Blackwell) 2000.

Schwedler, Jillian. *Faith in Moderation: Islamist Parties in Jordan and Yemen* (Cambridge; New York: Cambridge University Press) 2006.

Schwedler, Jillian. 'More Than a Mob: The Dynamics of Political Demonstrations in Jordan', *Middle East Report*, No. 226. Spring 2003.

Schwedler, Jillian. 'Don't Blink: Jordan's Economic Opening and Closing', *Middle East Report*, 3 July 2002.

Skocpol, Theda. 'Rentier State and Shi'a Islam in the Iranian Revolution', *Theory and Society*, Vol. 11. 1982.

Seale, Patrick. *Abu Nidal: A Gun for Hire* (London: Random Century Group) 1992.

Seale, Patrick. *The Shaping of an Arab Statesman: Sharif Abd al-Hamid Sharaf and the Modern Arab World* (London: Quartet Books) 1983.

Sela, Avrahim. *The Palestinian Ba'ath* (Jerusalem: The Magnes Press, Hebrew University) 1984.

Sheehi, Stephen. *Foundations of Modern Arab Identity* (Gainesville, FL: University Press of Florida) 2004.

Shiblak, Abbas. 'Residency Status and Civil Rights of Palestinian Refugees in Arab Countries', *Journal of Palestine Studies*, Vol. 25. No. 3. Spring 1996.

Shishani, Murad Batal and Cerwyn Moore. 'Jordan and Chechnya – An Unquestioned Relationship.' *Prague Watchdog*. 28 December 2005.

Shlaim, Avi. *The Iron Wall: Israel and the Arab World* (London: Allen Lane, the Penguin Press) 2000.

Shteiwi, Musa. 'Class Structure and Inequality in the City of Amman' in *Amman: Ville et Société*, Jean Hannoyer and Seteney Shami (eds.) (Beyrouth: Centre d'Études et des Recherches sur le Moyen-Orient Contemporain) 1996.

Simons, Geoff. *The Scourging of Iraq: Sanctions, Law and Natural Justice* (Basingstoke: Macmillan Press) 1998.

Smilansky, Gene. 'Palestinian Refugee Camps: Graveyards of Peace', *Yale Israel Journal*, No. 7. Summer 2005.

Smith, Anthony D. *Nationalism: Theory, Ideology, History* (Cambridge: Polity Press) 2001.

Smith, Anthony D. *National Identity* (London: Penguin Books) 1991.

Smith, Pamela Ann. 'The Palestinian Diaspora, 1948–1985', *Journal of Palestine Studies*, Issue 59. Spring 1986.

Suleiman, Yasir. *A War of Words: Language and Conflict in the Middle East* (Cambridge: Cambridge University Press) 2004.

Susser, Asher. 'Jordan: Preserving Domestic Order in a Setting of Regional Turmoil', *Middle East Brief*. No. 27. March 2008.

Susser, Asher. *Challenges to the Cohesion of the Arab State* (The Moshe Dayan Center: Tel Aviv University) 2008.

Susser, Asher. *Jordan: Case Study of a Pivotal State* (Washington, DC: Washington Institute for Near East Policy) 2000.

Swedenburg, Ted. *Memories of Revolt : The 1936–1939 Rebellion and the Palestinian National Past* (Fayetteville, AR: University of Arkansas Press) 1995.

Tal, Nachman. *Radical Islam in Egypt and Jordan* (Brighton: Sussex Academic Press/Jaffee Center for Strategic Studies) 2005.

Terrill, W. Andrew. 'The Political Mythology of the Battle of Karameh', *The Middle East Journal*, Vol. 55, No. 1. Winter 2001.

Tsimhoni, Daphne. *Christian Communities in Jerusalem and the West Bank since 1948: An Historical Social and Political Study* (Westport: Praeger) 1993.

Turki, Fawaz. *The Disinherited: Journal of a Palestinian Exile* (New York: Monthly Review Press) 1974.

Turki, Fawaz. *Exile's Return: the Making of a Palestinian American* (New York: Free Press) 1994.

Van Dijk, Jan. *The Network Society: Social Aspects of New Media* (London: SAGE) 2006.

Van Hear, Nicholas. *New Diasporas: The Mass Exodus: Dispersal and Regrouping of Migrant Communities* (London: University of Washington Press) 1998.

Van Hear, Nicholas. 'Mass Flight in the Middle East: Involuntary Migration and the Gulf Conflict, 1990–91', in *Geography and Refugees: Patterns and Processes of Change* R. Black and V. Robinson (eds.) (London: Belhaven) 1993.

Van Hear, Nicholas. 'The Return of Jordanian/Palestinian Nationals from Kuwait: Economic and Social Implications for Jordan.' *United Nations Economic and Social Commission for West Asia*, Mimeograph 1992.

Van Hear, Nicholas. 'Consequences of the forced Mass Repatriation of Migrant Communities: Recent Case from West Africa and the Middle East.' *Discussion Paper no. 38.* United Nations Research Institute for Social Development (UNRISD). January 1992.

Vatikiotis, P. J. *Conflict in the Middle East* (London: Allen and Unwin) 1971.

Vatikiotis, P. J. *Politics and the Military in Jordan: A Study of the Arab Legion, 1921–1957* (London: Cass) 1967.

Wagner, Donald E. *Dying in the Land of Promise: Palestine and Palestinian Christianity from Pentecost to 2000* (London: Melisende Press) 2001.

Wallach, John and Janet Wallach. *Arafat: In the Eyes of the Beholder* (Toronto, Birch Lane Press) 1997.

Weaver, Jace. 'Indigenousness and Indigeneity', in *A Companion To Postcolonial Studies*, Henry Schwarz and Sangeeta Ray (eds.) (Oxford: Blackwell) 2000.

Wilson, Rodney (ed.) *Politics and the Economy in Jordan* (School of Oriental and African Studies, Routledge) 1991.

Winckler, Barbara. 'France as a Role Model'. Qantara: http://bit.ly/aq9yI5 [Accessed: 12 September 2009].

Woodward, Kathryn. *Concepts of Identity and Difference* (London: SAGE) 1999.

World Bank. *Peace and the Jordanian Economy*, The International Bank for Reconstruction and Development (Washington, DC: The World Bank) 1994.

Yom, Sean L. 'Jordan: Ten More Years of Autocracy', *Journal of Democracy*, Vol. 20. No. 4. October 2009.

Young, Robert. *Colonial Desire: Hybridity in Theory, Culture, and Race* (London: Routledge) 1995.

Yorke, Valerie. *Domestic Politics and Regional Security: Jordan, Syria and Israel: The End of an Era?* (Aldershot: Gower for the International Institute for Strategic Studies) 1988.

Zaiotti, Ruben. 'Dealing with Non-Palestinian Refugees in the Middle East: Policies and Practices in an Uncertain Environment', *International Journal of Refugee Law*, Vol. 18. No. 2. June 2006.

Zdzisław, Mach. *Symbols, Conflict, and Identity: Essays in Political Anthropology* (Albany: State University of New York Press) 1993.

INDEX